The Apache Modules Book

Prentice Hall
Open Source Software Development Series

Arnold Robbins, Series Editor

"Real world code from real world applications"

Open Source technology has revolutionized the computing world. Many large-scale projects are in production use worldwide, such as Apache, MySQL, and Postgres, with programmers writing applications in a variety of languages including Perl, Python, and PHP. These technologies are in use on many different systems, ranging from proprietary systems, to Linux systems, to traditional UNIX systems, to mainframes.

The **Prentice Hall Open Source Software Development Series** is designed to bring you the best of these Open Source technologies. Not only will you learn how to use them for your projects, but you will learn *from* them. By seeing real code from real applications, you will learn the best practices of Open Source developers the world over.

Titles currently in the series include:

Linux® Debugging and Performance Tuning: Tips and Techniques
Steve Best
0131492470, Paper, © 2006

Understanding AJAX: Using JavaScript to Create Rich Internet Applications
Joshua Eichorn
0132216353, Paper, © 2007

Embedded Linux Primer
Christopher Hallinan
0131679848, Paper, © 2007

SELinux by Example
Frank Mayer, David Caplan, Karl MacMillan
0131963694, Paper, © 2007

UNIX to Linux® Porting
Alfredo Mendoza, Chakarat Skawratananond, Artis Walker
0131871099, Paper, © 2006

Linux Programming by Example: The Fundamentals
Arnold Robbins
0131429647, Paper, © 2004

The Linux® Kernel Primer: A Top-Down Approach for x86 and PowerPC Architectures
Claudia Salzberg, Gordon Fischer, Steven Smolski
0131181637, Paper, © 2006

The Apache Modules Book

Application Development with Apache

Nick Kew

PRENTICE
HALL

Upper Saddle River, NJ • Boston • Indianapolis • San Francisco
New York • Toronto • Montreal • London • Munich • Paris
Madrid • Cape Town • Sydney • Tokyo • Singapore • Mexico City

Many of the designations used by manufacturers and sellers to distinguish their products are claimed as trademarks. Where those designations appear in this book, and the publisher was aware of a trademark claim, the designations have been printed with initial capital letters or in all capitals.

The author and publisher have taken care in the preparation of this book, but make no expressed or implied warranty of any kind and assume no responsibility for errors or omissions. No liability is assumed for incidental or consequential damages in connection with or arising out of the use of the information or programs contained herein.

The publisher offers excellent discounts on this book when ordered in quantity for bulk purchases or special sales, which may include electronic versions and/or custom covers and content particular to your business, training goals, marketing focus, and branding interests. For more information, please contact:

> U.S. Corporate and Government Sales
> (800) 382-3419
> corpsales@pearsontechgroup.com

For sales outside the United States, please contact:

> International Sales
> international@pearsoned.com

 This Book Is Safari Enabled

The Safari® Enabled icon on the cover of your favorite technology book means the book is available through Safari Bookshelf. When you buy this book, you get free access to the online edition for 45 days.

Safari Bookshelf is an electronic reference library that lets you easily search thousands of technical books, find code samples, download chapters, and access technical information whenever and wherever you need it.

To gain 45-day Safari Enabled access to this book:

• Go to http://www.prenhallprofessional.com/safarienabled

• Complete the brief registration form

• Enter the coupon code JXAU-S8PC-6P3E-JZCP-CFH8

If you have difficulty registering on Safari Bookshelf or accessing the online edition, please e-mail customer-service@safaribooksonline.com.

Visit us on the Web: www.prenhallprofessional.com

Library of Congress Cataloging-in-Publication Data

Kew, Nick.
  The Apache modules book : application development with Apache / Nick Kew.
      p. cm.
  Includes bibliographical references and index.
  ISBN 0-13-240967-4 (pbk. : alk. paper)
  1. Apache (Computer file : Apache Group) 2. Web servers—Computer programs. 3. Application software—Development. I. Title.
  TK5105.8885.A63K49 2007
  005.7'1376—dc22

2006036623

ISBN 0-13-240967-4
Text printed in the United States on recycled paper at RR Donnelley in Crawfordsville, Indiana.
First printing, January 2007

To all who share my dream, and are working to help make it happen ...

... the dream of a world where your work, your colleagues, and your opportunities in life are not dictated by where you live or how far you commute. Where the old-fashioned office of the nineteenth and twentieth centuries has passed into history, along with its soul-destroying bums-on-seats culture and Dilbertian work practices. A world inclusive of those who cannot work in a standard office. A world inclusive of those who reject car-dependence, but embrace a full and active life. A world inclusive of those who seek to fit study and learning into a busy life, yet have no accessible library, let alone university. Of those who are housebound ...

Our information infrastructure is poised to liberate us all. We who develop with Apache are playing a small but exciting part in that. This work is dedicated to all of us!

Contents

Foreword

Nick's book is something that we've long been waiting for. The "Eagle Book," which came out in 1999, was a great book, but it focused primarily on mod_perl. Thus it was a rather different thing from this book.

And this book comes along at just the right time. With web applications needing more and more scalability, we're all looking for ways for our code to run faster, use fewer resources, have tighter integration with the webserver, and just plain be more robust.

It used to be sufficient to write Perl CGI programs to run even large websites, but over the years most of us have moved to mod_perl, PHP, Ruby on Rails, and other development tools that allow us to build bigger, faster, cheaper. Those of us looking for that next thing, wondering if it might be best to write our applications as an Apache module, tend to get frustrated with the lack of decent documentation and examples.

For the most part, when you ask on IRC for documentation of how to write an Apache module, the answers include looking at the code of some existing module, or looking at API documentation that was, at best, somewhat elderly and, for the most part, intended for Apache 1.3.

When Nick told me that he was going to write this book, I made sure to sign up for the first copy. I knew that Nick was the right person for the job because of his prolific module authoring and his numerous helpful tutorials.

For those of us who learn best by example and experimentation, this book is ideal—it provides many of the former and it encourages the latter. So make sure that you have your favorite editor and compiler ready as you dive in, as you'll encounter example code almost right away and will want to try it out. And don't be afraid to experiment.

You've picked the right book. This is sure to become the de facto standard document about how to write an Apache module.

—Rich Bowen
    September 2006

Preface

Introduction

The Apache Web Server (commonly known as "Apache") is, by most measures, the leading server on the Web today. For ten years it has been the unrivaled and unchallenged market leader, with approximately 70 percent of all websites running Apache. It is backed by a vibrant and active development community that operates under the umbrella of the Apache Software Foundation (ASF), and it is supported by a wide range of people and organizations, ranging from giants such as IBM down to individual consultants.

The key characteristics of Apache are its openness and diversity. The source code is completely open: Not only the current version, but also past versions and experimental development versions can be downloaded by anyone from apache.org. The development process is also open, with the exception of a few matters dealing with project management. Apache's diversity is a reflection of its user and developer communities: It is equally at home in an ultra-high-volume site that receives tens of thousands of hits per second, a complex and highly dynamic web application, a bridge to a separate application server, or a simple homepage host. The inclusion of developers from such diverse roles helps ensure that Apache continues to serve all of these widely differing environments successfully.

Yet that doesn't mean Apache follows a one-size-fits-all approach. Its highly modular architecture is built on a small core, which enables every user to tailor it to meet his or her own specific needs. Apache serves equally well as a stand-alone webserver or a component in some other system. Most importantly, it is a highly flexible and extensible applications platform.

Audience and Readership

This book is intended for software developers who are working with the Apache Web Server. It is the first such book published since March 1999, and the first and (to date) only developer book that is relevant to Apache 2.

The book's primary purpose is to serve as an in-depth textbook for module developers working with Apache. The narrative and examples deal with development in C, and a working knowledge of C is assumed. However, the Apache architecture and API are shared by major scripting environments such as mod_perl and mod_python, as well as C. With the exception of Chapter 3 (on the Apache Portable Runtime), much of this book should also be relevant to developers working with scripting languages at any level more advanced than standard CGI.

The current Apache release—version 2.2—is the primary focus of this book. Version 2.2.0 was released in December 2005 and, given Apache's development cycle, is likely to remain current for some time (the previous stable version 2.0 was released in April 2002). This book is also very relevant to developers who are still working with version 2.0 (the architecture and API are substantially the same across all 2.x versions), and is expected to remain valid for the foreseeable future.

Organization and Scope

This book comprises twelve chapters and three appendixes.

The first chapter is a nontechnical overview that sets the scene and introduces the social, cultural, and legal background of Apache. It is followed by an extended technical introduction and overview that is spread over the next three chapters. Chapter 2 is a technical overview of the Apache architecture and API. Chapter 3 introduces the Apache Portable Runtime (APR), a semi-autonomous library that is used throughout Apache and relieves the programmer of many of the traditional burdens of C programming. Chapter 4 discusses general programming techniques appropriate to working with Apache, to ensure that your modules work well across different platforms and environments, remain secure, and don't present difficulties to systems administrators.

The central part of the book moves from the general to the specific. Chapters 5–8 present detailed discussions of various aspects of the core function of a webserver—namely, processing HTTP requests. A number of real-life modules are developed in these chapters. Chapter 5 starts with a "Hello World" example and takes you to the point where you can duplicate the function of a CGI or PHP script as a module. Chapter 6 describes the request processing cycle and working with HTTP metadata. Chapter 7 goes into more detail about identifying users and handling access control. Chapter 8 presents the filter chain and techniques for transforming incoming and outgoing data; it includes a thorough theoretical exposition and several examples. Chapter 9 completes the core topics by describing how to work with configuration data.

Chapters 10 and 11 present more advanced topics that are nevertheless essential reading for serious application developers. Chapter 10 looks at the mechanics of how the API works, and describes how a module can extend it or introduce an entirely new API or service for other modules. Chapter 11 presents the DBD framework for SQL database applications. Chapter 12 briefly discusses troubleshooting and debugging techniques.

The appendixes include Apache legal documents reproduced from the Web. They are extremely relevant to the book but were not written by the author. Appendix A is the Apache License. Appendix B includes the Contributor License Agreements, which cover issues related to intellectual property. Finally, the authoritative Hypertext Transfer Protocol (HTTP/1.1) standard (RFC 2616) is reproduced in full in Appendix C as reference documentation for developers of web applications.

What the Book Does Not Cover

This book is firmly focused on applications development, so it has very little to say about systems programming for or with Apache. In particular, if your goal is to port Apache to a hitherto-unsupported platform, the book offers no more than a pointer to the areas of code you'll need to work on.

Apart from that, there is one important omission: The book limits itself to considering Apache as a server for HTTP (and HTTPS), the protocol of the Web. Although the server can be used to support other protocols, and implementations already exist for FTP, SMTP, and echo, this book has nothing to say on the subject. Nevertheless, if you are looking to implement or work with another protocol, the overview and the discussion of HTTP protocol handling should help you get oriented.

Sources

Some of the modules used as examples are written especially for this book or similar instructional materials:

- Chapter 5: mod_helloworld
- Chapter 6: mod_choices (derived from a non-open-source module)
- Chapter 7: mod_authnz_day
- Chapter 8: mod_txt (written originally for www.apachetutor.org)

These modules can be downloaded from www.apachetutor.org.

All of the more substantial modules are taken from real-life sources. Except where otherwise indicated and referenced by URL, all modules are taken from either the Apache standard distribution (httpd.apache.org) or the author's company's site (apache.webthing.com). Please note that the use of any source code in this book does not imply a license to copy it other than for purely personal use. Please refer to the license terms in the original sources of each module.

Acknowledgments

The Apache Web Server is the work of a worldwide community, on whose collective wisdom I have drawn in writing this book. I am privileged to work within this community as a developer and educator.

I am grateful to my series editor Arnold Robbins, and to reviewers Brian France, Brad Nicholes, Noirin Plunkett, and Ivan Ristic for drawing my attention to errors and other weaknesses in the original manuscript and suggesting improvements. I am especially grateful to Rich Bowen for agreeing to take the time to write a foreword (Rich is, of course, better known as the author of several well-respected Apache books, as well as much of the documentation at `apache.org`). Finally, thanks to my commissioning editor Catherine Nolan and her team at Prentice Hall for bringing this project from manuscript to publication.

The source code examples presented here are drawn mostly from my own work, but many are taken from the Apache core code and are the work of the larger Apache community. Likewise, the text is mostly mine, but draws in part on other sources:

The ASF overview (Section 1.2) is drawn from `www.apache.org`.

The brief introduction to buckets and brigades in Chapter 3 is drawn from the API documentation.

The introductions to Jeff Trawick's introspection modules in Chapter 12 are mostly Jeff's.

The entire texts of the three appendixes are reproduced verbatim from Web sources.

Appendix C is copyright by the Internet Society and is reproduced under the terms of its own copyright notice (C.21). All other third-party material used is reproduced here under the terms of the Apache License (Appendix A).

Source code used here is licensed under various licenses. Please refer to the original sources before copying code from this book other than for strictly personal use.

All illustrations used are the original work of the author. However, some are drawn from existing sources:

Chapter 2: Figures 2-2, 2-3, and 2-4 are reproduced from www.apachetutor.org.

Chapter 8: Figures 8-1 and 8-2 were first used in the author's tutorial presentations. Figures 8-3 and 8-4 are reproduced from documentation at httpd.apache.org.

Chapter 10: Figure 10-1 is reproduced from documentation at apache.webthing.com.

Chapter 11: Figure 11-1 is reproduced from documentation at httpd.apache.org.

About the Author

Nick Kew is a veteran developer, with more than twenty years' professional software and systems experience since graduating from Cambridge University. He is a member of the Apache Web Server core development team and Project Management Committee, and of the Apache Software Foundation. He is lead architect of the Apache DBD framework (Apache/SQL integration) and a major contributor to other subsystems—most notably, filtering and proxying. In addition to his work within the Apache team, Kew's company WebThing, Ltd., distributes more than twenty modules (specializing in smart XML and other markup-aware applications), and he is responsible for the well-respected ApacheTutor website.

Since the 1980s, Kew has been an enthusiastic proponent of the potential of a ubiquitous IT infrastructure to liberate us from enslavement to accidents of geography, and especially the misery of daily commuting. Now he is working to help make it happen. In addition to his work with Apache, he serves as Invited Expert with the World Wide Web Consortium in its accessibility and quality assurance (QA) activities, and is a member of the Web Design Group.

Kew founded WebThing, Ltd., in 1997 to pursue what had previously been a hobby. His primary professional activity is consultancy in the areas of Apache development and Web QA/accessibility.

Chapter 1

Applications Development with Apache

1.1 A Brief History of the Apache Web Server

1.1.1 Apache 1

The Apache Web Server was originally created in 1995. It was based on and derived from the earlier NCSA server, written by the National Center for Supercomputing Applications (which also developed the Mosaic browser, predecessor to most of today's browsers, with a direct line to Netscape and Mozilla, and considerable influence over others, including MSIE). The first production server under the Apache name was version 1.0.0, released in December 1995.

As a webserver, Apache was an immediate success. By April 1996, it had overtaken the NCSA server as the most widely used webserver on the Internet, a position it has occupied ever since. But it wasn't a general-purpose applications platform: The native API was fairly limiting, and the return on development effort for programmers was unattractive compared to some of the alternatives available as higher-level programming layers. Nevertheless, some useful application modules—most notably, the extraordinary mod_rewrite—were developed.

The first applications development framework to make a major splash was Perl, under both CGI and mod_perl. The main programming book and most application developers concentrated on Perl, because mod_perl presented the first really useful and easy-to-use API. The Java Servlet API and numerous other scripting languages, including the current market leader PHP, soon followed.

The last major new release of the original Apache server was version 1.3, which was introduced in June 1998. Apache 1.3 has continued in maintenance mode and remains popular today, although new development work has long since moved to Apache 2.

1.1.2 Apache 2

Recognizing the limitations of Apache's original, hackish architecture, the Apache developers began a major new codebase in 2000, leading to the first production release of Apache 2.0 in April 2002. Salient features of Apache 2 include the following:

- The native API is much improved and the APR library is a separate entity. This helps programmers overcome most of the drawbacks of C programming—in particular, the problems of cross-platform programming and resource management. Working with Apache 2, C programmers can expect levels of productivity more commonly associated with higher-level and scripting languages.

- A new extension architecture enables development of a whole new class of applications, as well as far cleaner implementations of existing modules and applications. This book will discuss in detail how to take advantage of this extension architecture.

- A new core architecture makes Apache 2 a truly cross-platform server. The operating system layer has itself become a module (the MPM), enabling it to be separately tuned for each operating system. Whereas Apache 1 was a UNIX application that was ported with many limitations to other platforms, Apache 2 is truly cross-platform and is not tied to UNIX features, some of which perform poorly on, for example, Windows or Netware. The introduction of threaded MPMs also improves scalability on UNIX in many applications.

The downside of Apache 2 is that the API is not backward compatible with Apache 1, so many third-party modules and applications have been slow to upgrade to version 2.

Apache 2.2 was released as a stable version in December 2005 and features further major enhancements. It preserves (and extends) the Apache 2.0 API, so that modules and applications written for Apache 2.0 will work with Apache 2.2. Notable improvements in version 2.2 include scalability and applications architecture. Where Apache 2.0 offered the foundations of a powerful applications platform, Apache 2.2 has added walls and a roof.

1.2 The Apache Software Foundation

The Apache Software Foundation (ASF) provides organizational, legal, and financial support for a broad range of open-source software projects. The ASF provides an established framework for intellectual property and financial contributions that simultaneously limits contributors' potential legal exposure. Through a collaborative and meritocratic development process, Apache projects deliver enterprise-grade, freely available software products that attract large communities of users. The pragmatic Apache License makes it easy for all users—whether commercial enterprises or individuals—to deploy Apache products.

Formerly known as the Apache Group, the ASF has been incorporated as a membership-based, not-for-profit corporation to ensure that the Apache projects continue to exist beyond the participation of individual volunteers. Individuals who have demonstrated a commitment to collaborative open-source software development, through sustained participation and contributions within the ASF's projects, are eligible for membership in the ASF. An individual is awarded membership after nomination and approval by a majority of the existing ASF members. Thus the ASF is governed by the community it most directly serves—the people collaborating within its projects.

The ASF members periodically elect a Board of Directors to manage the Foundation's organizational affairs, as accorded by the ASF bylaws. The Board, in turn, appoints officers who oversee the day-to-day operations of the ASF. A number of public records of the ASF's operations are made available to the community.

1.2.1 Meritocracy

Unlike many other software development efforts conducted under an open-source license, the Apache Web Server was not initiated by a single developer (for example, like the Linux Kernel or the Perl/Python languages), but rather started as a diverse group of people who shared common interests and got to know one another by exchanging information, fixes, and suggestions.

As the group started to develop its own version of the software, moving away from the NCSA version, more people were attracted to the effort. They started to help out, first by sending little patches, or suggestions, or replying to e-mail on the mail list, and later by making more important contributions.

When the group felt that a person had "earned" the right to be part of the development community, its members granted the individual direct access to the code repository. This approach both expanded the group and increased its ability to develop the Apache program and maintain it more effectively.

We call this basic principle *meritocracy*—literally, "government of merit." The meritocracy process scaled very well without creating friction. Unlike in other situations where power is a scarce and conservative resource, in the Apache group newcomers were seen as volunteers who wanted to help, rather than as people who wanted to steal a position.

At the same time, because there is no pressure to recruit more members, Apache is not scrabbling for scarce talent in a competitive environment. Instead, it can afford to restrict itself to people with a proven track record of contributions and a positive attitude. And because it is a virtual community, it is worldwide and not constrained by geography.

1.2.2 Roles

The meritocracy supports a variety of roles.

User

A user is someone who uses the software. Users contribute to the Apache projects by providing feedback to developers in the form of bug reports and feature suggestions. Users may also participate in the Apache community by helping other users on mailing lists and user support forums.

Developer

A developer is a user who contributes to a project by submitting code or documentation. Developers take extra steps to participate in a project, are active on the developer mailing list, participate in discussions, and provide patches, documentation, suggestions, and criticism. Developers are also known as contributors.

Committer

A committer is a developer who was given write access to the code repository and has a signed Contributor License Agreement (CLA) on file. All committers have an `apache.org` mail address. Not needing to depend on other people for the patches, these individuals actually make short-term decisions for the project, subject to oversight from the Project Management Committee (PMC).

PMC Member

A PMC member is a developer or a committer who was elected to the PMC on a merit basis, in recognition of his or her role in the evolution of the project and demonstration of commitment. PMC members have write access to the code repository, an `apache.org` mail address, the right to vote on community-related decisions, and the right to propose an active user for committer status. The PMC as a whole is the entity that controls the project.

ASF Member

An ASF member is a person who was nominated by current ASF members and elected due to merit based on his or her role in the evolution and progress of the ASF. Members care for the ASF itself. This concern is usually demonstrated through the roots of project-related and cross-project activities. Legally, a member is a "shareholder" of the Foundation, one of the owners. ASF members have the right to elect the Board of Directors, to stand as a candidate for the Board election, to propose a committer for membership, and to participate in a wide range of other roles within the ASF.

1.2.3 Philosophy

While there is not an official list, certain principles have been cited as the core beliefs of philosophy behind the ASF. These principles are sometimes referred to as "The Apache Way":

- Collaborative software development

- Commercial-friendly standard license

- Consistently high-quality software

- Respectful, honest, technical-based interaction

- Faithful implementation of standards

- Security as a mandatory feature

1.3 The Apache Development Process

Apache development is both a top-down and a bottom-up process. From the top come Big Ideas: major new features or capabilities that involve significant reworking or new components, and may take many months or even years to pass from inception to maturity. From the bottom come small patches, to deal with bugs or add features that are simple to support within the current software.

Somewhere between these extremes is the typical module: a self-contained plug-in implementing new features of interest to its author and often others. A module may implement core webserver functionality, a general-purpose service, a small but vital function, or a single-purpose application. A module that is of sufficiently general interest may, if offered, be incorporated into the core Apache distribution. However, that inclusion will not happen if the module adds external dependencies such as third-party libraries, or if any concerns arise regarding the module's licensing or intellectual property issues. Such modules may be distributed independently by their developers or by third parties, such as a company supporting Apache or the packagers of a Linux distribution.

1.3.1 The Apache Codebase

Like any other software project, Apache maintains a codebase. This codebase is divided into projects; those relevant to the webserver are `httpd` (which includes code, documentation, and build files) and `apr`.

1.3.1.1 Subversion

All Apache code is kept in a repository at `http://svn.apache.org/`. The code is managed by Subversion (SVN),[1] a modern revision-control system suitable for large-scale multi-developer projects. This is a relatively recent (2004) change from an older but broadly similar system, CVS.

Read access to the entire repository is public, but write access is limited to committers. Read access includes the ability to view any point in the development history of Apache, including reviewing any single or cumulative change, brief explanations of reasons for changes (e.g., bugs fixed, new capabilities, internal improvements), the date of the change, and the person responsible for making the change.

1.3.1.2 Branches: Trunk, Development, and Stable

The code repository contains a trunk and several different branches. The default version of any file is the trunk of the repository. In Apache, this version represents work in progress. It is, by definition, untested, and it generally includes experimental code in at least some areas.

The current stable branch is Apache httpd 2.2, which is found in `/branches/2.2.x/`. Also maintained (albeit minimally) are the older 2.0 and 1.3 branches, although neither is the subject of much developer effort.

New branches may also be created on an ad hoc basis for experimental code. For example, a substantial reworking of parts of the core code took place while Apache 2.2 was in beta testing, to support asynchronous I/O. This code was initially too experimental to develop in the trunk, so the developers involved in this work created a new development branch. The new codebase has subsequently stabilized and been merged into the trunk, and should eventually be included in the next stable release (version 2.4).

---

1. `http://subversion.tigris.org/`

1.3.1.3 Review and Consensus

The Apache developers operate under different development policies for stable and development code:

- Stable code is always Review-Then-Commit (RTC). That means any code going into a branch marked as stable—even the most trivial patch—*must* have been through a proper review process.

- Development code is Commit-Then-Review (CTR). That means code can be added, changed, or removed by a committer acting unilaterally, and reviewed in place by other developers (of course, SVN makes it easy to reverse a change where necessary). Nevertheless, major changes should be reviewed before committing, or worked on in a separate development branch.

1.3.1.4 Backports

New code is first added to the trunk. If a developer wants this code to become part of a stable branch (typically a minor enhancement or bug fix), it is proposed for backporting. The mechanism for this is a file called STATUS, which contains a list of current issues including votes for backport.

To qualify for backporting, any change must collect at least three positive votes from committers. A positive vote means that the voter has reviewed the change and is satisfied with it, so three such votes is a fairly good indicator that the change is sound. Even simple bug fixes are subject to this rule, which means that noncritical bugs can sometimes take a frustratingly long time to fix while awaiting attention from enough committers. Having collected three positive votes and no veto, a change may be added to a stable branch.

A committer who reviews a change and is not happy with it may note his or her reservations about it, or even veto the change. The rules require that a veto must be accompanied by an explanation and/or an alternative proposal for accomplishing the objectives of the change. A vetoed change may be either dropped or revised to deal with the objections and submitted for a new vote. A veto or a non-veto reservation will typically be resolved by discussion of the relevant issues in the developer forums.

1.3.1.5 Releases

From time to time, a new release of Apache is made available. Releases of the current stable codebase (versions 2.2.x at the time of this book's writing) give users the advantages of the most recent improvements and bug fixes. Such releases will be marked as the best available version and recommended to users. A release is usually prompted by developers thinking that enough minor changes have accumulated to warrant a new version, but may also be hurried if a security problem comes to the developers' attention. A developer will volunteer to be *release manager* to deal with the administrative issues and create the release, while others will concentrate on applying any approved and pending updates in the STATUS file for the stable codebase.

Current policy is that even-numbered branches are stable, while odd-numbered branches are intended for development. (This policy represents a change from earlier versions: Apache 1.3 is stable, but early 2.0 releases were not.) Thus 2.0.x (since April 2002) and 2.2.x releases are stable, while 2.1.x releases were intended for alpha testing and later beta testing for Apache 2.2. Version 2.1 was approximately 10 months in alpha testing and 3 months in beta testing before its final release as stable version 2.2.

A released version should build, install, and run cleanly on any supported platform. For stable releases, meeting these criteria is a must; for development releases, it is also the intention, though it is less critical. To ensure that the release satisfies these conditions, the release manager first creates a build for the release from the appropriate SVN branch, and then announces it to the Apache developers and testers. This allows enough time for many developers and testers to install and run the build version on a wide range of different hardware, operating systems, and applications before it is announced to the general public. If a serious problem arises in this testing, the build is not released.

All releases are PGP-signed by the release manager responsible. Public keys for many Apache developers, including all release managers, are available at http://www.apache.org/dist/httpd/KEYS.

1.3.2 Development Forums

The primary development forum for the Apache Web Server is the mailing list dev@httpd.apache.org. All technical matters of Apache development are discussed there. A similar development list, dev@apr.apache.org, serves APR development. These forums are 100% open and public, and all discussions are archived in several places (referenced at the end of this chapter).

Another popular development forum is Internet Relay Chat (IRC). The Apache developer channels are #httpd-dev and #apr on irc.freenode.net. These venues are also fully public and open.

The Apache Bugzilla at `http://issues.apache.org/` is a searchable database of bug reports, enhancement requests, and patches, both current and historical. This database is also fully open and public. Note that because it is fully open, it contains a significant proportion of bogus reports (some of which cannot be closed and are shown as "reopened") and nebulous reports that cannot be verified. It also contains a number of reports marked `PatchAvailable` that are deliberately left open, where it is felt that a patch might be useful for some users but is not appropriate for inclusion in the standard Apache distribution.

The full and accurate archive of all code additions and changes is the Subversion repository at `http://svn.apache.org/`. This repository is updated in real time as code is changed. Read access is fully open and public, but write access is limited to authorized committers. Noteworthy files in Subversion include STATUS, which contains current discussions and votes, and CHANGES, which provides the executive summary of changes to a stable/release branch.

1.3.3 Developers

It is important to Apache that the diversity of its users be reflected in its development community. There is no question of an Apache project becoming dominated by any one company or group of companies. Some developers (including this author) work either as freelance consultants or for very small companies. Other developers come from the larger vendors such as IBM, Red Hat, and Novell; from the big users such as Google, Yahoo!, and Ask Jeeves; and from universities and other noncommercial organizations. Whereas the majority of developers are employed by companies, the independents outnumber any single corporate contingent.

Perhaps more importantly, the developers reflect the wide range of roles that Apache fulfills. Those who are running it on ultra-busy sites such as CNN or HEAnet need to sustain loads of tens of thousands of concurrent users on a 24/7 basis, so they care about performance, scalability, and stability. Application sites, such as this author's Site Valet, are concerned with extending Apache beyond its original web-server role and using it as an application server. E-commerce sites are concerned with both security and reliability issues. Hosting companies need to support widely differing users and delegate control while maintaining security and stability. Having active developers from such a wide range of backgrounds ensures that Apache works well in all of these environments.

Finally, we are by no means an exclusive "hacker" community. Although software development and maintenance is the biggest single activity carried out by Apache developers, some members have risen to the top of the Apache hierarchy without writing a single line of C code! Support, documentation, and organizational roles are as highly valued as programming.

1.3.4 Participation

Participation in any of the Apache forums is open to anyone with a contribution to make. There are many ways to contribute, and all are highly valued:

- **Coding.** Patches for issues brought up in Bugzilla are very welcome. Contributions to current subjects of debate found on the developer lists, or highlighted in STATUS, are always welcome. The programmer looking for something to do is also invited to search the codebase in SVN for TODO or FIXME notes. Patches are most welcome when they can be applied cleanly (`diff -u` or `svn -diff` format) and are clearly motivated and explained. Patches can be posted to the developer list or to Bugzilla.

- **Documentation.** The documentation is held in SVN. All original documents are in an XML format that is a subset of DocBook. New documentation or improvements (patches) to existing documentation are always welcome.

- **Translation.** The documentation is provided in a number of languages, but not all pages are available in all languages. Neither are the translations always up to date with the originals. If you have the language skills, look for missing or outdated pages in your language, and fix them!

- **Testing.** Build and test code on your platform, particularly if you use an unusual platform. Build it with unusual environments and toolkits: Does it build and install cleanly? Stress-test it in all your most unusual tasks. If it fails, or if you find unexpected changes from an earlier version, try and diagnose what's going on. Report any bugs you find to the developer mailing list or Bugzilla. Try to ensure that whatever you describe is clear and reproducible behavior.

- **Build.** Maintaining the Apache build and installation setup is an important task, but one for which (at the time of this book's writing) we are not well equipped. Even the most widely used GNU autoconf-based installation for UNIX/Linux family platforms would benefit from an overhaul.

1.4 Apache and Intellectual Property

All Apache projects are copyrighted by the ASF and licensed under the Apache License. At the same time, the ASF and PMC take strong measures to ensure that no third-party intellectual property is used in Apache code without legally binding, written permission to distribute it under the Apache License. Note that while Apache holds the copyright for the entirety of a project, parts of a project may remain copyrighted by individual contributors and be licensed under ASF terms.

1.4.1 The Apache License

The Apache License (found in Appendix A) is a free software license, in the tradition of the older BSD and MIT software licenses, but with an important additional clause appropriate to our times. It satisfies all accepted definitions of free and open-source software.

Given that the language of free software may be confusing to some readers, let's pause to clarify some important points. Please note that this is just basic background information, and is certainly not legal advice for users in any particular country.

Free Speech, Not Free Beer

Free beer is nice. Free speech is important!

When we talk of software freedom, we are using the word in the sense of free speech. The key freedom in software is the freedom for every user to do whatever it takes to meet his or her own needs (or, of course, to hire someone to do that). Making the source code available is a necessary part of freedom.

Cost is not relevant to software freedom. Apache is available at a wide range of costs, from a no-cost download, to a package bundled in, for example, a commercial Linux distribution, to a fully paid product backed by a commercial support organization.

Not Public Domain

Like most other free software, Apache is *not* in the public domain. It is copyrighted by the ASF and subject to a license. The difference between this status and "traditional" commercial software licenses is that the Apache License is a great deal more friendly and less restrictive.

Not Shareware, Nagware, or Adware

Shareware and its modern variants are concepts alien to free software. They are commonly (though not always) associated with low-quality, amateur products, and today they are more likely to be driven by marketing than by engineering.

Not GPL

The oldest and best-known (but also much-misrepresented) free software license is the GNU General Public License (GPL), written and owned by the Free Software Foundation (FSF). The GPL introduced a concept known as *copyleft*. The basic principle can be summarized as follows: "We are granting you these freedoms, and you can't take them away from anyone else." This policy is sometimes seen as business unfriendly, because copyleft software cannot be incorporated willy-nilly into non-free products.[2] The Apache License is explicitly business friendly; it is *not* copyleft.

In fact, the Apache License is not even compatible with the GPL.[3] That is, each license includes provisions that are incompatible with the other license: GPL software cannot be distributed on ASF terms because copyleft is a restriction incompatible with ASF policy. ASF-licensed software cannot be distributed on GPL terms. Here's what the FSF has to say on the subject:

> This is a free software license but it is incompatible with the GPL. The Apache Software License is incompatible with the GPL because it has a specific requirement that is not in the GPL: it has certain patent termination cases that the GPL does not require. (We don't think those patent termination cases are inherently a bad idea, but nonetheless they are incompatible with the GNU GPL.[4])

Note that none of these issues is a problem for end users or for third parties such as module developers or distributors. Linux (GPL) vendors routinely include Apache in their products, and many Apache modules are GPL licensed. It's no problem for the Linux distributors to comply with both licenses, or for the module developers

---

2. This is a much-misunderstood topic. The GPL is a great deal less restrictive than it is often portrayed in the media. For details, see http://www.fsf.org/licensing/.

3. This discussion refers to GPL version 2 (1991). Version 3 is currently in preparation, and a draft has been posted for discussion. It appears likely that it will be possible to distribute Apache software under version 3 of the GPL, but not the reverse.

4. http://www.fsf.org/licensing/licenses/index_html#GPLIncompatibleLicenses

to apply their own choice of license to their work. Even the famously purist and legally meticulous Debian distribution[5] distributes GPL modules with Apache.

Where the incompatibility in licenses may pose a problem is in the interface with GPL software. Consider its implications for MySQL,[6] an SQL database package licensed under the GPL. To comply with the GPL requirements of MySQL, the Apache/APR driver[7] for MySQL is also GPL licensed and, therefore, cannot be distributed within Apache by the ASF. Instead, it is available as a separate download from the author's site or as a separate package from a third party. This is relevant to users who compile Apache themselves, but those users who install Apache from packages need never concern themselves with the details.

Patents and the Anti-Piracy Clause

The greatest danger to technology developers today comes from patents. This is particularly true in the United States, where the patent system was seen for many years as an instrument of economic imperialism: Let's grant thousands of patents to "our" companies, then enforce those patents worldwide through the World Trade Organization (WTO) treaties to gain a global competitive advantage. Consequently, the U.S. Patent Office has issued huge numbers of patents while making no attempt at effective scrutiny or quality control. Many of these patents are in the hands of people who have no interest in technology, but rather seek to extort money from legitimate businesses.

This is, in a very real sense, today's piracy. In the past, rulers of a country, province, or city would assert a claim over "their" seas, charge a substantial levy on foreign shipping to pass through their territory, and license privateers to enforce their property rights and seize any unlicensed ship passing through. Similarly, today's patent holders seek to charge levies to legitimate business, and use lawyers to enforce their property. In fact, the situation today is arguably worse than in the olden days, in that there are hugely more patents than there ever were nautical pirates, and there are no longer any safe shipping lanes.

One unusual restriction in the Apache License deals with this issue as far as possible. Acceptance of the Apache License requires the licensee not to assert any patent rights it may claim against the ASF or Apache users.

---

5. http://www.debian.org/
6. http://www.mysql.com/
7. See Chapter 11 for details.

To the best of my knowledge, Apache has remained clear of intellectual property lawsuits. This contrasts with the situation faced by Linux in the SCO lawsuits (although it appears likely that Linux will be vindicated[8]), and more strongly with the situation involving Microsoft, whose end users have paid substantial damages to third parties over patent infringements in Microsoft software.[9,10]

1.4.2 Third-Party Intellectual Property

Apache's intellectual property is protected by copyright and the license. Of course, it is also critically important that Apache doesn't violate anyone else's intellectual property. That means that all significant contributions to Apache must be properly donated:

- Before a developer can become a committer, he or she must sign a Contributor License Agreement (CLA) that gives the ASF all necessary rights to use that developer's contributions and to license them to third parties on ASF terms. The CLA also binds a contributor to ensure that contributions which are not their own original work are signed over to the ASF before including them in Apache. The full CLA appears in Appendix B.

- When a developer is not his or her own master (e.g., an employee whose employer may have rights over his or her work), a Corporate CLA signed by an authorized officer of the employer (e.g., CTO or IT Director) is also required. The full CCLA also appears in Appendix B.

- All relevant CLAs and CCLAs must be on file with the ASF before an individual can be granted commit access. These agreements serve to ensure that committers and their employers cannot prevent the ASF or Apache users making use of their contributed work.

---

8. SCO's main lawsuits are against UNIX and Linux developer IBM and former UNIX owner Novell, not end users. One of its two suits against Linux users (Daimler-Chrysler) has already been thrown out of court; the other (Autozone) is on hold pending the outcome of the IBM and Novell cases.
9. Starting in 1999, end users have paid tens of millions of dollars to Timeline, Inc., for patent infringements in Microsoft's SQL Server. Microsoft had licensed the patents for its own internal use but the license did not to extend to users of the software, according to a final court judgment in February 2003.
10. In 2005, Microsoft PR made a very public commitment to indemnify users against intellectual property lawsuits. Nevertheless, in January 2006, lawsuits over patent infringement in Microsoft DRM were filed by Softvault against Yahoo!, Microsoft, Napster, Creative Labs, Dell, Gateway, Iriver, Samsung, Toshiba, Digital Networks, Palm, Audiovox, Sandisk, and Thomson (http://www.theinquirer.net/?article=28990).

Responsibility

In the first instance, it is the responsibility of each committer to ensure that his or her contributions don't violate third-party intellectual property.

The overall responsibility lies with the PMC, which will query any contribution that raises doubts—in particular, major new contributions.

Audit

If despite all due care, problems with third-party intellectual property should arise, Apache has a full audit trail managed by Subversion. Thus, in the worst case, any problematic code can be identified and removed.

1.5 Further Reading

1.5.1 Interactive Online Forums

Public Mailing Lists

The Apache Module Developers list `modules-dev@httpd.apache.org` is an appropriate place for discussion of any module development issues. This list moved from `apache-modules@covalent.net` in September 2006, so check the archives of both lists.

The official developers list for the Apache Web Server is `dev@httpd.apache.org`. You are welcome to participate, but please stay on topic.

The official developers list for the Apache Portable Runtime is `dev@apr.apache.org`. You are welcome to participate, but please stay on topic.

The Apache users list `users@httpd.apache.org` is an appropriate forum for general discussion and user support questions.

Usenet

The `comp.infosystems.www.servers.[unix|windows|mac|misc]` newsgroups are appropriate for general discussion and questions about Apache on the respective platforms.

Online Chat

There are several channels relevant to Apache on **`irc://irc.freenode.net:`**

`#apache`—general support/unofficial helpdesk channel. Ask meaningful questions and wait for an answer. But do your homework first. In particular, look in the error log! Pay attention to fajita, the #apache 'bot; many of the regulars work by prompting her to answer your questions and/or post URLs to the relevant documentation pages.

`#apache-modules`—the channel for module development. It is likely to be appropriate for readers of this book.

`#apr`—the semi-official APR channel, including automated live notification of all changes to the APR repository.

`#httpd-dev`—the semi-official channel for webserver development, including automated live notification of all changes to the repository, including documentation and the website.

`#asfinfra`—the Apache infrastructure channel.

1.5.2 Conferences

The ASF organizes *ApacheCon* conferences devoted to ASF projects. These conferences bring together many of the developers (who know each other well from the online forums but may never otherwise meet face-to-face). Users may come just to learn, but some also bring new insights to the developers. A busy program of tutorials and talks by both developers and users is complemented by both organized and informal social events.

1.5.3 Websites

Official and Semi-official Apache Sites

`http://www.apache.org/`—Apache Software Foundation

`http://httpd.apache.org/`—Apache Web Server

`http://apr.apache.org/`—APR home site

`http://svn.apache.org/`—Apache code repository and complete history `http://issues.apache.org/`—Bugs and issues database

`http://modules.apache.org/`—Apache modules register

`http://asylum.zones.apache.org/modules/`—Updated modules register (work in progress)

`http://mail-archives.apache.org/`—Mailing list archives

`http://people.apache.org/`—Pages of individual Apache committers

`http://apachecon.com/`—ApacheCon conference

`http://perl.apache.org/`—mod_perl (Apache API in Perl)

`http://www.modpython.org/`—mod_python (Apache API in Python)

`http://tcl.apache.org/`—TCL language in Apache

`http://httpd.apache.org/cli/`—mod_aspdotnet (Microsoft's asp dot net)

Third-Party Extensions

`http://apache.webthing.com/`—More than 20 modules by the author of this book

`http://www.outoforder.cc/`—12 featured modules and other relevant work

`http://www.php.net/`—PHP language

`http://www.rubyonrails.org/`—Ruby on Rails

Developer Documentation

`http://docx.webperf.org/`—API reference

`http://www.apachetutor.org/dev/`—Developer tutorial site created and maintained by the author of this book

`http://dev.ariel-networks.com/apr/apr-tutorial/html/apr-tutorial.html`—A useful tutorial for APR, decoupling it from its role in the webserver

`http://www.apache-modules.com/`—Companion site to an Apache modules book that was never completed

Other Tutorials, News, and Articles

`http://www.onlamp.com/pub/q/all_apache_articles`—A wide range of articles

`http://www.apachelounge.com/`—News site together with Windows binary downloads (often available before the "official" ones)

`http://marc.theaimsgroup.com/`—Mailing list archives

1.6 Summary

This chapter examined the social, historical, and legal background of Apache and its culture. Specifically, Chapter 1 considered the following topics:

- The historical context of Apache `httpd`

- The Apache Software Foundation and its culture

- The Apache developers, processes, and resources for development and support, including how to participate

- Apache's approach to intellectual property, including the Apache License and the safeguards against misuse of third-party intellectual property

Chapter 1 was decidedly nontechnical. In contrast, the remainder of the book is all about programming with Apache, starting with a comprehensive overview, and moving to hands-on treatment of module and application development.

Chapter 2

The Apache Platform and Architecture

Apache runs as a permanent background task: a daemon (UNIX) or service (Windows). Start-up is a slow and expensive operation, so for an operational server, it is usual for Apache to start at system boot and remain permanently up. Early versions of Apache had documented support for an `inetd` mode (run from a generic superserver for every incoming request), but this mode was never appropriate for operational use.

2.1 Overview

The Apache HTTP Server comprises a relatively small core, together with a number of modules (Figure 2-1). Modules may be compiled statically into the server or, more commonly, held in a `/modules/` or `/libexec/` directory and loaded dynamically at runtime. In addition, the server relies on the Apache Portable Runtime (APR) libraries, which provide a cross-platform operating system layer and utilities,

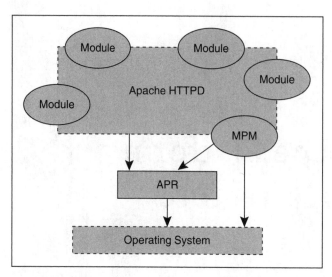

FIGURE 2-1
Apache architecture

so that modules don't have to rely on non-portable operating system calls. A special-purpose module, the Multi-Processing Module (MPM), serves to optimize Apache for the underlying operating system. The MPM should normally be the only module to access the operating system other than through the APR.

2.2 Two-Phase Operation

Apache operation proceeds in two phases: start-up and operational. System start-up takes place as `root`, and includes parsing the configuration file(s), loading modules, and initializing system resources such as log files, shared memory segments, and database connections. For normal operation, Apache relinquishes its system privileges and runs as an unprivileged user before accepting and processing connections from clients over the network. This basic security measure helps to prevent a simple bug in Apache (or a module or script) from becoming a devastating system vulnerability, like those exploited by malware such as "Code Red" and "Nimda" in MS IIS.

This two-stage operation has some implications for applications architecture. First, anything that requires system privileges must be run at system start-up. Second, it is good practice to run as much initialization as possible at start-up, so as to minimize the processing required to service each request. Conversely, because so many slow and expensive operations are concentrated in system start-up, it would be hugely inefficient to try to run Apache from a generic server such as `inetd` or `tcpserver`.

One non-intuitive quirk of the architecture is that the configuration code is, in fact, executed twice at start-up (although not at restart). The first time through checks that the configuration is valid (at least to the point that Apache *can* successfully start); the second pass is "live" and leads into the operational phase. Most modules can ignore this behavior (standard use of APR pools ensures that it doesn't cause a resource leak), but it may have implications for some modules. For example, a module that dynamically loads new code at start-up may want to do so just once and, therefore, must use a technique such as setting and checking a static flag to ensure that critical initialization takes place just once.

2.2.1 Start-up Phase

The purpose of Apache's start-up phase is to read the configuration, load modules and libraries, and initialize required resources. Each module may have its own resources, and has the opportunity to initialize those resources. At start-up, Apache runs as a single-process, single-thread program and has full system privileges.

2.2.1.1 Configuration

Apache's main configuration file is normally called `httpd.conf`. However, this nomenclature is just a convention, and third-party Apache distributions such as those provided as `.rpm` or `.deb` packages may use a different naming scheme. In addition, `httpd.conf` may be a single file, or it may be distributed over several files using the `Include` directive to include different configuration files. Some distributions have highly intricate configurations. For example, Debian GNU/Linux ships an Apache configuration that relies heavily on familiarity with Debian, rather than with Apache. It is not the purpose of this book to discuss the merits of different layouts, so we'll simply call this configuration file `httpd.conf`.

The `httpd.conf` configuration file is a plain text file and is parsed line-by-line at server start-up. The contents of `httpd.conf` comprise directives, containers, and comments. Blank lines and leading whitespace are also allowed, but will be ignored.

Directives

Most of the contents of `httpd.conf` are directives. A directive may have zero or more arguments, separated by whitespace. Each directive determines its own syntax, so different directives may permit different numbers of arguments, and different argument types (e.g., string, numeric, enumerated, Boolean on/off, or filename). Each directive is implemented by some module or the core, as described in Chapter 9.

For example:

```
LoadModule foo_module modules/mod_foo.so
```

This directive is implemented by `mod_so` and tells it to load a module. The first argument is the module name (string, alphanumeric). The second argument is a filename, which may be absolute or relative to the server root.

```
DocumentRoot /usr/local/apache/htdocs
```

This directive is implemented by the core, and sets the directory that is the root of the main document tree visible from the Web.

```
SetEnv hello "Hello, World!"
```

This directive is implemented by `mod_env` and sets an environment variable. Note that because the second argument contains a space, we must surround it with quotation marks.

```
Choices On
```

This directive is implemented by `mod_choices` (Chapter 6) and activates that module's options.

Containers

A container is a special form of directive, characterized by a syntax that superficially resembles markup, using angle brackets. Containers differ semantically from other directives in that they comprise a start and an end on separate lines, and they affect directives falling between the start and the end of the container. For example, the `<VirtualHost>` container is implemented by the core and defines a virtual host:

```
<VirtualHost 10.31.2.139>
   ServerName www.example.com
   DocumentRoot /usr/www/example
   ServerAdmin webmaster@example.com
   CustomLog /var/log/www/example.log
</VirtualHost>
```

The container provides a *context* for the directives within it. In this case, the directives apply to requests to `www.example.com`, but not to requests to any other names this server responds to. Containers can be nested unless a module explicitly prevents it. Directives, including containers, may be context sensitive, so they are valid only in some specified type of context.

Comments

Any line whose first character is a hash is read as a comment.

```
# This line is a comment
```

A hash within a directive doesn't in general make a comment, unless the module implementing the directive explicitly supports it.

If a module is not loaded, directives that it implements are not recognized, and Apache will stop with a syntax error when it encounters them. Therefore mod_so must be statically linked to load other modules. This is pretty much essential whenever you're developing new modules, as without `LoadModule` you'd have to rebuild the entire server every time you change your module!

2.2.2 Operational Phase

At the end of the start-up phase, control passes to the Multi-Processing Module (see Section 2.3). The MPM is responsible for managing Apache's operation at a systems level. It typically does so by maintaining a pool of worker processes and/or threads, as appropriate to the operating system and other applicable constraints (such as optimization for a particular usage scenario). The original process remains as "master," maintaining a pool of worker children. These workers are responsible for servicing incoming connections, while the parent process deals with creating new children, removing surplus ones as necessary, and communicating signals such as "shut down" or "restart."

Because of the MPM architecture, it is not possible to describe the operational phase in definite terms. Whereas the standard MPMs use worker children in some manner, they are not constrained to work in only one way. Thus another MPM could, in principle, implement an entirely different server architecture at the system level.

2.2.3 Shutdown

There is no shutdown phase as such. Instead, anything that needs be done on shutdown is registered as a cleanup, as described in Chapter 3. When Apache stops, all registered cleanups are run.

2.3 Multi-Processing Modules

At the end of the start-up phase, after the configuration has been read, overall control of Apache passes to a Multi-Processing Module. The MPM provides the interface between the running Apache server and the underlying operating system. Its primary role is to optimize Apache for each platform, while ensuring the server runs efficiently and securely.

As indicated by the name, the MPM is itself a module. But the MPM is uniquely a *systems-level* module (so developing an MPM falls outside the scope of a book on *applications* development). Also uniquely, every Apache instance must contain exactly one MPM, which is selected at build-time.

2.3.1 Why MPMs?

The old NCSA server, and Apache 1, grew up in a UNIX environment. It was a multiprocess server, where each client would be serviced by one server instance. If there were more concurrent clients than server processes, Apache would fork additional server processes to deal with them. Under normal operation, Apache would maintain a pool of available server processes to deal with incoming requests.

Whereas this scheme works well on UNIX-family[1] systems, it is an inefficient solution on platforms such as Windows, where forking a process is an expensive operation. So making Apache truly cross-platform required another solution. The approach adopted for Apache 2 is to turn the core processing into a pluggable module, the MPM, which can be optimized for different environments. The MPM architecture also allows different Apache models to coexist even within a single operating system, thus providing users with options for different usages.

---

1. Here and elsewhere in this book, terms such as "UNIX-family" imply both UNIX itself and other POSIX-centered operating systems such as Linux and MacOSX.

In practice, only UNIX-family operating systems offer a useful[2] choice: Other supported platforms (Windows, Netware, OS/2, BeOS) have a single MPM optimized for each platform. UNIX has two production-quality MPMs (Prefork and Worker) available as standard, a third (Event) that is thought to be stable for non-SSL uses in Apache 2.2, and several experimental options unsuitable for production use. Third-party MPMs are also available.

2.3.2 The UNIX-Family MPMs

- The **Prefork** MPM is a nonthreaded model essentially similar to Apache 1.x. It is a safe option in all cases, and for servers running non-thread-safe software such as PHP, it is the only safe option. For some applications, including many of those popular with Apache 1.3 (e.g., simple static pages, CGI scripts), this MPM may be as good as anything.[3]

- The **Worker** MPM is a threaded model, whose advantages include lower memory usage (important on busy servers) and much greater scalability than that provided by Prefork in certain types of applications. We will discuss some of these cases later when we introduce SQL database support and mod_dbd.

- Both of the stable MPMs suffer from a limitation that affects very busy servers. Whereas HTTP Keepalive is necessary to reduce TCP connection and network overhead, it ties up a server process or thread while the keepalive is active. As a consequence, a very busy server may run out of available threads. The **Event** MPM is a new model that deals with this problem by decoupling the server thread from the connection. Cases where the Event MPM may prove most useful are servers with extremely high hit rates but for which the server processing is fast, so that the number of available threads is a critical resource limitation. A busy server with the Worker MPM may sustain tens of thousands of hits per second (as happens, for example, with popular news outlets at peak times), but the Event MPM might help to handle high loads more easily. Note that the Event MPM will *not* work with secure HTTP (HTTPS).

---

2. MPMs are not necessarily tied to an operating system (most systems have some kind of POSIX support and might be able to use it to run Prefork, for instance). But if you try to build Apache with a "foreign" MPM, you're on your own!

3. This depends on the platform. On Linux versions without NPTL, Prefork is commonly reported to be as fast as Worker. On Solaris, Worker is reported to be much faster than Prefork. Your mileage may vary.

- There are also several experimental MPMs for UNIX that are not, at the time of this book's writing, under active development; they may or may not ever be completed. The **Perchild** MPM promised a much-requested feature: It runs servers for different virtual hosts under different user IDs. Several alternatives offer similar features, including the third-party **Metux**[4] and **Peruser**[5] MPMs, and (for Linux only) `mod_ruid`.[6] For running external programs, other options include `fastcgi/mod_fcgid`[7] and `suexec` (CGI). The author does not have personal knowledge of these third-party solutions and so cannot make recommendations about them.

2.3.3 Working with MPMs and Operating Systems

The one-sentence summary: MPMs are invisible to applications and should be ignored!

Applications developed for Apache should normally be MPM-agnostic. Given that MPM internals are not part of the API, this is basically straightforward, provided programmers observe basic rules of good practice (namely, write thread-safe, cross-process-safe, reentrant code), as briefly discussed in Chapter 4. This issue is closely related to the broader question of developing platform-independent code. Indeed, it is sometimes useful to regard the MPM, rather than the operating system, as the applications platform.

Sometimes an application is naturally better suited to some MPMs than others. For example, database-driven or load-balancing applications benefit substantially from connection pooling (discussed later in this book) and therefore from a threaded MPM. In contrast, forking a child process (the original CGI implementation or `mod_ext_filter`) creates greater overhead in a threaded program and, therefore, works best with the Prefork MPM. Nevertheless, an application should work even when used with a suboptimal MPM, unless there are compelling reasons to limit it.

If you wish to run Apache on an operating system that is not yet supported, the main task is to add support for your target platform to the APR, which provides the operating system layer. A custom MPM may or may not be necessary, but is likely to deliver better performance than an existing one. From the point of view of

---

4. `http://www.metux.de/mpm/`
5. `http://www.telana.com/peruser.php`
6. `http://websupport.sk/~stanojr/projects/mod_ruid/`
7. `http://fastcgi.coremail.cn/`

Apache, this is a systems programming task, and hence it falls outside the scope of an applications development book.

2.4 Basic Concepts and Structures

To work with Apache as a development platform, we need an overview of the basic units of webserver operation and the core objects that represent them within Apache. The most important are the **server,** the TCP **connection,** and the HTTP **request.** A fourth basic Apache object, the **process,** is a unit of the operating system rather than the application architecture. Each of these basic units is represented by a core data structure defined in the header file httpd.h and, like other core objects we encounter in applications development, is completely independent of the MPM in use.

Before describing these core data structures, we need to introduce some further concepts used throughout Apache and closely tied to the architecture:

- APR pools (apr_pool_t) are the core of resource management in Apache. Whenever a resource is allocated dynamically, a cleanup is registered with a pool, ensuring that system resources are freed when they are no longer required. Pools tie resources to the lifetime of one of the core objects. We will describe pools in depth in Chapter 3.

- Configuration records are used by each module to tie its own data to one of the core objects. The core data structures include configuration vectors (ap_conf_vector_t), with each module having its own entry in the vector. They are used in two ways: to set and retrieve permanent configuration data, and to store temporary data associated with a transient object. They are often essential to avoid use of unsafe static or global data in a module, as discussed in Chapters 4 and 9.

Having introduced pools and configuration records, we are now ready to look at the Apache core objects. In order of importance to most modules, they are

- request_rec
- server_rec
- conn_rec
- process_rec

The first two are by far the most commonly encountered in application development.

2.4.1 request_rec

A `request_rec` object is created whenever Apache accepts an HTTP request from a client, and is destroyed as soon as Apache finishes processing the request. The `request_rec` object is passed to every handler implemented by any module in the course of processing a request (as discussed in Chapters 5 and 6). It holds all of the internal data relevant to processing an HTTP request. It also includes a number of fields used internally to maintain state and client information by Apache:

- A request pool, for management of objects having the lifetime of the request. It is used to manage resources allocated while processing the request.

- A vector of configuration records for static request configuration (per-directory data specified in `httpd.conf` or `.htaccess`).

- A vector of configuration records for transient data used in processing.

- Tables of HTTP input, output, and error headers.

- A table of Apache environment variables (the environment as seen in scripting extensions such as SSI, CGI, `mod_rewrite`, and PHP), and a similar "notes" table for request data that should not be seen by scripts.

- Pointers to all other relevant objects, including the connection, the server, and any related request objects.

- Pointers to the input and output filter chains (discussed in Chapter 8).

- The URI requested, and the internal parsed representation of it, including the handler (see Chapter 5) and filesystem mapping (see Chapter 6).

Here is the full definition, from `httpd.h`:

```
/** A structure that represents the current request */
struct request_rec {
    /** The pool associated with the request */
    apr_pool_t *pool;
    /** The connection to the client */
    conn_rec *connection;
    /** The virtual host for this request */
    server_rec *server;

    /** Pointer to the redirected request if this is an external redirect */
    request_rec *next;
    /** Pointer to the previous request if this is an internal redirect */
    request_rec *prev;
```

```
/** Pointer to the main request if this is a sub-request
 * (see http_request.h) */
request_rec *main;

/* Info about the request itself... we begin with stuff that only
 * protocol.c should ever touch...
 */
/** First line of request */
char *the_request;
/** HTTP/0.9, "simple" request (e.g., GET /foo\n w/no headers) */
int assbackwards;
/** A proxy request (calculated during post_read_request/translate_name)
 *   possible values PROXYREQ_NONE, PROXYREQ_PROXY, PROXYREQ_REVERSE,
 *                   PROXYREQ_RESPONSE
 */
int proxyreq;
/** HEAD request, as opposed to GET */
int header_only;
/** Protocol string, as given to us, or HTTP/0.9 */
char *protocol;
/** Protocol version number of protocol; 1.1 = 1001 */
int proto_num;
/** Host, as set by full URI or Host: */
const char *hostname;

/** Time when the request started */
apr_time_t request_time;

/** Status line, if set by script */
const char *status_line;
/** Status line */
int status;

/* Request method, two ways; also, protocol, etc. Outside of protocol.c,
 * look, but don't touch.
 */

/** Request method (e.g., GET, HEAD, POST, etc.) */
const char *method;
/** M_GET, M_POST, etc. */
int method_number;

/**
 *  'allowed' is a bit-vector of the allowed methods.
 *
 *  A handler must ensure that the request method is one that
 *  it is capable of handling.  Generally modules should DECLINE
 *  any request methods they do not handle.  Prior to aborting the
 *  handler like this, the handler should set r->allowed to the list
 *  of methods that it is willing to handle. This bitvector is used
```

```
 *   to construct the "Allow:" header required for OPTIONS requests,
 *   and HTTP_METHOD_NOT_ALLOWED and HTTP_NOT_IMPLEMENTED status codes.
 *
 *   Since the default_handler deals with OPTIONS, all modules can
 *   usually decline to deal with OPTIONS.  TRACE is always allowed;
 *   modules don't need to set it explicitly.
 *
 *   Since the default_handler will always handle a GET, a
 *   module which does *not* implement GET should probably return
 *   HTTP_METHOD_NOT_ALLOWED.  Unfortunately this means that a Script GET
 *   handler can't be installed by mod_actions.
 */
apr_int64_t allowed;
/** Array of extension methods */
apr_array_header_t *allowed_xmethods;
/** List of allowed methods */
ap_method_list_t *allowed_methods;

/** byte count in stream is for body */
apr_off_t sent_bodyct;
/** body byte count, for easy access */
apr_off_t bytes_sent;
/** Last modified time of the requested resource */
apr_time_t mtime;

/* HTTP/1.1 connection-level features */

/**Sending chunked transfer-coding */
int chunked;
/** The Range: header */
const char *range;
/** The "real" content length */
apr_off_t clength;

/** Remaining bytes left to read from the request body */
apr_off_t remaining;
/** Number of bytes that have been read  from the request body */
apr_off_t read_length;
/** Method for reading the request body
 * (e.g., REQUEST_CHUNKED_ERROR, REQUEST_NO_BODY,
 *  REQUEST_CHUNKED_DECHUNK, etc.) */
int read_body;
/** reading chunked transfer-coding */
int read_chunked;
/** is client waiting for a 100 response? */
unsigned expecting_100;

/* MIME header environments, in and out.  Also, an array containing
 * environment variables to be passed to subprocesses, so people can
 * write modules to add to that environment.
 *
```

```
 * The difference between headers_out and err_headers_out is that the
 * latter are printed even on error, and persist across internal redirects
 * (so the headers printed for ErrorDocument handlers will have them).
 *
 * The 'notes' apr_table_t is for notes from one module to another, with no
 * other set purpose in mind...
 */

/** MIME header environment from the request */
apr_table_t *headers_in;
/** MIME header environment for the response */
apr_table_t *headers_out;
/** MIME header environment for the response, printed even on errors and
 * persist across internal redirects */
apr_table_t *err_headers_out;
/** Array of environment variables to be used for subprocesses */
apr_table_t *subprocess_env;
/** Notes from one module to another */
apr_table_t *notes;

/* content_type, handler, content_encoding, and all content_languages
 * MUST be lowercased strings.  They may be pointers to static strings;
 * they should not be modified in place.
 */
/** The content-type for the current request */
const char *content_type;   /* Break these out -- we dispatch on 'em */
/** The handler string that we use to call a handler function */
const char *handler;        /* What we *really* dispatch on */

/** How to encode the data */
const char *content_encoding;
/** Array of strings representing the content languages */
apr_array_header_t *content_languages;

/** variant list validator (if negotiated) */
char *vlist_validator;

/** If an authentication check was made, this gets set to the user name. */
char *user;
/** If an authentication check was made, this gets set to the auth type. */
char *ap_auth_type;

/** This response cannot be cached */
int no_cache;
/** There is no local copy of this response */
int no_local_copy;

/* What object is being requested (either directly, or via include
 * or content-negotiation mapping).
 */
/** The URI without any parsing performed */
```

```
char *unparsed_uri;
/** The path portion of the URI */
char *uri;
/** The filename on disk corresponding to this response */
char *filename;
/** The true filename, we canonicalize r->filename if these don't match */
char *canonical_filename;
/** The PATH_INFO extracted from this request */
char *path_info;
/** The QUERY_ARGS extracted from this request */
char *args;
/**  finfo.protection (st_mode) set to zero if no such file */
apr_finfo_t finfo;
/** A struct containing the components of URI */
apr_uri_t parsed_uri;

/**
 * Flag for the handler to accept or reject path_info on
 * the current request.  All modules should respect the
 * AP_REQ_ACCEPT_PATH_INFO and AP_REQ_REJECT_PATH_INFO
 * values, while AP_REQ_DEFAULT_PATH_INFO indicates they
 * may follow existing conventions.  This is set to the
 * user's preference upon HOOK_VERY_FIRST of the fixups.
 */
int used_path_info;

/* Various other config info which may change with .htaccess files.
 * These are config vectors, with one void* pointer for each module
 * (the thing pointed to being the module's business).
 */

/** Options set in config files, etc. */
struct ap_conf_vector_t *per_dir_config;
/** Notes on *this* request */
struct ap_conf_vector_t *request_config;

/**
 * A linked list of the .htaccess configuration directives
 * accessed by this request.
 * N.B.: always add to the head of the list, _never_ to the end.
 * That way, a sub-request's list can (temporarily) point to a parent's list
 */
const struct htaccess_result *htaccess;

/** A list of output filters to be used for this request */
struct ap_filter_t *output_filters;
/** A list of input filters to be used for this request */
struct ap_filter_t *input_filters;

/** A list of protocol level output filters to be used for this
 *  request */
```

```
    struct ap_filter_t *proto_output_filters;
    /** A list of protocol level input filters to be used for this
     *   request */
    struct ap_filter_t *proto_input_filters;

    /** A flag to determine if the eos bucket has been sent yet */
    int eos_sent;

/* Things placed at the end of the record to avoid breaking binary
 * compatibility.  It would be nice to remember to reorder the entire
 * record to improve 64-bit alignment the next time we need to break
 * binary compatibility for some other reason.
 */
};
```

2.4.2 server_rec

The `server_rec` defines a logical webserver. If virtual hosts are in use,[8] each virtual host has its own `server_rec`, defining it independently of the other hosts. The `server_rec` is created at server start-up, and it never dies unless the entire `httpd` is shut down. The `server_rec` does not have its own pool; instead, server resources need to be allocated from the process pool, which is shared by all servers. It does have a configuration vector as well as server resources including the server name and definition, resources and limits, and logging information.

The `server_rec` is the second most important structure to programmers, after the `request_rec`. It will feature prominently throughout our discussion of module programming.

Here is the full definition, from `httpd.h`:

```
/** A structure to store information for each virtual server */
struct server_rec {
    /** The process this server is running in */
    process_rec *process;
    /** The next server in the list */
    server_rec *next;

    /** The name of the server */
    const char *defn_name;
    /** The line of the config file that the server was defined on */
    unsigned defn_line_number;
```

---

8. Mass virtual hosting configurations use a single `server_rec` for all vhosts, which is why they don't have the flexibility of normal vhosts.

```
/* Contact information */

/** The admin's contact information */
char *server_admin;
/** The server hostname */
char *server_hostname;
/** for redirects, etc. */
apr_port_t port;

/* Log files -- note that transfer log is now in the modules... */

/** The name of the error log */
char *error_fname;
/** A file descriptor that references the error log */
apr_file_t *error_log;
/** The log level for this server */
int loglevel;

/* Module-specific configuration for server, and defaults... */

/** true if this is the virtual server */
int is_virtual;
/** Config vector containing pointers to modules' per-server config
 *  structures. */
struct ap_conf_vector_t *module_config;
/** MIME type info, etc., before we start checking per-directory info */
struct ap_conf_vector_t *lookup_defaults;

/* Transaction handling */

/** I haven't got a clue */
server_addr_rec *addrs;
/** Timeout, as an apr interval, before we give up */
apr_interval_time_t timeout;
/** The apr interval we will wait for another request */
apr_interval_time_t keep_alive_timeout;
/** Maximum requests per connection */
int keep_alive_max;
/** Use persistent connections? */
int keep_alive;

/** Pathname for ServerPath */
const char *path;
/** Length of path */
int pathlen;

/** Normal names for ServerAlias servers */
apr_array_header_t *names;
/** Wildcarded names for ServerAlias servers */
apr_array_header_t *wild_names;
```

```
/** limit on size of the HTTP request line    */
int limit_req_line;
/** limit on size of any request header field */
int limit_req_fieldsize;
/** limit on number of request header fields   */
int limit_req_fields;
};
```

2.4.3 conn_rec

The conn_rec object is Apache's internal representation of a TCP connection. It is created when Apache accepts a connection from a client, and later it is destroyed when the connection is closed. The usual reason for a connection to be made is to serve one or more HTTP requests, so one or more request_rec structures will be instantiated from each conn_rec. Most applications will focus on the request and ignore the conn_rec, but protocol modules and connection-level filters will need to use the conn_rec, and modules may sometimes use it in tasks such as optimizing the use of resources over the lifetime of an HTTP Keepalive (persistent connection).

The conn_rec has no configuration information, but has a configuration vector for transient data associated with a connection as well as a pool for connection resources. It also has connection input and output filter chains, plus data describing the TCP connection.

It is important to distinguish clearly between the request and the connection—the former is always a subcomponent of the latter. Apache cleanly represents each as a separate object, with one important exception, which we will deal with in discussing connection filters in Chapter 8.

Here is the full definition from httpd.h:

```
/** Structure to store things which are per connection */
struct conn_rec {
    /** Pool associated with this connection */
    apr_pool_t *pool;
    /** Physical vhost this conn came in on */
    server_rec *base_server;
    /** used by http_vhost.c */
    void *vhost_lookup_data;

    /* Information about the connection itself */
    /** local address */
    apr_sockaddr_t *local_addr;
    /** remote address */
    apr_sockaddr_t *remote_addr;
```

```
/** Client's IP address */
char *remote_ip;
/** Client's DNS name, if known.  NULL if DNS hasn't been checked;
 *   "" if it has and no address was found.  N.B.: Only access this through
 * get_remote_host() */
char *remote_host;
/** Only ever set if doing rfc1413 lookups.  N.B.: Only access this through
 *   get_remote_logname() */
char *remote_logname;

/** Are we still talking? */
unsigned aborted:1;

/** Are we going to keep the connection alive for another request?
 * @see ap_conn_keepalive_e */
ap_conn_keepalive_e keepalive;

/** Have we done double-reverse DNS? -1 yes/failure, 0 not yet,
 *   1 yes/success */
signed int double_reverse:2;

/** How many times have we used it? */
int keepalives;
/** server IP address */
char *local_ip;
/** used for ap_get_server_name when UseCanonicalName is set to DNS
 *   (ignores setting of HostnameLookups) */
char *local_host;

/** ID of this connection; unique at any point in time */
long id;
/** Config vector containing pointers to connections per-server
 *   config structures */
struct ap_conf_vector_t *conn_config;
/** Notes on *this* connection: send note from one module to
 *   another. Must remain valid for all requests on this conn. */
apr_table_t *notes;
/** A list of input filters to be used for this connection */
struct ap_filter_t *input_filters;
/** A list of output filters to be used for this connection */
struct ap_filter_t *output_filters;
/** Handle to scoreboard information for this connection */
void *sbh;
/** The bucket allocator to use for all bucket/brigade creations */
struct apr_bucket_alloc_t *bucket_alloc;
/** The current state of this connection */
conn_state_t *cs;
/** Is there data pending in the input filters? */
int data_in_input_filters;
};
```

2.4.4 process_rec

Unlike the other core objects discussed earlier, the `process_rec` is an operating system object rather than a web architecture object. The only time applications need concern themselves with it is when they are working with resources having the lifetime of the server, when the process pool serves all of the `server_rec` objects (and is accessed from a `server_rec` as `s->process->pool`). The definition appears in `httpd.h`, but is not reproduced here.

2.5 Other Key API Components

The header file `httpd.h` that defines these core structures is but one of many API header files that the applications developer will need to use. These fall into several loosely bounded categories that can be identified by naming conventions:

- **ap_** header files generally define low-level API elements and are usually (though not always) accessed indirectly by inclusion in other headers.

- **http_** header files define most of the key APIs likely to be of interest to application developers. They are also exposed in scripting languages through modules such as `mod_perl` and `mod_python`.

- **util_** header files define API elements at a higher level than **ap_**, but are rarely used directly by application modules. Two exceptions to that rule are `util_script.h` and `util_filter.h`, which define scripting and filtering APIs, respectively, and are commonly accessed by modules.

- **mod_** header files define APIs implemented by modules that are optional. Using these APIs may create dependencies. Best practice is discussed in Chapter 10.

- **apr_** header files define the APR APIs. The APR libraries are external but essential to the webserver, and the APR is required (directly or indirectly) by any nontrivial module. The APR is discussed in Chapter 3.

- Other header files generally define system-level APIs only.

- Third-party APIs may follow similar conventions (e.g., a **mod_** header file) or adopt their own.

As noted earlier, the primary APIs for application modules are the **http_*** header files.

- **http_config.h**—Defines the configuration API, including the configuration data structures, the configuration vectors, any associated accessors, and, in particular, the main APIs presented in Chapter 9. It also defines the module data structure itself and associated accessors, and the handler (content generator) hook. It is required by most modules.

- **http_connection.h**—Defines the (small) TCP connection API, including connection-level hooks. Most modules will access the connection through the conn_rec object, so this API is seldom required by application modules.

- **http_core.h**—Defines miscellaneous APIs exported by the Apache core, such as accessor functions for the request_rec object. It includes APIs exported for particular modules, such as to support mod_perl's configuration sections. This header file is rarely required by application modules.

- **http_log.h**—Defines the error logging API and piped logs. Modules will need it for the error reporting functions and associated macros.

- **http_main.h**—Defines APIs for server start-up. It is unlikely to be of interest to modules.

- **http_protocol.h**—Contains high-level functional APIs for performing a number of important operations, including all normal I/O to the client, and for dealing with aspects of the HTTP protocol such as generating the correct response headers. It also exports request processing hooks that fall outside the scope of http_request. Many modules will require this header file—for example, content generators (unless you use only the lower-level APIs) and authentication modules.

- **http_request.h**—Defines the main APIs discussed in Chapter 6. It exports most of the request processing hooks, and the subrequest and internal redirect APIs. It is required by some, but not all, modules.

- **http_vhost.h**—Contains APIs for managing virtual hosts. It is rarely needed by modules except those concerned with virtual host configuration.

- **httpd.h**—Contains Apache's core API, which is required by (probably) all modules. It defines a lot of system constants, some of them derived from local build parameters, and various APIs such as HTTP status codes and methods. Most importantly, it defines the core objects mentioned earlier in this chapter.

Other important API headers we will encounter include the following files:

- **util_filter.h**—The filter API, required by all filter modules (Chapter 8)
- **ap_provider.h**—The provider API (Chapter 10)
- **mod_dbd.h**—The DBD framework (Chapters 10 and 11)

Other API headers likely to be of interest to application developers include the following files:

- **util_ldap.h**—The LDAP API
- **util_script.h**—A scripting environment that originally supported CGI, but is also used by other modules that use CGI environment variables (e.g., mod_rewrite, mod_perl, mod_php) or that generate responses using CGI rules (e.g., mod_asis)

2.6 Apache Configuration Basics

Apache configuration is mostly determined at start-up, when the server reads httpd.conf (and any included files). Configuration data, including resources derived from them by a module (e.g., by opening a file), are stored on each module's configuration records.

Each module has two configuration records, either or both of which may be null (unused):

- The per-server configuration is stored directly on the server_rec, so there is one instance per virtual host. The scope of per-server directives is controlled by <VirtualHost> containers in httpd.conf, but other containers such as <Location>, <Directory>, and <Files> will be ignored.

- The per-directory configuration is stored indirectly and is available to modules via the request_rec object in the course of processing a request. It is the opposite of per-server configuration: Its scope is defined by containers such as <Location>, <Directory>, and <Files>.

To implement a configuration directive, a module must supply a function that will recognize the directive and set a field in one of the configuration records at system start-up time. After start-up, the configuration is set and should not be changed. In particular, the configuration records should generally be treated as read-only while processing requests (or connections). Changing configuration data during request processing violates thread safety (requiring use of programming techniques such as locking) and runs a high risk of introducing other bugs due to the increased complexity. Apache provides a separate configuration record on each `conn_rec` and `request_rec` for transient data.

Chapter 9 describes working with configuration records and data.

2.7 Request Processing in Apache

Most, though by no means all, modules are concerned with some aspect of processing an HTTP request. But there is rarely, if ever, a reason for a module to concern itself with every aspect of HTTP—that is the business of the `httpd`. The advantage of a modular approach is that a module can easily focus on a particular task but ignore aspects of HTTP that are not relevant to it.

2.7.1 Content Generation

The simplest possible formulation of a webserver is a program that listens for HTTP requests and returns a response when it receives one (Figure 2-2). In Apache, this job is fundamentally the business of a content generator, the core of the webserver.

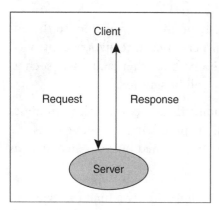

FIGURE 2-2
Minimal webserver

Exactly one content generator must be run for every HTTP request. Any module may register content generators, normally by defining a function referenced by a handler that can be configured using the `SetHandler` or `AddHandler` directives in `httpd.conf`. The default generator, which is used when no specific generator is defined by any module, simply returns a file, mapped directly from the request to the filesystem. Modules that implement content generators are sometimes known as "content generator" or "handler" modules.

2.7.2 Request Processing Phases

In principle, a content generator can handle all the functions of a webserver. For example, a CGI program gets the request and produces the response, and it can take full control of what happens between them. Like other webservers, Apache splits the request into different phases. For example, it checks whether the user is authorized to do something before the content generator does that thing.

Several request phases precede the content generator (Figure 2-3). These serve to examine and perhaps manipulate the request headers, and to determine what to do with the request. For example:

- The request URL will be matched against the configuration, to determine which content generator should be used.

- The request URL will normally be mapped to the filesystem. The mapping may be to a static file, a CGI script, or whatever else the content generator may use.

- If content negotiation is enabled, `mod_negotiation` will find the version of the resource that best matches the browser's preference. For example, the Apache manual pages are served in the language requested by the browser.

- Access and authentication modules will enforce the server's access rules, and determine whether the user is permitted what has been requested.

- `mod_alias` or `mod_rewrite` may change the effective URL in the request.

There is also a request logging phase, which comes after the content generator has sent a reply to the browser.

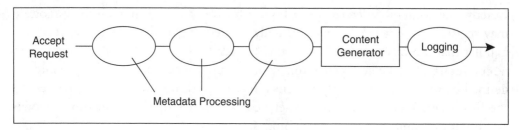

FIGURE 2-3
Request processing in Apache

2.7.2.1 Nonstandard Request Processing

Request processing may sometimes be diverted from the standard processing axis described here, for a variety of reasons:

- A module may divert processing into a new request or error document at any point before the response has been sent (Chapter 6).

- A module may define additional phases and enable other modules to hook their own processing in (Chapter 10).

- There is a `quick_handler` hook that bypasses normal processing, used by `mod_cache` (not discussed in this book).

2.7.3 Processing Hooks

The mechanism by which a module can influence or take charge of some aspect of processing in Apache is through a sequence of hooks. The usual hooks for processing a request in Apache 2.0 are described next.

post_read_request—This is the first hook available to modules in normal request processing. It is available to modules that need to hook very early into processing a request.

translate_name—Apache maps the request URL to the filesystem. A module can insert a hook here to substitute its own logic—for example, `mod_alias`.

map_to_storage—Since the URL has been mapped to the filesystem, we are now in a position to apply per-directory configuration (`<Directory>` and `<Files>` sections and their variants, including any relevant `.htaccess` files if enabled). This hook enables Apache to determine the configuration options that apply to this request. It applies normal configuration directives for all active modules, so few modules should ever need to apply hooks here. The only standard module to do so is `mod_proxy`.

`header_parser`—This hook inspects the request headers. It is rarely used, as modules can perform that task at any point in the request processing, and they usually do so within the context of another hook. `mod_setenvif` is a standard module that uses a `header_parser` to set internal environment variables according to the request headers.

`access_checker`—Apache checks whether access to the requested resource is permitted according to the server configuration (`httpd.conf`). A module can add to or replace Apache's standard logic, which implements the Allow/Deny From directives in `mod_access` (httpd 1.x and 2.0) or `mod_authz_host` (httpd 2.2).

`check_user_id`—If any authentication method is in use, Apache will apply the relevant authentication and set the username field `r->user`. A module may implement an authentication method with this hook.

`auth_checker`—This hook checks whether the requested operation is permitted to the authenticated user.

`type_checker`—This hook applies rules related to the MIME type (where applicable) of the requested resource, and determines the content handler to use (if not already set). Standard modules implementing this hook include `mod_negotiation` (selection of a resource based on HTTP content negotiation) and `mod_mime` (setting the MIME type and handler information according to standard configuration directives and conventions such as filename "extensions").

`fixups`—This general-purpose hook enables modules to run any necessary processing after the preceding hooks but before the content generator. Like `post_read_request`, it is something of a catch-all, and is one of the most commonly used hooks.

`handler`—This is the content generator hook. It is responsible for sending an appropriate response to the client. If there are input data, the `handler` is also responsible for reading them. Unlike the other hooks, where zero or many functions may be involved in processing a request, every request is processed by exactly one handler.

`log_transaction`—This hook logs the transaction after the response has been returned to the client. A module may modify or replace Apache's standard logging.

A module may hook its own handlers into any of these processing phases. The module provides a callback function and hooks it in, and Apache calls the function during the appropriate processing phase. Modules that concern themselves with the phases before content generation are sometimes known as metadata modules; they are described in detail in Chapter 6. Modules that deal with logging are known as logging modules. In addition to using the standard hooks, modules may define further processing hooks, as described in Chapter 10.

2.7.4 The Data Axis and Filters

What we have described so far is essentially similar to the architecture of every general-purpose webserver. There are, of course, differences in the details, but the request processing (metadata → generator → logger) phases are common.

The major innovation in Apache 2, which transforms it from a "mere" webserver (like Apache 1.3 and others) into a powerful applications platform, is the filter chain. The filter chain can be represented as a data axis, orthogonal to the request-processing axis (Figure 2-4). The request data may be processed by input filters before reaching the content generator, and the response may be processed by output filters before being sent to the client. Filters enable a far cleaner and more efficient implementation of data processing than was possible in the past, as well as separating content generation from its transformation and aggregation.

2.7.4.1 Handler or Filter?

Many applications can be implemented as either a handler or a filter. Sometimes it may be clear that one of these solutions is appropriate and the other would be non-sensical, but between these extremes lies a gray area. How does one decide whether to write a handler or a filter?

When making this decision, there are several questions to consider:

- Feasibility: Can it be made to work in both cases? If not, there's an instant decision.

- Utility: Is the functionality it provides more useful in one case than the other? Filters are often far more useful than handlers, because they can be reused with different content generators and chained both with generators and other filters. But every request has to be processed by some handler, even if it does nothing!

- Complexity: Is one version substantially more complex than the other? Will it take more time and effort to develop, and/or run more slowly? Filter modules are usually more complex than the equivalent handler, because a handler is in full control of its data and can read or write at will, whereas a filter has to implement a callback that may be called several times with partial data, which it must treat as unstructured chunks. We will discuss this issue in detail in Chapter 8.

For example, Apache 1.3 users can do an XSLT transformation by building it into handlers, such as CGI or PHP. Alternatively, they can use an XSLT module, but this is very slow and cumbersome (this author tried an XSLT module for Apache 1.3, but found it many hundreds of times slower than running XSLT in a CGI script operating on temporary files). Running XSLT in a handler works, but loses modularity and reusability. Any nontrivial application that needs it has to reinvent that

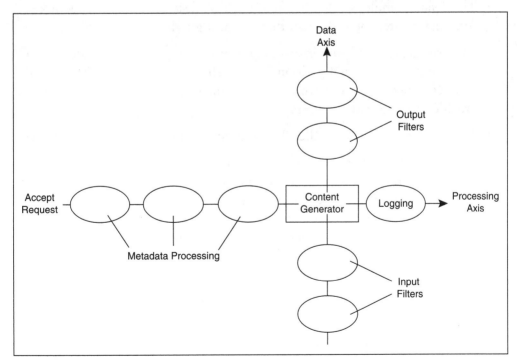

FIGURE 2-4
Apache 2 introduces a new data axis enabling a new range of powerful applications

wheel, using whatever libraries are available for the programming or scripting language used and often resorting to ugly hacks such as temporary files.

Apache 2, by contrast, allows us to run XSLT in a filter. Content handlers requiring XSLT can simply output the XML as is, and leave the transformation to Apache. The first XSLT module for Apache 2, written by Phillip Dunkel and released while Apache 2.0 was still in beta testing, was initially incomplete, but already worked far better than XSLT in Apache 1.3. It is now further improved, and is one of a choice of XSLT modules. This book's author developed another XSLT module.

More generally, if a module has both data inputs and outputs, and if it may be used in more than one application, then it is a strong candidate for implementation as a filter.

2.7.4.2 Content Generator Examples

- The default handler sends a file from the local disk under the `DocumentRoot`. Although a filter could do that, there's nothing to be gained.

- CGI, the generic API for server-side programming, is a handler. Because CGI scripts expect the central position in the webserver architecture, it has to be a handler. However, a somewhat similar framework for external filters is also provided by `mod_ext_filter`.

- The Apache proxy is a handler that fetches contents from a back-end server.

- Any form-processing application will normally be implemented as a handler—particularly those that accept POST data, or other operations that can alter the state of the server itself. Likewise, applications that generate a report from any back end are usually implemented as handlers. However, when the handler is based on HTML or XML pages with embedded programming elements, it can usefully be implemented as a filter.

2.7.4.3 Filter Examples

- `mod_include` implements server-side includes, a simple scripting language embedded in pages. It is implemented as a filter, so it can post-process content from any content generator, as discussed earlier with reference to XSLT.

- `mod_ssl` implements secure transport as a connection-level filter, thereby enabling all normal processing in the server to work with unencrypted data. This represents a major advance over Apache 1.x, where secure transport was complex and required a lot of work to combine it with other applications.

- Markup parsing modules are used to post-process and transform XML or HTML in more sophisticated ways, from simple link rewriting[9] through XSLT and Xinclude processing,[10] to a complete API for markup filtering,[11] to a security filter that blocks attempts to attack vulnerable applications such as PHP scripts.[12] Examples will be introduced in Chapter 8.

- Image processing can take place in a filter. This author developed a custom proxy for a developer of mobile phone browsers. Because the browser tells the proxy its capabilities, images can be reduced to fit within the screen space and, where appropriate, translated to gray scale, thereby reducing the volume of data sent and accelerating browsing over slow connections.

- Form-processing modules need to decode data sent from a web browser. Input filter modules, such as `mod_form` and `mod_upload`,[13] spare applications from reinventing that wheel.

- Data compression and decompression are implemented in `mod_deflate`. The filter architecture allows this module to be much simpler than `mod_gzip` (an Apache 1.3 compression module) and to dispense with any use of temporary files.

2.7.5 Order of Processing

Before moving on to discuss how a module hooks itself into any of the stages of processing a request/data, we should pause to clear up a matter that often causes confusion—namely, the order of processing.

---

9. `http://apache.webthing.com/mod_proxy_html/`
10. `http://www.outoforder.cc/projects/apache/mod_transform`
11. `http://apache.webthing.com/xmlns.html`
12. `http://modsecurity.org/`
13. `http://apache.webthing.com/`

The request processing axis is straightforward, with phases happening strictly in order. But confusion arises in the data axis. For maximum efficiency, this axis is pipelined, so the content generator and filters do not run in a deterministic order. For example, you cannot in general set something in an input filter and expect it to apply in the generator or output filters.

The order of processing centers on the content generator, which is responsible for pulling data from the input filter stack and pushing data onto the output filters (where applicable, in both cases). When a generator or filter needs to set something affecting the request as a whole, it must do so before passing any data down the chain (generator and output filters) or before returning data to the caller (input filters).

2.7.6 Processing Hooks

Now that we have an overview of request processing in Apache, we can show how a module hooks into it to play a part.

The Apache module structure declares several (optional) data and function members:

```
module AP_MODULE_DECLARE_DATA my_module = {
    STANDARD20_MODULE_STUFF,   /* macro to ensure version consistency */
    my_dir_conf,               /* create per-directory configuration record */
    my_dir_merge,              /* merge per-directory configuration records */
    my_server_conf,            /* create per-server configuration record */
    my_server_merge,           /* merge per-server configuration records */
    my_cmds,                   /* configuration directives */
    my_hooks                   /* register modules functions with the core */
};
```

The configuration directives are presented as an array; the remaining module entries are functions. The relevant function for the module to create request processing hooks is the final member:

```
static void my_hooks(apr_pool_t *pool) {
   /* create request processing hooks as required */
}
```

Which hooks we need to create here depend on which part or parts of the request our module is interested in. For example, a module that implements a content generator (handler) will need a handler hook, looking something like this:

```
ap_hook_handler(my_handler, NULL, NULL, APR_HOOK_MIDDLE) ;
```

Now `my_handler` will be called when a request reaches the content generation phase. Hooks for other request phases are similar.

The following prototype applies to a handler for any of these phases:

```
static int my_handler(request_rec *r) {
    /* do something with the request */
}
```

Details and implementation of this prototype are discussed in Chapters 5 and 6.

2.8 Summary

This basic introduction to the Apache platform and architecture sets the scene for the following chapters. We have now looked at the following aspects of Apache:

- The Apache architecture, and its relationship to the operating system

- The roles of the principal components: MPMs, APR, and modules

- The separation of tasks into initialization and operation

- The fundamental Apache objects and (briefly) the API header files

- Configuration basics

- The request processing cycle

- The data axis and filter architecture

Nothing in this general overview is specific to C programming, so Chapter 2 should be equally relevant to scripting languages. Together with the next two chapters (on the APR and programming techniques, respectively), it provides the essential basis for understanding the core information and advanced topics covered in Chapters 5–11. In those chapters, the concepts introduced here are examined in more detail, and demonstrated in the context of developing real applications.

Chapter 3

The Apache Portable Runtime

The Apache Portable Runtime (APR) and Utilities (APR-UTILS or APU) are a pair of libraries used by the Apache `httpd`, but autonomously developed and maintained within the ASF. Although many core developers are involved in both `httpd` (the webserver) and APR, the projects are separate. These libraries provide core functions that are not specific to webserving but are also useful in more general applications.

Apart from the webserver, the best-known APR application is Subversion, a revision and change control management system. Another is Site Valet, a suite of software for QA and accessibility audit on the Web; Site Valet was developed by this book's author.

This chapter discusses the APR as it applies to Apache modules. It does not go into subjects such as application initialization, which are necessary but are handled internally by the Apache core code. For developers working outside the webserver context, this usage is documented clearly within APR itself, and it is covered in the tutorial at `http://dev.ariel-networks.com/apr/apr-tutorial/html/apr-tutorial.html`.

3.1 APR

The main purpose of APR is to provide a portable, platform-independent layer for applications. Functions such as filesystem access, network programming, process and thread management, and shared memory are supported in a low-level, cross-platform library. Apache modules that use exclusively APR instead of native system functions are portable across platforms and can expect to compile cleanly—or at worst with a trivial amount of tidying up—on all platforms supported by Apache.

Each APR module comprises an application programming interface (API) shared between all platforms, together with implementations of the functions defined in the API. The implementations are often wholly or partly platform-specific, although this issue is of no concern to applications.

At the core of APR is Apache's resource management (pools), which are discussed in more detail later in this chapter. Table 3-1 provides a full list of the APR modules.

TABLE 3-1
APR Modules

Name	Purpose
apr_allocator	Used internally for memory allocation
apr_atomic	Atomic operations
apr_dso	Dynamic loading of code (.so/.dll)
apr_env	Reading/setting environment variables
apr_errno	Defines error conditions and macros
apr_file_info	Properties of filesystem objects and paths
apr_file_io	Filesystem I/O
apr_fnmatch	Filesystem pattern matching
apr_general	Initialization/termination; useful macros

Name	Purpose
apr_getopt	Command arguments
apr_global_mutex	Global locking routines
apr_hash	Hash tables
apr_inherit	File handle inheritance helpers
apr_lib	Odds and ends
apr_mmap	Memory mapping
apr_network_io	Network I/O (sockets)
apr_poll	Poll routines
apr_pools	Resource management
apr_portable	APR to native mapping conversion
apr_proc_mutex	Process locking routines
apr_random	Random numbers
apr_ring	Ring data struct and macros
apr_shm	Shared memory
apr_signal	Signal handling
apr_strings	String operations
apr_support	Internal support function
apr_tables	Table and array functions
apr_thread_cond	Thread conditions
apr_thread_mutex	Thread mutex routines
apr_thread_proc	Threads and process functions
apr_thread_rwlock	Reader/writer locking routines
apr_time	Time/date functions
apr_user	User and group ID services
apr_version	APR version
apr_want	Standard header support

3.2 APR-UTIL

APR-UTIL (also known as APU) is a second library in the APR project. It provides a small set of utilities, based on the APR and with a unified programming interface. APU doesn't have separate per-platform modules, but it does adopt a similar approach to some other commonly used resources, such as databases.

Table 3-2 provides a complete list of APU modules.

TABLE 3-2
APU Modules

Name	Purpose
apr_anylock	Transparent any lock flavor wrapper
apr_base64	Base-64 encoding
apr_buckets	Buckets/bucket brigades
apr_date	Date string parsing
apr_dbd	Common API for SQL databases
apr_dbm	Common API for DBM databases
apr_hooks	Hook implementation macros
apr_ldap	LDAP authentication APIs
apr_ldap_init	LDAP initialization APIs used mainly when initializing secure connections to the LDAP server
apr_ldap_option	APIs for setting LDAP options
apr_ldap_url	APIs for parsing and handling the LDAP URL
apr_md4	MD4 encoding
apr_md5	MD5 encoding
apr_optional	Optional functions
apr_optional_hooks	Optional hooks
apr_queue	Thread-safe FIFO queues
apr_reslist	Pooled resources
apr_rmm	Relocatable managed memory

Name	Purpose
apr_sdbm	SDBM library
apr_sha1	SHA1 encoding
apr_strmatch	String pattern matching
apr_uri	URI parsing/construction
apr_uuid	User identification
apr_xlate	Charset conversion (I18N)
apr_xml	XML parsing

3.3 Basic Conventions

APR and APR-UTIL adopt a number of conventions that give them a homogenous API and make them easy to work with.

3.3.1 Reference Manual: API Documentation and Doxygen

All of APR/APU is very well documented at the code level. Every public function and data type is documented in the header file that defines it, in doxygen[1]-friendly format. The header files themselves, or the doxygen-generated documentation, provide a full API reference for programmers. If you have doxygen installed, you can generate your own copy of the APR reference manual from the source code with the command make dox.

3.3.2 Namespacing

All APR/APU public interfaces are prefixed with the string "apr_" (data types and functions) or "APR_" (macros). This defines APR's "reserved" namespace.

Within the APR namespace, most of the APR and APU modules use secondary namespacing. This convention is often based on the name of the module in question. For example, all functions in module apr_dbd are prefixed with the string "apr_dbd_". Sometimes an obviously descriptive secondary namespace is used. For

---

1. http://www.doxygen.org/

example, socket operations in module `apr_network_io` are prefixed with
"`apr_socket_`".

3.3.3 Declaration Macros

Public functions in APR/APU are declared using macros such as `APR_DECLARE`,
`APU_DECLARE`, and `APR_DECLARE_NONSTD`. For example:

```
APR_DECLARE(apr_status_t) apr_initialize(void);
```

On most platforms, this is a null declaration and expands to

```
apr_status_t apr_initialize(void);
```

On platforms such as Windows with Visual C++, which require their own nonstandard keywords such as `_dllexport` to enable other modules to use a function,
these macros will expand to the required keywords.

3.3.4 apr_status_t and Return Values

A convention widely adopted in APR/APU is that functions return a status value
indicating success or an error code to the caller. The type is `apr_status_t`, which
takes integer values defined in `apr_errno.h`. Thus the usual prototype for an APR
function is

```
APR_DECLARE(apr_status_t) apr_do_something(...function args...);
```

Return values should routinely be tested, and error handling (recovery or graceful
failure) should be implemented. The return value `APR_SUCCESS` indicates success,
and we can commonly handle errors using constructs such as

```
apr_status_t rv;
...
rv = apr_do_something(... args ...);
if (rv != APR_SUCCESS) {
    /* log an error */
    return rv;
}
```

Sometimes we may do more. For example, if `do_something` was a nonblocking I/O
operation and returned `APR_EAGAIN`, we will probably want to retry the operation.

Some functions return a string value (`char*` or `const char*`), a `void*`, or `void`.
These functions are assumed to have no failure conditions or to return a null
pointer on failure as appropriate.

3.3.5 Conditional Compilation

By their very nature, a number of features of APR may not be supported on every platform. For example, prior to version 5.x, FreeBSD had no native thread implementation considered suitable for Apache; hence threads were not supported in APR (unless the relevant options were set manually for compilation).

To enable applications to work around this issue, APR provides `APR_HAS_*` macros for such features. When an application is concerned with such a feature, it should use conditional compilation based on these macros. For example, a module performing an operation that could lead to a race condition in a multithreaded environment might want to use something like this:

```
#if APR_HAS_THREADS
    rv = apr_thread_mutex_lock(mutex);
    if (rv != APR_SUCCESS) {
        /* Log an error */
        /* Abandon critical operation */
    }
#endif

    /* ... Execute critical section of code here ... */

#if APR_HAS_THREAD
    apr_thread_mutex_unlock(mutex);
#endif
```

3.4 Resource Management: APR Pools

The APR pools are a fundamental building block that lie at the heart of APR and Apache; they serve as the basis for all resource management. The pools allocate memory, either directly (in a `malloc`-like manner) or indirectly (e.g., in string manipulation), and, crucially, ensure that memory is freed at the appropriate time. But they extend much further, to ensure that other resources such as files or mutexes can be allocated and will always be properly cleaned up. They can even deal with resources managed opaquely by third-party libraries.

> NOTE It is common practice in Apache to assume that pool memory allocation never fails. The rationale for this assumption is that if the allocation does fail, then the system is not recoverable, and any error handling will fail, too.

3.4.1 The Problem of Resource Management

Every programmer knows that when you allocate a resource, you must ensure that it is released again when you've finished with it. For example:

```
char* buf = malloc(n) ;
... check buf is non null ...
... do something with buf ...
free(buf) ;
```

or

```
FILE* f = fopen(path, "r") ;
... check f is non null ...
... read from f ....
fclose(f) ;
```

Clearly, failure to free buf or to close f is a bug. In the context of a long-lasting program such as Apache, it would have serious consequences, up to and including bringing the entire system down. Obviously, it is important to get resource management right.

In trivial cases, this is straightforward. In a more complex case with multiple error paths, in which even the scope of a resource is uncertain at the time it is allocated, ensuring that cleanup takes place in every execution path is much more challenging. In such circumstances, we need a better way to manage resources.

Constructor/Destructor Model

One method of resource management is exemplified by the C++ concept of objects having a constructor and a destructor. Many C++ programmers make the destructor responsible for cleanup of all resources allocated by the object. This approach works well provided all dynamic resources are clearly made the responsibility of an object. But, as with the simple C approach, it requires a good deal of care and attention to detail—for example, where resources are conditionally allocated or shared between many different objects—and it is vulnerable to programming bugs.

Garbage Collection Model

A high-level method of resource management, typified by Lisp and Java, is garbage collection. This approach has the advantage of taking the problem away from the programmer and transferring it to the language itself, thereby completely removing the danger of crippling programming errors. The drawback is that garbage collection incurs a substantial overhead even where it isn't necessary, and it deprives the programmer of useful levels of control, such as the ability to control the lifetime of a resource. It also requires that all program components—including third-party libraries—be built on the same system, which is clearly not possible in an open system written in C.

3.4.2 APR Pools

The APR pools provide an alternative model for resource management. Like garbage collection, they liberate the programmer from the complexities of dealing with cleanups in all possible cases. In addition, they offer several other advantages, including full control over the lifetime of resources and the ability to manage heterogeneous resources.

The basic concept goes like this: Whenever you allocate a resource that requires cleanup, you register it with a pool. The pool then takes responsibility for the cleanup, which will happen when the pool itself is cleaned. In this way, the problem is reduced to one of allocating and cleaning up a single resource: the pool itself. Given that the Apache pools are managed by the server itself, the complexity is, therefore, removed from applications programming. All the programmer has to do is select the appropriate pool for the required lifetime of a resource.

Basic Memory Management

The most basic application of pools is for memory management. Instead of

```
mytype* myvar = malloc(sizeof(mytype)) ;
/* make sure it gets freed later in every possible execution path */
```

we use

```
mytype* myvar = apr_palloc(pool, sizeof(mytype)) ;
```

The pool automatically takes responsibility for freeing this resource, regardless of what may happen in the meantime. A secondary benefit is that pool allocation is faster than `malloc` on most platforms!

Basic memory management takes many forms in APR and Apache, where memory is allocated within another function. Examples include string-manipulation functions and logging, where we gain the immediate benefit of being able to use constructs such as the APR version of `sprintf()` without having to know the size of a string in advance:

```
char* result = apr_psprintf(pool, fmt, ...) ;
```

APR also provides higher-level abstractions of pool memory—for example, in the buckets used to pass data down the filter chain.

Generalized Memory Management

APR provides built-in functions for managing memory, as well as a few other basic resources such as files, sockets, and mutexes. However, programmers are not required to use these functions and resources. An alternative is to use native allocation functions and explicitly register a cleanup with the pool:

```
mytype* myvar = malloc(sizeof(mytype)) ;
apr_pool_cleanup_register(pool, myvar, free,
    apr_pool_cleanup_null) ;
```

or

```
FILE* f = fopen(filename, "r") ;
apr_pool_cleanup_register(pool, f, fclose, apr_pool_cleanup_null) ;
```

This code delegates responsibility for cleanup to the pool, so that no further action from the programmer is required. However, native functions may be less portable than the APR equivalents from `apr_pools` and `apr_file_io`, respectively, and `malloc` on most systems will be slower than using the pool.

This method of memory management generalizes to resources opaque to Apache and APR. For example, to open a MySQL database connection and ensure it is closed after use, you would write the following code:

```
MYSQL* sql = NULL ;
sql = mysql_init(sql) ;
if ( sql == NULL ) { log error and return failure ; }
apr_pool_cleanup_register(pool, sql, mysql_close,
        apr_pool_cleanup_null) ;

sql = mysql_real_connect(sql, host, user, pass,
    dbname, port, sock, 0) ;
if ( sql == NULL ) { log error and return failure ; }
```

Note that `apr_dbd` (which is discussed in Chapter 11) provides an altogether better method for managing database connections.

As a second example, consider XML processing:

```
xmlDocPtr doc = xmlReadFile(filename);
apr_pool_cleanup_register(pool, doc, xmlFreeDoc,
        apr_pool_cleanup_null) ;

/* Now we do things with doc, which may allocate further memory
 * managed by the XML library but will be cleaned by xmlFreeDoc
 */
```

Integrating C++ destructor-cleanup code provides yet another example. Suppose we have

```
class myclass {
public:
    virtual ~myclass() { do cleanup ; }
    // ....
} ;
```

We define a C wrapper:

```
void myclassCleanup(void* ptr) { delete (myclass*)ptr ; }
```

We then register this wrapper with the pool when we allocate `myclass`:

```
myclass* myobj = new myclass(...) ;
apr_pool_cleanup_register(pool, (void*)myobj, myclassCleanup,
        apr_pool_cleanup_null) ;

// Now we've hooked our existing resource management from C++
// into Apache and never need to delete myobj;
// pool cleanup will do the job for us
```

Implicit and Explicit Cleanup

Suppose we want to free our resource explicitly before the end of the request—for example, because we're doing something memory intensive but have objects we can free. We may want to do everything according to normal scoping rules and just use pool-based cleanup as a fallback to deal with error paths. However, because we registered the cleanup, it will run regardless of our intentions. In the worst-case scenario, it could possibly lead to a double-free and a segfault.

Another pool function, `apr_pool_cleanup_kill`, is provided to deal with this situation. When we run the explicit cleanup, we unregister the cleanup from the pool. Of course, we can be a little more clever about how we go about this task.

Here's the outline of a C++ class that manages itself based on a pool, regardless of whether it is explicitly deleted:

```
class poolclass {
private:
  apr_pool_t* pool ;
public:
  poolclass(apr_pool_t* p) : pool(p) {
      apr_pool_cleanup_register(pool, (void*)this,
          myclassCleanup, apr_pool_cleanup_null) ;
  }
  virtual ~poolclass() {
      apr_pool_cleanup_kill(pool, (void*)this, myclassCleanup) ;
  }
} ;
```

If you use C++ with Apache (or APR), you can derive any class from `poolclass`. Most APR functions do something equivalent to this, conducting register and kill operations whenever resources are allocated or cleaned up.

In simple C, we would use the following generic form:

```
/* Allocate something */
 my_type* my_res = my_res_alloc(args) ;
/* Handle errors */
if (my_res == NULL) {
    /* Log error and bail out */
}
/* Ensure it won't leak by registering a cleanup */
 apr_pool_cleanup_register(pool, my_res,
    my_res_free, apr_pool_cleanup_null) ;

/* ... Now use it as required ... */

/* OK, we're done with it, and we'd like to release it ASAP */
rv = my_res_free(my_res) ;
/* Since we freed it, we want to kill the cleanup */
apr_pool_cleanup_kill(pool, my_res, my_res_free) ;
/* Now handle errors and continue */
if (rv != APR_SUCCESS) { /* or whatever test may be appropriate */
    /* ... Log error and bail out or attempt recovery ... */
}
```

We can also streamline this form by running the cleanup and unregistering it with the pool using a single function:

```
apr_pool_cleanup_run(pool, my_res, my_res_free) ;
```

3.4.3 Resource Lifetime

When we allocate resources by using a pool, we automatically ensure that they get cleaned up at some point. But when? We need to make sure the cleanup happens at the right time—that is, neither while the resource is still in use, nor long after the resource is no longer required.

Apache Pools

Fortunately, Apache makes this process quite easy, by providing different pools for different types of resource. These pools are associated with relevant structures of the `httpd`, and they have the lifetime of the corresponding struct. Four general-purpose pools are always available in Apache:

- The request pool, with the lifetime of an HTTP request
- The process pool, with the lifetime of a server process
- The connection pool, with the lifetime of a TCP connection
- The configuration pool

The first three, which are associated with the relevant Apache structs, are accessed as `request->pool`, `connection->pool`, and `process->pool`, respectively. The fourth, `process->pconf`, is also associated with the process, but differs from the process pool in that it is cleared whenever Apache rereads its configuration.

The process pool is suitable for long-lived resources, such as those that are initialized at server start-up. The request pool is suitable for transient resources used to process a single request.

The connection pool has the lifetime of a connection, which normally consists of one or more requests. This pool is useful for transient resources that cannot be associated with a request—most notably, in a connection-level filter, where the `request_rec` structure is undefined, or in a non-HTTP protocol handler.

In addition to these standard pools, special-purpose pools may be created for other purposes, such as configuration and logging, or may be created privately by modules for their own use.

Using Pools in Apache: Processing a Request

All request-processing hooks take the form

```
int my_func(request_rec* r) {
  /* implement the request processing hook here */
}
```

This hook puts the request pool r->pool at our disposal. As discussed earlier, the request pool is appropriate for the vast majority of operations involved in processing a request. We pass it to Apache and APR functions that need a pool argument as well as our own.

The process pool is available as r->server->process->pool for operations that need to allocate long-lived resources—for example, caching a resource that should be computed once and subsequently reused in other requests. However, this process is a little more complex, and it is generally preferable to derive a subpool from the process pool, as discussed in Chapters 4 and 10.

The connection pool is r->connection->pool.

Using Pools in Apache: Initialization and Configuration

The internal workings of Apache's initialization are complex. As far as modules are concerned, however, the initialization can normally be treated as a simple procedure: Just set up a configuration, and everything is permanent. Apache makes that easy, because most of the relevant hooks have prototypes that pass the relevant pool as their first argument.

Configuration Handlers

```
static const char* my_cfg(cmd_parms* cmd, void* cfg, /* args */ )
```

Use the configuration pool, cmd->pool, to give a configuration the lifetime of the directive.

Pre-configuration and Post-configuration Hooks

These hooks are unusual in having several pools passed:

```
static int my_pre_config(apr_pool_t* pool,
    apr_pool_t* plog, apr_pool_t* ptemp)
```

For most purposes, just use the first pool argument. ptemp is suitable for resources used during configuration, but will be destroyed before Apache goes into operational mode. `plog` remains active for the lifetime of the server, but is cleaned up each time the configuration is read.

Child init

```
static void my_child_init(apr_pool_t* pool, server_rec* s).
```

The child pool is the first argument.

Monitor

```
static int my_monitor(apr_pool_t* pool)
```

The monitor is a special case: It runs in the parent process and is not tied to any time-limited structure. For this reason, resources allocated in a monitor function should be explicitly freed. If necessary, a monitor may create and free its own sub-pool and manage it as discussed in Chapter 4. Few applications will need to use the monitor hook.

Using Pools in Apache: Other Cases

Most Apache modules involve the initialization and request processing we have already discussed. There are two other cases to deal with, however: connection functions and filter functions.

Connection Functions

The `pre_connection` and `process_connection` connection-level hooks pass a `conn_rec` object as their first argument; they are directly analogous to request functions as far as pool resources are concerned. The `create_connection` connection-initialization hook passes the pool as its first argument. Any module implementing this hook takes responsibility for setting up the connection.

Filter Functions

Filter functions receive an `ap_filter_t` as their first argument. This object ambiguously contains both a `request_rec` and a `conn_rec` as members, regardless of whether it is a request-level or a connection-level filter. Content filters should normally use the request pool. Connection-level filters will get a junk pointer in `f->r` (the request doesn't exist outside the protocol layer; see Chapter 8) and must use the connection pool. Be careful: This can be a trap for the unwary.

3.4.4 Limitations of Pools

So far, we have seen the advantages of using pools for resource management. Naturally, there are also some limitations:

- Managing resources that have a lifetime that doesn't correspond to any of Apache's main objects requires more work. This issue is discussed further in Chapter 4.

- Allocating resources from a pool is not thread safe. This is rarely an issue, because most pool allocation by modules when Apache is running on a multithreaded basis uses a pool owned by an object (HTTP request or TCP connection) that is thread private at the time of use. Chapter 4 discusses some cases where thread safety is an issue.

- APR pools never return memory to the operating system until they are destroyed (they do, of course, reuse memory, so pool-based applications don't grow indefinitely). Thus it may sometimes make sense to use **malloc** rather than pools when allocating very large blocks of memory. Conversely, using **malloc** in your code may affect binary compatibility. On Windows, it may prevent your code from being linked with a binary compiled using a different version of Visual C++, due to incompatibilities in the runtime libraries.

3.5 Selected APR Topics

APR provides a direct alternative to functions that are familiar and almost certain to be available on your system without any need for APR. Nevertheless, there are good reasons to use the APR versions of these functions:

- APR functions are platform independent and provide for better portability.

- APR functions get the benefit of APR's pool-based resource management for free.

We won't go into detail here. For more information, see the excellent documentation in the header files.

3.5.1 Strings and Formats

The **apr_strings** module provides APR implementations of

- Common string functions: comparisons, substring matches, copying, and concatenation
- `stdio`-like functions: `sprintf` and family, including vformatters
- Parsing, including thread-safe `strtok`
- Conversion to and from other data types (e.g., `atoi`)

APR string handling is based on pools. This scheme brings with it a substantial simplification, as we very rarely need to worry about the size of a buffer. For example, to concatenate an arbitrary number of strings, we can use

```
result = apr_pstrcat(pool, str1, str2, str3, ..., NULL);
```

without the need to compute the length of `result` and allocate a buffer in advance. Similarly,

```
result = apr_psprintf(pool, fmt, ...) ;
```

requires altogether less tedious housekeeping than

```
length = [compute length here] ;
buf = malloc(length) ;
sprintf(buf, fmt, ...) ;
```

There is no regular expression support in APR (although there is in Apache), but the **apr_strmatch** module provides fast string matching that deals with the issues of case-insensitive (as well as case-sensitive) searches and non-null-terminated strings.

3.5.2 Internationalization

The **apr_xlate** module provides conversion between different character sets.

At the time of this book's writing, `apr_xlate` on the Windows platform relies on a third APR library, `apr_iconv`, because Windows lacks (or lacked) native internationalization support. This dependency is expected to be removed in the future.

3.5.3 Time and Date

The **apr_time** module provides a microsecond timer and clock. Because APR works in microseconds, its fundamental data type apr_time_t is a 64-bit integer and is not interchangeable with time_t. Macros provided for conversion include the following:

```
/** @return apr_time_t as a second */
#define apr_time_sec(time) ((time) / APR_USEC_PER_SEC)

/** @return a second as an apr_time_t */
#define apr_time_from_sec(sec) ((apr_time_t)(sec) * APR_USEC_PER_SEC)
```

Other data types include time intervals and a "struct tm" -like type apr_time_exp_t. APR time functions include

- Time now
- Any time as Greenwich Mean Time (GMT), local time, or a selected time zone
- Time arithmetic
- Sleep
- Time formatted as a ctime or RFC822 string

The **apr_date** module provides additional functions for parsing commonly used time and date formats.

3.5.4 Data Structs

Apache provides four data struct modules:

- **apr_table** provides tables and arrays.
- **apr_hash** provides hash tables.
- **apr_queue** provides first in, first out (FIFO) queues.
- **apr_ring** provides a ring struct, which is also the basis for APR bucket brigades.

3.5.4.1 Arrays

APR arrays are provided by the apr_array_header_t type, and can hold either objects or pointers. The array data type also serves as a stack. An array has a default size that is set when the array is created. Although it works most efficiently when it remains within that size, the array can grow as required. The most common operations supported are append (push) and iteration:

```
/* Allocate an array of type my_type */
apr_array_header_t* arr = apr_array_make(pool, sz, sizeof(my_type));

/* Allocate an uninitialized element on the array*/
my_type* newelt = apr_array_push(arr) ;

/* Now fill in the values of elt */
newelt->foo = abc ;
newelt->bar = "foo" ;

/* Pop the last-in element */
my_type* oldelt = apr_array_pop(arr) ;

/* Iterate over all elements */
for (i = 0; i < arr->nelts; i++) {
    /* A C++ reference is the clearest way to show this */
    my_type& elt = arr->elts[i] ;
}
```

Other array operations include the pop stack operation, copying (shallow copy), lazy copy, concatenation, append, and conversion to a string value (the latter is obviously meaningful only when the contents of the array are string values).

3.5.4.2 Tables

The apr_table_t is an intuitive, higher-level data type built on the array for storing key/value pairs. It supports adding elements (several variants), deleting elements (not efficient), lookup, iteration, and clearing an entire table. It also supports merge and overlay operations, and merging or elimination of duplicate entries.

Table keys are always case insensitive (in contrast to the keys in APR hash tables).

```
/* Allocate a new table */
apr_table_t* table = apr_table_make(pool, sz) ;

/* Set a key/value pair */
apr_table_setn(table, key, val) ;
```

Variants on apr_table_set include apr_table_setn, apr_table_add, apr_table_addn, apr_table_merge, and apr_table_mergen:

- **apr_table_setn** sets a value, overwriting any existing value for the key.
- **apr_table_addn** adds a new value, leaving duplicate keys if there was an existing value for the key.

- **apr_table_mergen** adds a new value, merging it with any existing value for the key.

- **apr_table_set** copies the data as they are entered in the table; **apr_table_setn** doesn't (and is therefore more efficient when the values are persistent or allocated on the same pool as the table). The same applies to the other functions.

```
/* Retrieve an entry */
val = apr_table_get(table, key) ;

/* Iterate over the table (see Chapter 5) */
apr_table_do(func, rec, table, NULL) ;

/* Clear the table */
apr_table_clear(table) ;

/* Merge tables */
newtable = apr_table_overlay(pool, table1, table2) ;

/* Prune duplicate entries */
apr_table_compress(table, flags) ;
```

The high-level API and the availability of functions such as apr_table_merge and apr_table_overlap provide the ideal foundations for manipulation of HTTP headers and environment variables in Apache.

3.5.4.3 Hash Tables

apr_hash_t also stores key/value pairs, but is a lower-level data type than apr_table_t. It has two advantages:

1. Keys and values can be of any data type (and, unlike with tables, are case sensitive).

2. Hash tables scale more efficiently as the number of elements grows.

Unlike the array and table, the hash table has no initial size. The most commonly used operations are insertion and lookup. Other operations supported include iteration, copy, overlay, and merge.

```
apr_hash_t* hash = apr_hash_make(pool) ;

/* key and value are pointers to arbitrary data types */
apr_hash_set(hash, key, sizeof(*key), value) ;
value = apr_hash_get(hash, key, sizeof(*key)) ;
```

There is one special case we commonly encounter: where the key is a character string. To ensure the proper string comparison semantics are used, we should use the macro APR_HASH_KEY_STRING in place of the size argument.

3.5.4.4 Queues

The apr_queue_t is a thread-safe, FIFO bounded queue. It is available only in threaded APR builds, and it enables multiple threads to cooperate in handling jobs. A queue has a fixed capacity, as set in apr_queue_create. The main queue operations are blocking and nonblocking push and pop.

3.5.4.5 Rings

APR_RING is not, in fact, a data type, but rather a collection of macros somewhat like a C++ template; these macros implement cyclic, doubly linked lists. The main ring example in Apache is the bucket brigade, which we'll introduce in Section 3.5.5 and discuss at length in Chapter 8. The bucket is an element in the ring, while the brigade is the ring structure itself. The following declarations implement the ring structure:

```
struct apr_bucket {
    /** Links to the rest of the brigade */
    APR_RING_ENTRY(apr_bucket) link;
    /** and, of course, the bucket's data fields */
};

/** A list of buckets */
struct apr_bucket_brigade {
    /** The pool to associate the brigade with.  The data is not allocated out
     *  of the pool, but a cleanup is registered with this pool.  If the
     *  brigade is destroyed by some mechanism other than pool destruction,
     *  the destroying function is responsible for killing the cleanup.
     */
    apr_pool_t *p;
    /** The buckets in the brigade are on this list. */
    /*
     * The apr_bucket_list structure doesn't actually need a name tag
     * because it has no existence independent of the struct apr_bucket_brigade.
     * The ring macros are designed so that you can leave the name tag
     * argument empty in this situation, but apparently the Windows compiler
     * doesn't like that.
     */
    APR_RING_HEAD(apr_bucket_list, apr_bucket) list;
    /** The freelist from which this bucket was allocated */
    apr_bucket_alloc_t *bucket_alloc;
};
```

3.5.5 Buckets and Brigades

Here's a one-sentence, buzzword-laden overview: Bucket brigades represent a complex data stream that can be passed through a layered I/O system without unnecessary copying.

Buckets and brigades form the basis of Apache's data handling, I/O, and filter chain (which are really three ways of saying the same thing). Use and manipulation of these is fundamental to filter modules, as is discussed in detail in Chapter 8.

A bucket brigade is a doubly linked list (ring) of buckets, so we aren't limited to inserting elements at the front and removing them at the end. Buckets are passed around only as members of a brigade, although singleton buckets can occur for short periods of time.

Buckets are data stores of various types. They can refer to data in memory, or part of a file or mmap area, or the output of a process, among other things. Buckets also have some type-dependent accessor functions:

The **read** function returns the address and size of the data in the bucket. If the data isn't in memory, then it is read in and the bucket changes type so that it can refer to the new location of the data. If all of the data cannot fit in the bucket, then a new bucket is inserted into the brigade to hold the rest of it.

The **split** function divides the data in a bucket into two regions. After a split, the original bucket refers to the first part of the data and a new bucket inserted into the brigade after the original bucket refers to the second part of the data. Reference counts are maintained as necessary.

The **setaside** function ensures that the data in the bucket has an adequate lifetime. For example, sometimes it is convenient to create a bucket referring to data on the stack in the expectation that it will be consumed (e.g., output to the network) before the stack is unwound. If that expectation turns out not to be valid, the setaside function is called to move the data somewhere safer.

The **copy** function makes a duplicate of the bucket structure as long as it's possible to have multiple references to a single copy of the data itself. Not all bucket types can be copied.

The **destroy** function maintains the reference counts on the resources used by a bucket and frees them if necessary.

> NOTE All of these functions have wrapper macros
> [`apr_bucket_read()`, `apr_bucket_destroy()`, and so on]. The
> wrapper macros should be used rather than using the function
> pointers directly.

To write a bucket brigade, we first turn the data into an `iovec`, so that we don't write too little data at one time. If we really want good performance, then we need to compact the buckets before we convert the data to an `iovec`, or possibly while we are converting to an `iovec`.

The following bucket types are supported natively in APR:

- **File**—bucket contents are a file. Commonly used when serving a static file.

- **Pipe**—bucket contents are a pipe (filesystem FIFO).

- **Socket**—bucket contents are a socket. Most commonly used by the network filters.

- **Heap**—bucket contents are heap memory. Used for `stdio`-like buffered I/O.

- **Mmap**—bucket contents are an mmapped file.

- **Immortal**—bucket contents are memory, which is guaranteed to be valid for at least the lifetime of the bucket.

- **Pool**—bucket contents are allocated on a pool.

- **Transient**—bucket contents may go out of scope and disappear.

- **Flush** (metadata)—the brigade's contents should be flushed before continuing. In Apache, that means passing whatever data is available to the next filter in the chain.

- **EOS** (metadata)—end of data.

Other types may also be implemented—indeed, additional metadata types are used internally in Apache. This author has implemented bucket types for SQL queries (using `apr_dbd`) and for script fragments; both of these types execute and convert data to another bucket type when read. A third-party library implementing a wide range of bucket types is **serf.**[2]

---

2. `http://svn.webdav.org/repos/projects/serf/trunk`

3.5.6 Filesystem

APR modules related to filesystems include the following:

- **apr_file_io** provides standard file operations: open/close, stdio-style read/write operations, locking, and create/delete/copy/rename/chmod. This module supports ordinary files, temporary files, directories, and pipes.

- **apr_file_info** provides filesystem information (stat), directory manipulation functions (e.g., open, close, read), file path manipulation, and relative path resolution.

- **apr_fnmatch** provides pattern matching for the filesystem, to support wildcard operations.

- **apr_mmap** mmaps a file.

We will see examples of these modules in later chapters.

A third-party extension is **apvfs**,[3] a library that implements a common, APR-based front end to a wide range of different (virtual) filesystems such as standard files, APR buckets, archives IPC, and databases.

3.5.7 Network

APR provides two modules related to networks:

- **apr_network_io** is a socket layer supporting IPv4, IPv6, and the TCP, UDP, and SCTP protocols. It supports a number of features subject to underlying operating system support, and will emulate them where not available. These features include send file, accept filters, and multicast.

- **apr_poll** provides functions for polling a socket (or other descriptor).

3.5.8 Encoding and Cryptography

APR does not provide a cryptographic library, and Apache's mod_ssl relies on the external OpenSSL package for implementation of transport-level security. APR

---

3. http://apvfs.sourceforge.net/

does support a number of data encoding and hashing techniques in its
apr_base64, **apr_md4**, **apr_md5**, and **apr_sha1** modules.

3.5.9 URI Handling

The **apr_uri** module defines a struct for URIs/URLs, and provides parsing and
unparsing functions:

```
/**
 * A structure to encompass all of the fields in a URI
 */
struct apr_uri_t {
    /** Scheme ("http"/"ftp"/...) */
    char *scheme;
    /** Combined [user[:password]\@]host[:port] */
    char *hostinfo;
    /** User name, as in http://user:passwd\@host:port/ */
    char *user;
    /** Password, as in http://user:passwd\@host:port/ */
    char *password;
    /** Hostname from URI (or from Host: header) */
    char *hostname;
    /** Port string (integer representation is in "port") */
    char *port_str;
    /** The request path (or "/" if only scheme://host was given) */
    char *path;
    /** Everything after a '?' in the path, if present */
    char *query;
    /** Trailing "#fragment" string, if present */
    char *fragment;

    /** Structure returned from gethostbyname() */
    struct hostent *hostent;

    /** The port number, numeric, valid only if port_str != NULL */
    apr_port_t port;

    /** Has the structure been initialized? */
    unsigned is_initialized:1;

    /** Has the DNS been looked up yet? */
    unsigned dns_looked_up:1;
    /** Has the DNS been resolved yet? */
    unsigned dns_resolved:1;
};
```

The main functions provided are apr_uri_parse and apr_uri_unparse, which
convert between a string and the apr_uri struct.

3.5.10 Processes and Threads

- **apr_thread_proc** provides process and thread management functions: creation, parent–child relationships including environment propagation, pipes, rendezvous, and wait.

- **apr_signal** provides basic signal handling.

- **apr_global_mutex** provides global locks that protect the calling thread both from other threads and processes.

Processes

- **apr_proc_mutex** provides locks for the calling process against other processes.

- **apr_shm** provides shared memory segments.

Threads

- **apr_thread_mutex** and **apr_thread_rwlock** provide thread locks/mutexes.

- **apr_thread_cond** provides thread conditions for synchronization of different threads in a process.

Modules should be able to run in a multiprocess and/or multithreaded environment. Although they will rarely need to create a new thread, they may need to use mutexes, shared memory, or other techniques to share resources and avoid race conditions. Techniques for working with threads and processes in Apache are discussed in Chapter 4.

3.5.11 Resource Pooling

The **apr_reslist** module manages a pool of persistent resources.

A database is a fundamental component of many web applications. Unfortunately, connecting to it incurs an overhead that affects traditional application architectures such as CGI and the environment commonly known as LAMP (Linux, Apache, MySQL, [Perl|PHP|Python]). Using apr_reslist (APR's resource pooling module) with Apache 2's threaded MPMs, we can achieve significant improvements in performance and scalability in applications using "expensive" resources such as databases, or back-end connections when proxying an application server.

Chapter 11 presents the DBD framework, which is one of the main applications of connection pooling.

3.5.12 API Extensions

The following modules serve to enable new APIs:

- **apr_hooks** provides Apache's hooks, a mechanism for exporting an API where an extension (module) can insert its own processing

- **apr_optional_hooks** provides optional hooks, enabling different modules to use each other's APIs when both are present without creating a dependency.

- **apr_optional** provides optional functions, so that a module can use functions exported by another module without creating a dependency.

These extensions are discussed in depth in Chapter 10.

3.6 Databases in APR/Apache

Readers of a certain age will recollect a time in the 1980s when every application for the PC came bundled with hundreds of different printer drivers on ever-growing piles of floppy disks. Eventually, the operating system implemented the sensible solution: a unified printing API, so that each printer had a single driver, and each application had a single print function that works with any driver.

The history of database support in Apache echoes this evolutionary path. At first, Apache had no database support, so every module needing it had to implement it. Apache 1.3 offered separate, yet virtually identical modules for authentication with NDBM and Berkeley DB, and a whole slew of different (third-party) authentication modules for popular SQL databases such as MySQL. Similarly, every scripting language—such as Perl, PHP and Python—had its own database management.

In time for the release of Apache 2.0, the apr_dbm module was developed to provide a unified interface for the DBM (simple key/value lookup) class of databases. Most recently, the apr_dbd module has been introduced, providing an analogous API for SQL databases. Just as with the printer drivers, the APR database classes eliminate the need for duplication and, as such, are the preferred means of database support for new applications in APR and Apache.

3.6.1 DBMs and apr_dbm

DBMs have been with us since the early days of computing, when the need for fast keyed lookups was recognized. The original DBM is a UNIX-based library and file format for fast, highly scalable, keyed access to data. It was followed (in order) by NDBM ("new DBM"), GDBM ("GNU DBM"), and the Berkeley DB. This last is by far the most advanced, and the only DBM under active development today. Nevertheless, all of the DBMs from NDBM onward provide the same core functionality used by most programs, including Apache. A minimal-implementation SDBM is also bundled with APR, and is available to applications along with the other DBMs.

Although NDBM is now old—like the city named New Town ("Neapolis") by the Greeks in about 600 B.C. and still called Naples today—it remains the baseline DBM. NDBM was used by early Apache modules such as the Apache 1.x versions of `mod_auth_dbm` and `mod_rewrite`. Both GDBM and Berkeley DB provide NDBM emulations, and Linux distributions ship with one or other of those emulations in place of the "real" NDBM, which is excluded for licensing reasons. Unfortunately, the various file formats are totally incompatible, and there are subtle differences in behavior concerning database locking. These issues led a steady stream of Linux users to report problems with DBMs in Apache 1.x.

Apache 2 replaces direct access to a DBM with a unified wrapper layer, `apr_dbm`. There can be one or more underlying databases; this determination is made at build time, either through a configuration option or by being detected automatically by the build scripts (the default behavior). The database to be used by an application may be passed as a parameter whenever a DBM is opened, so it is under direct programmer control (or administrator control, if the database is configurable) and can be trivially switched if that ever becomes necessary. Alternatively, for cases like authentication that are known to work well with any DBM, it can use a system default. Apache has to support only a single DBM interface, so, for example, a single DBM authentication module serves regardless of the underlying DBM used.

The `apr_dbm` layer, which is similar to the DBM APIs, is documented in `apr_dbm.h`. When programming with it, one should not assume any locking, although update operations are safe if the DBM is either GDBM or the original NDBM. Using a mutex for critical updates makes it safe in all cases.

The DBM functions supported in APR are basically the same as those common to all of the DBMs—namely, an API essentially equivalent to NDBM, GDBM, and early versions of Berkeley DB. Advanced capabilities of recent Berkeley DB versions, such as transactions, are not supported, so applications requiring them have to access DB directly.

Example

The function `fetch_dbm_value` in `mod_authn_dbm` looks up a value in a DBM database.

```
static apr_status_t fetch_dbm_value(const char *dbmtype,
                       const char *dbmfile,
                                     const char *user, char **value,
                                     apr_pool_t *pool)
{
    apr_dbm_t *f;
    apr_datum_t key, val;
    apr_status_t rv;

    rv = apr_dbm_open_ex(&f, dbmtype, dbmfile, APR_DBM_READONLY,
                    APR_OS_DEFAULT, pool);

    if (rv != APR_SUCCESS) {
        return rv;
    }

    key.dptr = (char*)user;
#ifndef NETSCAPE_DBM_COMPAT
    key.dsize = strlen(key.dptr);
#else
    key.dsize = strlen(key.dptr) + 1;
#endif

    *value = NULL;

    if (apr_dbm_fetch(f, key, &val) == APR_SUCCESS && val.dptr) {
        *value = apr_pstrmemdup(pool, val.dptr, val.dsize);
    }

    apr_dbm_close(f);

    return rv;
}
```

3.6.2 SQL Databases and apr_dbd

> NOTE The `apr_dbd` module is not available in APR0.x and,
> therefore, Apache 2.0. It requires APR 1.2 or higher, or the
> current version of CVS.

SQL is the standard for nontrivial database applications, and many such databases are regularly used with Apache in web applications. The most popular option is the lightweight open-source MySQL, but it is merely one choice among many possibilities.

SQL databases are altogether bigger and more complex than DBMs, and are not in general interchangeable, except where applications are explicitly designed to be portable (or in a limited range of simple tasks). Nevertheless, a unified API for SQL applications brings benefits analogous to the printer drivers.

The `apr_dbd` module is a unified API for using SQL databases in Apache and other APR applications. The concept is similar to Perl's DBI/DBD framework or `libdbi` for C, but `apr_dbd` differs from these in that APR pools are used for resource management. As a consequence, it is much easier to work with `apr_dbd` in APR applications.

The `apr_dbd` module is also unusual within APR in terms of its approach. Whereas the `apr_dbd` API is compiled into `libaprutil`, the drivers for individual databases may be dynamically loaded at runtime. Thus, when you install a new database package, you can install an APR driver for it without having to recompile the whole of APR or APR-UTIL.

At the time of this writing, `apr_dbd` supports the MySQL, PostgreSQL, SQLite, and Oracle databases. Drivers for other databases will likely be contributed in due course.

The MySQL Driver

Apache views MySQL as a special case. Because it is licensed under the GNU General Public License (GPL), a driver for MySQL must also be distributed under the GPL (or not at all). This requirement is incompatible with Apache licensing policy, because it would impose additional restrictions on Apache users.

The author has dealt with this issue by making a MySQL driver available separately[4] and licensing it under the GPL. Users requiring this driver should download it into the apr_dbd directory or folder and build it there. If MySQL is installed in a standard location, it should then be automatically detected and built by the standard APR-UTIL configuration process.

Usage

Apache modules should normally use apr_dbd through the provider module mod_dbd.

3.7 Summary

This chapter presented a brief overview of the APR and APR-UTIL (APU), focusing on those modules most likely to be of interest to developers of Apache applications. Many of the topics introduced here are discussed in more depth in later chapters where they become relevant—indeed essential—to the techniques presented there.

Specifically, this chapter identified the principal roles of APR:

- A platform-independent operating system layer
- A solution to resource management issues
- A utilities and class library

We took a detailed look at the following topics:

- APR conventions and style
- APR pools and resource management in Apache
- The APR database classes
- The principal APR types

We also engaged in a brief tour of other APR modules.

---

4. http://apache.webthing.com/database/

An appreciation of the APR is fundamental to all C programming in Apache, and the remainder of this book will use it extensively. For further reading on the APR, you can refer to the excellent API documentation generated automatically from the header files (available for browsing at `apr.apache.org`) and to INOUE Seiichiro's tutorial.[5]

---

5. `http://dev.ariel-networks.com/apr/apr-tutorial/html/apr-tutorial.html`

Chapter 4

Programming Techniques and Caveats

Before we start actually developing modules, we need to discuss matters of good practice for safe, efficient, and portable programming. There are a number of "gotchas" for the unwary, including thread safety and resource sharing between processes, that arise from the behavior of different MPMs. Some of the techniques in this chapter may be considered advanced, and the code examples will be easier to follow after reading some further relevant background in the following chapters, particularly Chapters 5, 6, and 9.

4.1 Apache Coding Conventions

A number of coding conventions apply within the Apache source code to ensure consistency and facilitate readability and review. These conventions are, of course, purely optional for third-party code, and examples used in this book may not always follow them.

4.1.1 Lines

- Lines of code should not exceed 80 characters, including any leading white-space. Where necessary, continuation lines are used.

- Continuation lines are indented to align with the first term in a continued expression or the first entry in a continued list.

- Separators (commas) appear in a continued line, but other binary operators appear in the continuation.

- No whitespace appears before the final semicolon.

- Whitespace is used within lines where appropriate and not prohibited.

```
static my_return_type *my_long_func_name(int arg1, foo *arg2,
                                         void **arg3)

if ((this != that) && (((x << 8) > y) || something_else++)
    && (error_code == 0)) {
  /* ... */
}
```

4.1.2 Functions

- Functions are always declared with ANSI-C style arguments.

- No whitespace is used before or after the brackets around the argument list.

- Arguments are separated by a comma and a single space.

- The function's opening and closing braces occupy their own lines, flush left.

```
static int my_func(int x, my_type *y)
{
    /* function code here */
}
```

4.1.3 Blocks

- Blocks are indented by four spaces from their surrounding blocks. Tabs are not permitted.

- Braces are always used, even where optional. Opening braces appear at the end of the line introducing a block. Closing braces appear in a line of their own, aligned with the code outside the block.

```
/* surrounding code */
status = do_something(args);
/* a block */
if (status != success) {
    /* handle an error condition */
    report_error(status);
}
```

4.1.4 Flow Control

- Flow control elements follow blocking rules.

- `case` statements are not indented in a `switch`, but their code is indented.

```
if (foo == bar) {
    /* do this */
}
else {
    /* do that */
}

switch (xyz) {
case X:
    /* code for X */
case Y:
    /* code for Y */
case Z:
    /* code for Z */
}
```

4.1.5 Declarations

- Declarations may include variable initialization where appropriate.

- Pointers are declared with the asterisk attached to the variable name, not to the type.

```
int x = 0;
const char *p;
my_type *my_var = apr_palloc(pool, sizeof(my_type));
```

4.1.6 Comments

- Comments always use C `/* ... */` style.

- Multiline comments have a * aligned at the start of each line, including the closing line of the comment.

- Comments are aligned with the block they are in.

```
/* A multiline comment
 * uses continuation lines like this
 */
```

4.2 Managing Module Data

When you first start programming, you learn about the scope of data. Typically (in C and most other lexically scoped languages), a variable declared within a function or block remains in scope until the end of the function or block, but thereafter is undefined. Variables may also have global scope and remain defined throughout the program. Of course, in terms of simple C programming, variables in Apache follow these rules.

4.2.1 Configuration Vectors

Apache modules are based on callbacks. C does not provide a mechanism to share data over two or more separate callback functions, other than global scope, which is, of course, not appropriate in a multithreaded environment. Apache provides an alternative means of managing data: the configuration vector (`ap_conf_vector_t`). The primary purpose of such vectors is, as the name suggests, to hold configuration data. They also serve a more general purpose.

4.2.2 Lifetime Scopes

The Apache architecture naturally defines a different kind of scope for data—namely, the core objects of process, server, connection, and request. Most data are naturally associated with one of these objects (or some subobject such as a filter). The Apache configuration vectors together with APR pools provide a natural framework for module data to be tied to an appropriate object. This deals nicely with two problems:

1. Using an appropriate configuration vector deals with the scoping issue, making data available wherever they are required.

2. Using an appropriate pool deals with the lifetime of resources, ensuring that they are properly cleaned up after use.

These techniques gives us three simple and useful associations: Variables and data can be associated with the server, the connection, or the request objects.

4.2.2.1 Configuration Data

Configuration data (Chapter 9) are set at server start-up, but can be accessed later by looking them up on the configuration vectors from `request_rec` or `server_rec`:

```
svr_cfg* my_svr_cfg =
    ap_get_module_config(server->module_config, &my_module);
dir_cfg* my_dir_cfg =
    ap_get_module_config(request->per_dir_config, &my_module);
```

When the server is running, configuration data should be treated as strictly read-only. Any changes will affect not only the current request, but also any other requests running concurrently or later in the same process.

4.2.2.2 Request Data

Apart from the configuration, the most common nontrivial case we have to deal with is where data need to be created in the course of processing a request, but scoped over more than one hook. Apache provides a pool and a configuration vector that are explicitly intended to enable modules to give variables the scope and lifetime of a request:

```
static int my_early_hook(request_rec* r) {
  req_cfg* my_req ;
  ...
  my_req = apr_palloc(r->pool, sizeof(req_cfg)) ;
  ap_set_module_config(r->request_config, &my_module, my_req);
  /* Set the data fields of my_req as required */
}

static int my_later_hook(request_rec* r) {
  req_cfg* my_req = ap_get_module_config(r->request_config, &my_module);
  /* Now we have all the data and we can do what we want with it */
}
```

And if we have a hook where the `req_cfg` may or may not be already set:

```
static int my_other_hook(request_rec* r) {
  req_cfg* my_req;
  ...
  my_req = ap_get_module_config(r->request_config, &my_module);
  if (my_req == NULL) {
    /* It hasn't been set yet */
    my_req = apr_palloc(r->pool, sizeof(req_cfg)) ;
    ap_set_module_config(r->request_config, &my_module, my_req);
    /* Set the data fields of my_req as required */
  }
  /* Now we have my_req, whether or not it was already set */
}
```

The lesson here is to get into the habit of using the request configuration vector whenever we have data that need to be scoped over more than one hook. The configuration struct itself is, of course, completely defined by the module, and it contains exactly what the module needs it to contain. If the module is complex and has multiple different hooks, each of which needs to set variables for later use, the different data should be combined in the configuration vector—for example, by giving each function its own substructure.

Note the standard use of the request pool to allocate the request configuration vector. The request configuration vector, therefore, will be freed at the end of the request, which is exactly what we want. Any data members that involve dynamic resource allocation should similarly use the request pool or register a cleanup on it, as discussed in Chapter 3 and illustrated in examples throughout this book. The request pool and request configuration solve the problem of resource management in request processing.

4.2.2.3 Connection Data

The connection is the other transient core object in Apache. It, too, presents a pool and a configuration vector for management of connection data. Use of the connection configuration and pool is exactly analogous to their use with the request.

4.2.2.4 Persistent Data

A more complex case arises where a module needs to manage persistent but non-constant data. Such data may be held on the `server_rec` object (separate from any configuration data fields), or even given global scope. In either case, thread-safety becomes an issue, and we need to use a mutex for any critical operations. We usually also need to define a pool for our module, as we should normally only use the process pool at server startup. The mutex and the pool will have the same scope and lifetime as the variable data. We'll discuss this in detail below.

4.3 Communicating Between Modules

Modules can communicate and interact in various ways. Chapter 10 presents a range of advanced methods for exporting an API and providing a service. For simpler needs, the `request_rec` object provides some straightforward methods we should look at first.

r->subprocess_env

r->subprocess_env is an apr_table that has the lifetime of a request and is shared by all modules. It was originally Apache's internal representation of the CGI environment; as such, it would be set whenever CGI or SSI was in use. It has subsequently acquired a much wider range of uses—in advanced configuration such as mod_rewrite and mod_filter, and in all the embedded scripting languages.

Any module can set values in the subprocess_env. Two, in particular, are noteworthy: mod_env and mod_setenvif are configuration modules whose purpose is to enable system administrators to determine environment variables.

In addition to the standard CGI/scripting environment, modules can define their own variables to enable another module or a system administrator to control some aspect of module behavior. Examples in the core distribution include mod_deflate responding to environment variables such as no-gzip and force-gzip to override default behavior, and even the core HTTP protocol module responding to nokeepalive. These environment variables are commonly determined using the Browsermatch directive, which is implemented by mod_setenvif.

Finally, mod_rewrite's **E** flag sets an environment variable in a RewriteRule. Modules can take advantage of this capability by using an environment variable to determine aspects of behavior. This gives system administrators access to the full power of mod_rewrite to configure the system dynamically.

r->notes

r->notes is another apr_table_t having the lifetime of a request. Its purpose is explicitly to enable modules to leave notes for each other. Unlike subprocess_env, it serves no other purpose. We'll see an example of its use in Chapter 6, where we use r->notes to set an error message that can be displayed in an error page returned to a user.

r->headers_in

r->headers_in holds the request headers; it is available to all modules. A module may "fake" request headers by manipulating them. For example:

- mod_headers reads "faked" headers set in the Apache configuration, and sets them in this internal table.

- `mod_auth_cookie`[1] sets a faked `Authorization` header from a cookie, so that Apache can authenticate the user using standard HTTP basic authentication.

r->headers_out

`r->headers_out` holds the response headers. Since these response headers describe exactly what Apache is returning to the client, modules should set them whenever they do something that affects the protocol. They are converted from the `apr_table_t` to simple text in the HTTP protocol core output filter.

r->err_headers_out

`r->err_headers_out` also holds response headers. However, whereas `r->headers_out` is discarded if request processing is diverted into an internal redirect or error document (Chapter 6), `r->err_headers_out` is preserved. As a consequence, it is suitable for tasks such as setting headers when redirecting a client.

4.4 Thread-Safe Programming Issues

For the most part, thread safety in Apache is the same as in any other software environment:

- Don't use global or static data (except for constants). Global data may be set during configuration or in a pre-configuration or post-configuration hook, but should not be modified thereafter. In almost all nontrivial situations, you should use the configuration vectors in preference to global variables.

- Don't call functions that are not themselves thread-safe and reentrant.

- If you ever need to violate either of the preceding guidelines, use a mutex to do so in a critical section, and prevent concurrent modifications by multiple threads.

One more rule applies in Apache: Don't change values of configuration data. Treat configuration variables with the same respect as you treat global variables. Stated in general terms, apply the same principles of thread safety in Apache as you would in any other environment.

---

1. `http://raburton.lunarpages.com/apache/mod_auth_cookie/`

Now let's formulate these rules for Apache in terms of dos rather than don'ts:

1. When processing a request, use the fields of the `request_rec`—in particular, the request pool and the request configuration vector. Treat everything else as read-only.

2. When processing a connection, use the fields of the `conn_rec`—in particular, the connection pool and the connection configuration vector. Treat everything else as read-only.

3. Use configuration functions or functions hooked to `post_config` to initialize constant module data, including values determined by the configuration.

4. Use module-private resources to manage data that outlive a request or connection yet cannot be treated as constant. Use a `child_init` hook to initialize such resources.

The last rule is the only one that requires us to do anything nontrivial. Let's take a closer look at it.

4.5 Managing Persistent Data

When we discussed data scoping with pools and configuration vectors earlier, we deferred our discussion of managing persistent data. Chapter 10 presents one important example: `mod_dbd` managing a pool of database connections. But in that case, all of the hard work is delegated to `apr_reslist`. How do we deal with this situation more generally? Let's consider a typical case where we're managing a dynamic cache in a hash table. We must deal with two issues in this scenario: providing thread safety and avoiding memory or other resource leaks.

4.5.1 Thread Safety

The crucial step is to use a `child_init` hook to set up the dynamic resource:

```
typedef struct {
    /* Server configuration as applicable */
    int foo;
    const char* bar;
```

```
    /* A persistent but variable resource */
    apr_pool_t *pool;
#if APR_HAS_THREADS
    apr_thread_mutex_t *mutex;
#endif
    apr_hash_t *cache;
} my_svr_cfg;

static void my_child_init(apr_pool_t *pchild, server_rec *s)
{
    apr_status_t rv;

    /* Get the config vector.  It already contains the configured
     * values of foo and bar, but the other fields are unset.
     */
    my_svr_cfg* svr =
        ap_get_module_config(s->module_config, &my_module);

    /* Derive our own pool from pchild */
    rv = apr_pool_create(&svr->pool, pchild);
    if (rv != APR_SUCCESS) {
        ap_log_perror(APLOG_MARK, APLOG_CRIT, rv, pchild,
                        "Failed to create subpool for my_module");
        return;
    }

    /* Set up a thread mutex for when we need to manipulate the cache */
#if APR_HAS_THREADS
    rv = apr_thread_mutex_create(&svr->mutex,
                        APR_THREAD_MUTEX_DEFAULT, pchild);
    if (rv != APR_SUCCESS) {
        ap_log_perror(APLOG_MARK, APLOG_CRIT, rv, pchild,
                        "Failed to create mutex for my_module");
        return;
    }
#endif

    /* Finally, create the cache itself (and prime it if applicable) */
    svr->cache = apr_hash_make(svr->pool);
}
```

The MPM code calls the `child_init` hook, after forking the child process but before entering operational mode and (in a threaded MPM) before creating threads. The pchild pool is created by the MPM as a process-wide subpool of the process pool itself (s->process->pool).

Now, when we want to add to the cache later, we are equipped to do so safely:

```
static int some_hook(request_rec *r)
{
    /* Get the server config vector.  This now serves two purposes:
     * it contains the configuration data foo and bar, and it holds the
     * dynamic part.
     */
    my_svr_cfg *svr =
        ap_get_module_config(s->module_config, &my_module);
    const char *key;
    my_data_t *val;

    key = compute_my_key(r);  /* set key from somewhere */

    /* Look up key in the cache */
    val = apr_hash_get(svr->cache, key, APR_HASH_KEY_STRING);

    if (val == NULL) {
#if APR_HAS_THREADS
        /* If it isn't cached, we need to compute it and save it to
         * the cache.  That's a critical section, so we need the mutex.
         */
        rv = apr_thread_mutex_lock(svr->mutex);
        if (rv != APR_SUCCESS) {
            ap_log_rerror(APLOG_MARK, APLOG_ERR, rv, r,
                        "Failed to acquire thread mutex");
            return HTTP_SERVICE_UNAVAILABLE;
        }

        /* In case of a race condition between cache lookup and
         * obtaining the lock, perform the lookup again.
         * Not a performance problem unless this happens a lot.
         */
        val = apr_hash_get(svr->cache, key, APR_HASH_KEY_STRING);

        if (val == NULL) {
            /* OK, we really do need to compute it */
            val = compute_my_val(r, svr);  /* do whatever it takes */
            apr_hash_set(svr->cache, key, APR_HASH_KEY_STRING, val);
        }
#else
        /* No threads = no risk of a race condition.  Just set it. */
        val = compute_my_val(r, svr);  /* do whatever it takes */
        apr_hash_set(svr->cache, key, APR_HASH_KEY_STRING, val);
#endif
    }

#if APR_HAS_THREADS
    rv = apr_thread_mutex_unlock(svr->mutex);
    if (rv != APR_SUCCESS) {
        /* Something is seriously wrong.  We need to log it,
         * but it doesn't -- of itself -- invalidate this request.
         */
```

```
        ap_log_rerror(APLOG_MARK, APLOG_ERR, rv, r,
                      "Failed to release thread mutex");
    }
#endif

    /* Now we have val, do whatever else this hook is doing */
    ...
    return OK;
}
```

If we want to change an existing value, we similarly need to use the mutex to protect our critical code.

4.5.2 Memory/Resource Management

As we saw in Chapter 3, APR pools provide a full and elegant solution to most resource management problems in Apache. Persistent resources are an exception, however, because they bring up a new problem: Are we leaking memory (or any other resource)? In the preceding code, if cache entries are ever deleted, the APR pool mechanism for managing resources fails us, because the pool lives on. This becomes a bug, which a server administrator will have to work around by limiting MaxRequestsPerChild to prevent an indefinite leak.

Several approaches are available to deal with this problem.

Garbage Collection

Instead of terminating the entire child, it is more efficient overall just to terminate our own resource from time to time and reclaim any possibly leaked resources. We can do so by tearing down the pool we've been using and starting anew. We'll need to make provision for this in our child_init function. In summary:

1. Add pchild to the my_svr_cfg struct.

2. Add a counter or a timeout to the my_svr_cfg struct.

3. Now we can clear garbage by winding up the module's pool, creating a new pool from pchild, and starting again. This activity must, of course, take place in a critical section, which is why the mutex needs to outlive the pool.

Let's take a look at a function to add garbage collection to our hash example. We call this function whenever an operation might leak, and we maintain a counter so that it does the real work only when it's got a decent amount of real work to do. Of course, any operation that might leak will be happening under mutex anyway.

```c
static apr_status_t do_garbage(my_server_cfg *svr)
{
    /* Call this only while we hold the mutex within some hook */

    apr_hash_index_t *index;
    const void *key;
    apr_ssize_t klen;
    my_val_type *val;
    apr_pool_t *newpool;
    apr_hash_t *newcache;
    apr_status_t rv;

    if (svr->count++ < svr->max_count) {
        return APR_SUCCESS;
    }
    /* Creating the new pool is actually a very slow leak on pchild */
    /* We can avoid this by creating and using a spare pool in place
     * of pchild (inefficient but doesn't leak) or, more simply, by
     * creating and destroying top-level pools.
     */
    rv = apr_pool_create(&newpool, svr->pchild);
    if (rv != APR_SUCCESS) {
        return rv ; /* We should also log an error message here */
    }

    /* Copy current cache entries */
    newcache = apr_hash_make(newpool);

    /* Deep-copy current entries in our cache */
    for (index = apr_hash_first(NULL, svr->cache); index != NULL;
         index = apr_hash_next(svr->cache)) {
        apr_hash_this(svr->cache, &key, &klen, &val);

        /* Now we need to deep-copy key and val.
         * Of course, we also need an application-specific
         * deep_copy function.
         */
        apr_hash_set(newcache, apr_pstrdup(newpool, key), klen,
                     deep_copy(newpool, val));
    }

    /* Clean up the old pool. Delete the old hash together
     * with any hitherto-leaked stuff.
     */
    apr_pool_destroy(svr->pool);

    /* Reset our data fields */
    svr->pool = newpool;
    svr->cache = newcache;
    svr->count = 0;

    /* All done successfully */
    return APR_SUCCESS;
}
```

Sometimes we can get away with much less. For example, if we have a hash of objects that time out, and re-creating them is not too expensive, we could dispense with copying anything at all. Then the preceding code reduces to the much simpler function shown here:

```
/* As in the more complex case, this maybe-garbage-collect
 * must always happen under thread mutex
 */
static apr_status_t do_garbage(my_server_cfg *svr)
{
    if (svr->count++ >= svr->max_count) {
        /* Just clean up everything, including the hash and its contents
         * along with whatever may have leaked.
         */
        apr_pool_clear(svr->pool);

        /* Re-initialize the cache and counter */
        svr->cache = apr_hash_new(svr->pool);
        svr->count = 0;
    }

    /* All done successfully */
    return APR_SUCCESS;
}
```

This is the "clean" alternative to leaking and using `MaxRequestsPerChild` as a workaround.

Use of Subpools

A variant on the garbage collection scheme is to use a subpool for every hash entry. With this approach, we can delete the subpool and reclaim resources whenever the entry itself is deleted. Because the subpools themselves incur overhead, this strategy is most likely to be appropriate when the number of resources is modest, but their size and complexity is such that they dominate relative to the overhead associated with the pools themselves.

Given that the subpools are allocated from the main pool, they are themselves a resource that needs to be managed and a potential source of memory leaks. Subpools offer a partial solution to the problem, but should be used in conjunction with one of the other solutions—for example, clearing and reusing the subpools.

Reuse of Resources

When the objects we are managing are of fixed size, we can manage the memory ourselves within the module:

- We can allocate an array of objects, together with an indexing array of free/in-use flags.

- When we need an object, we can claim it from the array. When we've finished with it, we can mark it as "free."

We can use this strategy with variable-sized objects by using subpools and managing the subpools themselves as the fixed-sized objects in the array. When we finish with an object, we run `apr_pool_clear`, but keep the pool itself for reuse.

Use of a Reslist

The `apr_reslist` serves to manage a pool of resources for reuse, providing a fully managed solution for us. It is most appropriate where the resources themselves carry a high cost. `mod_dbd` (see Chapter 10) is a usage example. For a case like our cache example, we could either use a reslist of subpools or manage blocks of memory and thereby avoid any dynamic allocation.

4.6 Cross-Platform Programming Issues

Provided we use the APR, cross-platform programming is basically straightforward. The problem, in this case, is equivalent to that seen with cross-MPM programming:

For example:

- The `apr_file_io`, `apr_file_info`, and `apr_fnmatch` modules provide a platform-independent filesystem layer.

- The `apr_time` module deals with timing issues.

- The `apr_user` module provides a platform-independent implementation of system users and groups.

- The `apr_*_mutex` modules provide cross-platform locks.

The lesson here: Avoid nonportable system calls and use these APR modules wherever they exist.

4.6.1 Example: Creating a Temporary File

Working on a UNIX or UNIX-like platform, we can create a temporary file, avoiding the widely deprecated `tmpfile()` system call:

```
FILE *create_tmpfile_BAD(apr_pool_t *pool)
{
    FILE *ret ;
    char *template = apr_pstrdup(pool, "/tmp/my-module.XXXXXX");
    int fd = mkstemp(template);

    if (fd == -1) {
        apr_log_perror(....);
        return NULL;
    }

    ret = fdopen(fd, "rw");
    if (ret == NULL) {
        apr_log_perror(....);
        close(fd);
        return NULL;
    }
    apr_pool_cleanup_register(pool, ret, (void*)fclose,
                    apr_pool_cleanup_null);
    return ret;
}
```

This code is fully correct and complete. We've created a temporary file using the standard secure mechanism, handled errors, and registered a cleanup to tie our temporary file to the lifetime of the pool. But it may not be fully portable:

1. The `/tmp/` directory is only valid in a UNIX or UNIX-like filesystem.

2. `fdopen` relies on POSIX.

3. The `FILE*` type, while valid across platforms, may support different and nonportable operations on some platforms.

Here's an APR-based version guaranteed to be portable across all supported platforms:

```
apr_file_t* create_tmpfile_GOOD(apr_pool_t *pool)
{
    apr_file_t *ret = NULL;
    const char *tempdir;
    char *template;
    apr_status_t rv;

    rv = apr_temp_dir_get(&tempdir, pool);
    if (rv != APR_SUCCESS) {
        ap_log_perror(APLOG_MARK, APLOG_ERR, rv, pool, "No temp dir!");
```

```
        return NULL;
    }

    rv = apr_filepath_merge(&template, tempdir, "my-module.XXXXXX",
                APR_FILEPATH_NATIVE, pool);
    if (rv != APR_SUCCESS) {
        ap_log_perror(APLOG_MARK, APLOG_ERR, rv, pool,
                "File path error!");
        return NULL;
    }

    rv = apr_file_mktemp(&ret, template, 0, pool);
    if (rv != APR_SUCCESS) {
        ap_log_perror(APLOG_MARK, APLOG_ERR, rv, pool,
                "Failed to open tempfile!");
        return NULL;
    }

    return ret;
}
```

A second reason for using APR functions here is to avoid binary compatibility issues, which may potentially arise when the module is compiled in a different environment to Apache/APR. For example, different versions of Microsoft's Visual C++ reportedly generate binary-compatible code if and only if the module avoids a wide range of native system calls, which it can do by delegating the system layer to APR.

4.7 Cross-MPM Programming Issues

As already hinted at, the MPM is really the platform for Apache. Because the APR deals with native platform issues such as the filesystem, the remaining MPM issues are the difficult ones. Principally, we have to deal with the consequences of running single or multiple processes, and implementing single or multiple threads within a process. This is not an "either/or" situation, however: Apache may also run with both multiple processes and multiple threads per process.

We've already discussed thread safety in Apache. The other major issue we need to deal with is coordinating between different processes. This coordination is generally expensive, and the types of interprocess interactions we can implement within the context of the standard Apache architecture are limited. Fortunately, such coordination is rarely necessary: While few modules need to concern themselves proactively with thread safety or resource management, fewer still need to concern themselves with interprocess issues.

There are two basic requirements you commonly have to consider:

- Global locks
- Shared memory

The APR provides Apache with support for both of these requirements.

4.7.1 Process and Global Locks

We've seen how using an APR thread mutex protects a critical section of code managing a server-based resource shared between threads. But APR provides two further mutexes: the process mutex `apr_proc_mutex` and the global mutex `apr_global_mutex`. When a module updates a globally shared resource (other than one with its own protection, such as an SQL database, or another server we are merely proxying), we need to use the latter mutex to protect critical sections of code. A case in which such a need often arises is when we are creating or updating files on the server.

The APR global mutex is more complex and more expensive than the thread mutex. The complexity lies in the initial setup of the mutex. First, it must be created in the parent process in the `post_config` phase. Second, each child has to attach to it in the `child_init` phase:

```
static int my_post_config(apr_pool_t *pool, apr_pool_t *plog,
              apr_pool_t *ptemp, server_rec *s)
{
    /* Several types of locks are supported; see apr_global_mutex.h
     * APR_LOCK_DEFAULT selects a lock type considered appropriate
     * for the platform we are running on.
     */
    apr_status_t rc;
    my_svr_cfg *cfg =
        ap_get_module_config(s->module_config, &my_module);

    rc = apr_global_mutex_create(&cfg->mutex, cfg->mutex_name,
                    APR_LOCK_DEFAULT, pool) ;
    if (rc != APR_SUCCESS) {
        ap_log_error(APLOG_MARK, APLOG_CRIT, rc, s,
                "Parent could not create mutex %s", cfg->mutex_name);
        return rc;
    }
#ifdef AP_NEED_SET_MUTEX_PERMS
    rc = unixd_set_global_mutex_perms(cfg->mutex);
    if (rc != APR_SUCCESS) {
        ap_log_error(APLOG_MARK, APLOG_CRIT, rc, cfg,
```

```
                        "Parent could not set permissions on global mutex:"
                        " check User and Group directives");
        return rc;
    }
#endif
    apr_pool_cleanup_register(pool, cfg->mutex,
            (void*)apr_global_mutex_destroy, apr_pool_cleanup_null) ;
    return OK ;
}

static void my_child_init(apr_pool_t *pool, server_rec *s)
{
    my_svr_cfg *cfg
        = ap_get_module_config(s->module_config, &my_module) ;
    apr_global_mutex_child_init(&cfg->mutex, cfg->mutex_name, pool) ;
}

static void my_hooks(apr_pool_t *pool)
{
    ap_hook_child_init(my_child_init, NULL, NULL, APR_HOOK_MIDDLE);
    ap_hook_post_config(my_post_config, NULL, NULL, APR_HOOK_MIDDLE) ;
    ap_hook_handler(my_handler, NULL, NULL, APR_HOOK_MIDDLE) ;
}
```

Now we've shown the two stages of global mutex creation and hooked an additional function: the content generator my_handler. A content generator is the most likely place in Apache to need a global mutex. Having set up our mutex in the server initialization, we can use it in the same manner as our thread mutex in any of our handlers:

```
static int my_handler(request_rec *r)
{
    /* Handler that edits some file on the server */
    apr_status_t rv;
    my_svr_cfg *cfg;

    cfg = ap_get_module_config(r->server->module_config, &my_module);

    /* Acquire the mutex */
    rv = apr_global_mutex_lock(cfg->mutex);
    if (rv != APR_SUCCESS) {
        ap_log_rerror(APLOG_MARK, APLOG_ERR, rv, r,
                "my_module: failed to acquire mutex!");
        return HTTP_INTERNAL_SERVER_ERROR;
    }
    /* Register a cleanup, so we don't risk holding the lock
     * forever if something bad happens to this request
     */
    apr_pool_cleanup_register(r->pool, cfg->mutex,
                    (void*)apr_global_mutex_unlock,
                    apr_pool_cleanup_null);
```

```
/* Now perform our file ops while we have the global lock */

/* If everything went OK, we can release the lock right now.
 * It may be worthwhile if there's much more processing yet to come
 * before this request is finished.
 */
rv = apr_global_mutex_unlock(cfg->mutex);
if ( rv != APR_SUCCESS ) {
    ap_log_rerror(APLOG_MARK, APLOG_ERR, rv, r,
            "my_module: failed to release mutex!");
}
apr_pool_cleanup_kill(r->pool, cfg->mutex, apr_global_mutex_unlock);

/* Further processing that doesn't require the mutex */

return OK;
}
```

4.7.2 Shared Memory

Many applications designers identify a shared resource as a requirement. Sometimes—as in the example case of editing a file—the shared resource has an independent existence. In other cases, the resource is internal to the webserver, as in a situation involving shared memory.

Consider, for example, the cache we examined earlier in this chapter. If our data are worth caching, presumably it's more expensive to compute them than to maintain a cache. So wouldn't it be better to share the cache over all processes, rather than duplicate it for every process?

The answer to this question is commonly "no." Shared memory is computationally expensive and too inflexible for the task of maintaining such a cache without incurring much more work. At the most fundamental level, there is no mechanism for memory allocation, and C pointers cannot meaningfully be shared. For all these reasons, you may want to avoid shared memory in your design.

Of course, sometimes you really do need shared memory. As usual, APR provides support for it.

Shared Memory: apr_shm

The APR shared memory module `apr_shm` serves well to share fixed-size data such as simple variables or structs comprising data members but no pointers.

Pointers in Shared Memory: apr_rmm

As mentioned earlier, pointers in `apr_shm` shared memory are meaningless, because the address space they point to is not shared. It is possible to implement pointers in shared memory by using another APR module, `apr_rmm`, to manage a block of memory allocated by `apr_shm`. As an example, `mod_ldap` uses this combination to manage a shared cache with dynamic allocation:

```
apr_status_t util_ldap_cache_init(apr_pool_t *pool, util_ldap_state_t *st)
{
#if APR_HAS_SHARED_MEMORY
    apr_status_t result;
    apr_size_t size;

    if (st->cache_file) {
        /* Remove any existing shm segment with this name. */
        apr_shm_remove(st->cache_file, st->pool);
    }

    size = APR_ALIGN_DEFAULT(st->cache_bytes);

    result = apr_shm_create(&st->cache_shm, size,
                st->cache_file, st->pool);
    if (result != APR_SUCCESS) {
        return result;
    }

    /* Determine the usable size of the shm segment */
    size = apr_shm_size_get(st->cache_shm);

    /* This will create an rmm "handler" to get into the shared memory area */
    result = apr_rmm_init(&st->cache_rmm, NULL,
                          apr_shm_baseaddr_get(st->cache_shm), size,
                          st->pool);
    if (result != APR_SUCCESS) {
        return result;
    }

#endif
    /* OMITTED FOR BREVITY */
    /* Register a cleanup on the pool to run apr_rmm_destroy
     * and apr_shm_destroy when apache exits.
     */

    /* More initialization for ldap */

    return APR_SUCCESS;
}
```

Now `mod_ldap` can use the `apr_rmm` functions (including versions of `malloc`, `calloc`, `realloc`, and `free`) and obtain pointers in shared memory. However, we are still working with a fixed-sized block, and our `apr_rmm` operations will be substantially slower than normal `apr_pool` allocation.

Fully Generic Shared Memory

If we wish to implement other APR and Apache data types in shared memory, we might want to implement an APR pool based on our `apr_rmm` functions. This is not possible in the APR as it stands, but such a strategy could, in principle, be made to work with modest modifications based on an alternative `apr_allocator` that uses the `apr_rmm` memory block and functions. Unfortunately, handling errors and managing pool lifetime are unlikely to be straightforward operations with this approach.

Persistent/Unlimited Shared Resources: apr_dbm and apr_memcache

DBM files are keyed lookup databases, typically based on hashing and fast lookup. They are (usually) held on the filesystem, so they can be used to share arbitrary data between processes. These databases, which represent an alternative to `apr_shm`/ `apr_rmm`, are better suited to management of larger shared resources or resources whose sizes cannot be set in the Apache configuration. They are also persistent, meaning that they will survive a restart of Apache.

The `apr_memcache` module is functionally similar (though by no means identical) to `apr_dbm`, but uses a (possibly remote) `memcached`[2] server instead of the local filesystem.

4.8 Secure Programming Issues

Warning

This section is not intended to serve as a general discussion of web and application security, nor even of programming modules for security-related tasks. Full coverage of these issues is beyond the scope of this book. Instead, we offer general good-practice tips and describe a few specific issues concerning programming for a

---

2. `http://www.danga.com/memcached/`

sometimes-hostile environment. For further reading, two books this author has reviewed and can recommend are Ryan C. Barnett's *Preventing Web Attacks with Apache* and Ivan Ristic's *Apache Security*.[3]

If you are responsible for running a server and are uncertain of the security of applications running on it, you should probably also consider deploying the web application firewall module `mod_security`.[4] However, matters of server administration fall outside the scope of this book.

4.8.1 The Precautionary Principle: Trust Nothing

Validate Inputs Proactively

Perl provides a superb aid to application security: taint checking. Taint checking causes external inputs to be treated as untrusted, so Perl will prevent them from being used in an unsafe operation. For example, you can print tainted data out to a browser, but you cannot use them in any `exec` or filesystem operation, as the tainted data might enable malicious input to compromise the system. Before you can use any input data in a potentially unsafe operation, it must first be untainted. That means proactively matching inputs to patterns—such as regular expressions—that determine exactly which inputs the application permits, and rejecting anything that doesn't match the specified patterns.

For example, an input representing a filename might be matched to a regular expression `[\w-_]{1-16}\.\w{3}`. That matching criterion is, of course, far more restrictive than is necessary under any modern filesystem. But this tougher standard is not a critical issue: It just means that the application is a little more restrictive, in an unimportant area, than is strictly necessary. More importantly, it prevents an attacker from using a carefully crafted filename to compromise system security—for example, reading "`../../../../../etc/passwd`" or executing a command with "`do_something_bad|`" [in Perl, the `|` turns `open()` into `popen()`].

Although no equivalent enforcement mechanism is available in C, the same principles apply whenever an Apache module uses input data, whether from request

---

3. `http://www.apachetutor.org/security/`
4. `http://www.modsecurity.org/`

headers, request entities (bodies), or any other source. Decide exactly what form the input data can take. Err on the side of caution where necessary. Check every input for conformance to allowed patterns. Refuse the request, typically by return-ing HTTP status 400 (bad request) if anything fails to match. To keep the input process reasonably user-friendly in case a legitimate user makes an honest mistake, you may want to construct an explanatory error page; of course, you can also del-egate that task to system administrators by advising them to use an appropriate `ErrorDocument`.

Use Inputs Safely

An important principle of security is not to rely on a single method of enforcement. No matter how carefully validated your inputs, it's worth using any means at your disposal to ensure they cannot be abused.

For example, consider authentication by SQL lookup with a statement like

```
statement = "SELECT password FROM authn WHERE user = '%s'"
```

together with a user value coming from the client.

If our module used something like

```
stmt = apr_psprintf(pool, statement, user);
apr_dbd_select(driver, pool, handle, &res, stmt, 0);
```

it would expose us to attacks such as an intruder adding himself to our database

```
user = "evil'; INSERT INTO authn VALUES (evil, password_for_evil);'"
```

or simply wiping the database in a similar manner.

In this case, the solution is obvious: Prepare the original statement, and pass the username as a parameter, so that the database treats the input as a string literal, eliminating this risk. In general, apply the same principle wherever possible: Ensure that inputs can never be treated as commands, only as data.

Apart from dbd, we must apply similar precautionary principles to logging, print-ing to the client, and—above all—system calls.

Don't Cut Corners!

Sloppy programming creates fertile ground for would-be security exploits. Ensure that *your* code is free of such vulnerabilities:

- Check the error status of all system calls and APR calls. Don't just ignore a return code. If there's no simple way to recover, abort request processing and return `HTTP_INTERNAL_SERVER_ERROR` to divert the request to an `ErrorDocument`. An internal error has occurred, and it's far better to admit that a problem exists than to cover it up and risk something far worse happening.

- Avoid buffer overflows. Never write to an already-allocated buffer without first checking that the data being written fit within the buffer.

Don't Be Afraid of Errors!

Sometimes you may be unsure what to do, as when dealing with an unexpected event in a complex situation. Your module should handle all events that you anticipate, but should also deal with events that seem unlikely or even impossible when the module is first written (maybe your impossible event will become possible in a future update). If it is not reasonable to think through every eventuality, just bail out with an error. With this approach, you've got a limitation, but you've also closed a potential security hole. Log an error message to help identify and fix it, should that ever become necessary.

4.8.2 Denial of Service: Limit the Damage

A denial of service (DoS) occurs when your server becomes too overloaded to manage its normal functions. Of course, it's very easy to initiate a DoS yourself: From the pure fork bomb to the elusive memory leak, programming bugs or deliberate misuse can bring a server to its knees. Unfortunately, it's almost as easy to initiate a DoS from a third-party server over the Internet. Causes can range from a targeted malicious attack to something perfectly innocent like the "slashdot effect," in which a site is suddenly inundated with higher levels of legitimate traffic than the server and network can handle. The worst form of attack is the distributed denial of service (DDoS), which occurs when an attacker has access to thousands of different machines around the world[5] and cobbles all of them together to mount a brute force attack.

---

5. Usually Windows machines where a virus enables the attacker to take control on demand.

The primary responsibility for protecting against DoS lies with system administrators, who may choose to deploy explicit DoS protection such as special-purpose modules. Modules for Apache include the following:

- `mod_evasive`[6] (formerly `mod_dosevasive`) is a sophisticated module that limits the amount of traffic per client IP the server will accept.

- `mod_cband`[7] is a general-purpose module that shapes traffic and manages bandwidth and numbers of connections.

- `mod_load_average`[8] is a simple module that avoids taking on heavy processing tasks when the server is already heavily loaded. Apache will return HTTP status `503` (the server is too busy) when processing the request normally would demand more of the system's resources.

- `mod_robots`[9] is a very simple module that denies access to badly behaved robots. It can also be used against spambots identifiable by `user-agent`.

For normal modules—those whose primary purpose isn't concerned with protecting the server—there is little you can or should do to protect them against DoS attacks. The main issue is to limit your module's total resource consumption:

- Manage expensive resources using `apr_reslist` or a similar means, so that the system administrator can set limits on the number of concurrent users.

- Use timeouts on client I/O, including network-level filters.

- Stream all I/O. If that is not possible, ensure that a system administrator can set limits on I/O size. Note that this approach may directly conflict with the use of `mod_security` to protect vulnerable applications such as PHP, because some uses of `mod_security` prevent I/O streaming.

- If your module supports large/long transactions (e.g., streaming media), reclaim memory and other resources regularly. This may mean using local pools and clearing them regularly and/or performing explicit cleaning of brigades in the filter chain.

---

6. `http://www.nuclearelephant.com/projects/mod_evasive/`
7. `http://cband.linux.pl/`
8. `http://force-elite.com/~chip/archives/mod_load_average-0.1.0-test3.tar.bz2`
9. `http://apache.webthing.com/svn/apache/misc/mod_robots.c`

4.8.3 Help the Operating System to Help You

It is up to system administrators to set up Apache securely, including using the protections provided by operating systems. The role of the application developer is to make as few demands as possible on the operating system that would be incompatible with security measures.

Privileges

Assume that Apache has no system privileges, such as a shell or ownership of any files or directories. If your module requires anything, it inevitably compromises best practices with regard to security.

Avoid requiring the identity or privileges of any system user, especially root. If your module absolutely *must* do something that requires root privileges,[10] it should run the privileged operations in a separate, ultra-simple, single-purpose process, so that Apache httpd doesn't have to be given privileges. The same guideline applies, albeit a little less strongly, to other users. CGI with suexec[11] is a good sandbox for applications requiring medium-level privileges.

Networking

Work with a firewall. If your module needs to perform its own network I/O, make sure that the system administrator can fix the ports and IP addresses used (subject to the constraints of your application), so that the firewall can be kept simple and tight.

Protect yourself from broken or malicious input from your own network I/O just as you would with incoming HTTP requests.

Filesystem

Use the precautionary principle in accessing the filesystem. Let the system administrator define (in httpd.conf) areas of the filesystem you will access, and never stray outside those areas.

Flags to enforce this restriction are available in the apr_filepath calls. For example, the following function from mod_include prevents SSI inclusion of unauthorized

---

10. This is *strongly* discouraged!
11. http://httpd.apache.org/docs/2.2/suexec.html

and possibly sensitive files. First we resolve the filename passed, rejecting anything that takes us out of the permitted area of the filesystem (e.g., paths such as "`../../../../etc/passwd`"). Then we perform a subrequest lookup (see Chapter 6) to check that the file really is available to Apache (and that it is found where we expect it to be), before allowing it to be served. If `find_file` returns a nonzero value, the directive accessing the file will fail.

```
static int find_file(request_rec *r, const char *directive,
    const char *tag, char *tag_val, apr_finfo_t *finfo)
{
    char *to_send = tag_val;
    request_rec *rr = NULL;
    int ret=0;
    char *error_fmt = NULL;
    apr_status_t rv = APR_SUCCESS;

    if (!strcmp(tag, "file")) {
        char *newpath;

        /* Be safe; only files in this directory or below allowed */
        rv = apr_filepath_merge(&newpath, NULL, tag_val,
                        APR_FILEPATH_NOTABOVEROOT |
                        APR_FILEPATH_SECUREROOTTEST |
                        APR_FILEPATH_NOTABSOLUTE, r->pool);

        if (rv != APR_SUCCESS) {
            error_fmt = "unable to access file \"%s\" "
                        "in parsed file %s";
        }
        else {
            /* Note: it is OK to pass NULL for the "next filter" because
               we never attempt to "run" this subrequest */
            rr = ap_sub_req_lookup_file(newpath, r, NULL);

            if (rr->status == HTTP_OK && rr->finfo.filetype != 0) {
                to_send = rr->filename;
                if ((rv = apr_stat(finfo, to_send,
                    APR_FINFO_GPROT | APR_FINFO_MIN, rr->pool))
                != APR_SUCCESS && rv != APR_INCOMPLETE) {
                    error_fmt = "unable to get information about \"%s\""
                        " in parsed file %s";
                }
            }
            else {
                error_fmt = "unable to look up information about \"%s\" "
                            "in parsed file %s";
            }
        }
    }
```

```
        if (error_fmt) {
            ret = -1;
            ap_log_rerror(APLOG_MARK, APLOG_ERR,
                            rv, r, error_fmt, to_send, r->filename);
        }

        if (rr) ap_destroy_sub_req(rr);

        return ret;
    }
    /* remainder of function irrelevant */
}
```

write and exec

The most serious exploits to have hit Apache servers in real life have involved saving an executable file to /tmp, and running it. It is not Apache itself, but rather applications (running under PHP) that give rise to this problem. Apache cannot prevent buggy applications from running, but you can and should protect against such serious consequences. The best advice to system administrators is to use filesystem security:

- Use file permissions and ownership to limit the Apache user's write access to designated areas.

- Ensure that those designated areas are on a device mounted with a noexec flag, so that the operating system prevents execution of a malicious file.

The role of the application developer here is, as usual, to avoid doing anything that could cause problems with this security. For example, do not write data anywhere that's not specified by the system administrator and that might therefore be inconvenient or impossible to have mounted with noexec.

chroot

Avoid doing anything that would prevent a system administrator from running Apache chroot. In other words, avoid making any assumptions about how the filesystem will look from Apache's perspective.

Running chroot is a relatively complex task for a system administrator, but has little relevance to most developers. Try this trick instead: Set up a minimal Apache installation to run in a chrooted test environment, and then add your module to the test server. If anything breaks, trace what caused the problem and try to fix it.

4.9 External Dependencies and Libraries

4.9.1 Third-Part Libraries

Administrators of many systems, including Apache, sometimes insist that more modules mean more complexity, and hence more trouble. Of course, more modules always mean a greater risk of bugs, simply because there's more code. The real problem, however, is the possibility that two modules will be mutually incompatible and cause each other to fail. *This should never happen!*

Third-party libraries are fertile ground for this kind of trouble, because two or more modules may access a library in mutually incompatible ways. Following some basic rules of good practice can help ensure that your module doesn't become the cuckoo in the nest that causes Apache to fail when it is used together with other modules from different sources.

4.9.2 Library Good Practice

Libraries, like modules, should always follow some basic rules of good practice. The most basic rule states that library functions should always return control to the caller in an orderly and properly documented manner. In particular, `exit()` is not an acceptable way to handle errors.

Unfortunately, some libraries—particularly older ones that may have been intended only for command line programs—may violate this principle. Examples are common in graphics libraries such as `libjpeg`.[12] Changing the library may pose a problem, but the conflict can be worked around by using `setjmp/longjmp`:

```
typedef struct {
    jmp_buf jmp;
    request_rec *r;
} my_ctx;
```

We need to set `libjpeg` to use `longjmp` rather than `exit()` when it encounters a fatal error:

```
static void jpeg_error_exit(j_common_ptr cinfo)
{
    my_ctx *ctx = (my_ctx*)cinfo->client_data;
    (*cinfo->err->output_message) (cinfo);
    longjmp(ctx->jmp, 1);
}
```

---

12. This is partially, but not entirely, solved in the higher-level gd library.

We also need to register a function to generate error messages from the library:

```
static void jpeg_output_message(j_common_ptr cinfo)
{
    char buffer[JMSG_LENGTH_MAX];
    my_ctx *ctx = (my_ctx*)cinfo->client_data ;

    (*cinfo->err->format_message) (cinfo, buffer);

    ap_log_rerror(APLOG_MARK, APLOG_ERR, 0, ctx->r,
            "JPEG Error: %s", buffer);
}
```

Now we need our handler to set up its own error handler with `libjpeg`:

```
static int my_jpeg_handler(request_rec* r)
{

    struct jpeg_compress_struct *cinfo;
    my_ctx *ctx;

    struct jpeg_error_mgr *errptr
            = apr_palloc(r->pool, sizeof(jpeg_error_mgr));
    errptr->output_message = jpeg_output_message;
    errptr->error_exit = jpeg_error_exit;

    /* Register handler with libjpeg */
    jpeg_std_error(errptr);

    /* Create a jpeg context and register a cleanup on the pool
     * (cleanup function omitted for brevity)
     */
    ctx = apr_palloc(r->pool, sizeof(my_ctx));
    cinfo = apr_palloc(r->pool, sizeof(struct jpeg_compress_struct));
    ctx->r = r;
    jpeg_create_compress(cinfo);
    cinfo->client_data = ctx;
    cinfo->err = errptr;
    apr_pool_cleanup_register(f->r->pool, cinfo,
                            (apr_status_t(*)(void*))cjpeg_cleanup,
                    apr_pool_cleanup_null);

    /* Set up other fields of cinfo (omitted) */

    /* Handle fatal errors from libjpeg */
    if (setjmp(ctx->jmp)) {
        ap_log_rerror(APLOG_MARK, APLOG_ERR, 0, r,
                "Fatal Error in libjpeg");
        return HTTP_INTERNAL_SERVER_ERROR ;
    }
```

```
    /* Now do our processing with libjpeg, including (of course)
     * always checking for nonfatal errors.
     * Fatal errors are now handled by longjmp setting the clock back
     * to our setjmp, so we'll log an error and return 500.
     */
}
```

C++ `throw`/`catch` is superficially a more elegant solution that accomplishes the same thing, but in this author's experience it doesn't work so well in Apache. Your mileage may vary.

Thread Safety

When using third-party libraries, the module developer is responsible for ascertaining whether the libraries are thread safe. If they are not, then your module will need to use a thread mutex for every library call (which may be prohibitively expensive). Alternatively, you can document the module as not being thread safe, and limit its use to the Prefork MPM. The best-known example that uses the latter approach is PHP.

Some libraries—for example, the MySQL client library `libmysqlclient`—come as more than one version: a "standard" version that is not thread safe, and an alternative that is fully thread safe and reentrant. When using such a library, you should ensure your users always select the thread-safe version.

Initialization and Termination

Some libraries may require per-process initialization and termination. These tasks can be handled in various places in Apache, including the module hooks function. Unfortunately, the double start-up followed by forking of children makes this strategy complex and sometimes unsuitable. A library that is initialized before configuration will first be initialized, then terminated, then initialized a second time, after which child processes will be forked. If that behavior is acceptable with your library, then it's a convenient way to handle initialization, because it makes the library available to the configuration functions.

Naturally, you will also need to register any termination function on the pool. If the library has a function whose signature is not compatible with a pool cleanup, you'll need to write a wrapper for it. Here's a typical outline for initialization:

```
static void register_hooks(apr_pool_t *pool)
{
    my_lib_init() ;
    apr_pool_cleanup_register(pool, NULL, my_lib_terminate,
                    apr_pool_cleanup_null);
    /* and of course register whatever this module exports */
}
```

When the start-stop-restart-fork process will cause trouble, the safest place to handle library initialization may be a function hooked to child_init. In this case, initialization happens after the fork but before entering operational mode. As with the other strategy, you'll need to call library initialization and register the termination function, this time on the child pool. If any configuration functions require the library, however, you may need to do something more complex, such as saving the configuration data "raw" in the configuration phase and then running any necessary library functions on the raw input data after initializing the library in the child_init phase.

Caution!

Bear in mind that your module may not be the only one to use the library. For most libraries, running initialization and global cleanup more than once does not pose a problem, so your module need not concern itself with this issue. If running either initialization or cleanup more than once will complicate life for the library, your module needs to be sensitive to whether another module is independently doing the same thing. One potential solution to this problem is to write a separate mini-module that specifically ensures that library functions are run exactly once.

Future Apache releases may provide a more elegant solution to this dilemma.

Library State Changes

If a library has global variables, any use of them is not thread safe.

A similar, more general issue arises when a library allows an application to change its state with global scope—for example, by registering callback functions for library events. This possibility is actually more than just a thread-safety issue, as it affects even the nonthreaded Prefork MPM.

To see how this problem arises, let's consider a real-life example. The XML (and HTML) parsing library libxml2 allows an application to register handlers for parse errors. If your module uses such handlers, they should always be registered in the context of a parser that is owned by your module. However, mod_php skimped on this requirement and registered the handlers globally.[13]

Now, when another module uses libxml2 in processing a request and encounters a parse error, the registered error handler is called. But that is PHP's handler! Because it wasn't a PHP request, there is no PHP context, and Apache will crash (segfault). PHP has become a cuckoo in the nest, and *other modules* had to take extra trouble to work around the bug if using the XML parser in a manner that might generate XML parse errors.

4.9.3 Building Modules with Libraries

When your module relies on a third-party library, it needs that library at runtime. You can provide the library by any of three means:

1. Link the library when building the module.

2. Use LoadFile to load the library into Apache.

3. Open the library from within your module code, using apr_dso.

If you are contemplating the third option, you are probably doing something unusual and have a good reason for making this choice. Options 1 and 2, by contrast, are largely interchangeable. Consider a module mod_foo that relies on an external library libfoo. Here's how it might look. These details are from an up-to-date Linux system, but the same principles apply on other platforms:

```
(1) apxs -c -lfoo mod_foo.c
ldd .libs/mod_foo.so
        linux-gate.so.1 =>  (0xffffe000)
        libfoo.so => /usr/lib/libfoo.so (0xb7fc9000)
        libc.so.6 => /lib/libc.so.6 (0xb7e22000)
        /lib/ld-linux.so.2 (0x80000000)
```

versus

```
(2) apxs -c mod_foo.c
ldd .libs/mod_foo.so
        linux-gate.so.1 =>  (0xffffe000)
        libc.so.6 => /lib/libc.so.6 (0xb7ec2000)
        /lib/ld-linux.so.2 (0x80000000)
```

---

13. http://marc.theaimsgroup.com/?1=php-dev&m=108258335530060&w=2

In example 1, the library is linked directly into the module. This approach is superficially simpler for end users: A single `LoadModule` directive suffices to load the module (we can even insert the directive within the build procedure, using the `-a` option to `apxs`). Some developers prefer this strategy, for this reason.

In example 2, the single `LoadModule` is no longer sufficient. Apache will try to load `mod_foo`, but will encounter unresolved symbols (from `libfoo`) and refuse to start. In this case, we need an additional `LoadFile` directive:

```
LoadFile      /usr/lib/libfoo.so
LoadModule    foo_module    modules/mod_foo.so
```

Although superficially more complicated, this second approach has a number of advantages, which are discussed next.

Flexibility

If a module is built on one computer but intended to run on another computer (e.g., a developer supplying binaries to a client), the linked library may be in a different place in the filesystem on the target computer. This becomes a headache for the system administrator to sort out, particularly when the libraries are controlled by a package manager. When the developer uses `LoadFile`, the filesystem layout is immaterial; all that matters is that `libfoo` is available somewhere on the system.

Side Effects (Stealth Libraries)

When a module links a third-party library, that library is imported into Apache with the module. This approach may have side effects for other modules that use the library, causing the library to load or fail according to the ordering of the `LoadModule` directives. Such behavior is, in this author's opinion, a clear violation of the principles of modularity. In some cases, it can also cause a module to load apparently successfully only to fail later, generating errors that are far more challenging to trace than an undefined symbol at start-up.

Versioning

When two or more modules link to a library, there is a risk of them linking to different versions of it. Even if the versions are fully binary compatible, this possibility causes major trouble: The overloading of the symbol table may lead to inexplicable, hard-to-trace segfaults. When a system administrator complains that supporting modules leads to trouble, this behavior is very likely to be the culprit.

In summary, it is recommended that you try to avoid linking any libraries into modules, and rely on `LoadFile` instead. If the setup is complex, shipping a configuration example with the module may be worthwhile. This tactic preserves modularity, leaves the system administrator in control, and makes conflicts and other serious problems both far less likely to happen and hugely easier to trace.

> NOTE Expert opinion is not unanimous on this subject, and even the core Apache distribution diverges from the principles of good practice suggested here. Your mileage may vary.

4.10 Modules Written and Compiled in Other Languages

Although all module examples in this book are written in C, it's entirely possible to write modules in other languages:

1. Any language that can be compiled to relocatable object code with C linkage can be used on exactly the same basis as C, with the C API. For example, C++, modern versions of FORTRAN, Modula 2/3, and a raft of obsolete languages can be used in this manner.

2. Scripting languages such as Perl, PHP, Python, Ruby, and Tcl are supported by their respective language modules, which expose the Apache API to support module programming. Perl's implementation of the API is probably the most complete of these options.

3. Any language can be supported as an external programming—for example, with CGI or a proxied back end such as Java's JSP and servlet APIs.

Only the first of these possibilities falls within the scope of this discussion. How do we compile and link a module written against the C API, given that `apxs` is fully compatible only with C?

This question is actually a platform-specific issue. On Windows, there is no `apxs`, and you can import a C++ module into VC++ exactly as you would a C module (I cannot speak for other languages on Windows). In our discussion here, we'll deal with UNIX-family platforms, where `apxs` is the usual build tool.

Building and loading are simple:

1. Export the C-compatible module symbol from your code, as you would in any module.

2. Compile the module for position-independent code and with Apache and APR include paths.

3. Link it as a shared object.

4. Copy it to your Apache modules directory.

5. Load it in `httpd.conf`.

For example, with gcc's options for C++, this process could be written as follows (don't forget to declare the `module` symbol with `extern "C"` to ensure C linkage):

```
$ c++ -g -O2 -Wall -fPIC -I/usr/local/apache/include mod_foo.cpp
$ c++ -shared -o mod_foo.so mod_foo.o
# cp mod_foo.so /usr/local/apache/modules/
```

If our module uses any of the API features implemented as macros, it will need a C-compatible preprocessor, which may not be compatible with the language. Two workarounds are possible in this case: expand the macros explicitly, or use C stubs.

Expanded Macros

When our use of macros is sufficiently simple, we may just expand the macros within our module code. Configuration directives (covered in Chapter 9) are easy to expand, for instance. An example is `mod_validator`, in which

```
AP_INIT_TAKE2("ValidatorDefault",
    (const char*(*)())ValidatorDefault, NULL, OR_ALL,
        "Default parser; default allowed parsers" ) ,
```

becomes

```
{ "ValidatorDefault",
    (const char*(*)(cmd_parms*, void*))ValidatorDefault,
    __null, (1|2|4|8|16), TAKE2,
    "Default parser; default allowed parsers" } ,
```

when expanded to work with a C++ compiler without a C99 preprocessor. (This step was required in Apache 2.2.0, but should no longer be necessary in future versions, as the C99 requirement shouldn't have affected C++ source.)

C Stubs

For complex macros, such as those that implement optional functions or hooks (covered in Chapter 10), we can again expand them inline. Sometimes, however, it may be more convenient to implement the macros in a C stubs file and then to link that file with our non-C module. Let's say we have a module written in language x, compiled with `xcompile`:

```
$ xcompile -xoptions mod_foo.x
$ cc -c -fPIC -g -O2 -I/usr/local/apache/include foo_stubs.c
$ cc -shared -o mod_foo.so mod_foo.o foo_stubs.o
# cp mod_foo.so /usr/local/apache/modules/
```

4.11 Summary

In this chapter, we discussed a number of important topics related to good practice and safe programming:

- The Apache `httpd` project's code style guidelines
- Management of transient and persistent module data, with regard to scope and lifetime
- Basic methods for communicating between modules
- Thread-safe and cross-process programming techniques
- Programming for security, and supporting the server administrator
- Working with third-party libraries and with languages other than C

We are now ready to move on to the more practically oriented section of the book and to develop real modules.

Chapter 5

Writing a Content Generator

In principle, one can do anything with the Common Gateway Interface (CGI).[1] But the range of problems for which CGI provides a *good* solution is much smaller!

The same is true of a content generator in Apache. It lies at the heart of processing a request and of building a web application. Indeed, it can be extended to do anything that the underlying system permits the webserver to do. The content generator is the most basic kind of module in Apache.

All of the major traditional applications normally work as content generators. For example, CGI, PHP, and application servers proxied by Apache are content generators.

---

1. `http://CGI-Spec.Golux.Com/`

5.1 The HelloWorld Module

In this chapter, we will develop a simple content generator. The customary `HelloWorld` example demonstrates the basic concepts of module programming, including the complete module structure, and use of the handler callback and `request_rec`.

By the end of the chapter, we will have extended our `HelloWorld` module to report the full details of the request and response headers, the environment variables, and any data posted to the server, and we will be equipped to write content generator modules in situations where we might otherwise have used a CGI script or comparable extension.

5.1.1 The Module Skeleton

Every Apache module works by exporting a module data structure. In general, an Apache 2.x module takes the following form:

```
module AP_MODULE_DECLARE_DATA some_module = {
    STANDARD20_MODULE_STUFF,
    some_dir_cfg,       /* create per-directory config struct */
    some_dir_merge,     /* merge per-directory config struct */
    some_svr_cfg,       /* create per-host config struct */
    some_svr_merge,     /* merge per-host config struct */
    some_cmds,          /* configuration directives for this module */
    some_hooks          /* register module's hooks/etc. with the core */
};
```

The `STANDARD20_MODULE_STUFF` macro expands to provide version information that ensures the compiled module will load into a server build only when it is fully binary compatible, together with the filename and reserved fields. Most of the remaining fields are concerned with module configuration; they will be discussed in detail in Chapter 9. For the purposes of our `HelloWorld` module, we need only the hooks:

```
module AP_MODULE_DECLARE_DATA helloworld_module = {
    STANDARD20_MODULE_STUFF,
    NULL,
    NULL,
    NULL,
    NULL,
    NULL,
    helloworld_hooks
};
```

Having declared the module structure, we now need to instantiate the hooks function. Apache will run this function at server start-up. Its purpose is to register our module's processing functions with the server core, so that our module's functions will subsequently be invoked whenever they are appropriate. In the case of `HelloWorld`, we just need to register a simple content generator, or handler,[2] which is one of many kinds of functions we can insert here.

```
static void helloworld_hooks(apr_pool_t *pool)
{
    ap_hook_handler(helloworld_handler, NULL, NULL, APR_HOOK_MIDDLE);
}
```

Finally, we need to implement `helloworld_handler`. This is a callback function that will be called by Apache at the appropriate point in processing an HTTP request. It may choose to handle or ignore a request. If it handles a request, the function is responsible for sending a valid HTTP response to the client and for ensuring that any data coming from the client are read (or discarded). This is very similar to the responsibilities of a CGI script—or, indeed, the responsibilities of the webserver as a whole.

Here's our simplest handler:

```
static int helloworld_handler(request_rec *r)
{
    if (!r->handler || (strcmp(r->handler, "helloworld") != 0)) {
        return DECLINED;
    }
    if (r->method_number != M_GET) {
        return HTTP_METHOD_NOT_ALLOWED;
    }
    ap_set_content_type(r, "text/html;charset=ascii");
    ap_rputs("<!DOCTYPE HTML PUBLIC \"-//W3C//DTD HTML 4.01//EN\">\n",
            r);
    ap_rputs("<html><head><title>Apache HelloWorld "
            "Module</title></head>", r);
    ap_rputs("<body><h1>Hello World!</h1>", r);
    ap_rputs("<p>This is the Apache HelloWorld module!</p>", r);
    ap_rputs("</body></html>", r);
    return OK;
}
```

---

2. Chapter 10 explains the meaning of registering the function with a hook.

This callback function starts with a couple of basic sanity checks. First, we check `r->handler` to determine whether the request is for us. If the request is not for us, we ignore it by returning DECLINED. Apache will then pass control to the next handler.

Second, we want to support only the HTTP GET and HEAD methods. We check for those cases and, if appropriate, return an HTTP error code indicating that the method is not allowed. Returning an error code here will cause Apache to return an error page to the client. Note that the HTTP standard (see Appendix C) defines HEAD as being identical to GET except for the response body, which is omitted in HEAD. Both methods are included in Apache's M_GET, and content generator functions should treat them as identical.

The order in which these checks are performed is important. If we reversed them, our module might cause Apache to return an error page in cases such as POST requests intended for another handler, such as a CGI script that accepts them.

Once we are satisfied that the request is acceptable and is meant for this handler, we generate the actual response—in this case, a trivial HTML page. Having done so, we return OK to tell Apache that we have dealt with this request and that it should not call any other handler.

5.1.2 Return Values

Even this trivial handler has three possible return values. In general, handlers provided by modules can return

- OK, to indicate that the handler has fully and successfully dealt with the request. No further processing is necessary.

- DECLINED, to indicate that the handler takes no interest in the request and declines to process it. Apache will then try the next handler. The default handler, which simply returns a file from the local disk (or an error page if that fails), never returns DECLINED, so requests are always handled by some function.

- An HTTP status code, to indicate an error. The handler has taken responsibility for the request, but was unable or unwilling to complete it.

An HTTP status code diverts the entire processing chain within Apache. Normal processing of the request is aborted, and Apache sets up an internal redirect to an error document, which may either be one of Apache's predefined defaults or be a document or handler specified by the ErrorDocument directive in the server configuration. Note that this diversion works only if Apache hasn't already started to send the response down the wire to the client—this can be an important design consideration in handling errors. To ensure correct behavior, any such diversion must take place before writing any data (the first ap_rputs statements in our case).

Where possible, it is good practice to deal with errors earlier in the request processing cycle. This consideration is discussed further in Chapter 6.

5.1.3 The Handler Field

Having to check r->handler may seem counterintuitive, but this step is generally necessary in all content generators. Apache will call all content generators registered by any module until one of them returns either OK or an HTTP status code. Thus it's up to each module to check r->handler, which tells the module whether it should process the request.

This scheme is made necessary by the implementation of Apache's hooks, which are designed to enable any number of functions (or nothing) to run on a hook. The content generator is unique among Apache's hooks in that exactly one content generator function must take responsibility for every request. Other hooks that share the implementation have different semantics, as we will see in Chapters 6 and 10.

5.1.4 The Complete Module

Putting it all together and adding the required headers, we have a complete mod_helloworld.c source file:

```
/* The simplest HelloWorld module */

#include <httpd.h>
#include <http_protocol.h>
#include <http_config.h>

static int helloworld_handler(request_rec *r)
{
    if (!r->handler || strcmp(r->handler, "helloworld")) {
        return DECLINED;
    }
```

```
    if (r->method_number != M_GET) {
        return HTTP_METHOD_NOT_ALLOWED;
    }
    ap_set_content_type(r, "text/html;charset=ascii");
    ap_rputs("<!DOCTYPE HTML PUBLIC \"-//W3C//DTD HTML 4.01//EN\">\n",
            r);
    ap_rputs("<html><head><title>Apache HelloWorld "
            "Module</title></head>", r);
    ap_rputs("<body><h1>Hello World!</h1>", r);
    ap_rputs("<p>This is the Apache HelloWorld module!</p>", r);
    ap_rputs("</body></html>", r);
    return OK;
}
static void helloworld_hooks(apr_pool_t *pool)
{
    ap_hook_handler(helloworld_handler, NULL, NULL, APR_HOOK_MIDDLE);
}
module AP_MODULE_DECLARE_DATA helloworld_module = {
        STANDARD20_MODULE_STUFF,
        NULL,
        NULL,
        NULL,
        NULL,
        NULL,
        helloworld_hooks
} ;
```

And that's all we need! Now we can build the module and insert it into Apache. We use the apxs utility, which is bundled with Apache and serves to ensure the compilation flags and paths are correct:

Compile the module

```
$ apxs -c mod_helloworld.c
```

and (working as root) install it:

```
# apxs -i mod_helloworld.la
```

Now configure it as a handler in httpd.conf:

```
LoadModule    helloworld_module    modules/mod_helloworld.so
<Location /helloworld>
    SetHandler helloworld
</Location>
```

This code causes any request to /helloworld on our server to invoke this module as its handler.

Note that the `helloworld_hooks` and `helloworld_handler` functions are both declared as `static`. This practice is typical—though not quite universal—in Apache modules. In general, only the module symbol is exported, and everything else remains private to the module itself. As a consequence, it is good practice to declare all functions as `static`. Exceptions may arise when a module exports a service or API for other modules, as discussed in Chapter 10. Another case arises when a module is implemented in multiple source files and needs some symbols to be common to those files. A naming convention should be adopted in such cases, to avoid symbol space pollution.

5.1.5 Using the request_rec Object

As we have just seen, the single argument to our handler function is the `request_rec` object. The same argument is used for all hooks involved in request processing.

The `request_rec` object is a large data structure that represents an HTTP request and provides access to all data involved in processing a request. It is also an argument to many lower-level API calls. For example, in `helloworld_handler`, it serves as an argument to `ap_set_content_type` and as an I/O descriptor-like argument to `ap_rputs`.

Let's look at another example. Suppose we want to serve a file from the local filesystem instead of a fixed HTML page. To do so, we would use the `r->filename` argument to identify the file. But we can also use file `stat` information to optimize the process of sending the file. Instead of reading the file and sending its contents with `ap_rwrite`, we can send the file itself, allowing APR to take advantage of available system optimizations:

```
static int helloworld_handler(request_rec *r)
{
    apr_file_t *fd;
    apr_size_t sz;
    apr_status_t rv;

    /* "Is it for us?" checks omitted for brevity */

    /* It's an error if r->filename and finfo haven't been set for us.
     * We could omit this check if we make certain assumptions concerning
     * use of our module, but if 'normal' processing is prevented by
     * some other module, then r->filename might be null, and we don't
     * want to risk a segfault!
     */
```

```
if (r->filename == NULL) {
    ap_log_rerror(APLOG_MARK, APLOG_ERR, 0, r,
            "Incomplete request_rec!") ;
    return HTTP_INTERNAL_SERVER_ERROR ;
}

ap_set_content_type(r, "text/html;charset=ascii");

/* Now we can usefully set some additional headers from file info
 * (1) Content-Length
 * (2) Last-Modified
 */
ap_set_content_length(r, r->finfo.size);
if (r->finfo.mtime) {
    char *datestring = apr_palloc(r->pool, APR_RFC822_DATE_LEN);
    apr_rfc822_date(datestring, r->finfo.mtime);
    apr_table_setn(r->headers_out, "Last-Modified", datestring);
}

rv = apr_file_open(&fd, r->filename,
            APR_READ|APR_SHARELOCK|APR_SENDFILE_ENABLED,
            APR_OS_DEFAULT, r->pool);
if (rv != APR_SUCCESS) {
    ap_log_rerror(APLOG_MARK, APLOG_ERR, 0, r,
            "can't open %s", r->filename);
    return HTTP_NOT_FOUND ;
}
ap_send_fd(fd, r, 0, r->finfo.size, &sz);

/* file_close here is purely optional. If we omit it, APR will close
 * the file for us when r is destroyed, because apr_file_open
 * registered a close on r->pool.
 */
apr_file_close(fd);
return OK;
}
```

5.2 The Request, the Response, and the Environment

Setting aside this little diversion into the filesystem, what else can a HelloWorld module usefully do?

Well, the module can report general information, in the manner of programs such as the printenv CGI script that comes bundled with Apache. Three of the most commonly used (and useful) sets of information in Apache modules are the request headers, the response headers, and the internal environment variables. Let's update the original HelloWorld module to print them in the response page.

Each of these sets of information is held in an APR table that is part of the request_rec object. We can iterate over the tables to print the full contents using apr_table_do and a callback. We'll use HTML tables to represent these Apache tables.

First, here's a callback to print a table entry as an HTML row. Of course, we need to escape the data for HTML:

```
static int printitem(void *rec, const char *key, const char *value)
{
    /* rec is a user data pointer.  We'll pass the request_rec in it. */
    request_rec *r = rec;
    ap_rprintf(r, "<tr><th scope=\"row\">%s</th><td>%s</td></tr>\n",
            ap_escape_html(r->pool, key),
            ap_escape_html(r->pool, value));
    /* Zero would stop iterating; any other return value continues */
    return 1;
}
```

Second, we provide a function that uses the callback to print an entire table:

```
static void printtable(request_rec *r, apr_table_t *t,
                const char *caption, const char *keyhead,
                const char *valhead)
{
    /* Print a table header */
    ap_rprintf(r, "<table><caption>%s</caption><thead>"
            "<tr><th scope=\"col\">%s</th><th scope=\"col\">%s"
            "</th></tr></thead><tbody>", caption, keyhead, valhead);

    /* Print the data: apr_table_do iterates over entries with
     * our callback
     */
    apr_table_do(printitem, r, t, NULL);

    /* Finish the table */
    ap_rputs("</tbody></table>\n", r);
}
```

Now we can wrap this functionality in our HelloWorld handler:

```
static int helloworld_handler(request_rec *r)
{
    if (!r->handler || (strcmp(r->handler, "helloworld") != 0)) {
        return DECLINED ;
    }
    if (r->method_number != M_GET) {
        return HTTP_METHOD_NOT_ALLOWED;
    }
```

```
    ap_set_content_type(r, "text/html;charset=ascii");
    ap_rputs("<!DOCTYPE HTML PUBLIC \"-//W3C//DTD HTML 4.01//EN\">\n"
             "<html><head><title>Apache HelloWorld Module</title></head>"
             "<body><h1>Hello World!</h1>"
             "<p>This is the Apache HelloWorld module!</p>", r);

    /* Print the tables */
    printtable(r, r->headers_in, "Request Headers", "Header", "Value");
    printtable(r, r->headers_out, "Response Headers", "Header", "Value");
    printtable(r, r->subprocess_env, "Environment", "Variable", "Value");

    ap_rputs("</body></html>", r);
    return OK;
}
```

5.2.1 Module I/O

Our `HelloWorld` module generates output using a `stdio`-like family of functions: `ap_rputc`, `ap_rputs`, `ap_rwrite`, `ap_rvputs`, `ap_vrprintf`, `ap_rprintf`, and `ap_rflush`. We have also seen the "send file" call `ap_send_file`. This simple, high-level API was inherited originally from earlier Apache versions, and it remains suitable for many content generators. It is defined in `http_protocol.h`.

Since the introduction of the filter chain, the underlying mechanism for generating output has been based on buckets and brigades, as discussed in Chapters 3 and 8. Filter modules employ different mechanisms for generating output, and these are also available to—and sometimes appropriate for—a content handler.

There are two fundamentally different ways to process or generate output in a filter:

- Direct manipulation of bucket and brigades
- Use of another `stdio`-like API (which is a better option than the `ap_r*` API, as backward compatibility isn't an issue)

We will describe these mechanisms in detail in Chapter 8. For now, we will look at the basic mechanics of using the filter-oriented I/O in a content generator.

There are three steps to using filter I/O for output:

1. Create a bucket brigade.

2. Populate the brigade with the data we are writing.

3. Pass the brigade to the first output filter on the stack (`r->output_filters`).

These steps can be repeated as many times as needed, either by creating a new brigade or by reusing a single brigade. If a response is large and/or slow to generate, we may want to pass it down the filter chain in smaller chunks. The response can then be passed through the filters and to the client in chunks, giving us an efficient pipeline and avoiding the overhead of buffering the entire response. Working properly with the pipeline whenever possible is an extremely useful goal for filter modules.

For our `HelloWorld` module, all we need to do is to create the brigade and then replace the `ap_r*` family calls with the alternative `stdio`-like API defined in `util_filter.h`: ap_fflush, ap_fwrite, ap_fputs, ap_fputc, ap_fputstrs, and ap_fprintf. These calls have a slightly different prototype: Instead of passing `request_rec` as a file descriptor, we have to pass both the destination filter we are writing to and the bucket brigade. We'll see examples of this scheme in Chapter 8.

5.2.1.1 Output

Here is our first trivial `HelloWorld` handler using filter-oriented output. This lower-level API is a little more complex than the simple `stdio`-like buffered I/O, and it may sometimes enable optimizations of the module (though in this instance, any difference will be negligible). We can also take advantage of slightly finer control by explicitly processing output errors.

```
static int helloworld_handler(request_rec *r)
{
    static const char *const helloworld =
        "<!DOCTYPE HTML PUBLIC \"-//W3C//DTD HTML 4.01//EN\">\n"
        "<html><head><title>Apache HelloWorld Module</title></head>"
        "<body><h1>Hello World!</h1>"
        "<p>This is the Apache HelloWorld module!</p>"
        "</body></html>";
    apr_status_t rv;
    apr_bucket_brigade *bb;
    apr_bucket *b;
    if (!r->handler || strcmp(r->handler, "helloworld")) {
        return DECLINED;
    }
    if (r->method_number != M_GET) {
        return HTTP_METHOD_NOT_ALLOWED;
    }
    bb = apr_brigade_create(r->pool, r->connection->bucket_alloc);
    ap_set_content_type(r, "text/html;charset=ascii");
    /* We could instead use the stdio-like filter API calls like
     * ap_fputs(r->filters_out, bb, helloworld);
     * which is basically the same as using ap_rputs and family.
     *
```

```
 * Alternatively, we can wrap our output in a bucket, append an
 * EOS, and pass it down the filter chain.
 */
b = apr_bucket_immortal_create(helloworld, strlen(helloworld),
                    bb->bucket_alloc);
APR_BRIGADE_INSERT_TAIL(bb, b);
APR_BRIGADE_INSERT_TAIL(bb,
                apr_bucket_eos_create(bb->bucket_alloc));
rv = ap_pass_brigade(r->filters_out, bb);
if (rv != APR_SUCCESS) {
    ap_log_rerror(APLOG_MARK, APLOG_ERR, rv, r, "Output Error");
    return HTTP_INTERNAL_SERVER_ERROR;
}
return OK;
}
```

5.2.1.2 Input

Module input is slightly different. Once again, we have at our disposal a legacy method inherited from Apache 1.x, but it is now treated as deprecated by most developers (although the method is still supported). In most cases, we would prefer to use the input filter chain directly in new code:

1. Create a bucket brigade.

2. Pull data into the brigade from the first input filter (`r->input_filters`).

3. Read the data in our buckets, and use it.

Both input methods are commonly found in existing modules, including modules for Apache 2.x. Let's introduce each in turn into our `HelloWorld` module. We'll update the module to support POSTs and count the number of bytes POSTed (note that this operation will usually—but not always—be available in a Content-Length request header). We won't decode or display the actual data; although we could do so, this task is usually best handled by an input filter (or by a library such as `libapreq`). The functions we use here are documented in `http_protocol.h`:

```
#define BUFLEN 8192
static int check_postdata_old_method(request_rec *r)
{
    char buf[BUFLEN];
    size_t bytes, count = 0;

    /* Decide how to treat input */
    if (ap_setup_client_block(r, REQUEST_CHUNKED_DECHUNK) != OK) {
```

```
        ap_log_rerror(APLOG_MARK, APLOG_ERR, 0, r, "Bad request body!");
        ap_rputs("<p>Bad request body.</p>\n", r);
        return HTTP_BAD_REQUEST;
    }
    if (ap_should_client_block(r)) {
        for (bytes = ap_get_client_block(r, buf, BUFLEN); bytes > 0;
            bytes = ap_get_client_block(r, buf, BUFLEN)) {
            count += bytes;
        }
        ap_rprintf(r, "<p>Got %d bytes of request body data.</p>\n",
                count);
    } else {
        ap_rputs("<p>No request body.</p>\n", r);
    }
    return OK;
}

static int helloworld_handler(request_rec *r)
{
    if (!r->handler || strcmp(r->handler, "helloworld")) {
        return DECLINED;
    }

    /* We could be just slightly sloppy and drop this altogether,
     * but it's good practice to reject anything that's not explicitly
     * allowed. It cuts off *potential* exploits for someone trying
     * to compromise the server.
     */
    if ((r->method_number != M_GET) && (r->method_number != M_POST)) {
        return HTTP_METHOD_NOT_ALLOWED;
    }
    ap_set_content_type(r, "text/html;charset=ascii");
    ap_rputs("<!DOCTYPE HTML PUBLIC \"-//W3C//DTD HTML 4.01//EN\">\n"
"<html><head><title>Apache HelloWorld Module</title></head>"
        "<body><h1>Hello World!</h1>"
      "<p>This is the Apache HelloWorld module!</p>", r);

    /* Print the tables */
    printtable(r, r->headers_in, "Request Headers", "Header", "Value");
    printtable(r, r->headers_out, "Response Headers", "Header", "Value");
    printtable(r, r->subprocess_env, "Environment", "Variable", "Value");

    /* Ignore the return value -- it's too late to bail out now
     * even if there's an error
     */
    check_postdata_old_method(r);

    ap_rputs("</body></html>", r);
    return OK ;
}
```

Here, finally, is `check_postdata` using the preferred method of direct access to the input filters, using functions documented in `util_filter.h`.

We create a brigade and then loop until EOS, filling the brigade from the input filters. We will see this technique again in Chapter 8.

```
static int check_postdata_new_method(request_rec *r)
{
    apr_status_t status;
    int end = 0;
    apr_size_t bytes, count = 0;
    const char *buf;
    apr_bucket *b;
    apr_bucket_brigade *bb;

    /* Check whether there's any input to read.  A client can tell
     * us that fact by using Content-Length or Transfer-Encoding.
     */
    int has_input = 0;
    const char *hdr = apr_table_get(r->headers_in, "Content-Length");
    if (hdr) {
        has_input = 1;
    }
    hdr = apr_table_get(r->headers_in, "Transfer-Encoding");
    if (hdr) {
        if (strcasecmp(hdr, "chunked") == 0) {
            has_input = 1;
        }
        else {
            ap_rprintf(r, "<p>Unsupported Transfer Encoding: %s</p>",
                ap_escape_html(r->pool, hdr));
            return OK; /* we allow this, but just refuse to handle it */
        }
    }
    if (!has_input) {
        ap_rputs("<p>No request body.</p>\n", r);
        return OK;
    }

    /* OK, we have some input data. Now read and count it. */
    /* Create a brigade to put the data into. */
    bb = apr_brigade_create(r->pool, r->connection->bucket_alloc);
    /* Loop until we get an EOS on the input */
    do {
        /* Read a chunk of input into bb */
        status = ap_get_brigade(r->input_filters, bb, AP_MODE_READBYTES,
                    APR_BLOCK_READ, BUFLEN);
        if ( status == APR_SUCCESS ) {
```

```
            /* Loop over the contents of bb */
            for (b = APR_BRIGADE_FIRST(bb);
                b != APR_BRIGADE_SENTINEL(bb);
                 b = APR_BUCKET_NEXT(b) ) {
                /* Check for EOS */
              if (APR_BUCKET_IS_EOS(b)) {
                      end = 1;
                      break;
              }
                /* Ignore other metadata */
            else if (APR_BUCKET_IS_METADATA(b)) {
              continue;
                }
            /* To get the actual length, we need to read the data */
              bytes = BUFLEN;
              status = apr_bucket_read(b, &buf, &bytes,
                          APR_BLOCK_READ);
              count += bytes;
            }
        }
        /* Discard data we're finished with */
        apr_brigade_cleanup(bb);
    } while (!end && (status == APR_SUCCESS));

    if (status == APR_SUCCESS) {
        ap_rprintf(r, "<p>Got %d bytes of request body data.</p>\n",
            count);
        return OK;
    }
    else {
        ap_rputs("<p>Error reading request body.</p>", r);
        return OK; /* Just send the above message and ignore the data */
    }
}
```

5.2.1.3 I/O Errors

What happens when we get an I/O error?

Filters (covered in Chapter 8) indicate an error to us by returning an APR error code; they may also set r->status. Our handler can detect such an event, as in the preceding examples, by checking the return values from ap_pass_brigade and ap_get_brigade. Normal behavior is to stop processing and return an appropriate HTTP error code. This behavior causes Apache to send an error document (discussed in Chapter 6) to the client. We should also log an error message, thereby helping the systems administrator diagnose the problem.

But what if the error was that the client connection was terminated? It's a waste of time trying to send an error document to a client that's gone away. We can detect this disconnection by checking r->connection->aborted, as demonstrated in the default handler found at the end of this chapter.

5.2.2 Reading Form Data

We now have the basis for reading input data. But the data are useful only if we know what to do with them. The most common form of data we need to handle on the Web is data sent to us by a web browser submitting an HTML form. Such data follow one of two standard formats supported by general-purpose browsers and controlled by the enctype attribute to the <form> element in HTML:

- application/x-www-form-urlencoded (normal web forms submitted either by POST or GET)

- multipart/form-data (Netscape's multipart format for file upload forms)

Historically, decoding form data in either of these formats is the responsibility of applications. For example, any CGI library or scripting module contains code for handling this task. Apache itself doesn't include this capability as standard, but it is provided by third-party modules such as mod_form and mod_upload.

Parsing Form Data

The format for standard form data (application/x-www-form-urlencoded) is a series of key/value pairs, separated by ampersands ("&"). Any character may be escaped using a %*nn* sequence, where *nn* is the hex representation of a byte, and some characters must be escaped. Parsing the data is complicated by the fact that keys are not always unique; for example, an HTML <select multiple> element may submit several values for a key.

The natural structure representing these data is a *table* of *bag*s. This structure can be represented in Apache as an apr_hash_t* (hash table) of apr_array_header_t* (array) values. We can parse input data into this representation as follows:

```
/* Parse form data from a string. The input string is NOT preserved. */
static apr_hash_t *parse_form_from_string(request_rec *r, char *args)
{
    apr_hash_t *form;
    apr_array_header_t *values;
```

```
char *pair;
char *eq;
const char *delim = "&";
char *last;
char **ptr;

if (args == NULL) {
    return NULL;
}

form = apr_hash_make(r->pool);

/* Split the input on '&' */
for (pair = apr_strtok(args, delim, &last); pair != NULL;
    pair = apr_strtok(NULL, delim, &last)) {
    for (eq = pair; *eq; ++eq) {
        if (*eq == '+') {
            *eq = ' ';
        }
    }
    /* split into Key / Value and unescape it */
    eq = strchr(pair, '=');

    if (eq) {
        *eq++ = '\0';
    ap_unescape_url(pair);
    ap_unescape_url(eq);
    }
    else {
        eq = "";
    ap_unescape_url(pair);
    }

  /* Store key/value pair in our form hash. Given that there
     * may be many values for the same key, we store values
     * in an array (which we'll have to create the first
     * time we encounter the key in question).
     */
    values = apr_hash_get(form, pair, APR_HASH_KEY_STRING);
    if (values == NULL) {
        values = apr_array_make(r->pool, 1, sizeof(const char*));
        apr_hash_set(form, pair, APR_HASH_KEY_STRING, values);
    }
    ptr = apr_array_push(values);
    *ptr = apr_pstrdup(r->pool, eq);
}
return form;
}
```

This scheme is based on parsing the entire input data from a single input buffer. It works well where the total size of a form submission is reasonably small, as is generally the case with normal web forms. We should guard against denial of service (DoS) attacks by limiting the size of inputs accepted this way (the maximum size of data to accept being specified by a server administrator). Alternative methods involving streamed parsing may be appropriate for larger forms, particularly those involving file upload that could involve megabytes or even gigabytes of data. The mod_upload[3] module provides a parser that is better suited to large uploads.

We can use the function we just defined to parse data submitted by GET:

```
static apr_hash_t* parse_form_from_GET(request_rec *r)
{
    return parse_form_from_string(r, r->args);
}
```

Parsing data submitted by POST is more work, because we have to read the data:

```
/* Get POSTed data. Assume we have already checked that the
 * content type is application/x-www-form-urlencoded.
 * Assume *form is null on entry.
 */
static int parse_form_from_POST(request_rec *r, apr_hash_t **form)
{
    int bytes, eos;
    apr_size_t count;
    apr_status_t rv;
    apr_bucket_brigade *bb;
    apr_bucket_brigade *bbin;
    char *buf;
    apr_bucket *b;
    const char *clen = apr_table_get(r->headers_in, "Content-Length");
    if (clen != NULL) {
        bytes = strtol(clen, NULL, 0);
        if (bytes >= MAX_SIZE) {
            ap_log_rerror(APLOG_MARK, APLOG_ERR, 0, r,
                    "Request too big (%d bytes; limit %d)",
                    bytes, MAX_SIZE);
            return HTTP_REQUEST_ENTITY_TOO_LARGE;
        }
    }
    else {
        bytes = MAX_SIZE;
    }
```

---

3. http://apache.webthing.com/mod_upload/

```
bb = apr_brigade_create(r->pool, r->connection->bucket_alloc);
bbin = apr_brigade_create(r->pool, r->connection->bucket_alloc);
count = 0;

do {
    rv = ap_get_brigade(r->input_filters, bbin, AP_MODE_READBYTES,
                        APR_BLOCK_READ, bytes);
    if (rv != APR_SUCCESS) {
        ap_log_rerror(APLOG_MARK, APLOG_ERR, rv, r,
                      "failed to read form input");
        return HTTP_INTERNAL_SERVER_ERROR;
    }
    for (b = APR_BRIGADE_FIRST(bbin);
         b != APR_BRIGADE_SENTINEL(bbin);
         b = APR_BUCKET_NEXT(b) ) {
        if (APR_BUCKET_IS_EOS(b)) {
            eos = 1;
        }
        if (!APR_BUCKET_IS_METADATA(b)) {
            if (b->length != (apr_size_t)(-1)) {
                count += b->length;
                if (count > MAX_SIZE) {
                    /* This is more data than we accept, so we're
                     * going to kill the request. But we have to
                     * mop it up first.
                     */
                        apr_bucket_delete(b);
                }
            }
        }
        if (count <= MAX_SIZE) {
            APR_BUCKET_REMOVE(b);
            APR_BRIGADE_INSERT_TAIL(bb, b);
        }
    }
} while (!eos);

/* OK, done with the data. Kill the request if we got too much data. */
if (count > MAX_SIZE) {
    ap_log_rerror(APLOG_MARK, APLOG_ERR, rv, r,
            "Request too big (%d bytes; limit %s)",
            bytes, MAX_SIZE);
    return HTTP_REQUEST_ENTITY_TOO_LARGE;
}

/* We've got all the data. Now put it in a buffer and parse it. */
buf = apr_palloc(r->pool, count+1);
rv = apr_brigade_flatten(bb, buf, &count);
if (rv != APR_SUCCESS) {
    ap_log_rerror(APLOG_MARK, APLOG_ERR, rv, r,
            "Error (flatten) reading form data");
      return HTTP_INTERNAL_SERVER_ERROR;
}
```

```
    buf[count] = '\0';
    *form = parse_form_from_string(r, buf);

    return OK;
}
```

At this point, we have laid the groundwork to ensure easy access to form data, and we can provide some accessor functions. mod_form performs a similar function, but uses techniques we haven't encountered yet to offer a cleaner API wherein the handler module need not concern itself with the hash.

The following example shows a function that returns all values for a key as a comma-separated string, a representation that will be familiar to users of scripting environments such as Perl (with CGI.pm) or PHP. Other high-level accessors are now similarly straightforward to write.

```
char *form_value(apr_pool_t *pool, apr_hash_t *form, const char *key)
{
    apr_array_header_t *v_arr = apr_hash_get(form, key,
                             APR_HASH_KEY_STRING);
    /* Caveat: this is ambiguous because values may contain commas */
    return apr_array_pstrcat(pool, v_arr, ',');
}
```

Combining these functions, we can update our HelloWorld handler to display form data. We'll assume that the form data consist of ASCII input, and substitute question marks for any non-ASCII characters:

```
static int helloworld_handler(request_rec *r)
{
    apr_hash_t *formdata = NULL;
    int rv = OK;

    if (!r->handler || (strcmp(r->handler, "helloworld") != 0)) {
        return DECLINED;
    }

    /* We could be just slightly sloppy and drop this altogether,
     * but it's good practice to reject anything that's not explicitly
     * allowed. It cuts off *potential* exploits for someone trying
     * to compromise the server.
     */
    if ((r->method_number != M_GET) && (r->method_number != M_POST)) {
        return HTTP_METHOD_NOT_ALLOWED;
    }
```

```
ap_set_content_type(r, "text/html;charset=ascii");
ap_rputs("<!DOCTYPE HTML PUBLIC \"-//W3C//DTD HTML 4.01//EN\">\n"
        "<html><head><title>Apache HelloWorld Module</title></head>"
        "<body><h1>Hello World!</h1>"
        "<p>This is the Apache HelloWorld module!</p>", r);

/* Print the tables */
printtable(r, r->headers_in, "Request Headers", "Header", "Value");
printtable(r, r->headers_out, "Response Headers", "Header", "Value");
printtable(r, r->subprocess_env, "Environment", "Variable", "Value");

/* Display the form data */
if (r->method_number == M_GET) {
   formdata = parse_form_from_GET(r);
}
else if (r->method_number == M_POST) {
   const char* ctype = apr_table_get(r->headers_in, "Content-Type");
   if (ctype && (strcasecmp(ctype,
                          "application/x-www-form-urlencoded")
                == 0)) {
      rv = parse_form_from_POST(r, &formdata);
   }
}

if (rv != OK) {
   ap_rputs("<p>Error reading form data!</p>", r);
}
else if (formdata == NULL) {
   ap_rputs("<p>No form data found.</p>", r);
}
else {
   /* Parsed the form successfully, so we have data to display */
   apr_array_header_t *arr;
   char *key;
   apr_ssize_t klen;
   apr_hash_index_t *index;
   char *val;
   char *p;

   ap_rprintf(r, "<h2>Form data supplied by method %s</h2>\n<dl>",
         r->method) ;
   for (index = apr_hash_first(r->pool, formdata); index != NULL;
       index = apr_hash_next(index)) {
     apr_hash_this(index, (void**)&key, &klen, (void**)&arr);
     ap_rprintf(r, "<dt>%s</dt>\n",ap_escape_html(r->pool, key));
     for (val = apr_array_pop(arr); val != NULL;
      val = apr_array_pop(arr)) {
        for (p = val; *p != '\0'; ++p) {
           if (!isascii(*p)) {
            *p = '?';
           }
```

```
        }
        ap_rprintf(r, "<dd>%s</dd>\n",
            ap_escape_html(r->pool, val));
      }
    }
    ap_rputs("</dl>", r) ;
  }
  ap_rputs("</body></html>", r) ;
  return OK ;
}
```

5.3 The Default Handler

So far, we've presented simple variants on a simple handler, and highlighted the tools required to develop a content handler equivalent to a normal CGI or PHP script. To conclude this chapter, we'll present Apache's default handler. Although it serves a file from the server's filesystem, this handler differs from our earlier functions in that it does quite a lot more housekeeping, illustrating more of the core API. Apache's default handler is more advanced than the handlers shown in the previous examples, and you may prefer to skip it on a first reading.

```
static int default_handler(request_rec *r)
{
    conn_rec *c = r->connection;
    apr_bucket_brigade *bb;
    apr_bucket *e;
    core_dir_config *d;
    int errstatus;
    apr_file_t *fd = NULL;
    apr_status_t status;

    int bld_content_md5;
```

`ap_get_module_config` retrieves the module's configuration (Chapter 9):

```
    d = (core_dir_config *)ap_get_module_config(r->per_dir_config,
                                      &core_module);
```

We can compute an MD5 hash if our system is configured to do so, but only if there isn't a filter that will transform the contents and invalidate our hash.

```
    bld_content_md5 = (d->content_md5 & 1)
            && r->output_filters->frec->ftype != AP_FTYPE_RESOURCE;
```

Because this is the handler of last resort, we can't just return DECLINED if we don't want the request.

```
ap_allow_standard_methods(r, MERGE_ALLOW,
    M_GET, M_OPTIONS, M_POST, -1);
```

This next check performs housekeeping tasks. It's not really necessary, because Apache will perform these tasks for us if unused input remains when it destroys the request.

```
/* If filters intend to consume the request body, they must
 * register an InputFilter to slurp the contents of the POST
 * data from the POST input stream.  It no longer exists when
 * the output filters are invoked by the default handler.
 */
if ((errstatus = ap_discard_request_body(r)) != OK) {
    return errstatus;
}

if (r->method_number == M_GET || r->method_number == M_POST) {
    if (r->finfo.filetype == 0) {
        ap_log_rerror(APLOG_MARK, APLOG_ERR, 0, r,
                    "File does not exist: %s", r->filename);
        return HTTP_NOT_FOUND;
    }
}
```

This handler serves only normal files; Apache handles directories differently. If a request for a directory reaches this handler, it's a configuration error.

```
/* Don't try to serve a directory. Some OSs do weird things
 * with raw I/O on a directory.
 */
if (r->finfo.filetype == APR_DIR) {
    ap_log_rerror(APLOG_MARK, APLOG_ERR, 0, r,
                "Attempt to serve directory: %s", r->filename);
    return HTTP_NOT_FOUND;
}
```

Deal with any extra junk on the end of the request URI.

```
if ((r->used_path_info != AP_REQ_ACCEPT_PATH_INFO) &&
    r->path_info && *r->path_info)
{
    /* default to reject */
    ap_log_rerror(APLOG_MARK, APLOG_ERR, 0, r,
                "File does not exist: %s",
                apr_pstrcat(r->pool, r->filename,
                    r->path_info, NULL));
    return HTTP_NOT_FOUND;
}
```

```
        /* We understood the (non-GET) method, but it might not be
           legal for this particular resource. Check whether the
           'deliver_script' flag is set. If so, then go ahead
           and deliver the file because
           it isn't really content (only GET normally returns content).

           Note: The only possible non-GET method
           at this point is POST. In the future, we should enable
           script delivery for all methods.  */
        if (r->method_number != M_GET) {
            core_request_config *req_cfg;

            req_cfg = ap_get_module_config(r->request_config,
                            &core_module);
            if (!req_cfg->deliver_script) {
                /* The flag hasn't been set for this request. Punt. */
                ap_log_rerror(APLOG_MARK, APLOG_ERR, 0, r,
                        "This resource does not accept the %s method.",
                            r->method);
                return HTTP_METHOD_NOT_ALLOWED;
            }
        }


        if ((status = apr_file_open(&fd, r->filename,APR_READ|APR_BINARY
#if APR_HAS_SENDFILE
                          | ((d->enable_sendfile == ENABLE_SENDFILE_OFF)
                                    ? 0 : APR_SENDFILE_ENABLED)
#endif
                                , 0, r->pool)) != APR_SUCCESS) {
            ap_log_rerror(APLOG_MARK, APLOG_ERR, status, r,
                "file permissions deny server access: %s", r->filename);
            return HTTP_FORBIDDEN;
        }
```

Now we set a few more standard headers:

```
        ap_update_mtime(r, r->finfo.mtime);
        ap_set_last_modified(r);
        ap_set_etag(r);
        apr_table_setn(r->headers_out, "Accept-Ranges", "bytes");
        ap_set_content_length(r, r->finfo.size);

        bb = apr_brigade_create(r->pool, c->bucket_alloc);
```

ap_meets_conditions carries out some useful checks, cross-referencing the file information to the request headers to determine whether we really need to send the file or just to confirm the validity of a client's cached copy. In exceptional circumstances, it may determine that our file is useless to the client and should be discarded.

```
        if ((errstatus = ap_meets_conditions(r)) != OK) {
            apr_file_close(fd);
            r->status = errstatus;
        }
        else {
            if (bld_content_md5) {
                apr_table_setn(r->headers_out, "Content-MD5",
                               ap_md5digest(r->pool, fd));
            }

            /* For platforms where the size of the file may be larger
             * than can be stored in a single bucket (where the
             * length field is an apr_size_t), split it into several
             * buckets */
            if (sizeof(apr_off_t) > sizeof(apr_size_t)
                && r->finfo.size > AP_MAX_SENDFILE) {
                apr_off_t fsize = r->finfo.size;
                e = apr_bucket_file_create(fd, 0, AP_MAX_SENDFILE,
                            r->pool, c->bucket_alloc);
                while (fsize > AP_MAX_SENDFILE) {
                    apr_bucket *ce;
                    apr_bucket_copy(e, &ce);
                    APR_BRIGADE_INSERT_TAIL(bb, ce);
                    e->start += AP_MAX_SENDFILE;
                    fsize -= AP_MAX_SENDFILE;
                }
                e->length = (apr_size_t)fsize;
                        /* Resize just the last bucket */
            }
            else {
                e = apr_bucket_file_create(fd, 0,
                            (apr_size_t)r->finfo.size,
                                    r->pool, c->bucket_alloc);
            }

#if APR_HAS_MMAP
            if (d->enable_mmap == ENABLE_MMAP_OFF) {
                (void)apr_bucket_file_enable_mmap(e, 0);
            }
#endif
            APR_BRIGADE_INSERT_TAIL(bb, e);
        }

        e = apr_bucket_eos_create(c->bucket_alloc);
        APR_BRIGADE_INSERT_TAIL(bb, e);

        status = ap_pass_brigade(r->output_filters, bb);
        if (status == APR_SUCCESS
            || r->status != HTTP_OK
            || c->aborted) {
            return OK;
        }
```

```
        else {
            /* No way to know what type of error occurred */
            ap_log_rerror(APLOG_MARK, APLOG_DEBUG, status, r,
                        "default_handler: ap_pass_brigade returned %i",
                        status);
            return HTTP_INTERNAL_SERVER_ERROR;
        }
    }
    else {                  /* unusual method (not GET or POST) */
        if (r->method_number == M_INVALID) {
            ap_log_rerror(APLOG_MARK, APLOG_ERR, 0, r,
                        "Invalid method in request %s", r->the_request);
            return HTTP_NOT_IMPLEMENTED;
        }
```

Another API call supports the `OPTIONS` method:

```
        if (r->method_number == M_OPTIONS) {
            return ap_send_http_options(r);
        }
        return HTTP_METHOD_NOT_ALLOWED;
    }
}
```

5.4 Summary

This chapter dealt with content generators and related topics:

- It introduced the Apache module structure.

- It showed how a module can register a handler function with the core.

- It described the basic handler API.

- It described the role of content generator modules and developed a simple module.

- It showed how a content generator works with the `request_rec` object to obtain information such as headers and environment variables, to perform I/O, and to access form data.

- It demonstrated basic error handling.

- It described basic housekeeping commonly encountered in modules.

- It introduced Apache's default handler, demonstrating slightly more advanced techniques to serve static files efficiently and with proper attention to the HTTP protocol.

At this point, you should be able to write an application as a module or rewrite a CGI script as a module. While we have introduced the overall structural skeleton of a module, our coverage has been punctuated with several blanks. The remaining parts of the module structure are concerned with configuration; they will be discussed in Chapter 9. The meaning of hooks and their registration are covered in Chapter 10. Next, Chapters 6, 7, and 8 complete our discussion of request handling fundamentals by introducing the request processing cycle, access and authentication, and the filter chain.

Chapter 6

Request Processing Cycle and Metadata Handlers

Before returning contents to the client, Apache needs to examine the HTTP request with reference to the server configuration. Much of the Apache standard code is concerned with this task, and sometimes we may need to write a new module to support different behavior. Such modules work by hooking into the early parts of request processing, before any content generator is invoked, and sometimes by diverting or aborting the entire request.

In this chapter, we will first review the metadata sent to the server in an HTTP request. We will then see how the standard modules in Apache deal with this in handling a request. Finally, we will develop a new module.

Note that there is no universally agreed-upon nomenclature here. Modules directly relevant to this chapter are classified into various categories in the Apache distribution:

- Mappers (modules that map from a request URL to the internal structure of the server and/or the filesystem)

- Metadata (modules that explicitly manipulate HTTP headers and/or Apache's internal state)

- AAA (access, authentication, and authorization modules—the most popular class of metadata modules; discussed in detail in Chapter 7)

This chapter deals with general issues concerning the request processing cycle and metadata handling. Of course, many modules with a different primary purpose (e.g., handlers) may include metadata hooks alongside other functions.

A great deal of folklore has arisen concerning certain uses of metadata and request handling—for example, methods for presenting different types of content to different visitors. At worst, adhering to these myths can lead to broken reimplementations of standard features (reinventing the wheel, but the new one isn't round)! Professional developers as well as hobbyists may be guilty of this. This chapter warns you about some of the more common misconceptions.

6.1 HTTP

To discuss HTTP request processing, we first need to understand some basics about the Hypertext Transfer Protocol (HTTP).

6.1.1 The HTTP Protocol

HTTP is one member of a broad family of networking protocols for passing messages, whose roots go back to the early days of the Internet. The oldest of these protocols still in general use today is SMTP, the e-mail standard known as RFC822 that dates from 1983. The protocol of the Web is HTTP, which is specified in RFC1945 (HTTP 1.0) and RFC2616 (HTTP/1.1, the current protocol version—see Appendix C). These protocols share some common overall characteristics, designed for the exchange of messages.

Envelopes, Cover Notes, Letters, and Enclosures

Before the Internet, we had other means of communicating over a distance. For those communication strategies to work, we needed two things:

- The contents of the communication: the letter, telegram, fax, or telephone conversation.

- The addressing information: the envelope, phone number, or fax number and cover sheet. This information ensures that the contents can be correctly sent to the intended recipient.

When the Internet messaging protocols were designed, a similar approach was adopted. A modern Internet message comprises an envelope, cover note, and message contents. The contents may be a single letter, a letter with enclosures, or empty.

Metadata Versus Data

When applying the letter metaphor to the Internet, we speak of data and metadata (information about the data). That is, a letter is data, or the contents of a message; the envelope and cover sheet are metadata, or information about the message.

HTTP metadata can be quite extensive. We will encounter examples of it in this chapter, though we will not present a detailed or thorough overview of it here. The authoritative specification dealing with HTTP metadata is RFC2616, which is included in this book as Appendix C.

Request and Response

One important characteristic of the RFC822 family of Internet protocols, including all versions of HTTP, is that all messages are two-way. In other words, every transaction includes both a request sent from the client to the server, and a response sent from the server to the client. A complete message comprising metadata and (optionally) data passes each way.

6.1.2 Anatomy of an HTTP Request

The first thing Apache must do upon receiving a request is to check the cover sheet (metadata) and decide how to deal with the request. The server configuration, together with HTTP rules, will determine how it proceeds.

In HTTP, we must deal with two sets of request metadata:

1. The request line (envelope)

2. The request headers (cover sheet)

The request line is a single line that specifies the request method and the resource requested. The request headers provide supplementary metadata that may be of relevance to the server in generating a response or in carrying out secondary tasks such as logging and analyzing usage patterns.

Let's consider a hypothetical request:

```
GET /index.html HTTP/1.1
Accept: text/html,application/xhtml+xml;q=0.9
Accept-Encoding: gzip
Accept-Language: en
Authorization: Basic DWB/2xgwF9e9
Cookie: prefs=laid-back
Host: www.example.com
If-Modified-Since: Sun Apr 24 11:12:15 GMT 2005
User-Agent: The Universal Proxy (Mozilla 7.2; Compatible)
X-foo: bar;wibble
```

> NOTE The `Host:` header is available in both HTTP/1.0 and 1.1. The fact that it's (technically) optional in HTTP/1.0 is a red herring: Support has been almost universal in both HTTP/1.0 and 1.1 clients since 1995.

The first line indicates a `GET` request for `/index.html` on the server. Combined with the `Host` header, it identifies the requested resource as `http://www.example.com/index.html` (which is necessary if and only if the server is running more than one virtual host on the IP address and port that the request came on).

The remaining headers, all of which are optional, illustrate the kind of metadata Apache may wish to deal with. No single module is likely to be concerned with all of the request headers, but many modules are concerned with at least some of these tasks:

*   Mapping `/index.html` to the filesystem or to a custom handler from the server configuration for `www.example.com`.

*   Selecting a response acceptable to the browser based on the various `Accept-*` headers.

- Checking whether the user is permitted to access the resource requested (`Authorization` header).

- Checking whether, from the information supplied, the client already has an up-to-date copy in cache (`If-Modified-Since`). If so, we just confirm that with a "`304 Not Modified`" response and save the bandwidth of returning the entire response body.

- Identifying private application data passed between this server and this particular client (`Cookie` and `X-anything` headers).

- Logging data (`User-Agent`).

To deal effectively with all these issues, Apache implements several request processing phases before content generation. Modules can hook into any of these phases to adjust, or take full control of, different aspects of request processing, just as our `HelloWorld` module hooked a content generator in Chapter 5.

6.2 Request Processing in Apache

We have already introduced the request processing cycle. A module can hook into this cycle in the following ways:

- **`post_read_request`**—General-purpose hook that runs immediately on creating the `request_rec` object.

- **`translate_name`**—Map the request URL to the filesystem.

- **`map_to_storage`**—Apply per-directory configuration.

- **`header_parser`**—Check the HTTP request headers. Another general-purpose hook after the configuration is fully available but before more specific phases begin.

- **`access_checker`**—Check whether access is permitted to the remote host.

- **`check_user_id`**—Authenticate the remote user (where applicable).

- **`auth_checker`**—Check whether the remote user is authorized to perform the attempted operation.

- **`type_checker`**—Apply configuration rules that determine the handler and response headers.

- **`fixups`**—General-purpose hook at the end of request preparation but before the handler is called.

- **`insert_filter`**—Insert content filters.
- **`handler`**—Handle the request and generate a response.
- **`logger`**—Log the transaction.

These can also be grouped into phases:

- The `post_read_request` phase marks the transition from the protocol to the request processing. The `request_rec` object is valid, but many of its fields are not yet set.
- The phases from `translate_name` to `fixups` are collectively known as the *request preparation* phase.
- The `insert_filter` and `handler` hooks represent the *handler* (*content generator*) phase.
- The `logger` is the final phase, being called after the request has run.

The request preparation phase can be further subdivided:

- `translate_name` and `map_to_storage` resolve the request to the filesystem and/or logical URL space defined for the server. The per-directory configuration doesn't exist at this point.
- `header_parser` is the first hook where the per-directory configuration is available and enables early processing that relies on it.
- `access_checker`, `check_user_id`, and `auth_checker` are the *security* phase; they determine whether the user is permitted to carry out the attempted operation.
- `type_checker` and `fixups` are the last part of the request and occur before the content generator is run.

Let's consider in more detail how the standard modules in Apache deal with our request.

6.2.1 Mapping to the Filesystem

The first task we identified was to map `/index.html` to the filesystem. By default, the Apache core will handle this task by appending the request in the path to the `DocumentRoot` (a configuration setting) at the end of the

translate_name phase. Thus, if /var/www/example.com/htdocs is our
DocumentRoot for www.example.com, then the default is to map that location
to a file /var/www/example.com/htdocs/index.html. A second default handler, at the end of map_to_storage, cross-references the file to <Directory>
and <Files> configuration and, if .htaccess files are enabled, merges them
into the configuration.

> WARNING Don't confuse URLs with filesystem paths. Although
> they may correspond (and do, by default, in Apache), this is
> never more than a matter of convention.
>
> Use <Directory> and <Files> with your filesystem paths to
> configure them for local contents. Use <Location> with URLs
> for virtual or nonlocal contents.

A standard module that can change the default behavior is mod_alias. The Alias
configuration directive is used to specify a different mapping to the filesystem for
selected request paths. Alias uses a translate_name hook that replaces the default
action of appending the request URL path to the document root. Subsequent processing, including the default map_to_storage handler, remains unchanged.

Here's the translate_name hook from mod_alias:

```
static int translate_alias_redir(request_rec *r)
{
    ap_conf_vector_t *sconf = r->server->module_config;
    alias_server_conf *serverconf = ap_get_module_config(sconf,
                                    &alias_module);
    char *ret;
    int status;

    if (r->uri[0] != '/' && r->uri[0] != '\0') {
        return DECLINED;
    }

    if ((ret = try_alias_list(r, serverconf->redirects, 1, &status))
                              != NULL) {
        if (ap_is_HTTP_REDIRECT(status)) {
            /* Include QUERY_STRING if any */
            if (r->args) {
                ret = apr_pstrcat(r->pool, ret, "?", r->args, NULL);
            }
            apr_table_setn(r->headers_out, "Location", ret);
        }
        return status;
    }
```

```
    if ((ret = try_alias_list(r, serverconf->aliases, 0, &status))
                                != NULL) {
        r->filename = ret;
        return OK;
    }

    return DECLINED;
}
```

This code calls the function `try_alias_list` twice: first to apply the `Redirect` directive and then to apply the `Alias` directive. If a directive matches, `try_alias_list` will return the redirected URL or pathname. An `Alias` directive will then simply set `r->filename`, whereas a `Redirect` directive will divert request processing into a separate processing path, using the error document mechanism described in Section 6.3.1.

6.2.2 Content Negotiation

Our second task was to select a response that will be acceptable to the browser, according to the `Accept-*` headers sent.

```
Accept: text/html,
    application/xhtml+xml
Accept-Encoding: gzip
Accept-Language: en
```

These conditions may be ignored, and will be if we use default processing without multiviews. This task may also be handled in other ways. For example, for dynamic contents, `gzip` encoding is determined by an output filter (`mod_deflate`), rather than by a metadata handler. Likewise, an XSLT output filter could deal with selection of content types. But a regular case we should consider (not least because it's a wheel that's been reinvented badly by many organizations that should know better) is standard content negotiation, in which Apache selects an appropriate static file from several available options.

> NOTE Take the time to read about content negotiation in the HTTP specification (Appendix C) and look at Apache's `mod_negotiation` module. This extra effort could save you and your clients or employers the embarrassment of a broken reinvention—some bad blunders are distressingly widespread!

Examples

Wrong: Sniff a user's hostname or IP address, look up a country based on that information, and serve the language you think someone in that country would like.

Right: Serve the language selected by the user in the browser preferences and supplied to the server in `Accept-Language`.

Wrong: Serve different contents to users by inferring client capabilities from a `User-Agent` string.

Right: Infer what a browser is capable of rendering from an `Accept:` header. But take care: Some browsers may lie. MS Internet Explorer (MSIE) is the main culprit. For example, it claims to accept all compressed contents and works fine with compressed HTML, yet chokes on other formats when they are compressed.

The module of interest here is `mod_negotiation`, which is typically used for the following purposes:

- For multilingual sites, to select a language specified in the user's browser preferences

- For sites supporting different devices (e.g., desktop PCs versus WAP devices), to select between HTML and XML variants, or between SVG and bitmap images.

The simplest use of `mod_negotiation` is just to create a choice of resources. For example, if we supply the files

`index.html.en` (English)

`index.html.fr` (French)

`index.html.de` (German)

`index.html.it` (Italian)

together with appropriate `AddLanguage` directives and `MultiViews`, then `mod_negotiation` will select one of the preceding files according to the `Accept-Language` header sent by the browser (and configured by the user in a preferences menu, or as supplied to the user localized by an ISP or other network administrator). `mod_negotiation` uses a `type_checker` handler to map `index.html` to one of the available variants. When a variant is chosen, it overwrites the request state with one that is identical except in that a new file has been selected.

Don't forget to set the `Vary` response header when your module serves negotiated contents, so that caches know there may be other variants better suited to another client requesting the same URL!

6.2.3 Security

The third task was to check that the user is authorized to access the resource. The access, authentication, and authorization phases of request processing check the client's credentials (if any) supplied in the request headers, together with the client's IP address, against any policies for the requested resource defined in `httpd.conf` or an applicable `.htaccess` file. This phase, which is a traditional favorite with module developers, will be discussed in detail in Chapter 7.

6.2.4 Caching

The fourth task was to check when the resource was last modified, so we don't have to resend the data if they are older than the version the client has cached, as indicated in the `If-Modified-Since` header. This is one of several HTTP headers concerned with caching and efficiency. By default, caching is dealt with only in the handler/content generator phase. Nevertheless, a module that is not concerned with the possible effects of another module's `fixups` operation could check this earlier.

6.2.5 Private Metadata

The fifth task was to deal with application-specific data, including cookies and any private HTTP extensions (`X-anything` headers). This task is entirely application-specific and cannot be generalized. Applications should always be sure to implement fallback behavior for clients that don't supply a cookie or a private header. A major blunder sometimes seen on websites is to redirect any client without a cookie to a page that sets one and then send the client into an infinite loop.

6.2.6 Logging

The final task is to log the request. Logging a request is the *only* appropriate use for a `User-Agent` string. One of the most common errors on the Web today is to attempt to infer client characteristics or capabilities from a `User-Agent` string. This behavior is wrong for many reasons. First, many browsers spoof their `User-Agent` strings to avoid being excluded from MSIE-only sites (ironically, MSIE still uses the `Mozilla` keyword, which is itself a spoof introduced originally to keep MSIE users from being excluded from Netscape-enhanced sites in the mid-1990s). Second, it fails to account for caching, including the likelihood that a single cache may serve many different user agents. Third, and most importantly, it is at best a poor reinvention of HTTP content negotiation, based on the preferences and capabilities stated in the `Accept-*` headers.

6.3 Diverting a Request: The Internal Redirect

The request processing cycle may be diverted at any point using a mechanism known as an internal redirect. An internal redirect replaces the current request with a new request for the new (redirected) resource.

The internal redirect mechanism emulates HTTP redirection (such as an HTTP 302 response), but without requiring an additional request from the browser. This behavior mirrors the distinction made through the dual nature of the CGI `Location` header:

```
Location: http://www.example.com/foo/
```

This causes Apache to send an HTTP redirection to the browser, including the HTTP `Location` header.

By contrast, a relative URL—which is illegal in HTTP—is allowed in CGI:

```
Location: /foo/
```

This generates an internal redirect, without involving the browser.

A module can divert request processing using one of the two internal redirection functions defined in `http_request.h`:

void ap_internal_redirect(const char *new_uri, request_rec *r)
This is the canonical internal redirection function, and the mechanism to use if you have no strong reason to make another choice. This function creates a new request object for the new URL, and then runs the new request as if `new_uri` had been requested in the first place.

```
void ap_internal_fast_redirect(request_rec *new_req, request_rec *r)
```

This function clones an existing request structure `new_req` into the running request `r`, so it can be used to set up a new request and simulate passing control to it. This mechanism is sometimes used to promote a subrequest (as discussed later in this chapter) to a main request.

Internal redirection can occur anywhere in the request processing cycle, provided that no data have been returned to the client as yet. The most common form of internal redirection is the error document, as described in Section 6.3.1.

Note that Apache's normal processing, including—where appropriate—functions implemented by your modules, will run within an internal redirect. Bear in mind that the configuration applied is that of the redirected URL, not the original URL. Your handlers can determine whether they are running in an internal redirect by examining the `r->prev` field. Normally, its value will be NULL; in an internal redirect, however, it contains the original `request_rec` from before the redirection. An internal redirection will also have an environment variable REDIRECT_STATUS set to the status code of the original request at the time of redirection.

```
static int my_func(request_rec* r) {
  ...
  /* Are we in an internal redirect? */
  request_rec *original = r->prev ;
  if (original != NULL) {
    /* We're in an internal redirect from "original" */
  }
  else {
    /* It's a normal request */
  }
  ...
}
```

6.3.1 Error Documents

In Chapter 5, we mentioned that if our handler returned an HTTP status code (or, indeed, any value other than OK or DECLINED), this would divert the entire request processing into an error path. Any function implementing an earlier hook in the request cycle may likewise return an HTTP status code. At that point, Apache sets up an internal redirection to the error document for the HTTP status code in question.

An error document is, by default, a predefined document that presents the user with a brief explanation of the error. A server administrator can change this document by using the `ErrorDocument` directive. Because an error document is treated internally as a different request, it can be served by any handler (such as a CGI or PHP script). To avoid going into an error loop, this functionality is not recursive: An error document will not divert the path to another error document by returning an HTTP status code itself. If that happens, it generates a predefined server error.

A special case involves error documents for HTTP 3xx status codes. These codes are not errors, but rather redirections and similar messages. Thus, in addition to an internal redirection, they generate an HTTP redirection. This operation is straightforward and perfectly normal, as illustrated by our earlier example in which `mod_alias` handles the `Redirect` directive.

6.3.2 Dealing with Malformed and Malicious Requests

A fundamental principle of security on the Web is always to exercise caution in what you accept from any unknown source. That includes HTTP requests coming from anywhere on the Web. Most of these requests will be legitimate, being generated by human-driven browsers, spiders such as Googlebot, proxy cache agents, QA tools such as Site Valet, and so on. Unfortunately, a significant number of HTTP requests represent attempts to exploit security vulnerabilities. Traces of some rather old IIS worms (e.g., Nimda, Code Red) are routinely seen in Apache logs, in which automated attacks attempt to use IIS bugs to take control of Windows servers. Although Apache has not suffered a comparable attack, it is every module developer's business to keep Apache clean! The basic rule is to determine which inputs, or pattern of inputs, an application will accept, and then to reject any request that fails to match an acceptable pattern.

Apache offers a ready-made solution that allows any module to deal with bad requests: Simply abort by returning HTTP status code 400 (Bad Request) or, where applicable, a more specific HTTP 4xx status code, as soon as you encounter the bad inputs. Don't even try to deal with the bad request directly—that way complexity and security vulnerabilities lie.

6.4 Gathering Information: Subrequests

A second form of diversion from normal request processing is the subrequest. A subrequest is a diversion to a new request. Unlike with internal redirection, however, processing returns to the original request after the subrequest completes.

Subrequests constituted an important tool in Apache 1.x, where they could be used to improvise a primitive form of filtering in which a module sets up a handler to run another handler in a subrequest, and intercepts incoming and/or outgoing data. In Apache 2.x, this kind of hack is no longer necessary. The main role of the subrequest now is to run a fast partial request, to gather information: "What would happen if we ran this request?" For example, `mod_autoindex` runs a subrequest to each file in a directory, producing a list of only those files that are accessible to the server. Of course, at the system level, we could achieve the same goal with a simple `stat`, but running a subrequest means that we can also ascertain whether the server configuration permits access.

The subrequest API in Apache 2 comprises four methods to create a subrequest from a request

- `ap_sub_req_lookup_uri`
- `ap_sub_req_lookup_file`
- `ap_sub_req_lookup_dirent`
- `ap_sub_req_method_uri`

together with a method to run it

- `ap_run_sub_req`

and a method to dispose of it when done

- `ap_destroy_sub_req`

When we create a subrequest using one of the first four methods, Apache goes through the request preparation phase (up to the `fixups` hook). This may be sufficient if the purpose of the subrequest is to gather information on "What would happen if we request this URL?" Running a subrequest is optional.

Destroying the subrequest can be a more complex issue. It is always required, whether or not the request was run. Modules can either run `ap_destroy_sub_req` explicitly or leave it to the pool cleanup when the parent request is destroyed. Take care when destroying a subrequest, as anything allocated on the subrequest's pool will die along with it!

Like the internal redirect and the error document, a subrequest will invoke functions from all modules hooked into the processing cycle, as appropriate. Your functions can tell when they are invoked in a subrequest by looking at the r->main field of the request_rec; its value is normally NULL, but in the context of a subrequest it holds the parent request_rec.

```
static int my_func(request_rec* r) {
  ...
  /* Are we in a subrequest? */
  request_rec *parent = r->main ;
  if (parent != NULL) {
    /* It's the parent, and we're in a subrequest */
  }
  else {
    /* It's a normal request */
  }
  ...
}
```

6.4.1 Example

The mod_include module demonstrates both forms of subrequests. The SSI <!--#include virtual="..."--> directive is implemented by a full subrequest to the included resource, whereas other directives such as <!--#fsize ...--> and <!--#flastmod ...--> use only a lookup to find information about the resource (metadata), without actually serving the resource to the client.

Here's the relevant subrequest code for processing <!--#include virtual...--> and <!--#include file ...--> directives in mod_include:

```
/*
 * <!--#include virtual|file="..." [virtual|file="..."] ... -->
 */
static apr_status_t handle_include(include_ctx_t *ctx, ap_filter_t *f,
                                   apr_bucket_brigade *bb)
{
    request_rec *r = f->r;

    /* Housekeeping DELETED FOR BREVITY */

    while (1) {
        char *tag      = NULL;
        char *tag_val = NULL;
        request_rec *rr = NULL;
        char *error_fmt = NULL;
        char *parsed_string;
```

```
ap_ssi_get_tag_and_value(ctx, &tag, &tag_val,SSI_VALUE_DECODED);
if (!tag || !tag_val) {
    break;
}
if (strcmp(tag, "virtual") && strcmp(tag, "file")) {
    ap_log_rerror(APLOG_MARK, APLOG_ERR,0,r,"unknown parameter "
            "\"%s\" to tag include in %s", tag, r->filename);
    SSI_CREATE_ERROR_BUCKET(ctx, f, bb);
    break;
}

parsed_string = ap_ssi_parse_string(ctx, tag_val, NULL, 0,
                                SSI_EXPAND_DROP_NAME);
if (tag[0] == 'f') {
    char *newpath;
    apr_status_t rv;

    /* Be safe; only files in this directory or below allowed */
    rv = apr_filepath_merge(&newpath, NULL, parsed_string,
                        APR_FILEPATH_NOTABOVEROOT |
                        APR_FILEPATH_SECUREROOTTEST |
                        APR_FILEPATH_NOTABSOLUTE, ctx->dpool);

    if (rv != APR_SUCCESS) {
        error_fmt = "unable to include file %s in parsed file %s";
    }
```

The next two `else` clauses create the subrequest: the first for `<!--#include file-->`, and the second for `<!--#include virtual-->`.

```
    else {
        rr = ap_sub_req_lookup_file(newpath, r, f->next);
    }
}
else {
    rr = ap_sub_req_lookup_uri(parsed_string, r, f->next);
}
```

At this point, the subrequest has not been run, but the lookup alone takes us through the process of constructing the subrequest and running it, up to and including the `fixups` phase. As a consequence, we know quite a lot about the subrequest: We know if it has failed or been denied (except for the case in which an error in its content generator causes it to fail), and we've got the file information we'd need for `<!--#fsize-->` or `<!--#flastmod-->`. But the subrequest has not (yet) touched the data, only the metadata.

```
    if (!error_fmt && rr->status != HTTP_OK) {
        error_fmt = "unable to include \"%s\" in parsed file %s";
    }

    if (!error_fmt && (ctx->flags & SSI_FLAG_NO_EXEC) &&
        rr->content_type && strncmp(rr->content_type, "text/", 5)) {

        error_fmt = "unable to include potential exec \"%s\" in "
            "parsed file %s";
    }

    /* See the kludge in includes_filter for why.
     * Basically, it puts a bread crumb in here, then looks
     * for the crumb later to see if it's been here.
     */
    if (rr) {
        ap_set_module_config(rr->request_config, &include_module,r);
    }
```

The second phase of the subrequest processing is to run the content generator. The subrequest's output will then be sent to the client. Other SSI directives such as `<!--#flastmod-->` and `<!--#fsize>` omit this step.

```
    if (!error_fmt && ap_run_sub_req(rr)) {
        error_fmt = "unable to include \"%s\" in parsed file %s";
    }

    if (error_fmt) {
        ap_log_rerror(APLOG_MARK, APLOG_ERR, 0, r, error_fmt,
                tag_val, r->filename);
        SSI_CREATE_ERROR_BUCKET(ctx, f, bb);
    }

    /* Do *not* destroy the subrequest here; it may have allocated
     * variables in this r->subprocess_env in the subrequest's
     * r->pool, so that pool must survive as long as this request.
     * Yes, this is a memory leak. */
```

The comment is noting that at this point, we would normally call `ap_destroy_sub_req`. The memory leak isn't really important, because it lasts only until the main request is itself destroyed.

```
    if (error_fmt) {
        break;
    }
    }

    return APR_SUCCESS;
}
```

6.5 Developing a Module

So far, we have breezed through a brief overview of the earlier phases of request processing. In the remainder of this chapter, we will develop a real example module.

6.5.1 Selecting Different Variants of a Document

The author's Site Valet product includes a facility through which users can publish reports to the server. These reports are part of a QA/audit process. As such, they are important but will be accessed infrequently, so system performance is not a major issue with the report generation process.

Reports are generated and stored on the server in an XML format used within Site Valet. Not surprisingly, the reports need to be accessible in other formats: HTML for web browsers and human readers, and EARL (RDF) for the Semantic Web. This reformatting is accomplished by applying an XSLT transformation on the fly when a document is served to anyone other than the Valet tools. The XSLT transformation is performed by `mod_transform`, which is a prerequisite for this module.

The problem we have to address here is, in a sense, the opposite of content negotiation. Instead of selecting one of many static resources according to the request headers, we must respond to the user's explicit request for a different URL.

Put explicitly, if an XML report is stored at `{DOCUMENT_ROOT}/reports/example`, then we need to map requested URLs as follows:

`http://server/reports/example`	→	XML (unchanged)
`http://server/reports/example.html`	→	HTML
`http://server/reports/example.rdf`	→	EARL

For additional flexibility, our module enables users to define other formats by introducing their own XSLT stylesheets. Let's call this module `mod_choices`.

The core of `mod_choices` is a `type_checker` hook. To set the scene for it, we need to define the relevant data structs. First, we define the module configuration:

```
typedef struct choices_cfg {
  int choices ;              /* Flag to turn this module on/off */
  apr_hash_t* transforms ;   /* Table of "extensions" known to
                              * this server
                              */
} choices_cfg ;
```

Second, we note that each "extension" is a record describing how to handle itself:

```
typedef struct choices_transform {
  const char* ctype ;   /* Content-Type for this extension */
  const char* xslt ;    /* Name of XSLT stylesheet for
                         * this extension.
                         */
} choices_transform ;
```

To implement .html and .rdf as described above, we will set up entries in the transforms table. The configuration will look something like this:

```
Alias reports /var/www/reports
<Directory /var/www/reports/>
    # set "choices" in choices_cfg
    Choices On

    # Set up choices_transform entries for HTML and RDF (EARL)
    ChoicesTransform html text/html;charset=utf-8 transforms/html.xslt
    ChoicesTransform rdf application/rdf+xml transforms/earl.xslt
</Directory>
```

Now we can present the main function:

```
static int choices_select(request_rec* r) {

  /* First, look up our module configuration */
  choices_cfg* cfg =
    ap_get_module_config(r->per_dir_config, &choices_module) ;

  if ( ! cfg->choices ) {
    /* This request has nothing to do with this module */
    return DECLINED ;
  }

  if ( r->method_number != M_GET ) {
    /* Other methods are allowed, but this hook isn't interested */
    return DECLINED ;
  }

  if ( ! r->filename ) {
    /* This can't happen; but if it does (e.g., a buggy third-party
     * module has messed up our request), a server error is better
     * than a server crash when we dereference a null pointer :-)
     */
    return HTTP_INTERNAL_SERVER_ERROR ;
  }

  /* Our request has been mapped to the filesystem, but it may not
   * match anything that's really there.  We can stat it to find out.
   */
  if ( apr_stat(&r->finfo, r->filename, APR_FINFO_SIZE, r->pool)
    == APR_SUCCESS ) {
```

```
  /* The request maps directly to a file.  We don't need to
   * do anything except serve it as XML.
   */
  ap_set_content_type(r, "application/xml;charset=utf-8") ;
} else {
  /* The request doesn't map to a file. We need to check whether we
   * can map to a file by stripping the "extension" off.
   *
   * First, we split the filename.
   */
  char* ext = strrchr(r->filename, '.') ;
  if ( ext ) {
    *ext++ = 0 ;
  } else {
    /* No such file and not a name we can parse as an extension */
    return HTTP_NOT_FOUND ;     /* (1) */
  }
  /* Now we can see whether we have a file we can map */
  if ( apr_stat(&r->finfo, r->filename, APR_FINFO_SIZE, r->pool)
   == APR_SUCCESS ) {
    /* OK, it's there.  Now check whether it's an extension we know. */
    choices_transform* fmt = apr_hash_get(cfg->transforms, ext,
                          APR_HASH_KEY_STRING) ;

    if ( fmt ) {
      /* OK, we have a transform for this extension.
       * We set request properties accordingly.
       */
    ap_set_content_type(r, fmt->ctype) ;

    /* this function is exported by mod_transform, and selects
     * an XSLT transform to run for this request
     */
      mod_transform_set_XSLT(r, fmt->name) ;

    /* Finally, we insert mod_transform in the output chain.
     * The filter name is also exported by mod_transform.
     */
      ap_add_output_filter(XSLT_FILTER_NAME, NULL, r, r->connection) ;
    } else {
    /* We don't know this extension, so we can't serve it.
     * If this was a negotiated resource, we'd return NOT_ACCEPTABLE
     * (HTTP 406) here.  Since it isn't, we return NOT_FOUND.
     */
    return HTTP_NOT_FOUND ;     /* (2) */
    }
  } else {
    /* apr_stat failed -- there's no underlying file to serve */
    return HTTP_NOT_FOUND ;     /* (3) */
  }
}
```

```
  /* OK, we've finished configuring this request */
  return OK ;
}
```

All we need to do now is to hook in the handler, together with its configuration. We'll show the remainder of the module here for completeness, but defer an explanation of it to Chapter 9, where we describe module configuration. We use `APR_HOOK_FIRST` to hook this handler in ahead of standard type checkers such as mod_mime.

```
static void choices_hooks(apr_pool_t* pool) {
  ap_hook_type_checker(choices_select, NULL, NULL, APR_HOOK_FIRST) ;
}
module AP_MODULE_DECLARE_DATA choices_module = {
        STANDARD20_MODULE_STUFF,
        choices_cr_cfg ,
        NULL ,
        NULL ,
        NULL ,
        choices_cmds ,
        choices_hooks
} ;

static void* choices_cr_cfg(apr_pool_t* pool, char* x) {
  choices_cfg* ret = apr_pcalloc(pool, sizeof(choices_cfg)) ;
  ret->transforms = apr_hash_make(pool) ;
  return ret ;
}
static const char* choices_transform_set(cmd_parms* cmd, void* cfg,
    const char* ext, const char* ctype, const char* xslt) {
  apr_hash_t* transforms = ((choices_cfg*)cfg)->transforms ;
  choices_transform* t
    = apr_palloc(cmd->pool, sizeof(choices_transform));
  t->ctype = ctype ;
  t->xslt = xslt ;
  apr_hash_set(transforms, ext, APR_HASH_KEY_STRING, t);
  return NULL;
}
static const command_rec choices_cmds[] = {
  AP_INIT_FLAG("Choices", ap_set_flag_slot,
    (void*)APR_OFFSETOF(choices_cfg, choices), ACCESS_CONF,
    "Enable document variant selection by extension"),
  AP_INIT_TAKE3("ChoicesTransform", choices_transform_set, NULL,
    ACCESS_CONF, "Define content-type and XSLT for an extension"),
  {NULL}
} ;
```

6.5.2 Error Handling and Reusability

The preceding module is adequate for our application. Anyone using this code will be accessing a URL generated by the application, so how we deal with failure to find a resource is unimportant. Of course, if we want to generalize our module a little, we could make a few changes. There's no problem with reusing it as is; it's just that the module is specific to a single project, so it is not very likely to be used on a more widespread basis.

There are three points at which we return an HTTP status of 404 (Not Found), thereby diverting processing into an error document. Points 1 and 3 indicate cases in which we fail to find any resource. Point 2 indicates the case in which we find the file but don't know what to do with the extension.

Now, mod_choices implements one scheme for dealing with variants on a resource; mod_negotiation implements another scheme; and another third-party module might provide an altogether different mapping. At points 1 and 3, we could return DECLINED instead of HTTP_NOT_FOUND to enable those modules to work alongside mod_choices.[1] At point 3, we would also need to restore r->filename to its original value first! If we do that, we can let Apache apply several different schemes until it finds one that works (or gives up).

We could do the same at point 2, but this failure is probably due to a server configuration that doesn't quite meet the client's expectations. As an example, suppose that the client requested

```
http://server/reports/example.html
```

but the ChoicesTransform line for html is missing from httpd.conf. In this scenario, a better option is to return HTTP_MULTIPLE_CHOICES, which will divert us into an error document. To be useful, our error document should tell the client which options are available, so we'll have to write our own handler for it, too. This handler needs the mod_choices configuration, so it'll be easiest to implement it in the same module.

---

1. mod_negotiation also uses APR_HOOK_FIRST, so we'd also have to hook mod_choices explicitly ahead of it to combine the two. See the discussion of hooks in Chapter 10.

Here's a minimal implementation:

```
static int choices_errordoc(request_rec* r) {

  /* This is an error handler we can use if we return
   * HTTP_MULTIPLE_CHOICES instead of HTTP_NOT_FOUND at (2) above
   */
  choices_cfg* cfg ;
  const char* ext ;
  apr_ssize_t len ;
  choices_transform* rec ;
  apr_hash_index_t* ht ;
  char* p;

  /* Ignore the request if we're not in an internal redirect */
  if ( ! r->prev || ! r->prev->uri ) {
    return DECLINED ;
  }

  /* Insist on being configured before we do anything */
  if ( strcmp(r->handler, "choices-errordoc") != 0 ) {
    return DECLINED ;
  }

  cfg = ap_get_module_config(r->prev->per_dir_config, &choices_module);

  ap_set_content_type(r, "text/html;charset=ascii") ;

  /* Now we can print an error page, listing the 'base' (XML)
   * document and other available variants.
   *
   * The base name is in r->prev->uri.
   * We just need to strip off the extensions.
   */
  p = strrchr(r->prev->uri, '.') ;
  if (p != NULL)
    *p = '\0' ;

  ap_rprintf(r, "<!DOCTYPE HTML PUBLIC \"-//W3C//DTD HTML 4.01//EN\">\n"
    "<html><head><title>No such format</title></head>"
    "<body><h1>Format not supported</h1>"
    "<p>mod_choices on this server is not configured to support "
    "the requested document format.  Available options are:</p>"
    "<table><thead><tr>"
    "<th scope=\"col\">Document Type</th>"
    "<th scope=\"col\">URL</th>"
    "</tr></thead><tbody>"
    "<tr><td>application/xml</td>"
    "<td><a href=\"%s\" type=\"application/xml\">%s</a></td></tr>",
    r->prev->uri, r->prev->uri) ;
```

```
/* We saw how to iterate over a table in Chapter 5.
 * For a hash table, we use a more traditional loop,
 * based on a hash index ht and the function apr_hash_this.
 */
for (ht = apr_hash_first(r->pool, cfg->transforms);
     ht; ht = apr_hash_next(ht)) {
  apr_hash_this(ht, (const void**)&ext, &len, (void**)&rec) ;
  ap_rprintf(r, "<tr><td>%s</td>"
      "<td><a href=\"%s.%s\" type=\"%s\">%s.%s</a></td></tr>\n",
      rec->ctype, r->prev->uri, ext, rec->ctype, r->prev->uri, ext) ;
}
ap_rputs("</tbody></table></body></html>" , r) ;
return OK ;
}
```

Now we just need to add this function to our hooks:

```
static void choices_hooks(apr_pool_t* pool) {
  ap_hook_type_checker(choices_select, NULL, NULL, APR_HOOK_FIRST) ;
  ap_hook_handler(choices_errordoc, NULL, NULL, APR_HOOK_MIDDLE) ;
}
```

Finally, we configure it:

```
Alias reports /var/www/reports
<Directory /var/www/reports/>
    # set "choices" in choices_cfg
    Choices On

    # Set up choices_transform entries for HTML and RDF (EARL)
    ChoicesTransform html text/html;charset=utf-8 transforms/html.xsl
    ChoicesTransform rdf application/rdf+xml transforms/earl.xsl

    # Set up ErrorDoc handling for Multiple Choices
    ErrorDocument 300     /reports/error300
    <Files     error300>
        SetHandler   choices-errordoc
        Choices      Off
    </Files>
</Directory>
```

6.6 Summary

This chapter presented an overview of the HTTP request processing cycle in Apache, covering both the standard processing path and diversions from it. As with content generators, the primary building blocks for metadata modules are callback functions attached to Apache's hooks. Specifically, we examined the following topics:

- The anatomy of an HTTP request
- Mapping the request to the server
- Handling HTTP request headers (metadata), including content negotiation
- The roles of the request processing phases, and hooking into them
- Diverting the request from the normal cycle
- Processing errors

Apache's hooks are explained in detail in Chapter 10, and configuration is addressed more fully in Chapter 9. Next, Chapter 7 offers a detailed look at the security phase of request processing.

Chapter 7

AAA: Access, Authentication, and Authorization

In terms of the main flow of this book, the Apache access, authentication, and authorization (AAA) framework falls broadly within the scope of metadata modules (Chapter 6). However, it has historically been an extremely popular area for module developers. Furthermore, it has changed significantly in Apache 2.1/2.2 compared to earlier versions. Given that this is the most substantial change since the original framework inherited from the NCSA HTTPD in 1995, it is of sufficient interest to merit its own chapter.

7.1 Security

Before we dig into the details of the security phase in Apache's request processing, we should perhaps take a broader look at the issue of security. Since a comprehensive discussion of security belongs in a book for system administrators—which this is not—we'll be very brief, but we should at least set the scene for what this chapter does and does not cover.

This chapter deals specifically with determining who is permitted to access a resource or perform an operation over the Web, including the concept of login. It discusses different methods of dealing with this issue, and widely different levels of security.

This chapter explicitly *does not* deal with other important aspects of web security, including these issues:

- Transport-layer security. Support for strong data encryption between the client and the server is provided by `mod_ssl` or `mod_gnutls`.[1]

- Operating system security. It is the business of the systems administrator to ensure the operating system offers the best possible protection against a bug in Apache—or any other program—becoming a backdoor to the system. This is an area in which UNIX-family operating systems in the hands of a competent administrator still offer major advantages over Windows.

- Safe programming techniques (see Chapter 4).

- Protection of vulnerable applications, particularly PHP. This is the main subject of a third-party module, `mod_security`.[2]

- People and processes. High security in the system is wasted when sensitive information such as passwords is revealed in an insecure medium such as an unencrypted email message, fax, or telephone conversation. Likewise, a password written down on paper or kept on a computer or in an organizer is only as secure as what it's written on. Similarly, if an attacker can physically access a machine via someone else's session, or trick someone into doing it for them, all your web security is in vain.

7.1.1 Authentication: Levels of Security

HTTP offers two levels of security for web authentication.

7.1.1.1 Basic

HTTP basic authentication is a simple, low-security method. The `username:` `password` combination is base-64 encoded and passed over the Web. It is secure to

---

1. `http://www.outoforder.cc/projects/apache/mod_gnutls/`
2. `http://www.modsecurity.org/`

the extent that the tokens passed are obscure and unmemorable to human readers, and will appear as gibberish to a non-computer-person such as the boss. But these tokens are trivial for a programmer to decode using, for example, Apache's `apr_base64`, and they can be reused verbatim to impersonate a user.

7.1.1.2 Digest

Digest authentication uses MD5 one-way encryption to protect passwords. This is cryptographically secure: A password cannot be reconstructed from an MD5 token, at least not without considerable resources. It is also secure against replay attacks, because passwords passed from the client to the server are constructed using a private token that is regenerated every few minutes. The downside (which is mostly historical and of little relevance today) is that digest authentication is harder to work with and carries a higher system overhead than basic authentication; also, browser support is not universal.

These methods of authentication can be supplemented by other measures, such as limited sessions with expiry times enforced by the server.

7.1.1.3 Authentication Dialog

Both basic and digest authentication are associated with authentication dialog pop-up boxes presented by browsers when challenged (Figure 7-1). These dialogs are firmly outside the scope of a site designer.

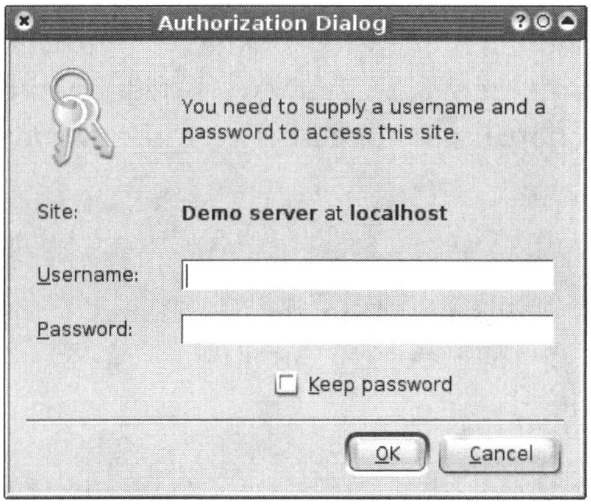

FIGURE 7-1
Authentication dialog pop-up box

Sometimes we may wish to avoid this dialog-based scheme and implement alternative authentication methods. We'll look at alternatives later in the chapter, but bear in mind that it is not possible to reproduce the level of cryptographic security of digest authentication, except by relying on nonstandard (and inevitably far less well-supported) client capabilities or by resorting to SSL/client certificates.

7.1.2 Login on the Web

The term *login* is sometimes used interchangeably with the term *authentication* on the Web. Strictly speaking, this is a misnomer: Login implies a session, but HTTP is a stateless protocol and so doesn't support sessions. Session management can be built on top of HTTP, but this requires that a session token is passed not just once at login time, but with *every request*. There is no way to avoid this duplication of effort.

We'll avoid confusing authentication as such with login, but at the end of the chapter we'll discuss session management under the title of login.

7.2 An Overview of AAA

The basic premise of access control and authentication is that we may wish to permit certain operations to some users, but deny them to others. Determining who a user is and whether that entity is permitted the current operation is the business of these aaa modules. Apache provides a number of standard modules for this purpose in the `modules/aaa` directory, and a wide range of third-party modules are also available. The number of third-party modules is likely to be reduced in Apache 2.2 compared to earlier versions, because the new AAA framework reduces the amount of duplication of very similar functionality required between the various modules.

Access control was originally determined in two ways:

- Host-based control permits or denies access based on the IP address from which the request originates (`REMOTE_HOST` or `REMOTE_ADDR`).

- User-based control identifies users by login/password (`REMOTE_USER`).

These two fundamental control methods still lie at the heart of Apache AAA, but the scope of the tasks has been greatly broadened. In particular, user-based control has been generalized to concepts such as sessions managed by a cookie or URL hash.

There are three request processing hooks concerned with access control:

- `ap_hook_access_checker`
- `ap_hook_check_user_id`
- `ap_hook_auth_checker`

These hooks are, respectively, responsible for three tasks:

- Determine whether the remote host is permitted access
- Determine who the remote user is, and verify the password
- Determine whether the now-identified remote user is permitted access

This underlying structure is common to all Apache versions to date, and reflects the forms of configuration available to AAA modules

Host Access

```
Order Deny, Allow
Deny from all
Allow from 192.168.1.11
```

Specifying an Authentication Protocol

```
AuthType Basic
AuthName "My Server"
```

Identifying the User

```
AuthUserFile /etc/apache/users
```

Determining Whether the Remote User Has Access

```
AuthGroupFile /etc/apache/groups
Require group example
```

Determining Whether to Require Both or Just One of Host and User

```
Satisfy Any
```

7.3 AAA in Apache 1.x and 2.0

Apache has traditionally supported two basic forms of access control:

1. Access by IP address is determined by `mod_access`.

2. Access by identified user is determined by `mod_auth`, or any of numerous equivalents from the standard `mod_auth_dbm` to a wide range of third-party options. These modules are responsible for both the `check_user_id` and `auth_checker` phases.

`mod_access` is configured using the `Order`, `Allow`, and `Deny` directives, which specify allowed or disallowed IP addresses. `mod_auth` is controlled primarily by the `Require` directive, which specifies users or groups permitted access. The two modules are linked by the `Satisfy` directive, which determines whether a request needs to satisfy both forms of access control or whether either one alone is sufficient.

In this framework, `mod_access` works cleanly and well, but the `mod_auth` family is less well specified. The basic problem with authentication is that each module has to perform several distinct tasks that would be better factored out into common functions.

HTTP distinguishes between basic and digest authentication by specifying different methods of encoding the user identification data. An authentication module has to decode the data according to the encoding used. This has left us with `mod_auth_digest` as separate from `mod_auth`, and other modules such as `mod_auth_dbm` not supporting digest authentication at all because it doesn't reimplement that code.

A module has first to identify the user using one of the above schemes or its own method (which could be something completely different, such as a cookie or a directory service) and then to determine whether the user is authorized for the attempted operation. That's two separate functions—indeed, two separate request processing hooks—in a single module.

7.4 AAA in Apache 2.1/2.2

Access, authentication, and authorization in Apache 2.1/2.2 have been refactored into a four-part process, as shown in Figure 7-2.

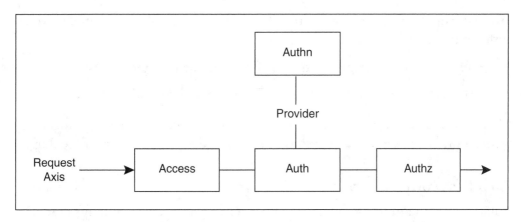

FIGURE 7-2
AAA: access control, authentication, and authorization

7.4.1 Host-Based Access Control

mod_access has been renamed to mod_authz_host ("host-based authorization"), but is otherwise not substantially changed. It is the only standard module to use the access_checker hook. Other modules implementing access control based on network or hardware information, such as a module implementing ARP lookup and permitting access by MAC address, would also use this hook.

7.4.2 Authentication: check_user_id

Authentication is the process of reading a token from the client, and converting it from the external representation sent over the wire to Apache's internal representation—in particular, setting the user field of the request_rec object. For example, mod_auth_basic implements HTTP basic authentication by extracting a username/password pair from a base-64-encoded token sent from the client. The process of verifying a password is now handled by a separate authorization (authn) module. The advantage of this approach is that it decouples password lookup from protocol support. Now, for example, mod_authn_dbd has only to look up passwords in an SQL database, and it automatically supports both basic and digest authentication.

Two standard modules implement the `check_user_id` hook. These are known as auth modules:

- `mod_auth_basic` implements HTTP basic authentication.

- `mod_auth_digest` implements HTTP digest authentication.

These two modules deal with implementing their respective HTTP protocols, as before, but differ from earlier versions in that they delegate the password lookup.

7.4.3 Password Lookup

Authentication (authn) modules are helpers for the auth (user-checking) modules. The authn API is an `ap_provider`, as introduced in Chapter 10. The standard Apache distribution includes the following authn modules:

- **`mod_authn_alias`**—support complex configuration options by delegating to other providers

- **`mod_authn_anon`**—permit arbitrary user-supplied passwords or variants such as anon-ftp style e-mail addresses

- **`mod_authn_dbd`**—look up passwords in an SQL database

- **`mod_authn_dbm`**—look up passwords in a DBM database

- **`mod_authn_default`**—a fallback to reject users if no other authn module deals with them

- **`mod_authn_file`**—look up passwords in a flat file (the old htpasswd/htdigest)

- **`mod_authnz_ldap`**—look up passwords in an LDAP directory

7.4.4 Authorization

Authorization (authz) is the decision of whether the user is authorized to carry out the attempted operation. The old `mod_access` module has become `mod_authz_host`, as it makes that decision based on the client host and `Allow/Deny From` directives. User-based authorization uses the `auth_checker` hook and grants or denies access based on the username, as set in the authentication phase.

Standard authorization modules are listed here.

- **mod_authz_dbd**—look up the user's groups in an SQL database (`"Require dbd-group"`) and provide hooks for login/logout

- **mod_authz_dbm**—look up the user's groups in a DBM database

- **mod_authz_default**—a fallback to reject users if no other authz module takes any decision

- **mod_authnz_ldap**—look up the user's groups in an LDAP directory

- **mod_authz_owner**—authorization based on the system user and group of a resource requested

- **mod_authz_user**—implements "`Require valid-user`" (allow anyone authenticated), as well as "`Require user`" and "`Require group`" (list of permitted users or groups, respectively)

7.5 AAA Logic

The logic of the security phase in the Apache core is shown here, in pseudocode form:

```
If (Satisfy Any) {
  run access_checker
  if (allowed by access checker) {
      ALLOW access; skip check_user_id and auth_checker hooks
  } else {
      if (configured for authentication) {
          run check_user_id
          if (user id is valid) {
            run auth_checker; outcome is ALLOW or DENY
          } else {
            DENY access
          }
      }
  }
} else { /* Satisfy ALL is the default */
  run access_checker
  if (allowed by access checker) {
      if (configured for authentication) {
          run check_user_id
          if (user id is valid) {
            run auth_checker; outcome is ALLOW or DENY
          } else {
            DENY access
          }
      }
  }
```

```
    } else {
        DENY access; skip check_user_id and auth_checker hooks
    }
}
```

This scheme is, of course, simplified, in that any hook can divert the processing into an internal error if a hook fails or if authentication is misconfigured. Nevertheless, the fundamental logic is sound: Host-based access control always runs, but user-based control may be skipped according to the configuration. At this level, the logic is unchanged in Apache 2.2 from earlier versions.

7.5.1 Authentication and Require

One bit of logic needs further explanation. What does it mean to be "configured for authentication"?

This is entirely predicated on the `Require` directive. If there is any `Require` directive in scope in `httpd.conf` or an applicable `.htaccess`, then some authentication is required. `Require` alone is not sufficient to configure authentication, but it is the arbiter of whether authentication is required. `Require` is implemented by the server core, which exports API methods for modules to use. The function that determines whether we are configured for authentication is `ap_some_auth_required`.

7.5.2 Denying Access

Apache uses three HTTP response codes to deny access in this phase:

- `401` (Unauthorized)
- `403` (Forbidden)
- `407` (Proxy Authentication Required)

Response code `403` is an unconditional denial of access: There is nothing the client can do to get in. This response is what will be returned when `mod_access` (now `mod_authz_host`) denies access based on a `Deny From` directive.

Response codes `401` and `407` tell the client that access was denied, but would be allowed if the client had sent the appropriate credentials (typically a username and password). The HTTP protocol requires that a `401` or `407` request *must* include an authentication challenge, which tells the client the authentication protocol to use.

This challenge, in turn, causes the client to display a username/password dialog when that client is a browser. Here is a typical response:

```
HTTP/1.1 401 Authorization Required
Date: Fri, 23 Dec 2005 20:01:34 GMT
Server: Apache/2.2.0 (Unix)
WWW-Authenticate: Basic realm="Demo server"
Accept-Ranges: bytes
Content-Length: 113
Connection: close
Content-Type: text/html; charset=ISO-8859-1
```

The crucial header here is the challenge `WWW-Authenticate`. It invites the browser to try again, using HTTP basic authentication. The realm is displayed by most browsers in a login dialog box, which varies a little between browsers but is basically the same.

A `407` response replaces `WWW-Authenticate` with `Proxy-Authenticate`, but is otherwise exactly the same.

7.5.3 Authentication Methods

The authentication method is part of the client/server communication protocol and is, therefore, constrained to be a method supported by browsers. On the Web, that means we have two options: Basic and digest authentication are implemented by `mod_auth_basic` and `mod_auth_digest`, respectively. Although we could implement a different method in Apache, it won't be useful (except perhaps within a specialist private network) because it will generate an authentication challenge that browsers won't understand and respond to.

If we are determined to implement a different "login" scheme, we can either "fake" HTTP basic authentication or avoid it altogether, provided we avoid sending a `401` or `407` response to the client.

7.6 Writing AAA Modules

Let's look at a nonstandard authentication task. Suppose we wish to develop a module that permits anonymous access on selected days specified by a server administrator, while requiring normal username/passwords to access the system on other days. Setting aside other possible implementations of this scheme, let's develop it using the authn/authz framework, which will integrate fully with standard authenticated access. Our goal is to create an authentication dialog appropriate for all users, so that users having normal username/password credentials can freely use either those data or anonymous access (using the name of the day as the username) on open days. We'll use the common convention for weekdays, and accept but ignore anything beyond the first three characters.

The pivotal control is the `Require` directive. We'll need a new keyword for our method. Let's use "`day`". Thus our configuration takes the following form:

```
Require day saturday sunday
```

7.6.1 A Basic Authentication Provider

Because we're integrating the new framework with normal authentication, we need to piggyback onto either basic or digest authentication. That means we want an authn provider to "verify" a "password" for the day. We'll allow a server administrator to configure the system to ignore passwords altogether or require today's date as a password. This approach is simpler than the normal authn function of looking up a password for the user.

```
static authn_status authn_check_day(request_rec *r, const char* user,
                                const char* password)
{
    int y, m, d;
    apr_time_exp_t today;
    const char* const wdays[7] =
            { "sun", "mon", "tue", "wed", "thu", "fri", "sat" };
    authnz_day_rec *cfg = ap_get_module_config(r->per_dir_config,
                                    &authnz_day_module);

    /* Get today's date, in local time.  If this fails, it's a server error. */
    if (apr_time_exp_lt(&today, apr_time_now()) != APR_SUCCESS) {
        return AUTH_GENERAL_ERROR;
    }

    /* Check the username is today */
    /* If not, disclaim any interest in this request and leave it
     * to normal authentication or fallback.
     */
    if ((strlen(user) < 3) || strncasecmp(user, wdays[today.tm_wday], 3)) {
        return AUTH_USER_NOT_FOUND;
    }

    /* Unless we're configured to ignore password, check this */
    if (!cfg->nopassword) {
        /* Read password, and reject anything not in 2005-11-03 format */
```

```
        if (sscanf(password, "%d-%d-%d", &y, &m, &d) != 3) {
            return AUTH_DENIED;
        }

        /* Check the password is today */
        if ((y != (today.tm_year+1900))
            || (m != (today.tm_mon+1))
            || (d != today.tm_mday)) {
            return AUTH_DENIED;
        }

    }
    /* If we got more than three letters, reduce it.  This doesn't affect
     * authentication, but avoids arbitrary and possibly spurious entries
     * in the log file.  For example, if we allow day-access on Mondays
     * and also have a registered user "Monica," we *accept* "Monica" as
     * an alias for Monday because we're looking at only three letters,
     * but we don't want Monica appearing in the logs when it's really
     * an anonymous user.
     *
     * For this reason, we want this provider to run *after* other authn
     * providers, so that when it's the real Monica her password is
     * checked for normal login before we allow anonymous access.
     */
    if (strlen(r->user) > 3) {
        r->user[3] = '\0';
    }

    /* Before returning, we'll set a flag to indicate that this is
     * an anonymous user.  The value is immaterial; it's just nonzero.
     */
    ap_set_module_config(r->request_config, &authnz_day_module, r);

    /* OK, we're happy. */
    return AUTH_GRANTED;
}
```

This function needs to be wrapped in an `ap_provider`:

```
static const authn_provider authn_day_provider =
{
    &authn_check_day,
    NULL
};
```

We register this in our module's `register_hooks` function:

```
static void register_hooks(apr_pool_t *p)
{
    ap_register_provider(p, AUTHN_PROVIDER_GROUP, "day", "0",
                         &authn_day_provider);
    .... ;
}
```

This provider will work with the standard `mod_auth_basic` module to implement the `check_user_id` hook and set `r->user`. We'll leave digest authentication for the time being.

7.6.2 An Authorization Function

`mod_auth_basic`, together with the authn provider developed in Section 7.6.1, will set the day's name as `r->user` and mark a "password" as accepted. But it won't check whether the day is, in fact, one for which access is permitted. To perform this task, we'll need an authorization (authz) handler. This is what actually implements our "`Require day`" directive:

```
static int authz_day(request_rec *r)
{
    authnz_day_rec *cfg = ap_get_module_config(r->per_dir_config,
                                    &authnz_day_module);

    char *day = r->user;
    int m = r->method_number;
    const apr_array_header_t *reqs_arr = ap_requires(r);
    require_line *reqs = reqs_arr ? (require_line *) reqs_arr->elts : NULL;
    char *w;
    const char *t;
    int i;
    int have_day = 0;

    /* Check flag: Is this an anonymous user authenticated by our provider?
     * If not, we're irrelevant.  Note that a 'normal' authz handler should
     * NOT make this kind of decision; it should work with any authn provider.
     */
    if (ap_get_module_config(r->request_config, &authnz_day_module) == NULL) {
        return DECLINED;
    }

    /* Require the first three letters; ignore any more */
    if (strlen(day) < 3) {
        return DECLINED;
    }

    /* Logic dictates this should be unnecessary: If there are no applicable
     * Requires, we won't be called.  But it's better to fail than crash in the
     * event of a bug elsewhere.
     */
    if (!reqs_arr) {
        return DECLINED;
    }
```

```
    /* Go through applicable Require directives */
    for (i = 0; i < reqs_arr->nelts; ++i) {

        /* Ignore this Require if it's in a <Limit> section
         * that excludes this method
         */
        if (!(reqs[i].method_mask & (AP_METHOD_BIT << m))) {
            continue;
        }

        /* Ignore if it's not a "Require day ..." */
        t = reqs[i].requirement;
        w = ap_getword_white(r->pool, &t);
        if (strcasecmp(w, "day")) {
            continue;
        }

        /* OK, we have a "Require day" to satisfy */
        have_day = 1;

        /* Loop over allowed days and match to today */
        while (*t) {
            w = ap_getword_white(r->pool, &t);
            if ((strlen(w) >= 3) && !strncasecmp(w, day, 3)) {

                /* Yep, anonymous access is allowed today */
                return OK;
            }
        }
    }

    /* If there weren't any "Require day" directives, we're irrelevant */
    if (!have_day) {
        return DECLINED;
    }

    /* OK, our decision is final and binding */
    ap_log_rerror(APLOG_MARK, APLOG_ERR, 0, r,
                  "Anonymous usage closed on %s", day);

    /* ap_note_auth_failure causes Apache to add an authentication challenge
     * to the response headers, as required by HTTP
     */
    ap_note_auth_failure(r);
    return HTTP_UNAUTHORIZED;
}
```

We need to register this handler as an `auth_checker`. We also need to be careful
here: We want to go before `mod_authz_user`, so that a "`Require valid-user`"
directive doesn't just automatically pass us. We do so by explicitly declaring that

`mod_authz_user` comes after us, whenever both modules are active. When put together with our authn provider, our register hooks function becomes

```
static void register_hooks(apr_pool_t *p)
{
    static const char *const aszSucc[] = { "mod_authz_user.c", NULL };

    ap_hook_auth_checker(authz_day, NULL, aszSucc, APR_HOOK_MIDDLE);

    ap_register_provider(p, AUTHN_PROVIDER_GROUP, "day", "0",
                         &authn_day_provider);
}
```

The configuration of this module is extremely simple; all we have to manage is the administrator choice of whether to require the date as the password. The remainder of the module is trivial:

```
typedef struct {
    int nopassword;
} authnz_day_rec;

static void *authnz_day_cr_conf(apr_pool_t *pool, char *x)
{
    return apr_pcalloc(pool, sizeof(authnz_day_rec));
}

static const command_rec authnz_day_cmds[] = {
    AP_INIT_FLAG("AuthnDayIgnorePassword", ap_set_flag_slot,
            (void *)APR_OFFSETOF(authnz_day_rec, nopassword), OR_AUTHCFG,
            "Set 'On' to ignore password; 'Off' (default) to require "
            "current date in 2005-11-03 format as a password."),
    {NULL}
};

module AP_MODULE_DECLARE_DATA authnz_day_module = {
    STANDARD20_MODULE_STUFF,
    authnz_day_cr_conf,         /* dir config creator */
    NULL,                       /* dir merger --- default is to override */
    NULL,                       /* server config */
    NULL,                       /* merge server config */
    authnz_day_cmds,            /* commands */
    register_hooks              /* register hooks */
}
```

Note that our module could (and normally would) have been two separate modules, as is the usual practice with the standard authentication and authorization modules. Of course, then we would have had to use a different mechanism for our authn provider to set a flag for the authz handler, or we would have had to implement an alternative logic.

7.6.3 Configuration

The configuration of our little module itself is trivial. But the point of it was to integrate our scheme with standard authentication. So how does that work?

First, let's configure for day-based anonymous authentication alone:

```
AuthType Basic
AuthName "Weekend Access"
AuthnBasicProvider day
Require day saturday sunday
```

Now suppose we have a large number of users having standard username/password access seven days a week, with their passwords being held in a DBM database. We want to combine this access method with our scheme allowing anonymous day-based authentication at weekends. This process is almost as simple, but raises some subtleties:

```
AuthType Basic
AuthName "My Server"
AuthBasicProvider dbm day
Require day saturday sunday
Require valid-user
```

Only one `AuthName` appears in the challenge, so for our normal users it would be misleading to call it "Weekend Access." We can, of course, call it anything we like—ideally something that describes the service being accessed.

The first interesting line here is `AuthBasicProvider`. This line can list multiple providers, which will run in order. We put `dbm` ahead of `day`, so our provider doesn't risk catching normal users (as noted in the comments).

The second point is the two `Require` lines. Their order is immaterial, as our authorization handler (rather than anything in the core) specifies the order in which these schemes run. Our handler runs first and deals with anonymous users, but passes any other users through to the module that implements the other `Require` directive.

7.6.4 Basic and Digest Authentication Providers

In the preceding example, we were able to fake basic authentication. This is a reasonably tried-and-tested approach: For example, cookie authentication modules and mod_auth_anon have used similar techniques since the 1990s. Digest authentication is more complex, and can be faked only if we know the actual password sent by the client.

Recall our authentication provider from `mod_authn_day`:

```
static const authn_provider authn_day_provider =
{
    &authn_check_day,
    NULL
};
```

This is an instance of `struct authn_provider`, defined in `mod_auth.h`:

```
typedef struct {
    /* For HTTP Basic Authentication
     * Given a username and password, expected to return AUTH_GRANTED
     * if we can validate this user/password combination.
     */
    authn_status (*check_password)(request_rec *r, const char *user,
                                   const char *password);

    /* For HTTP Digest Authentication
     * Given a user and realm, expected to return AUTH_USER_FOUND if we
     * can find a md5 hash of 'user:realm:password'
     */
    authn_status (*get_realm_hash)(request_rec *r, const char *user,
                                   const char *realm, char **rethash);
} authn_provider;
```

Whereas the first function `check_password` serves to *verify* a supplied *password* for the username, the second serves only to *look up* an *MD5 hash* and return it for `mod_auth_digest` to process. This approach works well when we are performing a simple lookup, and we can even fake it for `mod_authnz_day` (provided we drop the option of ignoring the password altogether). Of course, we can't just look up a password, because it's one-way encrypted and we can't extract it.

```
static authn_status authn_digest_day(request_rec *r, const char* user,
                                     const char* realm, char** hash)
{
    int y, m, d;
    apr_time_exp_t today;
    const char* unencoded;
    const char* const wdays[7]
    = { "sun", "mon", "tue", "wed", "thu", "fri", "sat" };
    authnz_day_rec *cfg = ap_get_module_config(r->per_dir_config,
                                               &authnz_day_module);

    /* Get today's date, in local time.  If this fails, it's a server error. */
    if (apr_time_exp_lt(&today, apr_time_now()) != APR_SUCCESS) {
        return AUTH_GENERAL_ERROR;
    }
```

```
    /* Check the username is today - needs an exact match this time */
    /* If not, disclaim any interest in this request */
    if (strcmp(user, wdays[today.tm_wday])) {
        return AUTH_USER_NOT_FOUND;
    }

    /* Allocate a buffer for the hash */
    *hash = apr_palloc(r->pool, APR_MD5_DIGESTSIZE);

    /* Now compute the MD5 hash of user:realm:password,
     * which in our scheme of things is day:realm:date
     */
    unencoded = apr_psprintf(r->pool, "%s:%s:%4.4d-%2.2d-%2.2d",
            wdays[today.tm_wday], realm, today.tm_year+1900,
            today.tm_mon+1, today.tm_mday);

    if (apr_md5(*hash, unencoded, strlen(unencoded)) != APR_SUCCESS) {
        return AUTH_GENERAL_ERROR;
    }

    /* Set a note that it's an anonymous user */
    ap_set_module_config(r->request_config, &authnz_day_module, r);

    /* OK, we're happy.  Note this isn't GRANTED as it was with basic
     * authentication, because we only 'looked up', not verified, the hash.
     */
    return AUTH_USER_FOUND;
}
```

Of course, this manufactured example is not typical. The usual function of an authn provider is to look up a password or hash from an authentication source such as a password file or directory, and most authorization providers implement group lookup for a user. Readers interested in examples of this functionality should look at the Apache source in /modules/aaa/ (this author recommends mod_authn_dbd and mod_authz_dbd, which he wrote, or mod_authn_file and mod_authz_user, which are the direct successors to the mod_auth of older Apache versions).

7.7 Implementing a Custom Login Scheme

The authentication dialog presented to the user by a typical browser is strongly reminiscent of logging in. However, this is an illusion: Login implies a session, but authentication doesn't give us one. In particular, there is no logout or relogin, unless we build it ourselves. Because HTTP is stateless, we cannot simply log a client out by unsetting or expiring a cookie or application-level token; a user can easily forge that data to access the system after logout. Neither should we just expire sessions on the server and invalidate a client's credentials. Although this approach secures the server, it is deeply unfriendly and confusing to deny access that the user legitimately believes to be authorized. We need to manage sessions twice over: once on the server, once on the client. The general Apache framework presented earlier in this chapter supports neither of those concepts, so we need to implement it ourselves.

7.7.1 Session Management with SQL

Although the general framework doesn't support sessions and login, one module that does support it is `mod_authz_dbd`, when used in conjunction with `mod_authn_dbd` for password lookup. The basis for this is that the users table in the authentication database should contain an additional "logged in" field, which is updated whenever a user logs in or out. Then `mod_authn_dbd` can use a query of the form

```
SELECT password FROM users WHERE username = %s AND login = 1
```

to allow access only when the user is logged in.

`mod_authz_dbd` supports this scheme by implementing custom `Require` variants,

```
Require dbd-login
Require dbd-logout
```

which cause it to execute SQL queries of the form

```
UPDATE users SET login = 1 WHERE username = %s
UPDATE users SET login = 0 WHERE username = %s
```

respectively.

This provides us with a basis for session management, but we're not there yet. Because authentication precedes authorization, the user is authenticated when the query runs, and the scheme basically works. However, for precisely the same reason, it's not secure. If a user has logged out but the browser still has the credentials, then hitting the login URL (e.g., by unwinding a browser history stack and using force-refresh) will *automatically* log the user in again!

If login is to be secure, we need an alternative method to check the user's credentials. For example, we could use an HTML form for login, with a handler in the content generator phase checking a one-time token (to prevent replay) together with the username and password entered before setting the login flag in the database. This can be coupled with setting the `ErrorDocument` for 401 responses to the login form.

The other part of the task is managing the client session. For this purpose, `mod_authnz_dbd` exports an optional hook that is run whenever a user successfully logs in or out (i.e., executes `dbd-login` or `dbd-logout`), as described in Chapter 10. This hook can be used to perform client-side session management such as setting and unsetting a login cookie.

7.7.2 Working Without Browser Authentication Dialogs

Sometimes we may wish to avoid browser built-in authentication dialogs altogether. Since the dialog is automatically triggered by an HTTP 401 or 407 response, we must avoid sending these codes to the client. It is no longer sufficient even to send a login form as `ErrorDocument`. Instead, we must either (a) present the unauthenticated user with a login form immediately, or (b) redirect the unauthenticated user to a login form with an HTTP 302 response.

In either case, we should embed the URL that the user originally tried into the challenge response, so that we can send the user back to the original resource after successful authentication.

The handler for the login form is then responsible for verifying the credentials entered, setting the client's credentials and (if a session is required) server-side session information, and redirecting the user back to the resource that was originally requested.

Once we have set the client-side credentials, we need to note that they are *not* in a standard HTTP form (only the authentication dialog can give us that). To use the token, we need to check for it ahead of the authentication phase, and set up "faked" basic authentication from it. The `header_parser` hook is the appropriate place for this operation. Let's see an example implementing it with a login cookie. The basic logic is

```
If (Basic authentication required) {
    if (No standard basic authentication present) {
        Look for an authentication cookie
        if ( cookie found ) {
            set Authorization header from it
            (this works because we run before the authentication phase)
        } else {
            redirect user to a login form
        }
    }
}
```

```c
static int cookie_authn(request_rec *r)
{
    login_cfg *cfg = ap_get_module_config(r->per_dir_config, &login_module);
    const char *authhdr;
    const char *cookies;
    const char *cookie = NULL;
    apr_size_t len;
    const char *location;
    const char *authtype;

    /* If no authentication is wanted, it's none of our business */
    if (!ap_some_auth_required(r)) {
        return DECLINED;
    }

    /* If the scheme is not basic authentication, it's none of our business */
    authtype = ap_auth_type(r);
    if (!authtype || strcasecmp(authtype, "Basic")) {
        return DECLINED;        /* authn not wanted at all */
    }

    /* If there's already an Authorization header, we're not needed */
    authhdr = apr_table_get(r->headers_in, "Authorization");
    if (authhdr != NULL) {
        return DECLINED;    /* normal basic authn */
    }

    /* Parse the cookies for an authentication token */
    cookies = apr_table_get(r->headers_in, "Cookie");
    if (cookies) {
        cookie = [ parse details omitted for brevity ]
    }

    if (cookie && *cookie) {
        /* Fake basic authentication credentials in this request */
        authhdr = apr_pstrcat(r->pool, "Basic ", cookie, NULL);
```

```
        apr_table_setn(r->headers_in, "Authorization", authhdr);
        return OK;

    } else if (cfg->login_form) {
        /* No credentials at all; redirect to login form */
        location = apr_pstrcat(r->pool, cfg->login_form, "?dest=",
                        login_redirect(r), NULL);
        apr_table_setn(r->err_headers_out, "Location", location);
        return HTTP_MOVED_TEMPORARILY;
    }
    /* No credentials and no login page.  Oh dear.
     * Unless some other module rides to the rescue, we'll never get in.
     */
    ap_log_rerror(APLOG_MARK, APLOG_WARNING, 0, r,
        "Client has no login credentials and server has no login page.");
    return DECLINED;
}
```

> CAUTION When using cookies for authentication (or anything
> else), take care to deal with users who have cookies disabled,
> either in the browser or in other privacy/security software (which
> the end user may not even be aware of). A surprisingly common,
> but serious, error is to send such users into a loop that sets a
> cookie, then on receiving a request without the cookie, redirects
> the user back to the set-cookie handler, and repeats ad infinitem.
> For general-purpose Web use, you should provide a cookie-free
> alternative. Failing that, send the cookie-free user to a page that
> explains why the user can't log in and what he or she may be able
> to do about it.

7.8 Summary

This chapter introduced the Apache 2.2 AAA framework and demonstrated the basics of writing authn and authz modules. The following topics were covered:

- The access, authentication, and authorization phases

- HTTP basic and digest authentication

- A historical perspective

- The Apache 2.2 architecture, which is based on four tasks and enables mix-and-match and multiple schemes running alongside each other

- HTTP challenge and client authentication dialog
- Writing AAA modules: password lookup (authn) providers for basic and digest authentication, and an authorization (authz) handler
- Session management and client login emulation, and working with HTTP's limitations

Now that you've seen this trivial case, you are equipped to read and understand the more complex authn/authz modules in the Apache distribution (`/modules/aaa/`) and to write your own. However, in view of the more modular framework, it is likely that fewer new authentication modules should be required for Apache 2.2 than for earlier versions. For example, the existence of the DBD authentication modules `mod_authn_dbd`/`mod_authz_dbd` obsoletes *all* existing modules for authenticating against an SQL database such as MySQL, PostgreSQL, or Oracle.

Chapter 8

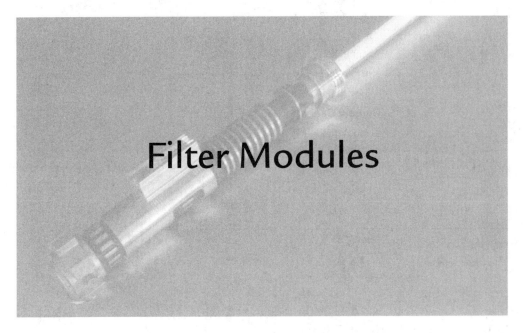

Filter Modules

In terms of application development, the most important innovation in Apache 2 is the filter architecture and the ability to chain multiple different data processing operations at will. In this chapter, we will take a detailed look at the filter chain and develop several illustrative filter modules.

Before going into details, let's review a few basics. In Chapter 2, we saw that filters operate on a "data" axis, orthogonal to the processing axis familiar from Apache 1 and other webservers (Figure 8-1). But this is not the whole story. Strictly speaking, it is really accurate only for content filters—that is, for those filters that operate on the body of an HTTP request or response. If your application is not concerned directly with processing HTTP requests, you may need to use filters that are not so clearly associated with the content generator.

Let's take a closer look at the filter chain. Filters are classified in two ways, as described in the following sections.

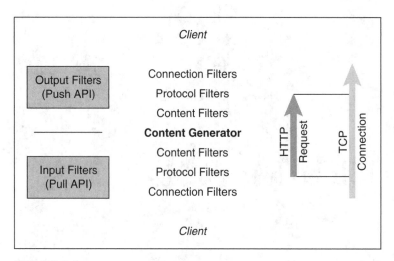

FIGURE 8-1
The filter axis

8.1 Input and Output Filters

Filters that process request data coming from a client are known as input filters. Filters that process response data as it is sent out to the client are known as output filters.

We will deal with the APIs for input and output filters in detail in this chapter.

8.2 Content, Protocol, and Connection Filters

Each filter chain (input and output) passes through predefined stages. Thus the same filter architecture can be used for different kinds of operation. In brief, from the content generator to the client, we have the following classes of filters:

- Content filters, which process document contents within a request. These are the filters most commonly relevant to applications programming.

- Protocol filters, which deal with details of the protocol but treat the contents as opaque. These filters are concerned with translating between HTTP data (as defined in RFC2616) and Apache's internal representation in the `request_rec` and associated structures.

- Connection filters, which process a TCP connection without reference to HTTP (either the protocol or contents). These filters are concerned with interfacing Apache with the network; they operate entirely outside the scope of HTTP or of any `request_rec`.

Although these filters have very different functions, moving from an applications level in the inner layers to a system level farther out, the API is the same throughout. There is just one important difference: The inner filters, working on HTTP, have a valid `request_rec` object, whereas connection-level filters have none. All filters have a `conn_rec` for the TCP connection.

In more detail, the output chain comprises the following stages in an enumeration in `util_filter.h` (the input chain is an exact mirror image of this sequence, and uses the same definitions):

- **AP_FTYPE_RESOURCE** is for content filters. These filters are the first to see content as it is produced by the content generator, and they serve to examine, modify, or even completely rewrite it. This is the most common form of application filter, and encompasses markup processing (such as SSI or XML filtering), image processing, or content assembly/aggregation. Resource filters may completely change the nature of the contents. For example, an XSLT filter might change the contents from XML to HTML or PDF.

- **AP_FTYPE_CONTENT_SET** is a second stage of content filtering. It is intended for operations concerned with packaging the contents, such as `mod_deflate` (which applies gzip compression).

Filters of type RESOURCE or CONTENT_SET operate on an HTTP response entity—that is, the body contents being returned to the client. The HTTP headers don't pass through these filters. The headers can be accessed in exactly the same way as in a content generator, via the headers tables in the `request_rec`.

- **AP_FTYPE_PROTOCOL** is the third layer of filtering. The normal function here is to insert the HTTP headers ahead of the data emerging from the content filters. This is dealt with by a core filter HTTP_HEADER (function `ap_http_header_filter`), so applications can normally ignore it. Apache also handles HTTP byte ranges[1] using a protocol filter.

---

1. Appendix C; section 19.2.

- **AP_FTYPE_TRANSCODE** is for transport-level packaging. Apache implements HTTP chunking[2] (where applicable) at this level.

- **AP_FTYPE_CONNECTION** filters operate on connections, at the TCP level (HTTP requests no longer exist). Apache (mod_ssl) uses it for SSL encoding. Another application is throttling and bandwidth control.

- **AP_FTYPE_NETWORK**, the final layer, deals with the connection to the client itself. This layer is normally dealt with by Apache's CORE output filter (function ap_core_output_filter).

The examples presented in detail in this chapter are all content filters, of types AP_FTYPE_RESOURCE and AP_FTYPE_CONTENT_SET. The essential principles of writing a filter are no different for other filters, with a few exceptions.

Protocol

Protocol filters are responsible for converting the input data from a byte stream to an HTTP request, and the output data back again. The input protocol filter populates r->headers_in, while the output protocol filter converts r->headers_out to a byte stream.

Headers and Entities

Filters of types AP_FTYPE_RESOURCE and AP_FTYPE_CONTENT_SET only see an HTTP request or response entity (body). The request and response headers may be accessed through the r->headers_in and r->headers_out tables, respectively.

> CAUTION r->headers_out will be converted to a set of response headers the first time the output HTTP protocol filter is invoked. Any changes made later will have no effect!
>
> By contrast, filters *outside* the protocol layer will not have r->headers_in and headers_out, but just a stream of bytes or lines. In fact, they won't have a request_rec at all, just an undefined pointer in f->r.

---

2. Appendix C; section 3.4.

Metadata Buckets

Inner filters will rarely see metadata buckets (except for EOS) and can commonly ignore them, although technically, flush buckets should be flushed immediately, and ignoring them *may* make a filter unsuitable for streaming media. Outer filters should respect all metadata buckets.

8.3 Anatomy of a Filter

8.3.1 Callback Function

The heart of a filter module is a callback function. How it is called differs between input and output filters:

- The input filter chain runs whenever the handler requests data from the client. Apache will call the callback function to request (pull) a chunk of data from it. Our filter must, in turn, pull a chunk of data from the next filter in the chain, process it, and return the requested data to the caller.

- The output filter chain runs whenever the handler sends a chunk of data to the client. This may be triggered explicitly by the handler (with `ap_pass_brigade`), or implicitly when a handler using the `stdio`-like APIs has filled a default (8K) buffer. Our filter should process the data, and send (push) a chunk to the next filter in the chain.

Apart from the callback, there is an optional initialization function. Also, filter modules may independently use other parts of the Apache API where necessary.

8.3.2 Pipelining

The basic principle of pipelining is that we should not have to wait for one stage of processing to complete before starting on the next stage (Figure 8-2). In the context of a webserver, where I/O commonly takes far more time than processing a request, this is an important performance issue.

In the Apache 2.x filter architecture, we don't have just the three stages to processing data—every filter is itself a stage. Thus there is still more to be gained by pipelining. As far as possible, we want to run the filters in parallel. To run filters on

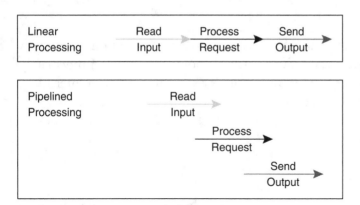

FIGURE 8-2
Linear versus pipelined processing

large documents without introducing scalability problems, we must avoid having to load an entire document into memory at once. Apache's filters, therefore, work on chunks of data rather than entire documents, and any general-purpose filter must deal with that behavior. Filters should always endeavor to cooperate with this pipelining. Ideally, a filter should always process a chunk of data and pass it on before the callback returns. Sometimes this is not possible, and a filter needs to buffer data over more than one call. For example, running an XSLT transform requires that the entire document be parsed into an in-memory structure, so an XSLT filter can't avoid breaking the pipeline.

Pipelining can be an important consideration when designing a module. If you are planning to use an external library, it's worth reviewing how well it will work with the pipeline. In the case of an input filter, that's usually straightforward: It can just pull in more data from the pipeline on demand. For an output filter, however, you need to look for an API that can accept arbitrary chunks of data. This author has written a number of XML- and HTML-parsing filters, and working with the Apache pipeline has a profound effect on the choice of a parser. Among markup processing libraries, `expat` and `libxml2` have parseChunk APIs and work well with Apache, but `Tidy`, `OpenSP`, and `Xerces-C` have no such APIs, and so cannot be used without breaking the pipeline.

8.4 The Filter API and Objects

As discussed in Section 8.3.2, the filter callback function differs between input and output filters. Let's deal with each case in turn.

8.4.1 Output Filters

The callback prototype for output filters is

```
apr_status_t my_output_filter_func(ap_filter_t* f,
                        apr_bucket_brigade* bb)
```

Here f is the filter object, and bb is a bucket brigade containing an arbitrary chunk (zero or more bytes) of data in APR buckets. The filter function should process the data in bb, and then pass the processed data to the next filter in the chain, f->next. We will see how to do this when we develop filter examples later in this chapter.

8.4.2 Input Filters

The input filter callback is a little more complex:

```
apr_status_t my_input_filter_func(
            ap_filter_t* f,
            apr_bucket_brigade* bb,
            ap_input_mode_t mode,
            apr_read_type_e block,
            apr_off_t readbytes
```

The first two arguments are the same as the output filter arguments, although the usage differs. This is a pull API, and our function is responsible for fetching a chunk of data from the next filter in the input chain, putting that data into the bucket brigade, and returning to the caller. Let's look at the other arguments.

mode is one of an enumeration:

```
typedef enum {
    /** The filter should return at most readbytes data. */
    AP_MODE_READBYTES,
    /** The filter should return at most one line of CRLF data.
     *  (If a potential line is too long or no CRLF is found, the
     *   filter may return partial data).
     */
    AP_MODE_GETLINE,
    /** The filter should implicitly eat any CRLF pairs that it sees. */
    AP_MODE_EATCRLF,
```

```
    /** The filter read should be treated as speculative and any returned
     *  data should be stored for later retrieval in another mode. */
    AP_MODE_SPECULATIVE,
    /** The filter read should be exhaustive and read until it cannot
     *  read any more.
     *  Use this mode with extreme caution.
     */
    AP_MODE_EXHAUSTIVE,
    /** The filter should initialize the connection if needed,
     *  NNTP or FTP over SSL for example.
     */
    AP_MODE_INIT
} ap_input_mode_t;
```

Clearly, not all of these modes are relevant to every filter. A filter that cannot support the mode it is called with is inappropriate, and may indicate a misconfiguration. It should normally remove itself from the filter chain and log a warning message for the administrator. A filter may often call the next filter using the same mode that it was called with, but this behavior is not always appropriate and a filter is free to do otherwise.

The `block` argument takes the value `APR_BLOCK_READ` or `APR_NONBLOCK_READ`. It determines whether the filter should block if data are not immediately available. Where set, `readbytes` is an indication of the (maximum) number of bytes the filter should return to its caller.

8.5 Filter Objects

The filter object (like others discussed in this chapter) is defined in `util_filter.h`.

```
/**
 * The representation of a filter chain. Each request has a list
 * of these structures, which are called in turn to filter the data.
 * Subrequests get an exact copy of the main request's filter chain.
 */
struct ap_filter_t {
    /** The internal representation of this filter.  This includes
     *  the filter's name, type, and the actual function pointer.
     */
    ap_filter_rec_t *frec;

    /** A place to store any data associated with the current filter */
    void *ctx;

    /** The next filter in the chain */
    ap_filter_t *next;
```

```
/** The request_rec associated with the current filter.  If a subrequest
 *  adds filters, then the subrequest is the request associated with the
 *  filter.
 */
request_rec *r;

/** The conn_rec associated with the current filter.  This is analogous
 *to the request_rec, except that it is used for connection filters.
 */
conn_rec *c;
};
```

The fields that most filter modules will use here are ctx, to store application data for the filter between calls, and request_rec, to access all the normal request data. (In the case of connection-level filters, there is no valid request_rec field, and the conn_rec serves a similar purpose.) The next field will be used to push data to the next filter in the output chain or to pull data from the next filter in the input chain.

The frec field can normally be treated as opaque by applications, but is necessary to our understanding of filter internals. Here it is:

```
/**
 * This structure is used for recording information about the
 * registered filters. It associates a name with the filter's callback
 * and filter type.
 *
 * At the moment, these are simply linked in a chain, so a ->next pointer
 * is available.
 *
 * It is used for any filter that can be inserted in the filter chain.
 * This may be either an httpd-2.0 filter or a mod_filter harness.
 * In the latter case, it contains provider and protocol information.
 * In the former case, the new fields (from providers) are ignored.
 */
struct ap_filter_rec_t {
    /** The registered name for this filter */
    const char *name;

    /** The function to call when this filter is invoked. */
    ap_filter_func filter_func;

    /** The function to call before the handlers are invoked. Notice
     * that this function is called only for filters participating in
     * the HTTP protocol. Filters for other protocols are to be
     * initialized by the protocols themselves.
     */
    ap_init_filter_func filter_init_func;
```

```
    /** The type of filter, either AP_FTYPE_CONTENT or AP_FTYPE_CONNECTION.
     * An AP_FTYPE_CONTENT filter modifies the data based on information
     * found in the content. An AP_FTYPE_CONNECTION filter modifies the
     * data based on the type of connection.
     */
    ap_filter_type ftype;

    /** The next filter_rec in the list */
    struct ap_filter_rec_t *next;

    /** Providers for this filter */
    ap_filter_provider_t *providers;

    /** Trace level for this filter */
    int debug;

    /** Protocol flags for this filter */
    unsigned int proto_flags;
};
```

The name is just an identifier for the filter configuration, which will be discussed
in Chapter 9. The filter_func is the main callback we've already introduced, and
the filter_init_func is a seldom-used initialization function that is called when
the filter is inserted and before the first data are available.

The final three fields were introduced with the smart filtering architecture in
Apache 2.2, as described in Section 8.7.

8.6 Filter I/O

Data passes through the filter chain on the bucket brigade. There are several strategies for dealing with the data in a filter:

- If the filter merely looks at the data but doesn't change anything, it can pass
  the brigade on as is.

- If the filter makes changes but preserve content length (e.g., a case filter for
  ASCII text), it can replace bytes in place.

- A filter that passes through most of the data intact but makes some changes
  can edit the data by direct bucket manipulation.

- A filter that completely transforms the data will often need to replace the
  data completely, by creating an entirely new brigade and populating it. It

can do so either directly or by using `stdio`-like functions. Two families of `stdio`-like functions are available: APR provides `apr_brigade_puts`/ `apr_brigade_write`/etc., while `util_filter` provides `ap_fwrite`/ `ap_fputs`/`ap_fprintf`/etc.

Management of I/O lies at the heart of filtering. It will be demonstrated at length when we develop example filters later in this chapter.

The key concepts in managing data are the *bucket* and the *brigade*. We have already encountered them in Chapter 3 and elsewhere. In this chapter, our examples will explore them in depth.

8.7 Smart Filtering in Apache 2.2

The original Apache 2.0 filter architecture presents problems when used with unknown content—whether in a proxy or with a local handler that generates different content types to order. The basic difficulty derives from the Apache configuration. Content filters need to be applied conditionally. For example, we don't want to pass images through an HTML filter. Apache 2.0 provides four generic configuration directives for filters:

- **SetOutputFilter**: Unconditionally insert a filter.

- **AddOutputFilter, RemoveOutputFilter**: Insert or remove a filter based on "extension."

- **AddOutputFilterByType**: Insert a filter based on content type. This directive is implemented in the `ap_set_content_type` function, and has complex side effects.

In the case of a proxy, extensions are meaningless, as we cannot know what conventions an origin server might adopt. Likewise, when the server generates content dynamically—or filters it dynamically with, for example, XSLT—it can be difficult or even impossible to configure the filter chain using the preceding directives. Instead, we have to resort to the unsatisfactory hack of inserting a filter unconditionally, checking the response headers from the proxy, and then having the filter remove itself where appropriate. Examples of filters that follow this approach include `mod_deflate`, `mod_xmlns`, `mod_accessibility`, and `mod_proxy_html`.

8.7.1 Preprocessing and Postprocessing

As with an origin server, it may be necessary to preprocess data before the data go through the main content-transforming filter and/or to postprocess the data afterward. For example, when dealing with gzipped content, we need to uncompress it for processing and then recompress the processed data. Similarly, in an image-processing filter, we need to decode the original image format and re-encode the processed data.

This may involve more than one phase. For example, when filtering text, we may need both to uncompress gzipped data and to transcode the character set before the main filter.

Potentially, then, we have a large multiplicity of filters: transformation filters, together with preprocessing and postprocessing for different content types and encodings (see Figures 8-3 and 8-4). To repeat the hack of each filter being inserted and determining whether to run or remove itself in such a setup goes beyond simple inelegance and into the absurd. An alternative architecture is required.

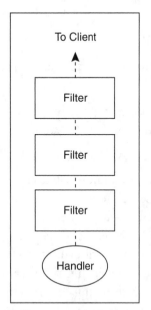

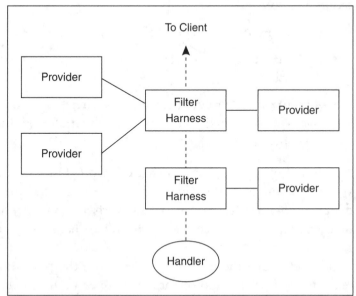

FIGURE 8-3
Apache 2.0 filter chain

FIGURE 8-4
Apache 2.2 smart filtering

8.7.2 mod_filter

The solution to this problem is implemented in Apache 2.2 in mod_filter. This module works by introducing indirection into the filter chain. Instead of inserting filters in the chain, we insert a filter harness, which in turn dispatches conditionally to a filter provider. Any content filter may be used as a provider to mod_filter; no change to existing filter modules is required (although it may be possible to simplify them). There can be multiple providers for one filter, but no more than one provider will run for any single request.

A filter chain comprises any number of instances of the filter harness, each of which may have any number of providers. A special case is that of a single provider with unconditional dispatch—this is equivalent to inserting the provider filter directly into the chain.

mod_filter is implemented only for output filters: The configuration problems it deals with are not relevant to the input chain. And although it can be applied anywhere in the output filter chain, it is really relevant only to content (application) filters. Neither the old nor the new filter configuration directives are generally used for the outer filters. For example, SSL (both input and output) is activated by mod_ssl's own configuration directives instead.

8.7.3 Filter Self-configuration

In addition to using the standard filter configuration provided by the core and mod_filter, a filter may be self-configuring.

The insert_filter Hook

A hook for inserting filters is provided in the content-handling phase of request processing, immediately before the content generator. mod_filter uses this hook to insert the filter harness for dynamically configured filters, but the same hook may also be used by other modules. Here is mod_filter's hook, which inserts all entries in the filter chain (as configured by the FilterChain directive) in order:

```
static void filter_insert(request_rec *r)
{
    mod_filter_chain *p;
    ap_filter_rec_t *filter;
    mod_filter_cfg *cfg = ap_get_module_config(r->per_dir_config,
                                               &filter_module);
```

```
        int ranges = 1;
        mod_filter_ctx *ctx = apr_pcalloc(r->pool, sizeof(mod_filter_ctx));
        ap_set_module_config(r->request_config, &filter_module, ctx);

        for (p = cfg->chain; p; p = p->next) {
            filter = apr_hash_get(cfg->live_filters,
                        p->fname, APR_HASH_KEY_STRING);
            ap_add_output_filter_handle(filter, NULL, r, r->connection);

            if (ranges && (filter->proto_flags
                        & (AP_FILTER_PROTO_NO_BYTERANGE
                            | AP_FILTER_PROTO_CHANGE_LENGTH))) {
                ctx->range = apr_table_get(r->headers_in, "Range");
                apr_table_unset(r->headers_in, "Range");
                ranges = 0;
            }
        }
        return;
}
```

It is hooked in as follows:

```
static void filter_hooks(apr_pool_t *pool)
{
    ap_hook_insert_filter(filter_insert, NULL, NULL, APR_HOOK_MIDDLE);
}
```

When other modules may use this hook, they should consider carefully where their filter should be inserted into the chain. They can explicitly run their `filter_insert` before or after `mod_filter`, to determine their position in the chain.

Configuration Using Environment Variables and Notes

Another strategy available to filters is to examine the request details themselves to determine whether to run or uninsert themselves. This approach was widely used in Apache 2.0 before `mod_filter` became available, and it may still be required when the configuration is more complex than can be delegated to `mod_filter`.

An example is the compression filter in `mod_deflate`. Since it is older than `mod_filter`, this module provides explicitly for control by environment variables (which could be set either in `httpd.conf` with `SetEnv` or similar or by another module). However, `mod_deflate` also provides some more complex logic that is better handled internally than in `httpd.conf`. Relevant code from `mod_deflate.c` is provided here:

```
    /* Only work on main request/no subrequests */
    if (!ap_is_initial_req(r)) {
        ap_remove_output_filter(f);
        return ap_pass_brigade(f->next, bb);
    }

    /* Some browsers might have problems, so set no-gzip
     * (with browsermatch) for them
     */
    if (apr_table_get(r->subprocess_env, "no-gzip")) {
        ap_remove_output_filter(f);
        return ap_pass_brigade(f->next, bb);
    }
    /* Let's see what our current Content-Encoding is.
     * If it's already encoded, don't compress again.
     * (We could, but let's not.)
     */
    encoding = apr_table_get(r->headers_out, "Content-Encoding");
    /* CHOPPED for brevity */
    /* Even if we don't accept this request based on it not having
     * the Accept-Encoding, we need to note that we were looking
     * for this header and downstream proxies should be aware of
     * that.
     */
    apr_table_mergen(r->headers_out, "Vary", "Accept-Encoding");

    /* force-gzip will just force it out regardless of whether the browser
     * can actually do anything with it.
     */
    if (!apr_table_get(r->subprocess_env, "force-gzip")) {
        /* DELETED FOR BREVITY
         * Remove the filter if the browser doesn't accept gzip */
    }
    /* For a 304 or 204 response there is no entity included in
     * the response and hence nothing to deflate. */
    if (r->status == HTTP_NOT_MODIFIED
        || r->status == HTTP_NO_CONTENT) {
        ap_remove_output_filter(f);
        return ap_pass_brigade(f->next, bb);
    }
    /* if we pass all those checks, we will compress it */
```

8.7.4 Protocol Handling

In Apache 2.0, each filter is responsible for ensuring that whatever changes it makes are correctly represented in the HTTP response headers, and that it does not run when it would make an illegal change. This requirement imposes a burden on filter authors to reimplement some common functionality in every filter. For example:

- Many filters will change the content, invalidating existing content tags, check-sums, hashes, and lengths.

- Filters that require an entire, unbroken response in input need to ensure that they don't get byte ranges from a back end.

- Filters that transform output in a proxy need to ensure that they don't violate a `Cache-Control: no-transform` header from the back end.

- Filters may make responses uncacheable.

`mod_filter` aims to offer generic handling of these details of filter implementation, reducing the complexity required of content filter modules. At the same time, `mod_filter` should not interfere with a filter that wants to handle all aspects of the protocol. By default (i.e., in the absence of any explicit instructions), `mod_filter` will leave the headers untouched.

Thus you as a filter developer have two options. If you handle all protocol considerations within your filter, then it will work with any Apache 2.x. However, if you are not concerned with backward compatibility, you can dispense with this approach and leave protocol handling to `mod_filter`. If you take advantage of this opportunity, please note that (at the time of this book's writing) `mod_filter`'s protocol handling is considered experimental: You should be prepared to verify that it works correctly with your module.

The API for filter protocol handling is simple. The protocol is defined in a bit field (unsigned int), which is passed as an argument when the filter is registered (in function `ap_register_output_filter_protocol`) or later in function `ap_filter_protocol`.

The following bit fields are currently supported:

- **`AP_FILTER_PROTO_CHANGE`**: filter changes the contents (thereby invalidating content-based metadata such as checksums)

- **`AP_FILTER_PROTO_CHANGE_LENGTH`**: filter changes the length of the contents

- **`AP_FILTER_PROTO_NO_BYTERANGE`**: filter requires complete input and cannot work on byte ranges

- **AP_FILTER_PROTO_NO_PROXY:** filter cannot run in a proxy (e.g., it makes changes that would violate mandatory HTTP requirements in a proxy)

- **AP_FILTER_PROTO_NO_CACHE:** filter output is non-cacheable, even if the input was cacheable

- **AP_FILTER_PROTO_TRANSFORM:** filter is incompatible with `Cache-Control: no-transform`

8.8 Example: Filtering Text by Direct Manipulation of Buckets

Our first example is a simple filter that manipulates buckets directly. It passes data straight through, but transforms it by manipulating pointers.

The purpose of this module is to display plain text files as HTML, prettified and having a site header and footer. So what the module has to do is this:

- Add a header at the top

- Add a footer at the bottom

- Escape the text as required by HTML

The header and footer are files specified by the system administrator who is responsible for the site.

8.8.1 Bucket Functions

First we introduce two functions to deal with the data insertions: one for the files and one for the simple entity replacements.

Creating a file bucket requires an open file handle and a byte range within the file. Since we're transmitting the entire file, we just `stat` its size to set the byte range. We open the file with a shared lock and with sendfile enabled for maximum performance.

```
static apr_bucket* txt_file_bucket(request_rec* r, const char* fname) {
  apr_file_t* file = NULL ;
  apr_finfo_t finfo ;
  if ( apr_stat(&finfo, fname, APR_FINFO_SIZE, r->pool)
       != APR_SUCCESS ) {
    return NULL ;
  }
```

```
  if ( apr_file_open(&file, fname,
        APR_READ|APR_SHARELOCK|APR_SENDFILE_ENABLED,
          APR_OS_DEFAULT, r->pool ) != APR_SUCCESS ) {
    return NULL ;
  }
  if (file == NULL) {
    return NULL ;
  }
  return apr_bucket_file_create(file, 0, finfo.size, r->pool,
        r->connection->bucket_alloc) ;
}
```

Creating the simple text replacements, we can just make a bucket of a string. By making the strings static, we avoid having to worry about their lifetime.

```
static apr_bucket* txt_esc(char c, apr_bucket_alloc_t* alloc) {
  static const char* lt = "&lt;" ;
  static const char* gt = "&gt;" ;
  static const char* amp = "&amp;" ;
  static const char* quot = "&quot;" ;
  switch (c) {
    case '<': return apr_bucket_immortal_create(lt, 4, alloc) ;
    case '>': return apr_bucket_immortal_create(gt, 4, alloc) ;
    case '&': return apr_bucket_immortal_create(amp, 5, alloc) ;
    case '"': return apr_bucket_immortal_create(quot, 6, alloc) ;
    default: return NULL ;        /* shut compilers up */
  }
}
```

8.8.2 The Filter

The main filter itself is largely straightforward, albeit with a number of interesting and unexpected points to consider. Since this function is a little longer than the utility functions given earlier, we'll comment it inline instead.

The txt_cfg struct used here is the module's configuration; it contains just the filenames for the header and footer. Given that this may be used concurrently by many threads, we access it on a read-only basis and use a second, private, txt_ctxt object to maintain our own state.

```
typedef struct txt_cfg {
  const char* head ;
  const char* foot ;
} txt_cfg ;
typedef struct txt_ctxt {
  int state ;
  const char* head ;
  const char* foot ;
} txt_ctxt ;
```

```
static int txt_filter(ap_filter_t* f, apr_bucket_brigade* bb) {
  apr_bucket* b ;
  txt_ctxt* ctxt = f->ctx ;
```

The filter context `f->ctx` is used to hold module variables over multiple calls to a filter. It is common practice to initialize it on the first call to the filter function, which is detected by checking for a NULL value (which our function then sets, as in this example). We could also initialize `f->ctx` in a filter initialization function, but that's rare in real filters.

```
if ( ctxt == NULL ) {
  txt_cfg* cfg = ap_get_module_config(f->r->per_dir_config,
                       &txt_module);
  ctxt = f->ctx = apr_pcalloc(f->r->pool, sizeof(txt_ctxt)) ;
  ctxt->head = cfg->head ;
  ctxt->foot = cfg->foot ;
}
```

The main loop here iterates over the incoming data in a manner common among filter functions:

```
for ( b = APR_BRIGADE_FIRST(bb);
      b != APR_BRIGADE_SENTINEL(bb);
      b = APR_BUCKET_NEXT(b) ) {

  const char* buf ;
  size_t bytes ;
```

As in any filter, we need to check for EOS. When we encounter it, we insert the footer in front of it. We shouldn't get more than one EOS, but just in case we do we'll note having inserted the footer. That means we're being error-tolerant.

```
if ( APR_BUCKET_IS_EOS(b) ) {
  /* End of input file - insert footer if any */
  if ( ctxt->foot && ! (ctxt->state & TXT_FOOT ) ) {
    ctxt->state |= TXT_FOOT ;
    APR_BUCKET_INSERT_BEFORE(b, txt_file_bucket(f->r, ctxt->foot));
  }
```

We can ignore other metadata buckets. If we get a flush bucket, it should be the last in our brigade, so we'll automatically exit the loop and pass it down the chain, thereby handling it correctly. If it's not the last bucket, then any damage we could have done by ignoring it has already been done by whatever sent us the brigade.

```
} else if ( APR_BUCKET_IS_METADATA(b) ) {
  /* Ignore it, but don't try to read data from it */
}
```

The main case is a bucket containing data. We can get it as a simple buffer, whose size is specified in bytes:

```
    } else if ( apr_bucket_read(b, &buf, &bytes, APR_BLOCK_READ)
        == APR_SUCCESS ) {
    /* We have a bucket full of text.  Just escape it
     * where necessary.
     */
    size_t count = 0 ;
    const char* p = buf ;
```

Now we can search for characters that need replacing, and replace them:

```
    while ( count < bytes ) {
        size_t sz = strcspn(p, "<>&\"") ;
        count += sz ;
```

Here comes the tricky bit—replacing a single character inline:

```
        if ( count < bytes ) {

        /* Split off buffer at the character */
          apr_bucket_split(b, sz) ;

        /* Skip over the before-buffer (where nothing changes) */
          b = APR_BUCKET_NEXT(b) ;

        /* insert the replacement for the character */
          APR_BUCKET_INSERT_BEFORE(b, txt_esc(p[sz],
                f->r->connection->bucket_alloc)) ;

        /* Split off the char we just replaced */
          apr_bucket_split(b, 1) ;

        /* ... and remove it */
          APR_BUCKET_REMOVE(b) ;

        /* Move cursor on to what remains, so it stays
         * in sequence with the main loop.
         */
          b = APR_BUCKET_NEXT(b) ;
        /* Finally, increment our counters */
          count += 1 ;
          p += sz + 1 ;
        }
      }
    }
  }
```

Now we insert the header if it hasn't already been inserted.

Be aware of the following points:

1. This insertion has to come after the main loop, to avoid the header itself getting parsed and HTML-escaped.

2. This approach works because we can insert a bucket anywhere in the brigade. In this case, we put it at the head.

3. As with the footer, we save the state to avoid inserting the header more than once.

```
if ( ctxt->head && ! (ctxt->state & TXT_HEAD ) ) {
  ctxt->state |= TXT_HEAD ;
  APR_BRIGADE_INSERT_HEAD(bb, txt_file_bucket(f->r, ctxt->head));
}
```

Note that we created a new bucket every time we replaced a character. Couldn't we have prepared four buckets in advance—one for each of the characters to be escaped—and then reused those buckets whenever we encounter the character?

The problem here is that each bucket is linked to its neighbors. Thus, if we reuse the same bucket, we lose the links, so that the brigade now jumps over any data between the two instances of it. Hence we do need a new bucket every time, which means this technique becomes inefficient when a high proportion of input data has to be changed.

Now we've finished manipulating data, we just pass it down the filter chain:

```
  return ap_pass_brigade(f->next, bb) ;
}
```

mod_txt was written one idle afternoon, after someone had asked on IRC whether such a module existed. It seemed such an obvious thing to do, and it is a great example to use here. Working with buckets and brigades is one of the most challenging parts of the Apache API, and it needs such a simple demonstrator module!

8.9 Complex Parsing

The parsing in the filter we just looked at is essentially trivial, in that each byte is treated as independent of its neighbors. A more complex task is to parse data where a pattern we want to match may span more than one bucket, or even more than one call to the filter function. Even a simple search-and-replace filter that matches words will need to save some context between calls, so as to avoid missing words that are split up. As an aside, this is a nontrivial task in general: Witness the number of spam messages that get past spam filters by breaking up words that might otherwise trigger their detection.

The simplest way to deal with this task is to collect the entire document body into memory. Unfortunately, this strategy is inefficient: It breaks Apache's pipelining architecture, and it scales very badly as document size grows. We should avoid it wherever possible.

A module that faces exactly this task is mod_line_edit,[3] a filter that provides text search-and-replace based on string or regular expression matching. This module works by rearranging its input into complete lines of text before editing it (the definition of a "line" is somewhat flexible, but it defaults to parsing normal lines of text). Let's look at this module for an example of more advanced bucket manipulation. For the purposes of this discussion, we'll present a simplified version that supports only the UNIX-family "\n" line-end character. The guiding principle of this filter is that it manipulates buckets and brigades at will (pointers are cheap), but moves or copies data only where unavoidable. This demonstrates some new techniques:

- Creating new bucket brigades for our own purposes
- Saving data between calls to the filter
- Flattening data into a contiguous buffer

Using this approach, we will need to rearrange any lines spanning more than one bucket, and save any partial lines between calls to the filter.

```
/* Filter to ensure we have no mid-line breaks that might be in the
 * middle of a search string causing us to miss it! At the same
 * time, we split into lines to avoid pattern matching over big
 * chunks of memory.
 */

/* We're parsing into lines, so let's have a brigade to put them in */
apr_bucket_brigade* bbline
    = apr_brigade_create(f->r->pool, f->c->bucket_alloc) ;
```

---

3. http://apache.webthing.com/mod_line_edit/

```
/* We're saving any incomplete lines for the next call, so we
 * store them on the filter context f->ctx.
 * We use a brigade ctx->bbsave so we don't have to touch the data.
 */
line_edit_ctx* ctx = f->ctx ;
if (ctx == NULL) {
  ctx = f->ctx = apr_palloc(f->r->pool, sizeof(line_edit_ctx)) ;
  ctx->bbsave = apr_brigade_create(f->r->pool, f->c->bucket_alloc) ;
}

/* Now the main loop over the input data */
b = APR_BRIGADE_FIRST(bb) ;

/* The end-of-loop condition is the same as last time */
while ( b != APR_BRIGADE_SENTINEL(bb) ) {
  if ( !APR_BUCKET_IS_METADATA(b) ) {
    if ( apr_bucket_read(b, &buf, &bytes, APR_BLOCK_READ)
      == APR_SUCCESS ) {
      while ( bytes > 0 ) {   /* parse loop */

      /* See if there's a line end in the bucket (simplified)! */
      le = memchr(buf, '\n', bytes) ;
        if (le != NULL) {

          /* There is a line end.  Extract what's before it. */
          offs = ((unsigned int)le-(unsigned int)buf)/sizeof(char)+1;
          apr_bucket_split(b, offs) ;

          /* Increment pointers for when we iterate the parse loop */
          bytes -= offs ;
          buf += offs ;
          b1 = APR_BUCKET_NEXT(b) ;

      /* Remove the line-ended bucket */
          APR_BUCKET_REMOVE(b);

          /* Is there any previous unterminated content? */
          if ( !APR_BRIGADE_EMPTY(ctx->bbsave) ) {

            /* Append this to any content waiting for a line end */
            APR_BRIGADE_INSERT_TAIL(ctx->bbsave, b) ;

        /* Assemble a complete line from the bits */
            rv = apr_brigade_pflatten(ctx->bbsave, &fbuf,
                &fbytes, f->r->pool) ;

            /* Make b a new bucket of the flattened stuff */
            b = apr_bucket_pool_create(fbuf, fbytes, f->r->pool,
                    f->r->connection->bucket_alloc) ;
```

```
                /* bbsave has been consumed, so clear it */
                apr_brigade_cleanup(ctx->bbsave) ;
            }

            /* b now contains exactly one line */
            /* Insert it into the lines brigade, and move the pointer */
            APR_BRIGADE_INSERT_TAIL(bbline, b);
            b = b1 ;

        } else {
            /* No line end found.  Remember the dangling content. */
            APR_BUCKET_REMOVE(b);
            APR_BRIGADE_INSERT_TAIL(ctx->bbsave, b);
            bytes = 0 ;
        }
    } /* Parse loop: while bytes > 0 */
  } else {
    /* Bucket read failed -- oops!  Let's remove it. */
    APR_BUCKET_REMOVE(b);
  }

/* This else means it's a metadata bucket.  The only metadata
 * we care about is EOS.
 */
} else if ( APR_BUCKET_IS_EOS(b) ) {
  /* If there's data to pass, send it in one bucket */
  if ( !APR_BRIGADE_EMPTY(ctx->bbsave) ) {
    rv = apr_brigade_pflatten(ctx->bbsave, &fbuf,
        &fbytes, f->r->pool) ;
    b1 = apr_bucket_pool_create(fbuf, fbytes, f->r->pool,
          f->r->connection->bucket_alloc) ;
    APR_BRIGADE_INSERT_TAIL(bbline, b1);
  }
  apr_brigade_cleanup(ctx->bbsave) ;
  /* Start again rather than segfault if a buggy
   * filter in front of us sent a bogus EOS
   */
  f->ctx = NULL ;

  /* Move the EOS to the new brigade */
  APR_BUCKET_REMOVE(b);
  APR_BRIGADE_INSERT_TAIL(bbline, b);
} else {  /* neither data nor EOS */
  /* Chop flush or unknown metadata bucket types */
  apr_bucket_delete(b);
}
/* Reset pointer to what's left (since we're not in a for loop) */
b = APR_BRIGADE_FIRST(bb) ;
}
```

```
/* Now we have a bunch of complete lines in bbline.
 * If we saw an EOS, we also have that
 * and a possibly unterminated last line.
 */

/* We can either process them here, or pass them to another filter
 * that requires its input to be in complete lines.
 */

/* Now pass it down the chain */
rv = ap_pass_brigade(f->next, bbline) ;

/* If we have leftover data, don't risk it going out of scope */
for ( b = APR_BRIGADE_FIRST(ctx->bbsave) ;
        b != APR_BRIGADE_SENTINEL(ctx->bbsave) ;
        b = APR_BUCKET_NEXT(b)) {
   apr_bucket_setaside(b, f->r->pool) ;
}

 return rv ;
}
```

8.10 Filtering Through an Existing Parser

An alternative to parsing data ourselves is to feed it to an existing parser, typically from a third-party library. This author's various markup-aware modules, including his most popular module, mod_proxy_html, work like this: The filter just reads each bucket and passes it to the library. This scheme works well because the library itself supports processing data in arbitrary chunks, so we don't have to worry about troublesome breaks in the input data disrupting the parse. Here's an example from mod_xmlns, which uses the expat library to parse XML. The core filter here is very simple, so we'll give it in full:

```
static int xmlns_filter(ap_filter_t* f, apr_bucket_brigade* bb) {
  apr_bucket* b ;
  const char* buf = 0 ;
  apr_size_t bytes = 0 ;

  xmlns_ctx* ctxt = (xmlns_ctx*)f->ctx ;
  if ( ! ctxt ) {
    xmlns_filter_init(f) ;
  }
  if ( ctxt = (xmlns_ctx*)f->ctx , ! ctxt )
    return ap_pass_brigade(f->next, bb) ;
```

```
for ( b = APR_BRIGADE_FIRST(bb) ;
      b != APR_BRIGADE_SENTINEL(bb) ;
      b = APR_BUCKET_NEXT(b) ) {
  if ( APR_BUCKET_IS_EOS(b) ) {
    if ( XML_Parse(ctxt->parser, buf, 0, 1) != XML_STATUS_OK ) {
      enum XML_Error err = XML_GetErrorCode(ctxt->parser) ;
      const XML_LChar* msg = XML_ErrorString(err) ;
      ap_log_rerror(APLOG_MARK, APLOG_ERR, 0, f->r,
        "Endparse Error %d: %s", err, msg) ;
    }
    APR_BRIGADE_INSERT_TAIL(ctxt->public->bb,
    apr_bucket_eos_create(ctxt->public->bb->bucket_alloc) ) ;
    ap_pass_brigade(ctxt->public->f->next, ctxt->public->bb) ;
  } else if ( APR_BUCKET_IS_FLUSH(b) ) {
    APR_BRIGADE_INSERT_TAIL(ctxt->public->bb,
      apr_bucket_flush_create(ctxt->public->bb->bucket_alloc) ) ;
  } else if ( apr_bucket_read(b, &buf, &bytes, APR_BLOCK_READ)
          == APR_SUCCESS ) {
    if ( XML_Parse(ctxt->parser, buf, bytes, 0) != XML_STATUS_OK ) {
      enum XML_Error err = XML_GetErrorCode(ctxt->parser) ;
      const XML_LChar* msg = XML_ErrorString(err) ;
      ap_log_rerror(APLOG_MARK, APLOG_ERR, 0, f->r,
        "Parse Error %d: %s", err, msg) ;
    }
  } else {
    ap_log_rerror(APLOG_MARK, APLOG_ERR, 0, f->r,
        "Error in bucket read") ;
  }
}
return APR_SUCCESS ;
}
```

This code takes the form of the now-familiar loop over input buckets, retrieving the bucket data (where applicable) into a buffer, and making a special case of EOS. But instead of parsing the data ourselves, we feed it to expat's chunk-parsing function XML_Parse. And we don't pass anything at all to the next brigade! So how does that work?

When we use the XML parser here, we basically lose the input data altogether. Our module must set up handlers with the library, but these receive XML events such as startElement, endElement, characters, cdata, and comment, rather than our input data. The filter has no option except to generate a new output stream from scratch. Of course, the expat library has no notion of Apache concepts such as buckets, brigades, requests, or filters, so whatever we do has to be done from scratch.

In this case, we could create a new bucket brigade and populate it with new buckets for each XML event.[4] But this is not an attractive option, for several reasons:

- Most markup events—for example, elements and attributes—involve generating just a few bytes of output per event. Creating new buckets for every few bytes becomes inefficient.

- We have no natural point at which to pass a brigade to the next filter. Either we have to break streaming or we have to do extra work to manage this ourselves.

- Creating buckets is an unduly awkward way to perform simple I/O.

This final reason alone could be considered compelling!

8.11 stdio-Like Filter I/O

Fortunately, the filter API provides an alternative, `stdio`-like way to write data and pass it down the chain. We still need to create a bucket brigade for output, but all we need to do with it is to pass it to the `stdio`-like calls, along with the filter we're writing to, in the manner of a file descriptor. The `stdio`-like functions are defined in `util_filter.h`:

```
ap_fflush(f, bb)
ap_fwrite(f, bb, buf, nbytes)
ap_fputs(f, bb, str)
ap_fputc(f, bb, c)
ap_fputstrs(f, bb, ...)      /* a NULL-terminated list of strings */
ap_fprintf(f, bb, fmt, ...)
```

Internally, the first time you use any of these calls, Apache creates a heap bucket (normally of size 8K) and writes your data to it. Subsequent writes append to the heap while sufficient space is available. When the heap space is exhausted, a second bucket of type transient is appended containing the data over and above the size of the heap bucket, and the two are flushed down the chain. This approach is the same as that followed by the `ap_rwrite`/etc. `stdio`-like API, and is the reason for the 8K default stream buffer size seen by many applications.

---

4. Since this passage was written, a module `mod_expat` has been developed that makes buckets of SAX events. But that module takes a different approach: The buckets are passed down the chain for another filter to interpret. `mod_expat` can be found at `http://www.heute-morgen.de/modules/mod_expat/`.

How does `mod_xmlns` use `stdio`-like I/O? Because it's a SAX2 filter, it has to generate all output from the SAX2 event callbacks. Let's look at the essentials of some of these callbacks. Our examples use two `#define` statements, which define the next filter in the chain and our output bucket brigade, respectively:

```
#define F ((xmlns_ctx*)ctx)->public->f->next
#define BB ((xmlns_ctx*)ctx)->public->bb
```

The simplest callback is the `default` callback—an `expat` callback that gets any data not passed to any other callback. Since we're registering callbacks for everything we need to process, anything passed to the default callback goes straight to the output:

```
static void xdefault(void* ctx, const XML_Char* buf, int len) {
  ap_fwrite(F, BB, buf, len) ;
}
```

The most complex handler is that for the `startElement` event. We'll quote it in full to show use of the API to simplify a lot of small, fiddly writes:

```
static void xstartElement(void* ctx, const XML_Char* name,
                          const XML_Char** atts) {
  parsedname name3 ;                    /* namespace, prefix, name */
  xmlns_active* ns ;

  xmlns_parsename(name, &name3) ;  /* parse the name expat gave us */
```

The next section is the heart of the module. `mod_xmlns` exports an API for other modules to register handlers for namespace events, of which the most important is `startElement`. So `lookup_ns` will return a non-null value if and only if another module has registered a handler for the namespace and it is marked as active.

```
  /* If a handler for this namespace is active, we dispatch to it */
  ns = lookup_ns((xmlns_ctx*)ctx, &name3) ;
  if ( ns && ns->handler->StartElement ) {
    if ( ns->handler->StartElement((xmlns_public*)CTX->public, &name3,
        (const xmlns_attr_t*)atts) != DECLINED )
      return ;
  }
```

The remainder of this function is just default behavior that reconstructs the element as is when no handler has handled it. It serves to demonstrate filter `stdio`-style output.

```
  /* Default: either no handler or it returned 0 to ask us to
   * produce default output
   */
  ap_fputc(F, BB, '<') ;
  if ( name3.nparts == 3 ) {  /* it's prefix:element */
```

```
      ap_fwrite(F, BB, name3.prefix, name3.prefixlen) ;
      ap_fputc(F, BB, ':') ;
    }
    ap_fwrite(F, BB, name3.elt, name3.eltlen) ;

    /* If there are any xmlns:foo="url" decls here, print them */
    if ( ns && ns->newns ) {
      if ( name3.nparts == 3 ) {
        ap_fputs(F, BB, " xmlns:") ;
        ap_fwrite(F, BB, name3.prefix, name3.prefixlen) ;
        ap_fputs(F, BB, "=\"") ;
        ap_fwrite(F, BB, name3.ns, name3.nslen) ;
        ap_fputc(F, BB, '"') ;
      } else if ( name3.nparts == 2 ) {
        ap_fputs(F, BB, " xmlns=\"") ;
        ap_fwrite(F, BB, name3.ns, name3.nslen) ;
        ap_fputc(F, BB, '"') ;
      }
      ns->newns = 0 ;
    }

    /* Now output any attributes */
    if ( atts ) {
      const XML_Char** a ;
      for ( a = atts ; *a ; a += 2 ) {
        parsedname a3 ;
        xmlns_parsename(*a, &a3) ;
        switch ( a3.nparts ) {
          case 1:    /* simple name="value" */
            ap_fputstrs(F, BB, " ", a[0], "=\"", a[1], "\"", NULL) ;
            break ;
          case 2:    /* namespace-uri:name="value" */
            ap_fputc(F, BB, ' ') ;
            ap_fwrite(F, BB, a3.ns, a3.nslen) ;
            ap_fputc(F, BB, ':') ;
            ap_fwrite(F, BB, a3.elt, a3.eltlen) ;
            ap_fputstrs(F, BB, "=\"", a[1], "\"", NULL) ;
            break ;
          case 3:    /* prefix:name="value" */
            ap_fputc(F, BB, ' ') ;
            ap_fwrite(F, BB, a3.prefix, a3.prefixlen) ;
            ap_fputc(F, BB, ':') ;
            ap_fwrite(F, BB, a3.elt, a3.eltlen) ;
            ap_fputstrs(F, BB, "=\"", a[1], "\"", NULL) ;
            break ;
        }
      }
    }
    ap_fputc(F, BB, '>') ;
}
```

The advantage that this API offers here is clear. We have lots of writes of just a few bytes, so direct manipulation of buckets would be insanely complex to write, not to mention inefficient. Classic buffered I/O is the ideal solution. And we lose nothing, because there simply isn't an input stream we could pass through without copying data.

Warning

Mixing `stdio`-like I/O with direct bucket manipulation in the same filter is not advisable. The buffering in the `stdio`-like API will cause the data to reach the next filter in an unexpected order, and it could cause data to be flushed at the wrong time. You would have to take great care to flush everything explicitly before switching modes, and you effectively get the worst of both worlds. Hence, although the function `xdefault` could explicitly create a new bucket (of type transient) to contain its data, it doesn't.

8.12 Input Filters and the Pull API

The input filter API differs from the output filter API we discussed earlier in several ways. As with the output filter, the heart of the input filter is a callback function, but the role of this function is different. Whereas the output filter accepts a chunk of data, processes it, and passes it to the next filter, the input filter requests data from the next filter in the chain, processes the data, and returns it to the caller. The basic form of an input filter can be demonstrated with a trivial, do-nothing filter:

```
int do_nothing_input_filter(ap_filter_t *f, apr_bucket_brigade *bb,
        ap_input_mode_t mode, apr_read_type_e block,
        apr_off_t readbytes) {
    int rv;
    rv = ap_get_brigade(f->next, bb, mode, block, readbytes);
    return rv;
}
```

We've already introduced the filter arguments. The first two are the same as for an output filter. The others will often be irrelevant to any particular filter, but are handled by Apache's core input filter and may be of use elsewhere.

8.12.1 Mode

`ap_input_mode_t mode`

Most filters will not want to support all input modes. For example, `mod_deflate`'s input filter, which serves to uncompress input that arrives compressed at the server, is entirely inappropriate to line-mode data. The correct behavior for an input filter called in an inappropriate mode is either to pass the data straight through or to remove itself from the chain:

```
/* Just get out of the way of things we don't want. */
if (mode != AP_MODE_READBYTES) {
    return ap_get_brigade(f->next, bb, mode, block, readbytes);
}
```

As a rule of thumb, a content filter will normally be called with `AP_MODE_READ-BYTES`. A connection filter will be called with `AP_MODE_GETLINE` until the HTTP headers are consumed by the protocol handler, and `AP_MODE_READBYTES` thereafter. But this behavior may vary, and cannot be relied on: Another filter or (more commonly) a content generator may use a different mode—hence the simple check in `mod_deflate`. MPMs may also use different input modes.

A module that supports multiple modes and modifies the data will typically need to use a switch statement or similar construct.

8.12.2 Block

`apr_read_type_e block`

Blocking versus nonblocking reads are only relevant to bucket types such as sockets where blocking is an issue. A filter should normally honor the block request and use the same value to retrieve data from the next filter. With due caution, however, it may override the request.

8.12.3 readbytes

`apr_off_t readbytes`

This is relevant to mode `AP_MODE_READBYTES`. A filter should not return more data than `readbytes`. In practice, it is sometimes treated as advisory: It is honored by the core input filter, but content filters sometimes ignore it. It may serve to optimize throughput of data by selecting a block size such as the widely used 8K default.

A filter to which `readbytes` may be highly relevant is `mod_deflate`, where the output data returned to the caller will often be many times greater than the input data from the next filter. `mod_deflate` deals with this issue by keeping a bucket brigade `proc_bb` in its filter context, and using the following logic:

```
/* All the 'main business' of this filter happens only
 * if ctx->proc_bb was empty on entry
 */
if (APR_BRIGADE_EMPTY(ctx->proc_bb)) {

    rv = ap_get_brigade(f->next, ctx->bb, mode, block, readbytes);

    /* Now inflate the data we just read into ctx->bb,
     * and put the inflated data into ctx->proc_bb
     */
}

/* At the end of the filter function, we partition ctx->proc_bb
 * so it has at most readbytes bytes of data, which we then
 * move to the caller's brigade bb.  We then save any remainder.
 */
if (!APR_BRIGADE_EMPTY(ctx->proc_bb)) {
    apr_bucket_brigade *newbb;

    /* May return APR_INCOMPLETE, which is fine by us */
    apr_brigade_partition(ctx->proc_bb, readbytes, &bkt);

    newbb = apr_brigade_split(ctx->proc_bb, bkt);
    APR_BRIGADE_CONCAT(bb, ctx->proc_bb);
    APR_BRIGADE_CONCAT(ctx->proc_bb, newbb);
}
```

8.12.4 Input Filter Example

To conclude this chapter, let's present the `mod_deflate` input filter we've drawn on for the preceding illustrations, with additional comments inserted where appropriate. The filter has been slightly reduced by replacing some of the detail relevant to `zlib` (the compression library used), but not to Apache, with comments.

```
/* This is the deflate input filter (inflates) */
static apr_status_t deflate_in_filter(ap_filter_t *f,
                                      apr_bucket_brigade *bb,
                                      ap_input_mode_t mode,
                                      apr_read_type_e block,
                                      apr_off_t readbytes)
{
    apr_bucket *bkt;
    request_rec *r = f->r;
```

```
deflate_ctx *ctx = f->ctx;
int zRC;
apr_status_t rv;
deflate_filter_config *c;

/* Just get out of the way of things we don't want */
if (mode != AP_MODE_READBYTES) {
    return ap_get_brigade(f->next, bb, mode, block, readbytes);
}

c = ap_get_module_config(r->server->module_config, &deflate_module);

if (!ctx) {
    int found = 0;
    char *token, deflate_hdr[10];
    const char *encoding;
    apr_size_t len;

    /* Only work on main request/no subrequests */
    if (!ap_is_initial_req(r)) {
        ap_remove_input_filter(f);
        return ap_get_brigade(f->next, bb, mode, block, readbytes);
    }

    /* Let's see what our current Content-Encoding is */
    encoding = apr_table_get(r->headers_in, "Content-Encoding");
    if (encoding) {
        const char *tmp = encoding;

        token = ap_get_token(r->pool, &tmp, 0);
        while (token && token[0]) {
            if (!strcasecmp(token, "gzip")) {
                found = 1;
                break;
            }
            /* Otherwise, skip token */
            tmp++;
            token = ap_get_token(r->pool, &tmp, 0);
        }
    }
    /* It wasn't gzipped anyway, so there's nothing to do */
    if (found == 0) {
        ap_remove_input_filter(f);
        return ap_get_brigade(f->next, bb, mode, block, readbytes);
    }

  /* Set up filter ctx */
    f->ctx = ctx = apr_pcalloc(f->r->pool, sizeof(*ctx));
    ctx->bb = apr_brigade_create(r->pool, f->c->bucket_alloc);
    ctx->proc_bb = apr_brigade_create(r->pool, f->c->bucket_alloc);
    ctx->buffer = apr_palloc(r->pool, c->bufferSize);
```

```
/* DELETED -- get 10 bytes from upstream and check the gzip header */

        /* Initialize deflate output buffer */
        ctx->stream.next_out = ctx->buffer;
        ctx->stream.avail_out = c->bufferSize;

        apr_brigade_cleanup(ctx->bb);
    }

    /* Main business happens if we don't already have data */
    if (APR_BRIGADE_EMPTY(ctx->proc_bb)) {
        rv = ap_get_brigade(f->next, ctx->bb, mode, block, readbytes);

        if (rv != APR_SUCCESS) {
            /* What about APR_EAGAIN errors? */
            inflateEnd(&ctx->stream);
            return rv;
        }

        for (bkt = APR_BRIGADE_FIRST(ctx->bb);
             bkt != APR_BRIGADE_SENTINEL(ctx->bb);
             bkt = APR_BUCKET_NEXT(bkt))
        {
            const char *data;
            apr_size_t len;

            /* If we actually see the EOS, that means we screwed up! */
            if (APR_BUCKET_IS_EOS(bkt)) {
                inflateEnd(&ctx->stream);
                return APR_EGENERAL;
            }

            if (APR_BUCKET_IS_FLUSH(bkt)) {
                apr_bucket *tmp_heap;
                zRC = inflate(&(ctx->stream), Z_SYNC_FLUSH);
                if (zRC != Z_OK) {
                    inflateEnd(&ctx->stream);
                    return APR_EGENERAL;
                }

                ctx->stream.next_out = ctx->buffer;
                len = c->bufferSize - ctx->stream.avail_out;

                ctx->crc = crc32(ctx->crc, (const Bytef *)ctx->buffer,
                        len);
                tmp_heap = apr_bucket_heap_create((char *)ctx->buffer,
                        len, NULL, f->c->bucket_alloc);
                APR_BRIGADE_INSERT_TAIL(ctx->proc_bb, tmp_heap);
                ctx->stream.avail_out = c->bufferSize;
```

```
                    /* Move everything to the returning brigade. */
                /* Could cause us to return more than readbytes. */
                    APR_BUCKET_REMOVE(bkt);
                    APR_BRIGADE_CONCAT(bb, ctx->bb);
                    break;
                }

                /* Read */
                apr_bucket_read(bkt, &data, &len, APR_BLOCK_READ);

                /* Pass through zlib inflate */
                /* DELETED for brevity.
                 * Inserts uncompressed data into ctx->proc_bb,
                 * and inserts an EOS bucket when it hits the end
                 * of the compressed input data stream
                 */
            }
        apr_brigade_cleanup(ctx->bb);
    }
    /* If we are about to return nothing for a 'blocking' read and
     * we have some data in our zlib buffer, flush it out so we can
     * return something.
     */
    if (block == APR_BLOCK_READ &&
        APR_BRIGADE_EMPTY(ctx->proc_bb) &&
        ctx->stream.avail_out < c->bufferSize) {

      /* DELETED for brevity */
    }
    if (!APR_BRIGADE_EMPTY(ctx->proc_bb)) {
        apr_bucket_brigade *newbb;

        /* May return APR_INCOMPLETE, which is fine by us */
        apr_brigade_partition(ctx->proc_bb, readbytes, &bkt);

        newbb = apr_brigade_split(ctx->proc_bb, bkt);
        APR_BRIGADE_CONCAT(bb, ctx->proc_bb);
        APR_BRIGADE_CONCAT(ctx->proc_bb, newbb);
    }
    return APR_SUCCESS;
}
```

8.13 Summary

Filters are one of the most powerful and useful innovations in Apache 2, and are the single biggest architectural change that helps transform Apache from a mere web-server to a powerful applications platform. Programming filters is not straightforward, but is essential to applications development with Apache. Note that there is a section on filter debugging in Chapter 12.

This chapter discussed the following topics:

- The data axis and filter chain
- Input and output filters
- Content, protocol and connection filters, with examples
- The filter APIs: principal objects and callbacks
- The importance of pipelining in filters
- Techniques for working with streamed data in the output chain push API
- Managing I/O in a filter
- Smart filtering, `mod_filter`, and self-configuration
- Filters and the HTTP protocol
- Working with buckets and brigades, including an example
- Filtering through a parser, and using a `stdio`-like buffer
- Input filtering: the pull API, with an example

This chapter completes the discussion of processing HTTP requests we started in Chapter 5. We are now ready to move on to the deferred discussion of Apache configuration in Chapter 9.

Chapter 9

Configuration for Modules

Most modules need to offer system administrators and users some means of configuring and controlling them. In some cases, this may even be the primary purpose of a module.

System administrators configure Apache using `httpd.conf`, while end users have more limited control through `.htaccess` files. Modules give control to both parties by implementing configuration directives that can be used in these files.

This chapter discusses how to implement configuration directives in a module and how to work with directives implemented by other modules.

9.1 Configuration Basics

From the system administrator's point of view, several kinds of directives exist. These can be broadly classified according to their scope and validity in the configuration files. In other words, some directives are valid for the server as a whole, whereas others apply within a scope such as `<VirtualHost>` or `<Directory>`.

Conflicting directives may override each other on the basis of order and specificity. For example, where there is a conflict, a directive in a `.htaccess` file overrides one set in the same scope in `httpd.conf` (provided the system administrator has enabled `.htaccess`). In most cases, this applies recursively, although this is controlled by individual modules whose behavior may differ.

Apache supports the following standard contexts:

Main Configuration

Directives appearing in `httpd.conf` but not inside any container, apply globally, except where overridden. This context is appropriate for setting system defaults such as MIME types, and for once-only setup such as loading modules. Most directives can be used here.

Virtual Host

Each virtual host has its (virtual) server-wide configuration set within a `<VirtualHost>` container. Most directives that are valid in the main configuration are also valid in a virtual host, and vice versa.

Directory

The `<Directory>`, `<Files>` and `<Location>` containers define a hierarchy within which configuration can be set and overridden at any level. This is the most usual form of configuration, and is orthogonal to the virtual hosts. In the interests of brevity, we'll refer to this configuration collectively as the directory hierarchy.

.htaccess

`.htaccess` files are an extension of the directory hierarchy that enables users to set directives for themselves, subject to permissions (the `AllowOverride` directive) set up by the server administrator. The `.htaccess` files also differ from normal configuration in that, when enabled, they are reread by Apache for every request. This scheme serves two purposes: Users don't have to bug the administrator to restart the server, and it avoids potential security issues of processing user inputs while Apache has root privilege. Setting `AllowOverride` to enable `.htaccess` files is always a compromise: It imposes a significant performance overhead and loses the security enjoyed by a tightly controlled configuration, but it empowers users who are not permitted to manipulate `httpd.conf`.

Additionally, modules may themselves implement their own containers. For example, `mod_proxy` implements `<Proxy>`, and `mod_perl` implements `<Perl>`.

9.2 Configuration Data Structs

As noted in Section 9.1, there are two orthogonal hierarchies of configuration directives: (virtual) hosts and directories. Internally, this dual hierarchy is based on having two different data structs: the per-server configuration and the per-directory configuration. In fact, every module has its own pointers for implementing each of these structs, although either or both can be unused (NULL), and it is unusual for a module to use both of them.

The per-server configuration is kept on the `server_rec`, of which there is one for each virtual host, created at server start-up. The per-directory configuration is exposed to modules via the `request_rec` and may be computed using the merge function for every request.

The configuration structs are instances of configuration vectors, as seen in Chapter 4. Those discussed in this chapter are used for configuration that is initialized at server start-up and should be accessed as read-only thereafter.

9.3 Managing a Module Configuration

9.3.1 Module Configuration

No less than five out of the six (usable) elements of the Apache module struct are concerned with configuration:

```
module my_module = {
  STANDARD20_MODULE_STUFF,
  my_create_dir_conf,          /* Create config rec for directory */
  my_merge_dir_conf,           /* Merge config rec for directory */
  my_create_svr_conf,          /* Create config rec for host */
  my_merge_svr_conf,           /* Merge config rec for host */
  my_cmds,                     /* Configuration directives */
  my_hooks
} ;
```

It is up to each module whether and how to define each configuration struct. Whenever a struct is defined, the module must implement an appropriate create function to allocate and (usually) initialize it:

```
typedef struct {
  ... ;
} my_svr_cfg ;

static void* my_create_svr_conf(apr_pool_t* pool, server_rec* s) {
  my_svr_cfg* svr = apr_pcalloc(pool, sizeof(my_svr_cfg));
  /* Set up the default values for fields of svr */
  return svr ;
}

typedef struct {
  ... ;
} my_dir_cfg ;

static void* my_create_dir_conf(apr_pool_t* pool, char* x) {
  my_dir_cfg* dir = apr_pcalloc(pool, sizeof(my_dir_cfg));
  /* Set up the default values for fields of dir */
  return dir ;
}
```

At this point, just allocating and returning a struct of the right size is often sufficient: Apache uses the return value. Now these values can be accessed at any time a server_rec or request_rec, respectively, is available:

```
my_svr_cfg* svr
    = ap_get_module_config(server->module_config, &my_module) ;
my_dir_cfg* dir
    = ap_get_module_config(request->per_dir_config, &my_module) ;
```

9.3.2 Server and Directory Configuration

So why does Apache have two separate configurations, how are they related, and which should your module use?

Most directives work in the directory hierarchy—for example, all the directives from our mod_choices and mod_txt modules in Chapters 6 and 8 do so. This approach offers the greatest flexibility to system administrators who want to control the configuration and to deploy different configurations in different areas of their server, with <Directory>, <Files>, <Location>, and pattern-matching versions such as `<DirectoryMatch>`, and, subject to `AllowOverride` settings, `.htaccess`. When in doubt, implementing a directive in the directory configuration is unlikely to be wrong!

The server hierarchy is simpler. There is no nesting, and only two levels are available: top level or inside a `<VirtualHost>`. This approach is appropriate in the following cases:

- Any configuration that needs to be accessed outside the scope of processing a request—for example, in a `post_config` or `child_init` hook

- Directives explicitly concerned with virtual host configuration

- Situations where the directory hierarchy is meaningless or irrelevant, such as in a forward proxy configuration

- Managing a persistent resource such as a database connection pool or a cache

Gotcha!

There is a subtle "gotcha" with directory configuration. When a directive is allowed to appear at the top level in `httpd.conf` (i.e., outside any `<Directory>`/etc. container), it is also syntactically valid inside a `<VirtualHost>`. But the `<VirtualHost>` container has no meaning in the directory hierarchy. Thus setting per-directory configuration in a virtual host requires a `<Directory>` or similar container, in addition to the `<VirtualHost>`. That's why, for example, most access and authentication control directives are disallowed at the top level.

Configuration directives on the server hierarchy can, and should, address this issue simply by making themselves syntactically invalid in a `<Directory>` context.

On a related theme, it is important not to confuse the two hierarchies. The `ProxyPassReverse` directive in early releases of Apache 2.0 `mod_proxy` offers a cautionary lesson. `ProxyPassReverse` directives were valid in a `<Location>` context, but were held in the per-server configuration. As a consequence, if multiple `ProxyPassReverse` directives appeared in different `<Location>` contexts, they would overwrite each other and only the last one would work.

9.4 Implementing Configuration Directives

The my_cmds field of the module struct mentioned earlier is a null-terminated array containing the commands implemented by the module. Normally, these commands are defined using macros defined in http_config.h. For example:

```
static const command_rec my_cmds[] = {
  AP_INIT_TAKE1("MyFirstDirective", my_first_cmd_func, my_ptr, OR_ALL,
        "This is My First Directive"),
  /* More directives as applicable */
  { NULL }
} ;
```

AP_INIT_TAKE1 is one of many such macros, all having the same prototype (more on that later). It has the following arguments:

1. Directive name

2. Function implementing the directive

3. Data pointer (often NULL)

4. Context in which this directive is allowed

5. A brief help message for the directive

9.4.1 Configuration Functions

An essential component of every directive is the function implementing it. Normally, the function serves to set some data field(s) in one of the configuration structs. The function prototype for AP_INIT_TAKE1 is the same, regardless of whether we're setting per-server or per-directory configuration:

```
const char* my_first_cmd_func(cmd_parms* cmd, void* cfg,
                    const char* arg)
```

cmd is a cmd_parms_struct comprising a number of fields used internally by Apache and available to modules. The following fields are most likely to be of interest in command functions:

*   void* info—contains my_ptr from the command declaration

*   apr_pool_t* pool—pool for permanent resource allocation

*   apr_pool_t* temp_pool—pool for temporary resource allocation

*   server_rec* server—the server_rec

Other fields are more commonly accessed through accessor functions on the rare occasions when a command function needs to be context sensitive. Here is the full declaration:

```
/**
 * This structure is passed to a command that is being invoked,
 * to carry a large variety of miscellaneous data that is all of
 * use to *somebody*...
 */
struct cmd_parms_struct {
    /** Argument to command from cmd_table */
    void *info;
    /** Which allow-override bits are set */
    int override;
    /** Which methods are <Limit>ed */
    apr_int64_t limited;
    /** Methods that are limited */
    apr_array_header_t *limited_xmethods;
    /** Methods that are xlimited */
    ap_method_list_t *xlimited;

    /** Config file structure */
    ap_configfile_t *config_file;
    /** The directive specifying this command */
    ap_directive_t *directive;

    /** Pool to allocate new storage in */
    apr_pool_t *pool;
    /** Pool for scratch memory; persists during configuration, but
     *  wiped before the first request is served...   */
    apr_pool_t *temp_pool;
    /** Server_rec being configured for */
    server_rec *server;
    /** If configuring for a directory, pathname of that directory.
     *  NOPE! That's what it meant previous to the existence of <Files>,
     * <Location>, and regex matching.  Now the only usefulness that can
     * be derived from this field is whether a command is being called
     * in a server context (path == NULL) or being called in a dir
     * context (path != NULL).
     */
    char *path;
    /** Configuration command */
    const command_rec *cmd;

    /** per_dir_config vector passed to handle_command */
    struct ap_conf_vector_t *context;
    /** Directive with syntax error */
    const ap_directive_t *err_directive;

    /** Which allow-override-opts bits are set */
    int override_opts;
};
```

cfg is the directory configuration rec, and **arg** is an argument to the directive set in the configuration file we are processing. Because we specified AP_INIT_TAKE1, there is exactly one argument. Thus, if we are setting per-directory configuration, we just cast the cfg argument. If we are setting per-server configuration, we need to retrieve this argument from the server_rec object in cmd_parms instead.

9.4.2 Example

We can now look at a simple example. Our mod_txt in Chapter 8 needs a user-defined header and footer, each of which is a separate file. Let's go ahead and implement the configuration for it. We would like to be able to specify different headers and footers at will, so that a user can apply different looks-and-feels to different areas of a site. Thus we need to implement these directives in the directory hierarchy.

```
typedef struct txt_cfg {
  const char* header ;
  const char* footer ;
} txt_cfg;

static const command_rec txt_cmds[] = {
  AP_INIT_TAKE1("TextHeader", txt_set_header, NULL, OR_ALL,
        "Header for prettified text files"),
  AP_INIT_TAKE1("TextFooter", txt_set_footer, NULL, OR_ALL,
        "Footer for prettified text files"),
  { NULL }
} ;
```

Now we need to implement the functions to set the header and footer. Just for the moment, we'll simply set them and ignore checking that they're really files, they're accessible to the server, and displaying them in a webpage won't be a security risk.

```
static const char* txt_set_header(cmd_parms* cmd, void* cfg,
    const char* val) {
  ((txt_cfg*)cfg)->header = val ;
  return NULL ;
}
static const char* txt_set_footer(cmd_parms* cmd, void* cfg,
    const char* val) {
  ((txt_cfg*)cfg)->footer = val ;
  return NULL ;
}
```

9.4.3 User Data in Configuration Functions

In the preceding example, we implemented two essentially identical functions to set different fields of the configuration. We can consolidate these functions into a single function by passing it a context variable in `cmd->info`. Apache (APR) provides a handy macro for passing a pointer to individual fields of a configuration struct, so we can just set its contents:

```
static const command_rec txt_cmds[] = {
  AP_INIT_TAKE1("TextHeader", txt_set_var,
    (void*)APR_OFFSETOF(txt_cfg, header),
    OR_ALL, "Header for prettified text files"),
  AP_INIT_TAKE1("TextFooter", txt_set_var,
    (void*)APR_OFFSETOF(txt_cfg, footer),
    OR_ALL, "Footer for prettified text files"),
  { NULL }
} ;
static const char* txt_set_var(cmd_parms* cmd, void* cfg,
                      const char* val)
{
  int offset = (int)(long)cmd->info;
  *(const char **)((char *)cfg + offset) = val;
  return NULL ;
}
```

9.4.4 Prepackaged Configuration Functions

In general, we write our own function to implement a directive. This step is not always necessary, however. When a directive simply sets a field in the directory configuration, we can use one of the prepackaged functions to set a field, based on the type of the field to be set: `ap_set_string_slot`, `ap_set_string_slot_lower`, `ap_set_int_slot`, `ap_set_flag_slot`, or `ap_set_file_slot`.

Our earlier function `txt_set_var` is, in fact, an exact copy of `ap_set_string_slot`. Since the fields we are setting are actually filenames, we should instead use `ap_set_file_slot`. This means that the user can specify either absolute or relative pathnames for the file, and Apache will resolve them correctly according to the underlying filesystem and server root. So we can reduce our `mod_txt` configuration to the following code:

```
static const command_rec txt_cmds[] = {
  AP_INIT_TAKE1("TextHeader", ap_set_file_slot,
    (void*)APR_OFFSETOF(txt_cfg, header),
    OR_ALL, "Header for prettified text files"),
  AP_INIT_TAKE1("TextFooter", ap_set_file_slot,
    (void*)APR_OFFSETOF(txt_cfg, footer),
    OR_ALL, "Footer for prettified text files"),
  { NULL }
} ;
```

We've improved our configuration without writing any configuration functions at all!

These functions are provided for directives in the directory hierarchy. There are no equivalent functions for implementing configuration directives in the server hierarchy, so we always have to write our own.

9.4.5 Scope of Configuration

The preceding example used OR_ALL to say that TxtHeader/TxtFooter can be used anywhere in httpd.conf or in any .htaccess file (provided htaccess is enabled on the server). We could instead have used any of these options:

- **RSRC_CONF**: httpd.conf at top level or in a VirtualHost context. All directives using server configuration should use this option, as other contexts are meaningless for a server configuration.

- **ACCESS_CONF**: httpd.conf in a directory context. This option is appropriate to per-directory configuration directives for a server administrator only. It is often combined (using OR) with RSRC_CONF to allow its use anywhere within httpd.conf, giving rise to the "gotcha" mentioned earlier related to directives appearing in ambiguous contexts.

- **OR_LIMIT**, **OR_OPTIONS**, **OR_FILEINFO**, **OR_AUTHCFG**, **OR_INDEXES**: extend ACCESS_CONF to allow use of the directive in .htaccess, where permitted by the AllowOverride setting.

An additional value, **EXEC_ON_READ**, can be ORed with any of the preceding options to take control of parsing httpd.conf into a module. We can use this to implement containers in configuration, as described in Section 9.7.

9.4.6 Configuration Function Types

The preceding example used the AP_INIT_TAKE1 macro, which defines a function having a single string argument. This is one of several such macros defined in http_config.h:

- **AP_INIT_NO_ARGS**—no arguments

- **AP_INIT_FLAG**—a single On/Off argument

- **AP_INIT_TAKE1**—a single string, file or numeric argument

- **AP_INIT_TAKE2**, **AP_INIT_TAKE3**—two/three arguments
- **AP_INIT_TAKE12**, and so on—directives taking variable numbers of arguments
- **AP_INIT_ITERATE**—function will be called repeatedly with each of an unspecified number of arguments
- **AP_INIT_ITERATE2**—function will be called repeatedly with two arguments
- **AP_INIT_RAW_ARGS**—function will be called with arguments unprocessed

Let's look at some examples. We've already seen a TAKE1 case. The other AP_INIT_TAKE* functions are similar but have different numbers of arguments (those with variable numbers of arguments simply work by passing NULL values where no argument was specified in the configuration).

AP_INIT_FLAG

In the directory hierarchy, this function can generally be dealt with using ap_set_flag_slot. For example, in our mod_choices module from Chapter 6, we need to implement the directive Choices On|Off. Recall that we have a per-directory configuration record:

```
typedef struct choices_cfg {
  int choices ;                 /* Flag to turn this module on/off */
  apr_hash_t* transforms ;    /* Table of "extensions" known to
                               * this server
                               */
} choices_cfg ;
```

All we need to implement the directive is

```
AP_INIT_FLAG("Choices", ap_set_flag_slot,
     (void*)APR_OFFSETOF(choices_cfg, choices), ACCESS_CONF,
     "Enable document variant selection by extension" )
```

In the server hierarchy, you would have to supply a function to set the configuration value, as in an AP_INIT_TAKE1.

AP_INIT_ITERATE

The function is called once for each argument, so it is suitable for directives with variable arguments, all of which have the same semantics.

There are several examples in `mod_proxy`, where you can supply a list of addresses or ports to which a proxy is or isn't allowed to connect. For example:

```
AllowConnect 21 80 443 8000 8080
```

This is declared as iterating over the arguments:

```
AP_INIT_ITERATE("AllowCONNECT", set_allowed_ports, NULL, RSRC_CONF,
  "A list of ports which CONNECT may connect to")
```

Here's the function: It's very simple because it has to deal with only one argument at a time. Note that this function is also an example of a directive in the server hierarchy, where we have to look up the `server_rec` object from the `cmd_parms` supplied.

```
/*
 * Set the ports CONNECT can use
 */
static const char *
    set_allowed_ports(cmd_parms *parms, void *dummy, const char *arg)
{
    server_rec *s = parms->server;
    proxy_server_conf *conf =
        ap_get_module_config(s->module_config, &proxy_module);
    int *New;

    if (!apr_isdigit(arg[0]))
        return "AllowCONNECT: port number must be numeric";

    New = apr_array_push(conf->allowed_connect_ports);
    *New = atoi(arg);
    return NULL;
}
```

AP_INIT_ITERATE2

This is similar to `AP_INIT_ITERATE`. It is a two-argument form that takes the first argument from the configuration every time, while iterating over the remaining arguments.

An example is `mod_proxy_html` (version 3). The primary purpose of this output filter is to rewrite HTML links into a reverse proxy's address space. Thus the module needs to know which markup attributes are links and may, therefore, need to be rewritten.

Originally, `mod_proxy_html` supported HTML4 and XHTML1, with knowledge of the markup taken directly from the authoritative DTDs (published by the World

Wide Web Consortium) and embedded in the module. As its popularity grew beyond those able to adapt it themselves, a frequently requested feature was to support proprietary extensions to HTML. Version 3 accommodates this request by removing the knowledge of HTML from the module and delegating it to the configuration. A configuration directive `ProxyHTMLLinks` reads the specification to find out which attributes need to be processed.

A configuration excerpt is bundled with `mod_proxy_html` and duplicates the knowledge that was hard-coded into earlier versions:

```
ProxyHTMLLinks a href
ProxyHTMLLinks img src longdesc usemap
ProxyHTMLLinks form action
ProxyHTMLLinks link href
ProxyHTMLLinks script src for
ProxyHTMLLinks base href
ProxyHTMLLinks area href
ProxyHTMLLinks input src usemap
ProxyHTMLLinks frame src longdesc
ProxyHTMLLinks iframe src longdesc
ProxyHTMLLinks object classid codebase data usemap
ProxyHTMLLinks q cite
ProxyHTMLLinks blockquote cite
ProxyHTMLLinks ins cite
ProxyHTMLLinks del cite
ProxyHTMLLinks head profile
ProxyHTMLLinks body background
ProxyHTMLLinks applet codebase
```

The arguments to `ProxyHTMLLinks` consist of an HTML element followed by a variable number of attributes. We implement this using an ITERATE2 function:

```
static const char* set_links(cmd_parms* cmd, void* CFG,
        const char* elt, const char* att) {
  apr_hash_t* elts = ((my_conf*)CFG)->links ;
  apr_array_header_t* attrs = apr_hash_get(elts, elt,
                             APR_HASH_KEY_STRING) ;
  tattr* attr ;

  if (!attrs) {
    attrs = apr_array_make(cmd->pool, 2, sizeof(tattr)) ;
    apr_hash_set(elts, elt, APR_HASH_KEY_STRING, attrs) ;
  }
  attr = apr_array_push(attrs) ;
  attr->val = att ;
  return NULL ;
}
```

The underlying representation of HTML links used here is an APR hash table of elements, each having an APR array of attributes to be processed. The function first looks up the hash entry for the element (first argument), creates one if none is found, and then appends the attribute (second argument) to the attributes array.

AP_INIT_RAW_ARGS

Raw arguments are needed where a directive's syntax is highly variable and needs to be fully parsed in the configuration function. Such functions by their nature are often long and complex. Instead of giving a real-life example here, we'll show how to reimplement the previously mentioned set_links function using raw arguments. The key to this approach is a utility function ap_getword_conf, which deals with the complexities of parsing arguments that may include whitespace, escape characters, and quotes.

```
static const char* set_links_raw_args(cmd_parms* cmd, void* CFG,
                            const char* args)
{
  const char* attname;
  apr_hash_t* elts = ((my_conf*)CFG)->links ;

  /* The first argument is the element name */
  const char* elt = ap_getword_conf(cmd->pool, &args) ;

  /* Create an array of attributes for the element */
  apr_array_header_t* attrs
        = apr_array_make(cmd->pool, 2, sizeof(tattr)) ;
  apr_hash_set(elts, elt, APR_HASH_KEY_STRING, attrs) ;

  /* Now there could be any number of further arguments,
   * so we handle them in a loop.  We push each argument
   * onto the attributes array.
   */
  for (attname = ap_getword_conf(cmd->pool, &args);
     attname != NULL;
     attname = ap_getword_conf(cmd->pool, &args)) {
    tattr* attr = apr_array_push(attrs) ;
    attr->val = attname ;
  }
  return NULL;
}
```

9.5 The Configuration Hierarchy

The next topic we need to deal with is managing the configuration hierarchy: how directives set at different levels interact with each other. This is the purpose of the merge functions in the module struct.

A merge function is called whenever directives appear in more than one container in `httpd.conf`. It resolves conflicts between directives in the various containers that may be applicable.

Normal behavior in the directory hierarchy meets the following criteria:

1. Any applicable `<Directory>` or `<Location>` overrides a configuration that isn't in any container.

2. A `.htaccess` file (if enabled) overrides `httpd.conf` for the same directory.

3. A directory's configuration overrides a parent directory's configuration.

4. Any applicable `<Location>` overrides `<Files>`, which overrides `<Directory>` and `.htaccess`.

5. The `<Location>` and `<Files>` containers override each other based not on specificity, but rather on the order in which they appear in `httpd.conf`.

6. Where configuration values are not explicitly set, they are inherited rather than overridden.

7. These relationships may be influenced by a module such as `mod_alias` hooking a relevant function before the `map_to_storage` phase.

> NOTE It is strongly recommended that `<Directory>` and `<Location>` containers should never have an overlapping scope: That way confusion lies! But that's an issue for system administrators to manage.

Normal behavior in the server hierarchy is simpler: We just need to merge `<VirtualHost>` containers with the top-level configuration.

Consider the following example:

```
typedef struct {
  int a , b , c ;
} my_dir_cfg;
```

with directives to set a, b, and c, and used with the configuration

```
DocumentRoot /var/www/
<Directory> /var/www/somewhere/>
    SetMyB    456
</Directory>
<Directory /var/www/somewhere/else/again/>
    SetMyC    789
```

```
</Directory>
<Directory /var/www/>
    SetMyA    123
    SetMyC    321
</Directory>
```

We normally want a request to /somewhere/else/again/ to have the following behavior:

1. At the top level, a is set to 123 and c is set to 321; b is unset.

2. The first merge sets b to 456. Because a and c are not set (overridden) at this level, the previous values are inherited in the merge.

3. There are no configuration directives at /var/www/somewhere/else/, so this level simply inherits from the parent without any need for a merge.

4. The second merge sets the value of c by overriding the previous setting, while inheriting the previous values of a and b. Now we have a = 123, b = 456, and c = 789.

If we use <Location> instead of <Directory>, then the precedence changes, and the last <Location> overrides the earlier ones despite being less specific.

Because only the module itself knows the semantics of its own configuration directives, only the module itself can actually implement this behavior. This task is the business of a merge_config function, which Apache will call whenever directives applicable to the module appear in more than one container. If no such function is provided by the module, configuration cannot be inherited. Thus, in the preceding example, c is set to 789 at /var/www/somewhere/else/again/ but a and b are unset.

The merge function follows this generic form:

```
static void* my_merge_dir_conf(apr_pool_t* pool, void* BASE, void* ADD) {
    my_dir_cfg* base = BASE ;
    my_dir_cfg* add = ADD ;
    my_dir_cfg* conf = apr_palloc(pool, sizeof(my_dir_cfg)) ;

    /* UNSET is defined to something that won't be used --
     * e.g., -1 if all our integers are positive.  We initialize
     * everything to UNSET in our create_conf function.
     */
    conf->a = ( add->a == UNSET ) ? base->a : add->a ;
    conf->b = ( add->b == UNSET ) ? base->b : add->b ;
    conf->c = ( add->c == UNSET ) ? base->c : add->c ;
    return conf ;
}
```

Often we may need to do something a little more complex—for example, merge non-trivial structures, or deal with cases where there is no meaningful UNSET value to test. When merging structures that involve pointers, take care when modifying the originals: It's safer to make a copy unless you're using a standard APR data type and its merge functions. You'll have to make this decision for each case based on its merits.

The next example demonstrates the potential pitfalls in merging structures. Consider a module that supports an unlimited number of some kind of rule in its configuration, and uses a linked list in the configuration struct to represent them:

```
typedef struct myrule {
  void* next;  /* Another myrule*, void to avoid circular declaration */
  /* data fields */
} myrule;
typedef struct {
  myrule* rules;
  /* other configuration data fields */
} my_conf;
```

The configuration function for setting a myrule is simple enough: We append the new rule at the end of the list, to ensure the rules are applied in the same order as they appear in httpd.conf:

```
static const char* set_myrule( [args] ) {
  my_conf* cfg = (my_conf*)CFG ;
  myrule* newrules = apr_palloc(cmd->pool, sizeof(myrule) ) ;
  ...
  if ( cfg->rules != NULL ) {
    for ( ptr = cfg->rules ; ptr->next != NULL; ptr = ptr->next
    ptr->next = newrules ;
  } else
    cfg->rules = newrules ;
  /* And, of course, set the data fields of newrules */
}
```

When we perform the merge, we want the add rules to take precedence, so we put them first. But there's a pitfall awaiting us if we try to merge using pointers without copying:

```
static void* BAD_merge(apr_pool_t* pool, void* BASE, void* ADD) {
  my_conf* base = (my_conf*) BASE ;
  my_conf* add = (my_conf*) ADD ;
  my_conf* conf = apr_palloc(pool, sizeof(my_conf)) ;

  if (add->rules && base->rules) {
    /* Append base to add */
    for (ptr = conf->rules = add->rules; ptr->next; ptr = ptr->next)
        ;
    ptr->next = base->rules;
```

```
  } else {
    conf->rules = add->rules ? add->rules : base->rules ;
  }
  /* Deal with other fields as appropriate */
}
```

This code fails in the general case, because when we appended the base list to conf, we actually modified the add list itself. Add a nontrivial configuration into the mix, and we could easily end up appending add to itself, leading to a circular list and causing Apache to spin as soon as it applies the rules in processing a request with the merged list.

To avoid this risk, our merge function needs to copy the entire list:

```
static void* GOOD_merge(apr_pool_t* pool, void* BASE, void* ADD) {
  my_conf* base = (my_conf*) BASE ;
  my_conf* add = (my_conf*) ADD ;
  my_conf* conf = apr_palloc(pool, sizeof(my_conf)) ;

  if (add->rules && base->rules ) {
    myrule* a ;
    conf->rules = NULL ;
    for ( a = base->rules ; a ; a = a->next ) {
      myrule* save = conf->rules ;
      conf->rules = apr_pmemdup(pool, a, sizeof(myrule)) ;
      conf->rules->next = save ;
    }
    for ( a = add->rules ; a ; a = a->next ) {
      myrule* save = conf->rules ;
      conf->rules = apr_pmemdup(pool, a, sizeof(myrule)) ;
      conf->rules->next = save ;
    }
  } else {
    conf->rules = add->rules ? add->rules : base->rules ;
  }
  /* Deal with the other fields as appropriate */
}
```

Note that we could have simplified this example by using appropriate APR types. In this case, we could have used the APR array type apr_array_header_t in place of our linked list, and we could have then used apr_array_append in our merge function:

```
static void* ARRAY_merge(apr_pool_t* pool, void* BASE, void* ADD) {
  my_conf* base = (my_conf*) BASE ;
  my_conf* add = (my_conf*) ADD ;
  my_conf* conf = apr_palloc(pool, sizeof(my_conf)) ;
```

```
    /* With an APR data type we can delegate all the real work to APR */
    conf->rules = apr_array_append(pool, base->rules, add->rules);
    /* etc */
}
```

9.6 Context in Configuration Functions

For most purposes, the configuration we've introduced here offers ample control. Configuration directives don't care where they appear so long as they are syntactically correct and follow the rules of the appropriate hierarchy (directory or server). Apache itself will manage the hierarchy, and all the module should do is provide a merge function. But occasionally a directive might care where it appears. For example, if it concerns support for a virtual filesystem, it might want to know if it's within the filesystem in question. And what is the effect of a directive appearing in a context such as `<Limit>` that is not part of either hierarchy?

9.6.1 Context Checking

If a configuration function needs to know its context, the information is available in the `cmd_parms` struct. The most useful way to access this information, however, is through the function `ap_check_cmd_context` from `http_config.h`. It provides us with the promised workaround for directory-hierarchy directives appearing misleadingly in a `<VirtualHost>` container: We can permit our directive to appear at the top level with `RSRC_CONF` or `OR_ALL`, yet generate a syntax error if our directive appears in a `<VirtualHost>`:

```
static const char* my_conf(cmd_parms* cmd, void* cfg, ...) {
  const char* errmsg;
  errmsg = ap_check_cmd_context(cmd, NOT_IN_VIRTUALHOST);
  if (errmsg != NULL) {
    return errmsg;
  }
  /* OK, not in a <VirtualHost>; go ahead and process the directive */
  return NULL;
}
```

`NOT_IN_VIRTUALHOST` is one of several macros we can test in this manner. Others include `NOT_IN_LIMIT`, `NOT_IN_DIRECTORY`, `NOT_IN_LOCATION`, `NOT_IN_FILES`, `NOT_IN_DIR_LOC_FILE`, and `GLOBAL_ONLY`. These macros can be used with a logical OR, and `ap_check_cmd_context` will return `NULL` if and only if the conditions are satisfied.

9.6.2 Method and <Limit>

> CAUTION <Limit> is traditionally associated with authen-
> tication and access control. After an example was published,
> it became cargo-cult knowledge, and even today some sources
> imply that it is an integral part of authentication. In fact, <Limit>
> is rarely useful in a regular webserver and, in the context of secu-
> rity, it can be dangerous. Examples of good <Limit> usage can
> be found in DAV and Subversion.

The <Limit> and <LimitExcept> containers provide a context in which directives
may or may not apply, depending on the HTTP method used. Unlike with the
standard hierarchy containers, this usage is not automatic, but rather requires coop-
eration from modules.

Configuration functions can find out if they are in a <Limit> section by checking
the "limited" field of the cmd_parms: It is set to −1 when not in a <Limit> or
<LimitExcept>, or to a bit field of <Limit>ed method numbers. You might wish
to use this approach when a directive is applicable only to certain methods, to generate a syntax error if the directive is <Limit>ed to inappropriate methods:

```
/* Example: Directive that is meaningless except in a POST or PUT */
if ( cmd->limited != -1) {  /* We're happy if not in <Limit> at all. */
  /* When in <Limit>, insist that at least one of POST/PUT applies. */
  mask = (AP_METHOD_BIT<<M_POST) | (AP_METHOD_BIT<<M_PUT) ;
  if ( !(cmd->limited & mask) ) {
    return "Directive is relevant only in POST or PUT context" ;
  }
}
```

Alternatively, a directive may unconditionally refuse to work in a <Limit> by using
ap_check_command_context with NOT_IN_LIMIT.

Modules more commonly want to know whether they are <Limit>ed later, when
processing a request. At this point, there is an actual request, and hence a method
to check against the <Limit>.

The most common example of a directive that works with <Limit> is Require. It
is implemented by the core, and accessed by authorization modules (Chapter 7).
First, the configuration function records any <Limit>:

```
static const char *require(cmd_parms *cmd, void *c_, const char *arg)
{
  require_line *r;
  core_dir_config *c = c_;

  if (!c->ap_requires) {
    c->ap_requires = apr_array_make(cmd->pool, 2, sizeof(require_line));
  }

  r = (require_line *)apr_array_push(c->ap_requires);
  r->requirement = apr_pstrdup(cmd->pool, arg);
  r->method_mask = cmd->limited;

  return NULL;
}
```

Second, the authorization handlers check the request method against the limit mask of the `Require` directive:

```
static int some_authz_handler(request_rec* r) {
  const apr_array_header_t *reqs_arr = ap_requires(r);
  require_line *reqs = (require_line *)reqs_arr->elts;
  loop over reqs {
     if (!(reqs[n].method_mask & (AP_METHOD_BIT << r->method_number))) {
        /* We're in a <Limit> that excludes this Require directive,
         * so we'll just ignore it
         */
        continue;
     }
     /* If we reach here, this Require applies to this request method */
  }
  /* etc. */
}
```

9.7 Custom Configuration Containers

So far, we have discussed the standard configuration containers that define the two hierarchies. But an `httpd.conf` may contain other sections as well:

```
<Limit> ... </Limit>

<IfDefine> ... </IfDefine>

<Proxy> ... </Proxy>

<Perl> .... </Perl>
```

In terms of its implementation, a container is simply an extended form of a directive. We can process its entire contents with AP_INIT_RAW_ARGS, setting the EXEC_ON_READ flag to indicate that we will do something other than just passively consume the line.

The simplest example of a container is <Comment>, from mod_comment:[1]

```
<Comment>
        Anything here is commented out. This can be useful when hacking
        configurations, to comment out whole chunks rather than just line-by-
        line.
</Comment>
```

This container is implemented as a directive <Comment. Note that the directive here includes the opening angle bracket, but not the closing one: This is because arguments to a container directive will precede the closing bracket.

```
static const command_rec comment_cmds[] =
{
  AP_INIT_RAW_ARGS("<Comment", start_comment, NULL,
                 EXEC_ON_READ | OR_ALL, "Container for comments"),
  {NULL}
};
```

Now, of course, the start_comment function applies to the opening <Comment. But instead of consuming a single line, it takes over processing the input, returning control to the caller only when it reaches the closing </Comment>.

```
static const char *start_comment(cmd_parms *cmd, void *dummy,
                                 const char *arg)
{
    const char *endp;


    /* Complain if the <Comment> directive is not well formed */
    endp = ap_strrchr_c(arg, '>');
    if (endp == NULL) {
        return apr_pstrcat(cmd->pool, cmd->cmd->name,
                         "> directive missing closing '>'", NULL);
    }
    *(ap_directive_t **)dummy = NULL;

    /* Now ignore everything until </Comment> */
    return ap_soak_end_container(cmd, "<Comment");
}
```

---

1. https://ssl.bulix.org/projects/rici/browser/apache/mod_comment.c

A particularly interesting example of a container is <Macro>, from mod_macro.[2] It introduces macros into Apache configuration. A complementary Use directive instantiates the macro with arguments matching the <Macro> template. For example, if we have lots of virtual hosts with similar configurations, we could save ourselves from a lot of repetition by making the basic virtual host skeleton into a macro.

First, we define vhost as a macro:

```
<Macro vhost $host $dir $admin>
  <VirtualHost 192.168.23.90>
    ServerName $host
    DocumentRoot $dir
    ServerAdmin $admin

    <Directory $dir>
      Order allow,deny
      Allow from all
    </Directory>

  </VirtualHost>
</Macro>
```

Next, we use it to declare virtual hosts using just a single line per host:

```
Use vhost www.example.com /usr/www/example.com webmaster@example.com
Use vhost www.example.org /usr/www/example.org webmaster@example.org
```

To implement this, mod_macro defines a macro_t type:

```
typedef struct {
  char * name;            /* case-insensitive name of the macro */
  apr_array_header_t * arguments; /* of char* */
  apr_array_header_t * contents;
  char * location;            /* of the macro definition */
} macro_t;
```

The handler for <Macro creates and populates a macro_t structure, while Use activates the macro's contents with the arguments supplied. The module is too complex to include here in detail (and to do so would also require its license to be reproduced in full), so we'll just look at it in outline form.

_____

2. http://www.coelho.net/mod_macro/

The function implementing the `<Macro>` container is `macro_section`. The function implementing the `Use` directive is `use_macro`. Both functions are declared as `AP_INIT_RAW_ARGS` with `EXEC_ON_READ`.

```
static const char *macro_section(cmd_parms * cmd,
                                 void * dummy,
                                 const char * arg)
{
    /* Check that the <Macro ...> line is well formed
     * (same check as mod_comment)
     */

    /* The macro name is the first argument */
     name = ap_getword_conf(cmd->temp_pool, &arg);

    /* Check that we don't already have a macro of the same name */

    /* Allocate the macro_t struct and set the macro name */

    /* Read the remainder of the line into the macro's arguments
     * using ap_getword_conf as in the RAW_ARGS example above
     */

    /* Run sanity checks on arguments (no duplicate names, etc.) */

    /* Read lines until </Macro> into the macro contents,
     * discarding blank lines and comments, using ap_cfg_getline
     */
    while (!ap_cfg_getline(line, MAX_STRING_LEN, config_file)) {
        /* Run a range of checks on line */
        /* Store line in macro's contents */
    }

    /* Run sanity checks on macro contents */

    return NULL;
}
static const char *use_macro(cmd_parms * cmd,
                             void * dummy,
                             const char * arg)
{
    /* The macro name is the first argument */

    /* Retrieve the macro_t record for this name */

    /* Check for recursion */

    /* Read the argument values from the remainder of the line */

    /* Check that the number of arguments matches the macro prototype */
```

```
    /* Process macro contents by copying line-by-line into
     * a new array and substituting argument values for variables
     */

    /* Incorporate the contents into a custom context, and pass
     * it to ap_pcfg_open_custom to consume the contents as if
     * it were read directly from httpd.conf
     */

    return NULL;
}
```

The prototype for `ap_pcfg_open_custom` is

```
AP_DECLARE(ap_configfile_t *) ap_pcfg_open_custom(apr_pool_t *p,
    const char *descr,
    void *param,
    int(*getc_func)(void*),
    void *(*gets_func) (void *buf, size_t bufsiz, void *param),
    int(*close_func)(void *param));
```

The preparation for it is omitted here for the sake of brevity, but is based on passing the contents in the `param` argument, and supplying functions to read from those contents.

9.8 Alternative Configuration Methods

Whereas single-line directives and (occasionally) containers serve well for most modules, sometimes we may want to use more complex forms of configuration, or read the configuration from a standard format such as SQL or XML that may be well suited to a particular module's requirements. A simple way to take advantage of different formats is to use a configuration directive that takes the name of a configuration file as an argument. The configuration function then reads the file. Variants on this approach include querying a database or running an XPath query on an XML module-configuration file.

Modules can also rely on variables in the Apache core for configuration. For example:

- Content generators check the `r->handler` field to determine whether to accept a request (as we saw in Chapter 5), so we never need to implement our own directive for this purpose.

- `mod_deflate` reads environment variables such as `nogzip` to determine whether to compress a document when the compression filter is active. This approach delegates configuration to modules that set environment variables, and enables configuration using directives such as `BrowserMatch`.

9.9 Summary

Configuration is a basic topic, and one that is essential to nearly every module and application. Apache's configuration is largely straightforward once you appreciate how the hierarchies work and how they relate to one another. Implementing the configuration directives for your modules is usually simple. Although this holds some subtleties (such as `<Limit>` sections), these exist largely to maintain backward compatibility among the standard modules, and can usually be ignored by applications.

Specific topics we have looked at in this chapter include the following:

- The directory and server configurations
- Configuration data structs
- The `command_rec`, and defining and implementing commands
- Configuration macros and function prototypes
- Custom and prepackaged configuration functions
- The configuration hierarchy and merge functions
- Context, scope, limitations, and availability of configuration records
- Configuration containers

This chapter complements the discussion of HTTP request processing in Chapters 5–8, and concludes our presentation of core topics. In the next chapters, we move on to more advanced topics that may be of interest to many, but not all, applications developers: providing a new API or service for other modules, and working with an SQL database.

Chapter 10

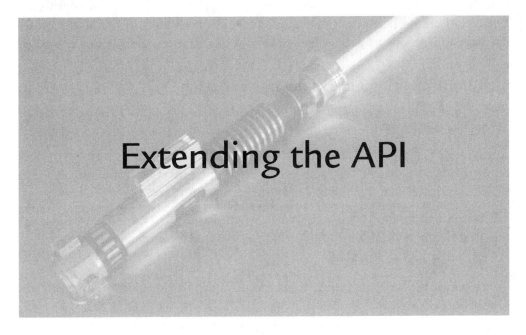

Extending the API

One of the major innovations in Apache 2 is the flexible and extensible API, which brings a hugely enhanced level of modularity and an applications architecture that is limited only by the developer's imagination. We have encountered Apache's hooks in earlier chapters, but we haven't yet seen the full power they offer us, nor the other mechanisms for extending not merely the program, but also the API.

In this chapter, we will demonstrate a number of ways to extend the Apache API:

- Implementing new API functions
- Taking a closer look at hooks
- Implementing new hooks
- The provider API
- Providing a service

You should familiarize yourself with these techniques, as selecting an appropriate extension framework may mean the difference between an ill-fitting and hard-to-maintain application architecture and one that is elegant, maintainable, and extensible.

10.1 Implementing New Functions in Apache

10.1.1 Exporting Functions

Any module can export a function for use by other modules. At its simplest, it need only provide a header file that defines exported functions. Other modules can then `#include` the relevant header file and use the functions.

We saw an example of this in Chapter 6, where our `mod_choices` used functions exported by the XSLT filter module `mod_transform` to select a stylesheet:

```
mod_transform_set_XSLT(r, fmt->name);
```

To support this, all `mod_transform` has to do is export the relevant functions in a header file `mod_transform.h`:

```
AP_DECLARE(void) mod_transform_set_XSLT(request_rec* r,
                            const char* name) ;
AP_DECLARE(void) mod_transform_XSLTDoc(request_rec* r, xmlDocPtr doc) ;
```

In this instance, `mod_choices` depends explicitly on `mod_transform`, so this simple approach is sufficient. It does, however, introduce one support issue: `mod_choices` cannot be loaded before `mod_transform` in `httpd.conf`. To do so would cause a fatal error, because the symbol `mod_transform_set_XSLT` is unresolved when `mod_choices` tries to load.

In other cases, this approach can be more of a problem. Let's look at a couple of examples:

- `mod_include` requires a CGI module (`mod_cgi` or `mod_cgid`) if it is to process `<!--#exec cgi=...-->` directives. But these directives are rarely used, and `mod_include` can do everything else it needs without CGI. Thus it is undesirable for `mod_include` to *require* CGI support.

- `mod_publisher` can work with form inputs provided that `mod_form` has parsed them into an appropriate `apr_table`. However, most users of `mod_publisher` leave the task of working with form inputs to the content generator. As a consequence, we should be able to run `mod_publisher` without having to install `mod_form`.

- `mod_authnz_ldap` depends on `mod_ldap` for basic LDAP functions. Earlier versions of Apache required `mod_ldap` to be loaded before other LDAP modules. In Apache 2.2, LDAP modules can be loaded in any order.

10.1.2 Optional Functions

APR provides a solution to this dilemma: Optional functions can be exported by one module and imported by another without creating a dependency. To see how this process works, let's consider the simple example of `mod_form`, a module whose purpose is to parse data from an HTML form (`application/x-www-form-urlencoded`) into an `apr_table`.

`mod_form` provides two functions to other modules:

- `form_data` returns the table of all key/value pairs parsed.

- `form_value` returns the value of a given key in the table.

`mod_form` could, of course, export these functions the simple way:

```
AP_DECLARE(apr_table_t*) form_data(request_rec* r) ;
AP_DECLARE(const char*) form_value(request_rec* r, const char* key) ;
```

Unfortunately, that creates a dependency we prefer to avoid. Instead, `mod_form` exports them as optional functions, using the following declarations:

```
#include <apr_optional.h>
APR_DECLARE_OPTIONAL_FN(apr_table_t*, form_data, (request_rec*) ) ;
APR_DECLARE_OPTIONAL_FN(const char*, form_value,
                        (request_rec*, const char*) ) ;
```

Implementing the Functions

Implementing these functions requires two things in `mod_form` itself. First, it needs the functions, which are straightforward and can be declared as `static`:

```
static apr_table_t* form_data(request_rec* r) {
  form_ctx* ctx = ap_get_module_config(r->request_config, &form_module);
  return ctx ? ctx->vars : NULL ;
}
static const char* form_value(request_rec* r, const char* arg) {
  form_ctx* ctx = ap_get_module_config(r->request_config, &form_module);
  if ( ! ctx || ! ctx->vars )
    return NULL ;
  return apr_table_get(ctx->vars, arg) ;
}
```

Here, `ctx->vars` is the table into which `mod_form` has parsed any available form data.

Second, `mod_form` needs to export the functions as optional functions by registering them in the `form_hooks` callback (where, of course, the module's own callbacks are also registered):

```
static void form_hooks(apr_pool_t* pool) {
  ap_hook_fixups(form_fixups, NULL, NULL, APR_HOOK_MIDDLE) ;
  ap_register_input_filter("form-vars", form_filter, NULL,
                           AP_FTYPE_RESOURCE) ;
  APR_REGISTER_OPTIONAL_FN(form_data) ;
  APR_REGISTER_OPTIONAL_FN(form_value) ;
}
```

Using the Functions

Now, a client module such as `mod_sql` or `mod_publisher`, having `#included` `mod_form.h`, just needs to retrieve the optional function. Both modules just retrieve the data to their own tables, during per-request initialization:

```
typedef struct my_ctxt {
  ....
  apr_table_t* form_vars;
  ....
};

static int my_init_function(ap_filter_t* f) {
  apr_table_t* (*form_vars)(request_rec*) ;
  my_ctxt* ctx = f->ctx = apr_pcalloc(f->r->pool, sizeof(my_ctxt)) ;
  ....
  form_vars = APR_RETRIEVE_OPTIONAL_FN(form_data);
  if (form_vars != NULL) {
    /* The function returns the table of data, so in future we can just
     * look things up as we would with request headers or subprocess env
     */
    ctx->form_vars = form_vars(f->r) ;
  }
  ....
  return OK;
}
```

In this case, if `mod_form` isn't available, the client modules will still work, albeit without the capability of accessing data from form inputs.

10.2 Hooks and Optional Hooks

In the preceding chapters, we discussed the Apache processing hooks. In Apache 1.x, this would have been the whole story: A fixed sequence of hooks was hard-wired into the server.

Likewise, Apache 2 has a de facto "standard" sequence of hooks that are available in a default installation, and that reflect the older architecture. However, hooks in Apache 2 serve a more general purpose. Any module can extend the API by providing additional hooks or optional hooks, extending an invitation to other modules to provide their own behavior at this point. For example, `mod_proxy` provides hooks into the request it is making to the back-end server, and `mod_dav` provides optional hooks for implementing additional HTTP methods. Both modules are characterized by being extensible—that is, you can plug in more modules. In fact, they depend on additional modules implementing the hooks provided. They are extending the API by providing these additional hooks.

10.2.1 A Closer Look at Hooks

Before we look at implementing a new hook, let's take a closer look at the kind of hooks we've seen already. Recall these examples from Chapters 5 and 6:

```
ap_hook_handler(helloworld_handler, NULL, NULL, APR_HOOK_MIDDLE);
ap_hook_type_checker(choices_select, NULL, NULL, APR_HOOK_FIRST);
```

Both of these hooks appear in a `register_hooks` function, which is run at server start-up. The respective modules are registering their own functions to play some part in Apache's behavior. But what exactly does that mean?

A hook is simply a point in Apache's processing where a module can insert its own function to implement new behavior. Any module can extend the API by providing additional hooks or optional hooks, thereby extending an invitation to other modules to provide their own behavior at this point. The calling code implements one of the following logics:

- Run all functions registered on this hook in order.

- Run functions registered on this hook until one returns any value other than `DECLINED`.

- Run all functions until and unless one returns an error (that is, anything other than `OK` or `DECLINED`).

Implementing a hook is done by means of macros defined in `apr_hooks.h`, `apr_optional_hooks.h`, and `ap_config.h`. The three logics, respectively, are associated with

- `AP_IMPLEMENT_EXTERNAL_HOOK_VOID`

- `AP_IMPLEMENT_EXTERNAL_HOOK_RUN_FIRST`

- `AP_IMPLEMENT_EXTERNAL_HOOK_RUN_ALL`

(or their APR versions when working outside the context of `httpd`).

For reasons we'll discuss later in this chapter, a module outside the Apache core should normally implement any hooks as optional hooks. Only one standard macro is defined for optional hooks, but any of the previously mentioned functions can also be treated as an optional hook by client modules.

When a module implements a hook (though not an optional hook), it exports a hook function such as `ap_hook_handler` or `ap_hook_translate_name`. As we saw in Chapter 6, a sequence of them appear in the request processing cycle. The core also implements other standard hooks.

Initialization at Server Start-up

- **test_config**—hook into configuration testing

- **optional_fn_retrieve**—run before anything else after all modules are loaded

- **pre_config**—run before processing configuration directives

- **post_config**—run after processing configuration directives

- **open_logs**—run when Apache opens its log files

- **pre_mpm**—run ahead of the MPM launching worker processes and/or threads

- **child_init**—run after an `httpd` child has forked, but before it becomes multithreaded or starts to accept connections

Hooks into the Core Exported by mpm_common

- **monitor**—polled in the parent process

- **fatal_exception**—run when Apache crashes

There are also hooks into connection creation and processing, request creation, and protocol handling. In addition, a number of hooks are exported not by the core, but rather by the standard modules. The latter functions are implemented as optional hooks.

10.2.2 Order of Execution

Returning to the hooks in our earlier modules, we had

```
ap_hook_handler(helloworld_handler, NULL, NULL, APR_HOOK_MIDDLE);
ap_hook_type_checker(choices_select, NULL, NULL, APR_HOOK_FIRST);
```

In each case, the first argument is the function we are hooking in to Apache. The other three arguments are concerned with the order of execution when multiple modules have inserted functions on the same hook.

The final argument is an expression indicating where the function should run. For the majority of modules, it really doesn't matter whether their functions run before or after others on the same hook; such modules should use APR_HOOK_MIDDLE. Other modules may need to run a function either before or after "all other" functions on the same hook have run; these modules can use APR_HOOK_FIRST or APR_HOOK_LAST. The values APR_HOOK_REALLY_FIRST and APR_HOOK_REALLY_LAST are also available, although they are seldom appropriate and may give unexpected behavior. For example, a REALLY_LAST function may never run if it follows an Apache standard function that never returns DECLINED.

The two NULL values are the *predecessors* and *successors* of our function, and they offer fine control. Instead of expressing a general desire to run before or after other (unspecified) modules, they offer the opportunity to name other modules explicitly. They are appropriate for closely related modules whose functions, if both modules are present, *must* run in a particular order. These arguments take the form of a NULL-terminated list of modules that must run before or after ours.

An example arises in the authorization modules, where several modules require mod_authz_owner (if present) to run before their own hooks. Here's how mod_authz_groupfile declares it:

```
static void register_hooks(apr_pool_t *p)
{
    static const char * const aszPre[]={ "mod_authz_owner.c", NULL };
    ap_hook_auth_checker(check_user_access, aszPre,
                NULL, APR_HOOK_MIDDLE);
}
```

10.2.3 Optional Hooks Example: mod_authz_dbd

mod_authz_dbd is, in part, a standard authorization (authz) module, implementing group access by means of SQL queries (i.e., checking an SQL database for
whether a user is a member of a group). In addition to this standard function, it
implements login and logout functions that work by setting a flag in the database
to indicate whether the user is currently logged in.

Although mod_authz_dbd manages the server state, it doesn't care about the client.
Nevertheless, a server that implements login/logout may also wish to manage the
client state—for example, by setting a cookie or other session token. Ideally, the
client session should be tied to the server session, so the two always remain in agreement. mod_authz_dbd supports this approach by exporting an optional hook. A
module managing a client session can use this hook to implement its client-side
login and logout exactly when the server successfully performs these functions.

Exporting an Optional Hook

mod_authz_dbd exports the hook by declaring it in a header file and implementing it in the C file. This is made very simple by the macros from apr_hooks.h and
apr_optional_hooks.h.

First, here is the declaration in mod_authz_dbd.h:

```
APR_DECLARE_EXTERNAL_HOOK(authz_dbd, AP, int, client_login,
                     (request_rec *r, int code, const char *action))
```

This declares an external hook called client_login, with arguments consisting of
the preprocessor namespace AP (implemented by Apache) and the C namespace
authz_dbd. The template for a client_login function is also determined by the
arguments:

```
int func(request_rec*, int, const char*)
```

The implementation in mod_authz_dbd.c is almost as simple. A macro expands
to implement a function authz_dbd_run_client_login:

```
APR_IMPLEMENT_OPTIONAL_HOOK_RUN_ALL(authz_dbd, AP, int, client_login,
                     (request_rec *r, int code, const char *action),
                     (r, code, action), OK, DECLINED)
```

Finally, there is a call to run the functions registered for the hook in the function
implementing server-side login/logout:

```
static int authz_dbd_login(request_rec *r, authz_dbd_cfg *cfg,
              const char *action)
```

```
{
    /* code omitted -- perform database login/logout */
    if (successful) {
        authz_dbd_run_client_login(r, code, action);
    }
    return code ;
}
```

That's all! Now a module implementing client sessions can hook a function straight into `authz_dbd_login`:

```
static int client_cookie(request_rec *r, int code, const char *action) {
    if (strcmp(action, "login") == 0) {
        /* Set authentication token in client session cookie */
    }
    else if (strcmp(action, "logout") == 0) {
        /* Clear session cookie */
    }
    return OK;
}
static void register_hooks(apr_pool_t *pool) {
    APR_OPTIONAL_HOOK(authz_dbd, client_login, client_cookie,
                NULL, NULL, APR_HOOK_MIDDLE);
}
```

Now our `client_cookie` function runs whenever someone successfully logs in or out through `mod_authz_dbd`.

We could have implemented this function as a non-optional hook, by replacing the macro `APR_IMPLEMENT_OPTIONAL_HOOK_RUN_ALL` with `APR_IMPLEMENT_EXTERNAL_HOOK_RUN_ALL` from `apr_hooks.h`. Then a client function could use the familiar form of declaration:

```
static void register_hooks(apr_pool_t *pool) {
    authz_dbd_hook_client_session(client_cookie,
                    NULL, NULL, APR_HOOK_MIDDLE);
}
```

The drawback is that this approach would cause a fatal link error if the client session module is loaded before `mod_authz_dbd`. Hence we follow the general advice to use optional hooks in non-core modules.

> NOTE This has nothing to do with security, for which only the server protection matters. The session is managed from both the server side and the client side for the convenience of legitimate users accessing the system as designed.

10.3 The Provider API

The `ap_provider` API provides yet another means for modules to extend the Apache API in a manner slightly reminiscent of exporting a Java interface or C++ virtual base class. A module exporting a new API defines an interface and leaves it to others to implement providers for the interface. A provider is typically implemented in another module, and it instantiates the interface with its own behavior.

The provider API is most useful when we need to support several distinct behaviors in a particular situation, and it works well when the available options will be controlled directly by a server administrator in `httpd.conf`. It ensures that new modules can add new behaviors without affecting existing code or users.

Within the Apache core distribution, the main example demonstrating the `ap_provider` API is the authentication framework (others occur in `mod_proxy` and `mod_cache`). Authentication in Apache 2.2 comprises several well-defined tasks (see Chapter 7). One of those tasks is looking up a username/password to verify the credentials presented. This lookup can be done in many ways, so we need an API for modules to implement it. This functionality is implemented by exporting a provider API. Each lookup module works by registering its own implementation of the provider.

Two standard modules export the API:

- **mod_auth_basic** implements HTTP basic authentication.
- **mod_auth_digest** implements HTTP digest authentication.

The standard lookup modules that implement providers include the following:

- **mod_authn_file** looks up a username/password in a classic `htpasswd` file.
- **mod_authn_dbm** looks it up in a DBM database (with `apr_dbm`).
- **mod_authn_dbd** looks it up in an SQL database (with `apr_dbd`).
- **mod_authn_ldap** looks it up in an LDAP directory.
- **mod_authn_anon** allows anonymous authentication, by substituting simple rules for any lookup.

These lookup modules can be used with either of the modules exporting the API.

A slightly more complex example is the XML namespace framework. It is based on an output filter that parses XML on the fly using a SAX2 parser, and it enables modules to process different XML namespaces in the markup. This offers a modular and far faster alternative to XSLT filtering for a range of applications involving post-processing of XML, as well as options for embedded processing and scripting.

At the time of writing, two modules export the namespace framework:

- **mod_xmlns** is a minimal implementation.

- **mod_publisher** implements the namespace framework in the context of an extremely feature-rich, general-purpose rewriting module for both HTML and XML.

Namespace modules will work with either of those modules.

To illustrate the provider API, let's look at the XML namespace API (Figure 10-1). The module providing the namespace filter is a SAX2 parser; current implementations are mod_publisher and mod_xmlns. Let's look at mod_xmlns, whose sole function is to provide the namespace API. In Figure 10-1, we show XHTML, annotations, SQL queries, and Dublincore metadata, each of which is implemented by a separate module. The key part of the API is for mod_xmlns to enable these modules to register themselves and take charge of processing selected markup.

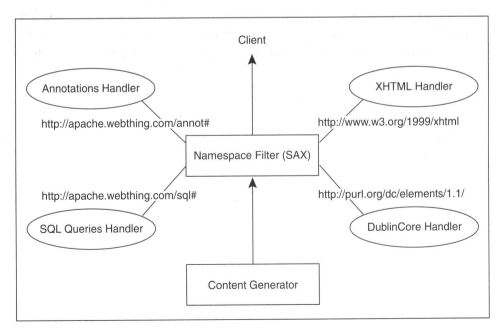

FIGURE 10-1
XML namespace API

The key configuration directive provided by `mod_xmlns` is

```
XMLNSUseNamespace namespace-uri [action] [version]
```

A namespace module works by registering a provider for `namespace-uri` with the server. `XMLNSUseNamespace` then activates the provider as a handler for XML elements in the namespace. For example,

```
XMLNSUseNamespace http://www.w3.org/1999/xhtml On 1.0
```

activates handler version 1.0 of provider `http://www.w3.org/1999/xhtml` (which ensures that XHTML is Appendix C–compliant and can be served to real-life Web browsers as HTML). Other events may be handled by another handler. For example, if the source document also provides metadata as RDF (such as `mod_choices`), any Dublincore[1] metadata elements can be served to HTML browsers as <META> elements with

```
XMLNSUseNamespace http://purl.org/dc/elements/1.1/ On xhtml
```

which registers a handler for the Dublincore namespace.

10.3.1 Implementation

Unlike the API extensions we have looked at so far, the provider API works solely on a global lookup table. It doesn't need to export any function declarations, and in principle it might not need a header file at all, although in practice it is likely to export a declaration of the provider structure it implements.

In the case of `mod_xmlns`, the provider implements a configuration directive, so the API is exported from a configuration handler function:

```
static const command_rec xmlns_cmds[] = {
  AP_INIT_TAKE123("XMLNSUseNamespace", use_namespace, NULL, OR_ALL, NULL) ,
  ....
}
static const char* use_namespace(cmd_parms* cmd, void* cfg,
       const char* uri, const char* action, const char* version) {
  xmlns_rec* rec;
  void* handler = ap_lookup_provider("xmlns", uri, version) ;
  if ( !handler ) {
     return "Can't use namespace: not loaded or incompatible version" ;
  }
```

---

1. `http://dublincore.org/`

```
    /* Code omitted here, including checking the namespace is compiled
     * to the same version of the API as us and won't just segfault
     */

    rec = apr_hash_get(((xmlns_cfg*)cfg)->namespaces,
            uri,APR_HASH_KEY_STRING) ;
    if ( ! rec ) {
        rec = apr_palloc(cmd->pool, sizeof(xmlns_rec) ) ;
        rec->handler = handler ;
        apr_hash_set(((xmlns_cfg*)cfg)->namespaces, uri,
                APR_HASH_KEY_STRING, rec) ;
    }
  rec->onoff = onoff ;
  return NULL;
}
```

The key to the API is `ap_lookup_provider`. If a module implementing a provider for the requested URI and version is loaded, it will be configured as active for XML events in the URI's namespace according to the value of `onoff`. The parser will then dispatch every XML event in the namespace to the registered provider when a document is parsed.

10.3.2 Implementing a Provider

The `handler` in the preceding example is treated as `void*`, but, of course, it is known to `mod_xmlns`. It is actually a struct, defined in the header file `xmlns.h` (which is common to both `mod_publisher` and `mod_xmlns`):

```
typedef struct xmlns {
  /* Version helps ensure we don't load a provider that's compiled to
   * an API version that isn't binary-compatible with the version of
   * mod_xmlns/mod_publisher in use
   */
  int version;

/* SAX2 Events */
  int (*StartElement) ( xmlns_public*, const parsedname*,
                const xmlns_attr_t*) ;
  int (*EndElement) ( xmlns_public*, const parsedname*) ;
  void (*StartNamespace) ( xmlns_public*,
        const xml_char_t*, const xml_char_t* ) ;
  void (*EndNamespace) ( xmlns_public*, const xml_char_t* ) ;

/* Allow a comment handler. Many people put a function in
 * comments, and mod_xmlns will dispatch to this comment handler if
 * this prefix is non-null and the start of the comment matches it.
 */
  const char* comment_prefix ;
  int (*CommentHandler) (xmlns_public*, const xml_char_t*) ;
```

```
/* We may want to set up custom handlers for characters and
 * cdata.  These are kept on a stack, with the innermost namespace
 * in control.
 */
  int (*CharactersHandler)(xmlns_public*, const xml_char_t*, int len) ;
  int (*CdataHandler)(xmlns_public*, const xml_char_t*, int len) ;
} xmlns ;
```

A provider module works by implementing one or more xmlns structures, and registering them as providers for xmlns. An example is mod_xhtml, which registers three providers for two namespaces:

```
/* Process XHTML to ensure Appendix C compliance, and at the same
 * time process server-side include (SSI) directives.
 * This duplicates the function of mod_includes, but means we
 * can run both the SSI and Appendix C tasks in a single parse.
 */
static xmlns xmlns_xhtml_ssi = {
  XMLNS_VERSION ,          /* Version of xmlns.h */
  xhtml_start ,          /* StartElement */
  xhtml_end ,            /* EndElement  */
  ssi_init ,             /* StartNSDecl  */
  ssi_term ,             /* EndNSDecl    */
  "#" ,                  /* Comment identifier */
  ssi_comment ,          /* Comment handler */
  NULL, NULL             /* Characters and CDATA */
} ;

/* SSI maps trivially to an XML namespace. For no additional effort, we can
implement it that way, and give content developers the choice of which form
to use.
*/
static xmlns xmlns_ssi = {
  XMLNS_VERSION ,           /* Version of xmlns.h */
  ssi_start ,            /* StartElement */
  ssi_end ,             /* EndElement   */
  ssi_init ,            /* StartNSDecl  */
  ssi_term ,            /* EndNSDecl    */
  NULL ,                /* Comment identifier */
  NULL ,                /* Comment handler */
  NULL, NULL            /* Characters and CDATA */
} ;

/* XHTML Appendix C only; no SSI support */
static xmlns xmlns_xhtml10 = {
  XMLNS_VERSION ,           /* Version of xmlns.h */
  xhtml_start ,         /* StartElement */
  xhtml_end ,           /* EndElement   */
  NULL ,                /* StartNSDecl  */
  NULL ,                /* EndNSDecl    */
  NULL ,                /* Comment identifier */
```

```
  NULL ,                 /* Comment handler */
  NULL, NULL             /* Characters and CDATA */
} ;

static void xhtml_hooks(apr_pool_t* pool) {

  /* Register the bare provider for XHTML as version "1.0" */
  /* XHTML10 is #defined as "http://www.w3.org/1999/xhtml" */
  ap_register_provider(pool, "xmlns", XHTML10 , "1.0", &xmlns_xhtml10) ;

  /* Register provider for XHTML with SSI support as version "ssi" */
  ap_register_provider(pool, "xmlns", XHTML10 ,
             "ssi", &xmlns_xhtml_ssi) ;

  /* Register a provider for a separate SSI namespace */
  ap_register_provider(pool, "xmlns", SSI , "ssi", &xmlns_ssi) ;
}
```

As we can see, the xmlns struct is closer to the module struct itself than to the single-purpose optional function or hook. In general, the provider API is well suited to supporting new classes of applications, in which implementing a provider will be the sole or main purpose of a new module. Similarly, within the standard Apache 2.2 distribution, each of the mod_authn_* modules implements a provider for authentication.

10.4 Providing a Service

The final way to extend Apache for the benefit of other modules is to provide a general-purpose service. This doesn't offer a separate means of extending the API, but rather represents an optional extension of the Apache core implemented in a module. In fact, most of Apache's core functions are implemented by a number of standard modules, so we could simply describe this approach as extending the Apache core.

10.4.1 Example: mod_dbd

A prime example is mod_dbd, which is Apache's provider for the database framework (Chapter 11). The purpose of mod_dbd is to provide a service to modules needing an SQL back end. It improves the efficiency and scalability of Apache + SQL architectures over classic LAMP in two important ways:

- It provides a dynamic pool of connections that can be shared across threads in an efficient manner.

- It provides connections that can be shared by different modules using a database, including authentication, scripting languages such as PHP and Perl, and logging.

mod_dbd exports a simple API that hides the complexities of managing the connections, including the pool itself and the alternative single persistent connection when running on a nonthreaded platform. The core of mod_dbd is an apr_reslist, the APR structure for managing a dynamic pool of resources. The reslist is the key to the service provided by mod_dbd.

To implement a reslist service, mod_dbd must

- Provide a constructor and a destructor function for the reslist.

- Call apr_reslist_create to set up the reslist.

- Provide accessor functions to acquire a resource from the reslist, and then return it or mark it as invalid.

- Ensure apr_reslist_destroy is called at process shutdown to clean up.

Caution

This discussion is focused on the apr_reslist. However, mod_dbd also needs to work when the APR has been built without threads, such that apr_reslist is not available. The actual mod_dbd code uses constructs like

```
#if APR_HAS_THREADS
  .... reslist-based code ...
#else
  .... implement a single persistent connection ...
#endif
```

in many places. We'll ignore these cases for the sake of brevity.

10.4.2 Implementing the reslist

First. let's consider the constructor and destructor. These functions are callbacks for apr_reslist, which determines their function signatures:

```
/* An apr_reslist_constructor for SQL connections.
 * Also use this for opening in non-reslist modes, since it gives
 * us all the error handling in one place.
 */
static apr_status_t dbd_construct(void **db, void *params,
                        apr_pool_t *pool)
{
    svr_cfg *svr = (svr_cfg*) params;
    ap_dbd_t *rec = apr_pcalloc(pool, sizeof(ap_dbd_t));
    apr_status_t rv;
```

```
    /* This pool allows dbd_close to destroy the prepared statements */
    rv = apr_pool_create(&rec->pool, pool);
    if (rv != APR_SUCCESS) {
        ap_log_perror(APLOG_MARK, APLOG_CRIT, rv, pool,
                        "DBD: Failed to create memory pool");
        return rv;
    }

/* The driver is loaded at config time, so get_driver just
 * checks a hash, and the error checking is unnecessary.
 * We keep it in case this situation changes in future.
 */
    rv = apr_dbd_get_driver(rec->pool, svr->name, &rec->driver);
    switch (rv) {
    case APR_ENOTIMPL:
        ap_log_perror(APLOG_MARK, APLOG_CRIT, rv, rec->pool,
                        "DBD: driver for %s not available", svr->name);
        return rv;
    case APR_EDSOOPEN:
        ap_log_perror(APLOG_MARK, APLOG_CRIT, rv, rec->pool,
                        "DBD: can't find driver for %s", svr->name);
        return rv;
    case APR_ESYMNOTFOUND:
        ap_log_perror(APLOG_MARK, APLOG_CRIT, rv, rec->pool,
                "DBD: driver for %s is invalid or corrupted", svr->name);
        return rv;
    default:
        ap_log_perror(APLOG_MARK, APLOG_CRIT, rv, rec->pool,
                    "DBD: mod_dbd not compatible with apr in get_driver");
        return rv;
    case APR_SUCCESS:
        break;
    }

    /* Open the database. This could very easily fail (e.g., if the
     * back end is down or unreachable), so we have to handle it.
     */
    rv = apr_dbd_open(rec->driver, rec->pool, svr->params,&rec->handle);
    switch (rv) {
    case APR_EGENERAL:
        ap_log_perror(APLOG_MARK, APLOG_CRIT, rv, rec->pool,
                        "DBD: Can't connect to %s", svr->name);
        return rv;
    default:
        ap_log_perror(APLOG_MARK, APLOG_CRIT, rv, rec->pool,
                        "DBD: mod_dbd not compatible with apr in open");
        return rv;
    case APR_SUCCESS:
        break;
    }
```

```
    /* This is what we're setting for the reslist */
    *db = rec;

    /* Initialize prepared statements from httpd.conf with the back end */
    rv = dbd_prepared_init(rec->pool, svr, rec);

    return rv;
}
```

dbd_destruct is a wrapper having the signature required by the reslist, whereas dbd_close can be passed to apr_pool_cleanup functions.

```
static apr_status_t dbd_close(void *CONN)
{
    ap_dbd_t *conn = CONN;
    apr_status_t rv = apr_dbd_close(conn->driver, conn->handle);
    apr_pool_destroy(conn->pool);
    return rv;
}
static apr_status_t dbd_destruct(void *sql, void *params,
                        apr_pool_t *pool)
{
    return dbd_close(sql);
}
```

Now that we have our callbacks, let's look at the function that creates the reslist. Note that svr->dbpool here is an apr_reslist_t*.

```
static apr_status_t dbd_setup(apr_pool_t *pool, svr_cfg *svr)
{
    apr_status_t rv;

    /* Create a pool just for the reslist from a process-lifetime pool;
     * that pool (s->process->pool in the dbd_setup_lock case,
     * whatever was passed to ap_run_child_init in the dbd_setup_init
     * case) will be shared with other threads doing other non-mod_dbd
     * things, so we can't use it for the reslist directly.
     */
    rv = apr_pool_create(&svr->pool, pool);
    if (rv != APR_SUCCESS) {
        ap_log_perror(APLOG_MARK, APLOG_CRIT, rv, pool,
                    "DBD: Failed to create reslist memory pool");
        return rv;
    }

    rv = apr_reslist_create(&svr->dbpool, svr->nmin, svr->nkeep,
                svr->nmax, apr_time_from_sec(svr->exptime),
                        dbd_construct, dbd_destruct, svr, svr->pool);
    if (rv == APR_SUCCESS) {
```

```
            apr_pool_cleanup_register(svr->pool, svr->dbpool,
                                      (void*)apr_reslist_destroy,
                                      apr_pool_cleanup_null);
    }
    else {
        ap_log_perror(APLOG_MARK, APLOG_CRIT, rv, svr->pool,
                      "DBD: failed to initialize");
        apr_pool_destroy(svr->pool);
        svr->pool = NULL;
    }

    return rv;
}
```

This function in itself is not thread safe: It sets a field in the server configuration, which is common to all threads. The appropriate hook for it in the Apache architecture is `child_init`, which runs after an Apache child process is created but before it creates its own pool of threads or (crucially) accepts asynchronous incoming connections. This order of operations should be normal practice for modules using a `reslist`.

In the case of `mod_dbd`, there's an additional complication: The `dbd_setup` function may fail. We want it to recover smoothly if the database is down when Apache is started, but becomes available later. Specifically, if the database access fails, we want to try again each time a client module asks for a connection, until we find that the database is up:

```
if (!svr->dbpool) {
    if (dbd_setup(pool, s) != APR_SUCCESS) {
        return NULL;
    }
}
```

But now we're working in a thread, so we need to acquire a thread mutex before running `dbd_setup`.

At this point, we have the core of our service: a `reslist` managing the objects we're interested in. The remainder of the module consists of two components:

- Client API: the functions we export for other modules

- Configuration functions for a systems administrator to manage the resource

For the purposes of our discussion here, the most important consideration is the API. It comprises five functions: `ap_dbd_open`, `ap_dbd_close`, `ap_dbd_acquire`, `ap_dbd_cacquire`, and `ap_dbd_prepare`. We'll explore usage of these functions in

Chapter 11. For now, we're just interested in implementing them. Here are the basic open and close functions:

```
DBD_DECLARE_NONSTD(ap_dbd_t*)
        ap_dbd_open(apr_pool_t *pool, server_rec *s)
{
    ap_dbd_t *arec;
    void *rec = NULL;
    svr_cfg *svr = ap_get_module_config(s->module_config, &dbd_module);
    apr_status_t rv = APR_SUCCESS;
    const char *errmsg;

    if (!svr->persist) {
        /* Return a once-only connection */
        rv = dbd_construct(&rec, svr, s->process->pool);
        arec = rec;
        return (rv == APR_SUCCESS) ? arec : NULL;
    }
```

If the database is down when we try to connect at server start-up, `svr->dbpool` will be `NULL`. We try to make this connection again now. If successful, this request takes the overhead of connecting to the database, but subsequent requests are spared it.

```
    if (!svr->dbpool) {
        if (dbd_setup_lock(pool, s) != APR_SUCCESS) {
            return NULL;
        }
    }
```

The core of this function is the acquisition of a resource from the `reslist`. Normally, we will just get an `ap_dbd_t*` from the pool, but `apr_reslist` may call our constructor internally if sufficient connections are not available in the pool.

```
    rv = apr_reslist_acquire(svr->dbpool, &rec);
    if (rv != APR_SUCCESS) {
        ap_log_perror(APLOG_MARK, APLOG_ERR, rv, pool,
                      "Failed to acquire DBD connection from pool!");
        return NULL;
    }
```

We also check that the connection is valid, provided the driver supports this ability. If a database connection has been lost, we mark it as invalid, so `apr_reslist` can destroy it and remove it from the pool.

```
    arec = rec;
    rv = apr_dbd_check_conn(arec->driver, pool, arec->handle);
    if ((rv != APR_SUCCESS) && (rv != APR_ENOTIMPL)) {
        errmsg = apr_dbd_error(arec->driver, arec->handle, rv);
        if (!errmsg) {
            errmsg = "(unknown)";
        }
```

```
        ap_log_perror(APLOG_MARK, APLOG_ERR, rv, pool,
                      "DBD[%s] Error: %s", svr->name, errmsg );
        apr_reslist_invalidate(svr->dbpool, rec);
        return NULL;
    }
    return arec;
}
```

The corresponding close function is simple:

```
DBD_DECLARE_NONSTD(void) ap_dbd_close(server_rec *s, ap_dbd_t *sql)
{
    svr_cfg *svr = ap_get_module_config(s->module_config, &dbd_module);
    if (!svr->persist) {
        dbd_close((void*) sql);
    }
    else {
        apr_reslist_release(svr->dbpool, sql);
    }
}
```

To make this functionality work in the context of a request, we want a slightly higher-level API. A module should be able to acquire a resource from the pool without having to worry about when to close it or whether this or another module also uses the same resource earlier or later in the same request. For this reason, we provide a wrapper function that performs the following tasks:

- Registers a cleanup to run when the request is destroyed (apr_pool_cleanup_register).

- Reserves the connection to the request, and keeps it for the duration of the request. When we open a connection, we store it with ap_set_module_config, so each subsequent call to ap_dbd_acquire need merely retrieve the stored pointer.

This requires an auxiliary struct and a cleanup function that can be passed to apr_pool_cleanup_register:

```
typedef struct {
    ap_dbd_t *conn;
    apr_reslist_t *dbpool;
} dbd_pool_rec;
static apr_status_t dbd_release(void *REQ)
{
    dbd_pool_rec *req = REQ;
    apr_reslist_release(req->dbpool, req->conn);
    return APR_SUCCESS;
}
```

```
DBD_DECLARE_NONSTD(ap_dbd_t*) ap_dbd_acquire(request_rec *r)
{
    svr_cfg *svr;
    dbd_pool_rec *req
        = ap_get_module_config(r->request_config, &dbd_module);
    if (!req) {
        req = apr_palloc(r->pool, sizeof(dbd_pool_rec));
        req->conn = ap_dbd_open(r->pool, r->server);
        if (req->conn) {
            svr = ap_get_module_config(r->server->module_config,
                            &dbd_module);
            ap_set_module_config(r->request_config, &dbd_module, req);
            if (svr->persist) {
                req->dbpool = svr->dbpool;
                apr_pool_cleanup_register(r->pool, req, dbd_release,
                                    apr_pool_cleanup_null);
            }
            else {
                apr_pool_cleanup_register(r->pool, req->conn, dbd_close,
                                    apr_pool_cleanup_null);
            }
        }
    }
    return req->conn;
}
```

At this point, we have written a set of core functions accessing DBD through a reslist, along with some accessor functions. Together, these functions provide a service for modules of many kinds, as described in Chapter 11. Our final task is to export the API in mod_dbd.h. But before doing so, let's take a look at those declarations.

10.5 Cross-Platform API Builds

All of the preceding examples, as well as many provided elsewhere in this book, use a range of macros in declaring their public/API functions. For example:

```
AP_DECLARE(void) mod_transform_set_XSLT(request_rec* r,
                        const char* name);
DBD_DECLARE_NONSTD(ap_dbd_t*) ap_dbd_acquire(request_rec *r);
module AP_MODULE_DECLARE_DATA helloworld_module;
```

Why aren't these standard C declarations?

```
void mod_transform_set_XSLT(request_rec* r, const char* name);
ap_dbd_t *ap_dbd_acquire(request_rec *r);
module helloworld_module;
```

The answer lies in Apache's cross-platform support, and specifically in its support for Windows. Whereas most target platforms (e.g., UNIX, Linux, MacOS, BeOS, OS2, Netware) support standard C and use build options to determine the linkage of the compiled and linked module, Microsoft's Visual C++ uniquely requires some of its build options to be hard-coded into the source. Thus, although it is possible to write modules for any platform using standard C, C++, or any other language with C linkage, those modules cannot be linked on Windows to an executable (dll) that will load as an Apache module. Of course, if we insert the proprietary keywords required by VC++, that's a syntax error in any standard C compiler.

10.5.1 Using Preprocessor Directives

Apache and APR work around this problem by using preprocessor directives. These directives follow a standard form, and any module that exports functions may have to define a new set. Here are the declarations from mod_dbd.h:

```
/* Create a set of DBD_DECLARE(type), DBD_DECLARE_NONSTD(type), and
 * DBD_DECLARE_DATA with appropriate export and import tags for the
 * platform
 */
#if !defined(WIN32)
#define DBD_DECLARE(type)            type
#define DBD_DECLARE_NONSTD(type)     type
#define DBD_DECLARE_DATA
#elif defined(DBD_DECLARE_STATIC)
#define DBD_DECLARE(type)            type __stdcall
#define DBD_DECLARE_NONSTD(type)     type
#define DBD_DECLARE_DATA
#elif defined(DBD_DECLARE_EXPORT)
#define DBD_DECLARE(type)            __declspec(dllexport) type __stdcall
#define DBD_DECLARE_NONSTD(type)     __declspec(dllexport) type
#define DBD_DECLARE_DATA             __declspec(dllexport)
#else
#define DBD_DECLARE(type)            __declspec(dllimport) type __stdcall
#define DBD_DECLARE_NONSTD(type)     __declspec(dllimport) type
#define DBD_DECLARE_DATA             __declspec(dllimport)
#endif
```

When building on non-Windows platforms, we can simply ignore these macros, as the preprocessor will remove them (or—usually easiest—leave it all to apxs, which ensures that you have the right build options for your platform). On Windows, the build may want some preprocessor macros defined. So, for a Windows build of mod_dbd, we define DBD_DECLARE_EXPORT to export API symbols from mod_dbd.

We do not define AP_DECLARE_EXPORT or any other such symbols, so API functions from the core, from APR, or from any other module are declared as imports.

Here's what some of the declarations look like in the headers included in mod_dbd.

Before the Preprocessor
```
/* an exported symbol */
DBD_DECLARE_NONSTD(ap_dbd_t*) ap_dbd_acquire(request_rec*);

/* an imported symbol */
APR_DECLARE(void *) apr_palloc(apr_pool_t *p, apr_size_t size);
```

After the Preprocessor (Standard C)
```
/* an exported symbol */
ap_dbd_t* ap_dbd_acquire(request_rec*);

/* an imported symbol */
void * apr_palloc(apr_pool_t *p, apr_size_t size);
```

After the Preprocessor (Windows)
```
/* an exported symbol */
__declspec(dllexport) ap_dbd_t* ap_dbd_acquire(request_rec*);

/* an imported symbol */
__declspec(dllimport) __stdcall void *
            apr_palloc(apr_pool_t *p, apr_size_t size);
```

10.5.2 Declaring the Module API

Now that we have dealt with the API macros, we can specify in full the API for our service module mod_dbd:

```
#ifndef DBD_H
#define DBD_H

/* Create a set of DBD_DECLARE(type), DBD_DECLARE_NONSTD(type), and
 * DBD_DECLARE_DATA with appropriate export and import tags for the
 * platform
 */
#if !defined(WIN32)
#define DBD_DECLARE(type)             type
#define DBD_DECLARE_NONSTD(type)      type
#define DBD_DECLARE_DATA
#elif defined(DBD_DECLARE_STATIC)
#define DBD_DECLARE(type)             type __stdcall
#define DBD_DECLARE_NONSTD(type)      type
#define DBD_DECLARE_DATA
```

```
#elif defined(DBD_DECLARE_EXPORT)
#define DBD_DECLARE(type)              __declspec(dllexport) type __stdcall
#define DBD_DECLARE_NONSTD(type)       __declspec(dllexport) type
#define DBD_DECLARE_DATA               __declspec(dllexport)
#else
#define DBD_DECLARE(type)              __declspec(dllimport) type __stdcall
#define DBD_DECLARE_NONSTD(type)       __declspec(dllimport) type
#define DBD_DECLARE_DATA               __declspec(dllimport)
#endif
#include <httpd.h>
#include <apr_optional.h>
#include <apr_hash.h>

typedef struct {
    apr_dbd_t *handle;
    const apr_dbd_driver_t *driver;
    apr_hash_t *prepared;
    apr_pool_t *pool;
} ap_dbd_t;

/* Export functions to access the database */

/* Acquire a connection that MUST be explicitly closed.
 * Returns NULL on error.
 */
DBD_DECLARE_NONSTD(ap_dbd_t*) ap_dbd_open(apr_pool_t*, server_rec*);

/* Release a connection acquired with ap_dbd_open */
DBD_DECLARE_NONSTD(void) ap_dbd_close(server_rec*, ap_dbd_t*);

/* Acquire a connection that will have the lifetime of a request
 * and MUST NOT be explicitly closed.  Return NULL on error.
 * This is the preferred function for most applications.
 */
DBD_DECLARE_NONSTD(ap_dbd_t*) ap_dbd_acquire(request_rec*);

/* Acquire a connection that will have the lifetime of a connection
 * and MUST NOT be explicitly closed.  Return NULL on error.
 * This is the preferred function for most applications.
 */
DBD_DECLARE_NONSTD(ap_dbd_t*) ap_dbd_cacquire(conn_rec*);

/* Prepare a statement for use by a client module during
 * the server start-up/configuration phase. Can't be called
 * after the server has created its children (use apr_dbd_*).
 */
DBD_DECLARE_NONSTD(void) ap_dbd_prepare(server_rec*, const char*,
                          const char*);

/* Also export them as optional functions for modules that prefer it */
APR_DECLARE_OPTIONAL_FN(ap_dbd_t*, ap_dbd_open,
                    (apr_pool_t*, server_rec*));
```

```
APR_DECLARE_OPTIONAL_FN(void, ap_dbd_close, (server_rec*, ap_dbd_t*));
APR_DECLARE_OPTIONAL_FN(ap_dbd_t*, ap_dbd_acquire, (request_rec*));
APR_DECLARE_OPTIONAL_FN(ap_dbd_t*, ap_dbd_cacquire, (conn_rec*));
APR_DECLARE_OPTIONAL_FN(void, ap_dbd_prepare,
                    (server_rec*, const char*, const char*));

APR_DECLARE_EXTERNAL_HOOK(dbd, DBD, int, construct, (ap_dbd_t *handle))

#endif
```

10.6 Summary

This chapter dealt with several advanced topics:

- Exporting functions from a module

- Optional functions

- A detailed look at hooks

- Optional hooks

- The provider API: exporting an interface

- Providing a service

- Cross-platform builds and declaration macros

Even if these issues are not obviously relevant to your current needs, it is worth familiarizing yourself with these basic techniques. The discussions in Chapter 10 are complemented by some of the techniques covered in Chapter 4, and mod_dbd is an important part of the database infrastructure discussed next, in Chapter 11.

Chapter 11

The Apache Database Framework

Many web applications involve an SQL database back end. The classic architecture for this is LAMP: Linux, Apache, MySQL, and Perl, Python, or PHP. LAMP has been in widespread use for a full decade, and in terms of its fundamental architecture has remained essentially unchanged since `mod_perl` introduced the persistent database connection in 1996. In addition to LAMP and other applications, databases are used in a number of stand-alone applications, such as authentication, logging, and dynamic configuration.

This chapter describes the Apache database framework, by exploring the following topics:

- The need for a new framework

- The DBD architecture

- The `apr_dbd` API (database operations)

- The `ap_dbd` API (database connection management)

- Applications (i.e., using DBD in your modules)

- Writing a DBD driver to support a back-end database

11.1 The Need for a New Framework

11.1.1 Apache 1.x/2.0 Versus Apache 2.2

With Apache 1.x and 2.0, modules requiring an SQL back end had to take responsibility for managing it themselves. Apart from reinventing the wheel, this approach can be very inefficient, for example, when each of several modules maintains its own connection. An analogy can be drawn to MS-DOS in the late 1980s, when every software application was supplied on a huge pile of floppy disks comprising mostly different drivers for every possible printer. This situation was eventually resolved when the operating system provided a single printing API to which both applications and printer drivers were expected to conform, thereby relieving application developers of an unnecessary burden.

Another reason for updating the original LAMP architecture was to improve the scalability of database applications. LAMP itself improved on the simplest CGI model by providing a persistent database connection, which is ideal for the Apache 1.x architecture (and the nonthreaded Prefork MPM in Apache 2). But the threaded MPMs in Apache 2 enable an altogether more efficient and scalable architecture, based on *connection pooling*.

Apache 2.2 and later provide the `ap_dbd` API for managing database connections (including optimized strategies for threaded and nonthreaded MPMs), while APR 1.2 and later provide the `apr_dbd` API for interacting with the database. New modules *should* use these APIs for all SQL database operations. Existing applications *should* be upgraded to use them where feasible, either transparently or as a recommended option to their users.

11.1.2 Connection Pooling

There is a fundamental mismatch between the (connectionless and stateless) HTTP protocol and the connection-oriented architecture of most, if not all, databases. This can easily lead to inefficiency in web-database applications.

11.1.2.1 The Simple CGI Model

The simplest form of dynamic web application is exemplified by CGI, in which a script external to the webserver takes responsibility for processing a request. If the script needs to use a database, it has to open and log into the database server, do its work, and then close the connection when it's finished. Creating a new connection for every request imposes a heavy overhead, and it makes CGI unsuitable for any but low-volume database applications.[1]

11.1.2.2 The Classic LAMP Model

The LAMP architecture deals with this problem by opening a persistent database connection and reusing it over many requests. In this way, it avoids the overhead of opening a new connection for every request. Unfortunately, this scheme brings its own problem: The overhead incurred by holding a large number of database connections open seriously limits the scalability of this architecture. This situation is made worse by the fact that every server process has to maintain its connection even when serving requests that make no use of the database, since such requests represent the vast majority of requests at most sites (even when pages are database-driven, contents such as images and stylesheets are usually static).

11.1.2.3 Taking Advantage of Apache 2

With Apache 2 and threaded MPMs, a range of altogether more efficient and scalable options become possible. Starting from what we already have, we can list our options:

- Classic CGI: one connection per request

- Classic LAMP: one persistent connection per thread

- Alternative LAMP: one persistent connection per process, with a mechanism for a thread to take and lock it for the duration of a request

- Connection pooling: more than one connection per process, but fewer than one per thread, with a mechanism for a thread to take and lock a connection from the pool

- Dynamic connection pooling: a variable-size connection pool, which will grow or shrink according to actual database traffic levels

---

1. This description applies to simple CGI, as implemented by Apache's mod_cgi. Other CGI implementations, such as fastcgi, provide workarounds for this problem.

Looking at these options in order, we can see the advantages and drawbacks of each one. We have already dealt with the first two possibilities. The third dispenses with the LAMP overhead at the cost of preventing parallel accesses to the back end. It may be an efficient solution in some cases, but it clearly presents its own problems when servicing concurrent requests.

The fourth and fifth options present an optimal solution whose scalability is limited only by the available hardware and operating system. The ratio of back-end connections to threads can reflect the proportion of the total traffic that requires the back end. Put in simple terms, if one in every five requests to the webserver requires the database, then a pool might have one connection per five threads. The optimal solution to managing back-end connections is a dynamic pool whose size is driven by actual demand rather than best-guess configuration.

11.2 The DBD Architecture

Figure 11-1 shows the four-layer DBD architecture in Apache. At the top, application modules implement functionality requiring use of the database. mod_dbd manages the database connections on behalf of modules, and apr_dbd provides an API for common SQL/database operations. Finally, drivers provide implementations of the API based on various SQL database packages, using the functions provided by the respective databases' client libraries.

Drivers are available at the time of writing for PostgreSQL 7+, MySQL 4.1+, SQLite 2/3, and Oracle 8+. If your application wants to use a database for which no apr_dbd driver is yet available, you are strongly urged to write a driver for your back end, so that other DBD applications will have the option to reuse it. We describe how to write a driver at the end of this chapter.

11.3 The apr_dbd API

apr_dbd is a simple unified API for accessing SQL databases, in the tradition of Perl's DBI/DBD. The nearest C equivalent, libdbi,[2] has sometimes been used for Apache modules, but is not an ideal fit for working with Apache; it is also licensed on terms that would make it problematic for the ASF to distribute. apr_dbd is, by design, integrated with Apache and APR, and it is built on key APR structures. In

---

2. http://libdbi.sourceforge.net/

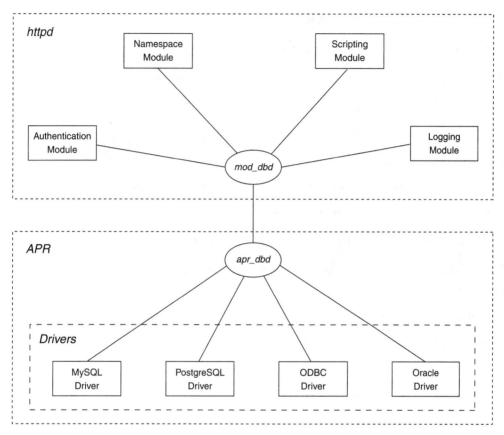

FIGURE 11-1
Apache DBD architecture

particular, all resource management in apr_dbd is based on APR pools, making it easy to use safely in Apache.

apr_dbd is a small API that supplies only a limited number of core functions likely to be of general interest. Modules that need to perform functions not supported have several options:

- Extend the apr_dbd API. If you think your extensions are of general interest, you might consider proposing them for inclusion in a future release of the standard API.

- Use apr_dbd_native() to obtain a "native" database handle. This gives you the full API of the underlying database, albeit at the expense of portability.

- Implement functions as SQL statements.
- Implement functions in an embedded language provided by the database.

The API defines six data types, which are used as opaque pointers in applications:

- `apr_dbd_driver_t`—a driver
- `apr_dbd_t`—a database handle
- `apr_dbd_prepared_t`—an SQL-prepared statement
- `apr_dbd_results_t`—a results set from a select statement
- `apr_dbd_row_t`—a row from a results set
- `apr_dbd_transaction_t`—an SQL transaction

Instantiation of the types is the responsibility of driver modules, and is different for each driver.

The anatomy of a typical `apr_dbd` application is, in outline form:

1. Initialize (`apr_dbd_init`).
2. Get a driver handle (`apr_dbd_get_driver`).
3. Open a database connection (`apr_dbd_open`).
4. Perform database operations (query, select, and so on).
5. Close the connection (`apr_dbd_close`).

When writing an application module, we delegate initialization and the management of drivers and connections to `mod_dbd`. All the application needs to deal with is the required database operations and (optionally) preparing statements in advance.

11.3.1 Database Operations

The database operations fall into several categories:

- Preparing SQL statements
- SQL statements that don't return a results set

- SQL statements that do return a results set
- Operations on a results set
- SQL transactions
- Miscellaneous operations (escape strings, handle errors)

Let's look at each of these in turn.

11.3.1.1 SQL Statements, Format Strings, Data Types, and Labels

apr_dbd uses the word *Query* to describe a database query (such as SQL INSERT or UPDATE) that doesn't return a results set, and *Select* for a query such as SELECT that returns results. There are three variants of each Query and Select:

- apr_dbd_query and apr_dbd_select execute an SQL statement supplied verbatim.
- apr_dbd_pquery and apr_dbd_pselect execute a prepared statement with arguments supplied in an argc/argv form.
- apr_dbd_pvquery and apr_dbd_pvselect execute a prepared statement with arguments supplied as a NULL-terminated varargs list.

Different database drivers support different statement formats. Consider, for example, a simple statement to look up a password for a user. The statement, though trivial, differs for different drivers:

- MySQL: SELECT password FROM users WHERE username = ?
- PostgreSQL: SELECT password FROM users WHERE username = $1
- Oracle: SELECT password FROM users WHERE username = :user

apr_dbd_prepare supports a unified format for all drivers:

- apr_dbd: SELECT password FROM users WHERE username = %s

This is based on stdio-like format string syntax, so an integer variable is %d, a floating-point number is %f, and a large object is %L. At present, there is no consistency between different drivers in what they support beyond the basic %s. Drivers *may* also support a "%123s" format, to indicate that a field in the database is of (maximum) size 123 and so cannot accommodate a larger value.

A prepared statement in any driver may be assigned a label in `apr_dbd_prepare`. This parameter is optional (it may be NULL) and may materially affect how the statement is prepared. Applications must follow two rules to use this technique efficiently:

- When preparing a statement for regular reuse (e.g., at server start-up), assign it a label.

- When preparing a statement for one-off use (e.g., during processing of a connection or request), *do not* assign it a label.

When assigning statements in a module, you should take care to ensure that all labels are *globally* unique for the connection. Recommended practice is to use a namespace associated with your module, together with a counter. For example:

```
static const char *make_label(apr_pool_t *pool)
{
    /* We normally use a label only when preparing statements at
     * server start-up.  If we use this function later, we'll need
     * to make it thread safe.
     */
    static unsigned int counter = 0;
    return apr_psprintf(pool, "my_module_%d", ++counter);
}
```

11.3.1.2 Results Sets (Cursors)

Each successful select operation will create a results set, corresponding to an SQL cursor. Queries may run synchronously and permit random access to any row by number, or they may run asynchronously and permit only sequential access to rows. Asynchronous operation is generally faster (especially for larger queries) with drivers that support it. This determination is made by a `random` argument to the `apr_dbd_select`-family functions. Applications expecting unspecified or large results sets should set this parameter to 0 (sequential access only), as this approach may be significantly faster and more efficient. For example, the PostgreSQL driver uses asynchronous operation when random access is not required.

There is no explicit `apr_dbd` function to clear or destroy a cursor, but it is important that you do one of the following:

- In sequential access mode, you must loop through all results until `apr_dbd_get_row` returns -1, indicating the end of the results.

- In random access mode, accessing an invalid row number with `apr_dbd_get_row` will clear the cursor.

11.3.1.3 Transactions

Transactions in `apr_dbd` correspond closely to SQL transactions. Transaction behavior depends on transaction mode, which is either `APR_DBD_TRANSACTION_COMMIT` (the default) or `APR_DBD_TRANSACTION_ROLLBACK`; either of these modes can be ORed with `APR_DBD_TRANSACTION_IGNORE_ERRORS`. Transactions follow these rules:

- When not in a transaction, all database operations are treated as in auto-commit-on-success mode.

- The transaction maintains a success-or-error state. If any database operation generates an error, the transaction is put into an error state.

- When the transaction is in an error state, no further database operations are performed while the transaction is in effect, and attempted operations will immediately return with an error. `APR_DBD_TRANSACTION_IGNORE_ERRORS` can be used to override this behavior.

- When a transaction is ended, it will either COMMIT or ROLLBACK. If the transaction is in an error state or if `APR_DBD_TRANSACTION_ROLLBACK` is set, it will ROLLBACK; otherwise, it will COMMIT. Within a transaction, nothing is committed or rolled back (unless you execute an SQL COMMIT or ROLLBACK using `apr_dbd_query`).

A limitation of the current implementation is that you cannot reliably have more than one concurrent transaction open on a single database connection (although some drivers may support this behavior). This constraint is not a problem in most modules, but it does mean that modules should follow some simple guidelines:

- When a module implements more than one hook involving database access, do not leave a transaction open between hooks.

- Filters execute effectively in parallel, so you should not use transactions except within a single call.

If you need to violate these rules, you'll have to open a private connection for your module with `ap_dbd_open`. Otherwise, this tactic is generally worth avoiding, as it is inefficient for a request to use more than one database connection.

11.3.2 API Functions

The full `apr_dbd` API is defined in `apr_dbd.h`. Note that some functions return an `int` instead of `apr_status_t`. Unless otherwise indicated, these functions return zero to indicate success or an error number from the underlying database on error. These error numbers can be used with `apr_dbd_error` to return a printable error message from the underlying database.

```
APU_DECLARE(apr_status_t) apr_dbd_init(apr_pool_t *pool);
```

Once-only initialization. Use the pool to register cleanups for shutdown.

```
APU_DECLARE(apr_status_t) apr_dbd_get_driver(apr_pool_t *pool,
          const char *name, const apr_dbd_driver_t **driver);
```

Get a driver by name.

```
APU_DECLARE(apr_status_t) apr_dbd_open(const apr_dbd_driver_t *driver,
          apr_pool_t *ptmp, const char *params, apr_dbd_t **handle);
```

Open a connection to a back end. `ptmp` is a working pool, and `params` is a driver-dependent connection string. Returns a connection in `handle`.

```
APU_DECLARE(apr_status_t) apr_dbd_close(const apr_dbd_driver_t *driver,
                              apr_dbd_t *handle);
```

Close a back-end connection.

```
APU_DECLARE(const char*) apr_dbd_name(const apr_dbd_driver_t *driver);
```

Get the name of a driver.

```
APU_DECLARE(void*) apr_dbd_native_handle(const apr_dbd_driver_t *driver,
                              apr_dbd_t *handle);
```

Return a native database handle of the underlying database.

```
APU_DECLARE(int) apr_dbd_check_conn(const apr_dbd_driver_t *driver,
            apr_pool_t *pool, apr_dbd_t *handle);
```

Check the status of a database connection. This function may attempt to reconnect if an error is encountered; it may also return APR_ENOTIMPL.

```
APU_DECLARE(int) apr_dbd_set_dbname(const apr_dbd_driver_t *driver,
            apr_pool_t *pool, apr_dbd_t *handle, const char *name);
```

Select a database name. This may be a no-op if it is not supported.

```
APU_DECLARE(int) apr_dbd_transaction_start(
            const apr_dbd_driver_t *driver, apr_pool_t *pool,
            apr_dbd_t *handle, apr_dbd_transaction_t **trans);
```

Start a transaction if supported. This may be a no-op. If a non-null *trans argument is supplied, it will be reused.

```
APU_DECLARE(int) apr_dbd_transaction_end(const apr_dbd_driver_t *driver,
                                         apr_pool_t *pool,
                                         apr_dbd_transaction_t *trans);
```

End a transaction, executing a COMMIT if all is well, or a ROLLBACK if there's an error or if the transaction mode is rollback.

```
APU_DECLARE(int) apr_dbd_transaction_mode_get(
    const apr_dbd_driver_t *driver, apr_dbd_transaction_t *trans);
```

Return the transaction mode.

```
APU_DECLARE(int) apr_dbd_transaction_mode_set(
                    const apr_dbd_driver_t *driver,
                        apr_dbd_transaction_t *trans, int mode);
```

Set the transaction mode (commit/rollback; ignore or abort on error). Returns the transaction mode we just set.

```
APU_DECLARE(int) apr_dbd_query(const apr_dbd_driver_t *driver,
            apr_dbd_t *handle, int *nrows, const char *statement);
```

Execute an SQL query statement that doesn't return a results set, passed as a literal string. Sets *nrows to the number of rows affected.

```
APU_DECLARE(int) apr_dbd_select(const apr_dbd_driver_t *driver,
          apr_pool_t *pool, apr_dbd_t *handle, apr_dbd_results_t **res,
          const char *statement, int random);
```

Execute an SQL query that returns a results set in `*res`. The query is a literal string `statement`. If `random` is zero, the query may run asynchronously and all results must be accessed in a for-next loop; if it is nonzero, the query runs synchronously and results can be accessed by row number.

```
APU_DECLARE(int) apr_dbd_num_cols(const apr_dbd_driver_t *driver,
                              apr_dbd_results_t *res);
```

Return the number of columns in a results set.

```
APU_DECLARE(int) apr_dbd_num_tuples(const apr_dbd_driver_t *driver,
                              apr_dbd_results_t *res);
```

Return the number of rows in a results set, or `-1` if the query was asynchronous.

```
APU_DECLARE(int) apr_dbd_get_row(const apr_dbd_driver_t *driver,
          apr_pool_t *pool, apr_dbd_results_t *res,
          apr_dbd_row_t **row, int rownum);
```

Get a row from a results set. If the query was synchronous, it gets row `rownum`; otherwise, `rownum` is ignored. If the query was asynchronous or if `rownum` is `-1`, it gets the next row. The function returns `0` on success, `-1` for `rownum` out of range or end-of-data, or an error. It automatically deletes the results set when `-1` is returned.

```
APU_DECLARE(const char*) apr_dbd_get_entry(
          const apr_dbd_driver_t *driver, apr_dbd_row_t *row, int col);
```

Return an entry from a row.

```
APU_DECLARE(const char*) apr_dbd_get_name(
                              const apr_dbd_driver_t *driver,
                                   apr_dbd_results_t *res, int col);
```

Return the name of a column in the results set.

```
APU_DECLARE(const char*) apr_dbd_error(const apr_dbd_driver_t *driver,
                                apr_dbd_t *handle, int errnum);
```

Get the current error message (if any). errnum is an error code from the operation that returned an error, but it may be ignored by the driver.

```
APU_DECLARE(const char*) apr_dbd_escape(const apr_dbd_driver_t *driver,
            apr_pool_t *pool, const char *string, apr_dbd_t *handle);
```

Escape a string so it is safe for query/select. The returned string is allocated
from pool.

```
APU_DECLARE(int) apr_dbd_prepare(const apr_dbd_driver_t *driver,
            apr_pool_t *pool, apr_dbd_t *handle, const char *query,
            const char *label, apr_dbd_prepared_t **statement);
```

Prepare a statement, allocated from pool and returned in statement. If
label is non-null, supply a label for it.

```
APU_DECLARE(int) apr_dbd_pquery(const apr_dbd_driver_t *driver,
            apr_pool_t *pool, apr_dbd_t *handle, int *nrows,
            apr_dbd_prepared_t *statement, int nargs, const char **args);
```

Like apr_dbd_query, but executes a prepared query, with arguments supplied
using the argc/argv convention.

```
APU_DECLARE(int) apr_dbd_pselect(const apr_dbd_driver_t *driver,
            apr_pool_t *pool, apr_dbd_t *handle, apr_dbd_results_t **res,
            apr_dbd_prepared_t *statement, int random,
            int nargs, const char **args);
```

Like apr_dbd_select, but executes a prepared query, with arguments supplied using the argc/argv convention.

```
APU_DECLARE(int) apr_dbd_pvquery(const apr_dbd_driver_t *driver,
            apr_pool_t *pool, apr_dbd_t *handle, int *nrows,
            apr_dbd_prepared_t *statement, ...);
```

Like apr_dbd_pquery, but uses arguments supplied in a varargs list.

```
APU_DECLARE(int) apr_dbd_pvselect(const apr_dbd_driver_t *driver,
            apr_pool_t *pool, apr_dbd_t *handle, apr_dbd_results_t **res,
            apr_dbd_prepared_t *statement, int random, ...);
```

Like apr_dbd_pselect, but uses arguments supplied in a varargs list.

11.4 The ap_dbd API

Whereas `apr_dbd` provides an API for SQL operations, `ap_dbd` is exported by `mod_dbd` (Chapter 10) and manages database connections on behalf of a module. Its work includes management of a dynamic pool of persistent database connections (or of a single persistent connection, in the case of a nonthreaded platform), so that application modules never need concern themselves with connection management.

The `ap_dbd` API provides one data type and five functions.

```
typedef struct {
    apr_dbd_t *handle;
    const apr_dbd_driver_t *driver;
    apr_hash_t *prepared;
} ap_dbd_t;
```

The `ap_dbd_t` object comprises a driver handle, a database handle, and a hash table of prepared statements indexed by label. These are available for use in `apr_dbd` operations.

The functions are shown here:

```
/* Acquire a connection that MUST be explicitly closed.
 * Returns NULL on error.
 */
ap_dbd_t* ap_dbd_open(apr_pool_t*, server_rec*);

/* Release a connection acquired with ap_dbd_open */
void ap_dbd_close(server_rec*, ap_dbd_t*);

/* Acquire a connection that will have the lifetime of a request
 * and MUST NOT be explicitly closed. Return NULL on error.
 * This is the preferred function for most applications.
 */
ap_dbd_t* ap_dbd_acquire(request_rec*);

/* Acquire a connection that will have the lifetime of a connection
 * and MUST NOT be explicitly closed. Return NULL on error.
 */
ap_dbd_t* ap_dbd_cacquire(conn_rec*);

/* Prepare a statement for use by a client module during
 * the server start-up/configuration phase. The const char*
 * args are the Statement and a Label. Can't be called
 * after the server has created its children (use apr_dbd_*).
 */
void ap_dbd_prepare(server_rec*, const char*, const char*);
```

Given that most modules concern themselves with processing an HTTP request or, more rarely, a TCP connection, they should normally use `ap_dbd_acquire` or `ap_dbd_cacquire`. These functions can be used any number of times within the processing of a request or connection, and are guaranteed to return the same connection handle every time they are called within the lifetime of the request. For example, a database authentication module, a content generator, and a database logging module will all share a single connection, making for efficient use of resources. This scheme is strongly recommended for most modules.

By contrast, `ap_dbd_open` obtains a different database connection in every call. Modules using `ap_dbd_open` will be those needing a connection with a lifetime incompatible with the `acquire`/`cacquire` functions, and those whose use of `apr_dbd_transactions` is incompatible with the guidelines given previously.

Finally, `ap_dbd_prepare` is intended *only* for the configuration phase; it will not work if used later.

11.5 An Example Application Module: mod_authn_dbd

The DBD framework evolved in public for two years before the release of Apache 2.2 made it a standard component. As a consequence, a number of applications have been developed using precursors to the current DBD framework. These include this author's `mod_sql`, a module implementing a namespace for SQL in XML using the xmlns filter framework,[3] so that queries can be embedded in XML and executed in a filter. Let's use DBD authentication as a simple example here.[4]

`mod_authn_dbd` is an authentication module. As described in Chapter 7, its purpose is to verify a password supplied by a user. The module implements an `ap_provider` comprising two functions to retrieve an encrypted password from an SQL database: one for a user (HTTP basic authentication) and one for a user+realm (digest authentication). In the interest of brevity, we'll confine our discussion to one of these functions.

---

3. `http://apache.webthing.com/xmlns/`
4. Since this chapter was written, a similar but improved and up-to-date module `mod_sqil` has been developed (`http://www.heute-morgen.de/modules/mod_sqil/`).

Authentication is a task that involves frequent repetition of a small number of SQL queries that can be specified in the server configuration, so preparing the statements at start-up time offers obvious benefits in this case. We will do so by exposing the SQL queries as configuration directives, and then using ap_dbd_prepare from our handler for those directives. First, here are our directives:

```
static const command_rec authn_dbd_cmds[] =
{
    AP_INIT_TAKE1("AuthDBDUserPWQuery", authn_dbd_prepare,
            (void *)APR_OFFSETOF(authn_dbd_conf, user), ACCESS_CONF,
            "Query used to fetch password for user"),
    AP_INIT_TAKE1("AuthDBDUserRealmQuery", authn_dbd_prepare,
            (void *)APR_OFFSETOF(authn_dbd_conf, realm), ACCESS_CONF,
            "Query used to fetch password for user+realm"),
    {NULL}
};
```

They will typically take the following form:

```
AuthDBDUserPWQuery "SELECT password FROM authn WHERE username = %s"
```

To prepare that SQL statement for frequent reuse, our configuration function uses ap_dbd_prepare as an optional function:

```
static ap_dbd_t *(*authn_dbd_acquire_fn)(request_rec*) = NULL;
static void (*authn_dbd_prepare_fn)
                (server_rec*, const char*, const char*) = NULL;

...

static const char *authn_dbd_prepare(cmd_parms *cmd, void *cfg,
                            const char *query)
{
    static unsigned int label_num = 0;
    char *label;

    if (authn_dbd_prepare_fn == NULL) {
      /* Retrieve the optional functions once only */
        authn_dbd_prepare_fn = APR_RETRIEVE_OPTIONAL_FN(ap_dbd_prepare);
        if (authn_dbd_prepare_fn == NULL) {
            return "You must load mod_dbd to enable AuthDBD functions";
        }
        authn_dbd_acquire_fn = APR_RETRIEVE_OPTIONAL_FN(ap_dbd_acquire);
    }

    /* Create a label we can access it by */
    label = apr_psprintf(cmd->pool, "authn_dbd_%d", ++label_num);
```

```
    /* Prepare it */
    authn_dbd_prepare_fn(cmd->server, query, label);

    /* Save the label here for our own use */
    return ap_set_string_slot(cmd, cfg, label);
}
```

When we need to authenticate a user, we will execute one of the queries we just prepared. Here's the function to look up a user's password in the database:

```
static authn_status authn_dbd_password(request_rec *r, const char *user,
                                       const char *password)
{
    apr_status_t rv;
    const char *dbd_password = NULL;
    char *colon_pw;
    apr_dbd_prepared_t *statement;
    apr_dbd_results_t *res = NULL;
    apr_dbd_row_t *row = NULL;

    authn_dbd_conf *conf = ap_get_module_config(r->per_dir_config,
                                                &authn_dbd_module);

    /* Get a database handle from mod_dbd */
    ap_dbd_t *dbd = authn_dbd_acquire_fn(r);
    if (dbd == NULL) {
        ap_log_rerror(APLOG_MARK, APLOG_ERR, 0, r,
                    "Error looking up %s in database", user);
        return AUTH_GENERAL_ERROR;
    }
    /* conf->user is the label we saved when we prepared the statement */
    if (conf->user == NULL) {
        ap_log_rerror(APLOG_MARK, APLOG_ERR, 0, r,
                "No DBD Authn configured!");
        return AUTH_GENERAL_ERROR;
    }

    statement = apr_hash_get(dbd->prepared, conf->user,
                    APR_HASH_KEY_STRING);
    if (statement == NULL) {
        ap_log_rerror(APLOG_MARK, APLOG_ERR, 0, r,
                "No DBD Authn configured!");
        return AUTH_GENERAL_ERROR;
    }

    /* Execute a pvselect with sequential access to results */
    if (apr_dbd_pvselect(dbd->driver, r->pool, dbd->handle, &res,
                statement, 0, user, NULL) != 0) {
        ap_log_rerror(APLOG_MARK, APLOG_ERR, 0, r,
                    "Error looking up %s in database", user);
        return AUTH_GENERAL_ERROR;
    }
```

```
/* Loop over all rows (we expect there to be only one, but
 * that's irrelevant)
 */
for (rv = apr_dbd_get_row(dbd->driver, r->pool, res, &row, -1);
     rv != -1;
     rv = apr_dbd_get_row(dbd->driver, r->pool, res, &row, -1)) {
    if (rv != 0) {
        ap_log_rerror(APLOG_MARK, APLOG_ERR, rv, r,
                    "Error looking up %s in database", user);
        return AUTH_GENERAL_ERROR;
    }
    if (dbd_password == NULL) {
        dbd_password = apr_dbd_get_entry(dbd->driver, row, 0);
    }
    /* We can't break out here or res won't get cleaned up
 * and we'll leave a dangling cursor in the database
     */
}

if (!dbd_password) {
    return AUTH_USER_NOT_FOUND;
}

rv = apr_password_validate(password, dbd_password);

if (rv != APR_SUCCESS) {
    return AUTH_DENIED;
}
return AUTH_GRANTED;
}
```

11.6 Developing a New DBD Driver

Sometimes you may wish to use Apache with a particular database that isn't currently supported by the DBD framework. The recommended way to do so is to add support for your database to Apache/APR by writing a new driver. This approach offers several benefits over simply managing the database from within your own module:

- **Architecture:** You get the benefit of mod_dbd's connection strategies optimized for performance and scalability on both threaded and nonthreaded platforms.

- **Reusability:** By writing an apr_dbd driver, you make support for your chosen back end available to other modules, including your own, those distributed with Apache itself, and third-party modules.

- **Scrutiny:** If you write a new driver and contribute it to the ASF (subject to any relevant intellectual property concerns), your work will be seen by other programmers, and it may be extended and improved.

Let's look at the anatomy of a driver. Third-party authors to date have most often taken the PostgreSQL driver as a reference implementation. We'll take the MySQL driver[5] as a case study to explain the elements of a driver.

11.6.1 The apr_dbd_internal.h Header File

As we saw earlier, applications access the apr_dbd API by including apr_dbd.h. Besides the public API, drivers need additional declarations in an extended API private to the apr_dbd subsystem. It is exposed in a private header file apr_dbd_internal.h (which, in turn, includes apr_dbd.h). This serves two purposes over and above the public API:

- It defines the apr_dbd_driver_t struct, which every driver implements.

- It exports a thread mutex for the apr_dbd system.

The apr_dbd_driver_t object is a struct comprising a name together with a number of functions corresponding to the apr_dbd API. The role of a driver is to export an apr_dbd_driver_t object, along with implementations of the functions. Partial implementations may be adequate for some purposes, so some functions may do nothing except return APR_ENOTIMPL.

11.6.2 Exporting a Driver

Given that the purpose of our driver is to export an apr_dbd_driver_t object, let's start by doing exactly that. Here's the declaration from the MySQL driver:

```
APU_DECLARE_DATA const apr_dbd_driver_t apr_dbd_mysql_driver = {
    "mysql",
    dbd_mysql_init,
    dbd_mysql_native,
    dbd_mysql_open,
    dbd_mysql_check_conn,
    dbd_mysql_close,
    dbd_mysql_select_db,
    dbd_mysql_transaction,
    dbd_mysql_end_transaction,
    dbd_mysql_query,
    dbd_mysql_select,
    dbd_mysql_num_cols,
    dbd_mysql_num_tuples,
    dbd_mysql_get_row,
```

---

5. This is as originally written for MySQL 4.1. The current driver has some conditional sections (omitted for brevity here) to support differences in MySQL 5.

```
    dbd_mysql_get_entry,
    dbd_mysql_error,
    dbd_mysql_escape,
    dbd_mysql_prepare,
    dbd_mysql_pvquery,
    dbd_mysql_pvselect,
    dbd_mysql_pquery,
    dbd_mysql_pselect,
    dbd_mysql_get_name,
    dbd_mysql_transaction_mode_get,
    dbd_mysql_transaction_mode_set
};
```

To complete the driver, all that remains is to implement each of these `apr_dbd` functions using the MySQL client API. To do so, we need to implement the `apr_dbd` data types. Apart from the driver (which is defined by `apr_dbd_internal.h`), these data types are private to the driver module itself, and will differ between drivers. Here are the definitions we use for MySQL (these are probably the simplest of any driver):

```
struct apr_dbd_prepared_t {
    MYSQL_STMT* stmt;
};
struct apr_dbd_transaction_t {
    int mode;
    int errnum;
    apr_dbd_t *handle;
};
struct apr_dbd_t {
    MYSQL* conn ;
    apr_dbd_transaction_t* trans ;
};
struct apr_dbd_results_t {
    int random;
    MYSQL_RES *res;
    MYSQL_STMT *statement;
    MYSQL_BIND *bind;
};
struct apr_dbd_row_t {
    MYSQL_ROW row;
    apr_dbd_results_t *res;
};
```

In summary, and setting aside housekeeping, we're mapping the `apr_dbd` API to MySQL:

- The handle object `apr_dbd_t` is a `MYSQL` handle.

- The `apr_dbd` prepared statement is a `MYSQL_STMT`.

- The `apr_dbd` results and row objects map to multiple MySQL objects.

11.6.3 The Driver Functions

To complete our driver, let's describe the functions.

init

`dbd_mysql_init` is called once only, when the driver is initialized. MySQL requires us to initialize it with `my_init` to ensure the client library will be thread safe and reentrant, and to call another function on exit:

```
static void dbd_mysql_init(apr_pool_t *pool)
{
    my_init();
    apr_pool_cleanup_register(pool, NULL, (void*)mysql_thread_end,
                    apr_pool_cleanup_null);
}
```

native

`dbd_mysql_native` returns a native handle for applications wanting functionality beyond the scope of the `apr_dbd` API:

```
static void *dbd_mysql_native(apr_dbd_t *handle)
{
    return handle->conn;
}
```

open

`dbd_mysql_open` opens a new connection to a back-end database. Because the API constrains the parameters to be passed in a single string argument, this function has to be parsed to extract the arguments to the native function `mysql_real_connect`. This parsing may be reused in other drivers—for example, the Oracle driver copied this code.

```
static apr_dbd_t *dbd_mysql_open(apr_pool_t *pool, const char *params)
{
    static const char *const delims = " \r\n\t;|,";
    const char *ptr;
    int i;
    const char *key;
    size_t klen;
    const char *value;
    size_t vlen;
    struct {
        const char *field;
        const char *value;
```

```
    } fields[] = {
        {"host", NULL},
        {"user", NULL},
        {"pass", NULL},
        {"dbname", NULL},
        {"port", NULL},
        {"sock", NULL},
        {NULL, NULL}
    };
    unsigned int port = 0;
    apr_dbd_t *sql = apr_pcalloc(pool, sizeof(apr_dbd_t));
    sql->conn = mysql_init(sql->conn);
    if ( sql->conn == NULL ) {
        return NULL;
    }
    for (ptr = strchr(params, '='); ptr; ptr = strchr(ptr, '=')) {
        for (key = ptr-1; isspace(*key); --key); /* strip whitespace */
        klen = 0;
        while (isalpha(*key)) {
            /* Don't parse past the start of the string */
            if (key == params) {
                --key;
                ++klen;
                break;
            }
            --key;
            ++klen;
        }
        ++key;
        for (value = ptr+1; isspace(*value); ++value);
        vlen = strcspn(value, delims);
        for (i=0; fields[i].field != NULL; ++i) {
            if (!strncasecmp(fields[i].field, key, klen)) {
                fields[i].value = apr_pstrndup(pool, value, vlen);
                break;
            }
        }
        ptr = value+vlen;
    }
    if (fields[4].value != NULL) {
        port = atoi(fields[4].value);
    }
    sql->conn = mysql_real_connect(sql->conn,
                                   fields[0].value, /* host */
                                   fields[1].value, /* user */
                                   fields[2].value, /* pass */
                                   fields[3].value, /* dbname */
                                   port,
                                   fields[5].value, /* sock */
                                   0);

    return sql;
}
```

check_conn

This function checks that a connection is still good. If the back end doesn't support such an operation, it may return APR_ENOTIMPL.

```
static apr_status_t dbd_mysql_check_conn(apr_pool_t *pool,
                                         apr_dbd_t *handle)
{
    /* mysql_ping checks a connection, and also attempts to
     * reestablish it if it was stale
     */
    return mysql_ping(handle->conn) ? APR_EGENERAL : APR_SUCCESS;
}
```

close

This function closes a back-end connection.

```
static apr_status_t dbd_mysql_close(apr_dbd_t *handle)
{
    mysql_close(handle->conn);
    return APR_SUCCESS;
}
```

select_db

This optional function selects a different database.

```
static int dbd_mysql_select_db(apr_pool_t *pool, apr_dbd_t* handle,
                               const char* name)
{
    return mysql_select_db(handle->conn, name);
}
```

transaction_start

This function starts an SQL transaction. We do so using the C API, but could also have implemented it by executing an SQL statement.

```
static int dbd_mysql_transaction(apr_pool_t *pool, apr_dbd_t *handle,
                                 apr_dbd_transaction_t **trans)
{
    /* Don't try recursive transactions here */
    if (handle->trans) {
        dbd_mysql_end_transaction(handle->trans) ;
    }
    if (!*trans) {
        *trans = apr_pcalloc(pool, sizeof(apr_dbd_transaction_t));
    }
    (*trans)->errnum = mysql_autocommit(handle->conn, 0);
```

```
    (*trans)->handle = handle;
    (*trans)->mode = APR_DBD_TRANSACTION_COMMIT;
    handle->trans = *trans;
    return (*trans)->errnum;
}
```

transaction_end

This function ends a transaction, issuing a COMMIT if the transaction has executed successfully, or a ROLLBACK if an error occurred or if the mode was rollback.

```
static int dbd_mysql_end_transaction(apr_dbd_transaction_t *trans)
{
    int ret = -1;
    if (trans) {
        if (trans->errnum || TXN_DO_ROLLBACK(trans)) {
            trans->errnum = 0;
            ret = mysql_rollback(trans->handle->conn);
        }
        else {
            ret = mysql_commit(trans->handle->conn);
        }
    }
    ret |= mysql_autocommit(trans->handle->conn, 1);
    return ret;
}
```

transaction_mode_get

This function returns the current transaction mode.

```
static int dbd_mysql_transaction_mode_get(apr_dbd_transaction_t *trans)
{
    if (!trans)
        return APR_DBD_TRANSACTION_COMMIT;

    return trans->mode;
}
```

transaction_mode_set

This function sets the transaction mode.

```
static int dbd_mysql_transaction_mode_set(apr_dbd_transaction_t *trans,
                                          int mode)
{
    if (!trans)
        return APR_DBD_TRANSACTION_COMMIT;

    return trans->mode = (mode & TXN_MODE_BITS);
}
```

query

This function executes a one-off SQL query supplied as a simple string.

```
static int dbd_mysql_query(apr_dbd_t *sql, int *nrows, const char *query)
{
    int ret;
    if (sql->trans && sql->trans->errnum) {
        return sql->trans->errnum;
    }
    ret = mysql_query(sql->conn, query);
    if (ret != 0) {
        ret = mysql_errno(sql->conn);
    }
    *nrows = mysql_affected_rows(sql->conn);
    if (TXN_NOTICE_ERRORS(sql->trans)) {
        sql->trans->errnum = ret;
    }
    return ret;
}
```

select

This function executes a one-off query that returns a results set. The last argument seek determines whether random access to results (i.e., get a row by row number) is required, or whether we will simply process results sequentially. This decision determines whether our driver uses mysql_store_result or the more efficient mysql_use_result.

```
static int dbd_mysql_select(apr_pool_t *pool, apr_dbd_t *sql,
                            apr_dbd_results_t **results,
                            const char *query, int seek)
{
    int sz;
    int ret;
    if (sql->trans && sql->trans->errnum) {
        return sql->trans->errnum;
    }
    ret = mysql_query(sql->conn, query);
    if (!ret) {
        if (sz = mysql_field_count(sql->conn), sz > 0) {
            if (!*results) {
                *results = apr_palloc(pool, sizeof(apr_dbd_results_t));
            }
            (*results)->random = seek;
            (*results)->statement = NULL;
            if (seek) {
                (*results)->res = mysql_store_result(sql->conn);
            }
            else {
```

```
                (*results)->res = mysql_use_result(sql->conn);
            }
            apr_pool_cleanup_register(pool, (*results)->res,
                                      (void*)mysql_free_result,
                                      apr_pool_cleanup_null);
        }
    }
    if (TXN_NOTICE_ERRORS(sql->trans)) {
        sql->trans->errnum = ret;
    }
    return ret;
}
```

num_cols

This function returns the number of columns in a results set.

```
static int dbd_mysql_num_cols(apr_dbd_results_t *res)
{
    if (res->statement) {
        return mysql_stmt_field_count(res->statement);
    }
    else {
        return mysql_num_fields(res->res);
    }
}
```

num_tuples

This function returns the number of rows in a results set. If random access is not available (so that rows are accessed sequentially in a loop), it returns -1.

```
static int dbd_mysql_num_tuples(apr_dbd_results_t *res)
{
    if (res->random) {
        if (res->statement) {
            return (int) mysql_stmt_num_rows(res->statement);
        }
        else {
            return (int) mysql_num_rows(res->res);
        }
    }
    else {
        return -1;
    }
}
```

get_row

This function retrieves a row from a results set. If random access is available, we can select a row by number; otherwise, we simply get the next row.

A return value of -1 indicates end-of-data, and any other nonzero return value indicates an error. Drivers *must* clear the results set when this happens, to avoid a resource leak.

```
static int dbd_mysql_get_row(apr_pool_t *pool, apr_dbd_results_t *res,
                             apr_dbd_row_t **row, int rownum)
{
    MYSQL_ROW r;
    int ret = 0;

    if (res->statement) {
        if (res->random) {
            if (rownum >= 0) {
                mysql_stmt_data_seek(res->statement,
                             (my_ulonglong)rownum);
            }
        }
        ret = mysql_stmt_fetch(res->statement);
    }
    else {
        if (res->random) {
            if (rownum >= 0) {
                mysql_data_seek(res->res, (my_ulonglong) rownum);
            }
        }
        r = mysql_fetch_row(res->res);
        if (r == NULL) {
            ret = 1;
        }
    }
    if (ret == 0) {
        if (!*row) {
            *row = apr_palloc(pool, sizeof(apr_dbd_row_t));
        }
        (*row)->row = r;
        (*row)->res = res;
    }
    else {
        mysql_free_result(res->res);
        apr_pool_cleanup_kill(pool, res->res, (void*)mysql_free_result);
        ret = -1;
    }
    return ret;
}
```

get_entry

This function returns a value from the row, as a string.

```
static const char *dbd_mysql_get_entry(const apr_dbd_row_t *row, int n)
{
    MYSQL_BIND *bind;
    if (row->res->statement) {
        bind = &row->res->bind[n];
        if (mysql_stmt_fetch_column(row->res->statement, bind, n, 0)
                                   != 0) {
            return NULL;
        }
        if (*bind->is_null) {
            return NULL;
        }
        else {
            return bind->buffer;
        }
    }
    else {
        return row->row[n];
    }
    return NULL;
}
```

get_name

This function gets the name of a column in the results set.

```
static const char *dbd_mysql_get_name(const apr_dbd_results_t *res,
                        int n)
{
    if ((n < 0) || (n >= mysql_num_fields(res->res))) {
        return NULL;
    }

    return mysql_fetch_fields(res->res)[n].name;
}
```

error

In the event of a database error, this function returns a human-readable error message.

```
static const char *dbd_mysql_error(apr_dbd_t *sql, int n)
{
    return mysql_error(sql->conn);
}
```

escape

This function escapes any characters in a string that would be unsafe or ambiguous to store as is in the database or to use in a query.

```
static const char *dbd_mysql_escape(apr_pool_t *pool, const char *arg,
                                    apr_dbd_t *sql)
{
    unsigned long len = strlen(arg);
    char *ret = apr_palloc(pool, 2*len + 1);
    mysql_real_escape_string(sql->conn, ret, arg, len);
    return ret;
}
```

prepare

This function prepares an SQL statement. As discussed earlier, it supports %s format for arguments to a statement as well as the native ? form. This driver (currently) makes no attempt to support different data types, and it makes no use of the label argument.

```
static int dbd_mysql_prepare(apr_pool_t *pool, apr_dbd_t *sql,
                             const char *query, const char *label,
                             apr_dbd_prepared_t **statement)
{
    /* Translate from apr_dbd to native query format */
    char *myquery = apr_pstrdup(pool, query);
    char *p = myquery;
    const char *q;
    for (q = query; *q; ++q) {
        if (q[0] == '%') {
            if (isalpha(q[1])) {
                *p++ = '?';
                ++q;
            }
            else if (q[1] == '%') {
                /* reduce %% to % */
                *p++ = *q++;
            }
            else {
                *p++ = *q;
            }
        }
        else {
            *p++ = *q;
        }
    }
    *p = 0;
```

```
    if (!*statement) {
        *statement = apr_palloc(pool, sizeof(apr_dbd_prepared_t));
    }
    (*statement)->stmt = mysql_stmt_init(sql->conn);
    apr_pool_cleanup_register(pool, *statement, (void*)mysql_stmt_close,
                              apr_pool_cleanup_null);
    return mysql_stmt_prepare((*statement)->stmt, myquery,
                    strlen(myquery));
}
```

pvquery and pquery

These functions execute a prepared statement using arguments supplied either as
argc/argv (pquery) or varargs (pvquery). The latter form may support different data types (the Oracle driver does), but in this case we support only strings.
These two functions are almost identical, so we'll just reproduce one of them here.

```
static int dbd_mysql_pvquery(apr_pool_t *pool, apr_dbd_t *sql,
                             int *nrows, apr_dbd_prepared_t *statement,
                             va_list args)
{
    MYSQL_BIND *bind;
    char *arg;
    int ret;
    int nargs = 0;
    int i;
    my_bool is_null = FALSE;

    if (sql->trans && sql->trans->errnum) {
        return sql->trans->errnum;
    }
    nargs = mysql_stmt_param_count(statement->stmt);

    bind = apr_palloc(pool, nargs*sizeof(MYSQL_BIND));
    for (i=0; i < nargs; ++i) {
        arg = va_arg(args, char*);
        bind[i].buffer_type = MYSQL_TYPE_VAR_STRING;
        bind[i].buffer = arg;
        bind[i].buffer_length = strlen(arg);
        bind[i].length = &bind[i].buffer_length;
        bind[i].is_null = &is_null;
        bind[i].is_unsigned = 0;
    }

    ret = mysql_stmt_bind_param(statement->stmt, bind);
    if (ret != 0) {
        *nrows = 0;
    }
    else {
```

```
        ret = mysql_stmt_execute(statement->stmt);
        *nrows = mysql_stmt_affected_rows(statement->stmt);
    }
    if (TXN_NOTICE_ERRORS(sql->trans)) {
        sql->trans->errnum = ret;
    }
    return ret;
}
```

pselect and pvselect

These functions execute a prepared statement that returns a results set. As is the case with pquery/pvquery, they are essentially identical. In this driver, unlike the simple select function, no distinction is made between random and sequential access in the MySQL client library. Thus all we do with the random argument is save it for the benefit of the num_tuples and get_row functions.

```
static int dbd_mysql_pvselect(apr_pool_t *pool, apr_dbd_t *sql,
                              apr_dbd_results_t **res,
                              apr_dbd_prepared_t *statement, int random,
                              va_list args)
{
    int i;
    int nfields;
    char *arg;
    my_bool is_null = FALSE;
    my_bool *is_nullr;
    int ret;
    const int FIELDSIZE = 255;
    unsigned long *length;
    char **data;
    int nargs;
    MYSQL_BIND *bind;

    if (sql->trans && sql->trans->errnum) {
        return sql->trans->errnum;
    }

    nargs = mysql_stmt_param_count(statement->stmt);
    bind = apr_palloc(pool, nargs*sizeof(MYSQL_BIND));

    for (i=0; i < nargs; ++i) {
        arg = va_arg(args, char*);
        bind[i].buffer_type = MYSQL_TYPE_VAR_STRING;
        bind[i].buffer = arg;
        bind[i].buffer_length = strlen(arg);
        bind[i].length = &bind[i].buffer_length;
        bind[i].is_null = &is_null;
        bind[i].is_unsigned = 0;
    }
```

```
ret = mysql_stmt_bind_param(statement->stmt, bind);
if (ret == 0) {
    ret = mysql_stmt_execute(statement->stmt);
    if (!ret) {
        if (!*res) {
            *res = apr_pcalloc(pool, sizeof(apr_dbd_results_t));
            if (!*res) {
                while (!mysql_stmt_fetch(statement->stmt));
                return -1;
            }
        }
        (*res)->random = random;
        (*res)->statement = statement->stmt;
        (*res)->res = mysql_stmt_result_metadata(statement->stmt);
        apr_pool_cleanup_register(pool, (*res)->res,
                (void*)mysql_free_result, apr_pool_cleanup_null);
        nfields = mysql_num_fields((*res)->res);
        if (!(*res)->bind) {
            (*res)->bind = apr_palloc(pool,
                    nfields*sizeof(MYSQL_BIND));
            length = apr_pcalloc(pool,
                    nfields*sizeof(unsigned long));
            data = apr_palloc(pool, nfields*sizeof(char*));
            is_nullr = apr_palloc(pool, nfields*sizeof(my_bool));
            length = apr_pcalloc(pool, nfields);
            for ( i = 0; i < nfields; ++i ) {
                (*res)->bind[i].buffer_type = MYSQL_TYPE_VAR_STRING;
                (*res)->bind[i].buffer_length = FIELDSIZE;
                (*res)->bind[i].length = &length[i];
                data[i] = apr_palloc(pool, FIELDSIZE*sizeof(char));
                (*res)->bind[i].buffer = data[i];
                (*res)->bind[i].is_null = is_nullr+i;
            }
        }
        ret = mysql_stmt_bind_result(statement->stmt, (*res)->bind);
        if (!ret) {
            ret = mysql_stmt_store_result(statement->stmt);
        }
    }
}
if (TXN_NOTICE_ERRORS(sql->trans)) {
    sql->trans->errnum = ret;
}
return ret;
}
```

11.7 Summary

The DBD API is one of the most recent innovations in Apache, having first appeared in Apache 2.2. It represents probably the most important fundamental advance in architecture for database applications since `mod_perl` introduced (what is now known as) LAMP in the mid-1990s. In this chapter we looked at the following topics:

- The need for a new framework
- The DBD architecture: a common API, plus connection pooling
- The `apr_dbd` API (database objects and operations)
- The `ap_dbd` API (database connection management)
- An example of using DBD in a module
- Writing a DBD driver to support a back-end database

It is anticipated that the DBD framework will support a new generation of web-database applications, including both C modules and LAMP applications running under the scripting modules. Programmers working in scripting languages should see the database objects and `apr_dbd` methods exposed in their language. In a case such as Perl, which has its own mature DBI/DBD framework, `apr_dbd` will be presented as a DBD provider instance such as `DBD::APR`. However, the details of scripting implementations are the business of the developers of the scripting modules and, therefore, are outside the scope of this book.

Chapter 12

Module Debugging

In the preceding chapters, we have looked at the Apache platform and architecture, the API and APR, and important aspects of developing applications with Apache. Of course, knowing the application and the platform is just part of the development process. Before we have a working module, we have to debug it!

For those modules whose installation, configuration, and usage are (or may be) not straightforward, we have a second debugging problem to consider: What can we provide to help system administrators using our module? Even a one-off module that will never be seen outside the IT department that wrote it may need to deal with changes to the system and network the module is working in, and hence require reconfiguration, so debugging is not something we can just ignore.

12.1 Logging for Debugging

The first technique to consider—and in some ways the most important—is to generate diagnostic and debugging information from within the code itself. Apache offers a well-established logging mechanism for this purpose: the error log. We've used the error log in our examples throughout this book, but let's take a closer look at it now.

> TIP Whenever you encounter a problem running Apache, with or without your own applications, always look first in the error log for information!

12.1.1 The Error Log

The error log is normally a file, possibly accessed through a piped logger that deals with log rotation, and specified by the system administrator in the Apache configuration. Modules can and should write messages to the error log whenever they have to report diagnostic information concerning an error. Of course, like system logs, the error log serves a wider purpose, including debugging.

The API for the error log, which is defined in `http_log.h`, provides four variants of a `printf`-like logging function for normal usage by modules. These variants serve different originating contexts: request, connection, server, or anywhere we have a pool.

```
AP_DECLARE(void) ap_log_error(const char *file, int line, int level,
                              apr_status_t status, const server_rec *s,
                              const char *fmt, ...)
                              __attribute__((format(printf,6,7)));
AP_DECLARE(void) ap_log_perror(const char *file, int line, int level,
                               apr_status_t status, apr_pool_t *p,
                               const char *fmt, ...)
                               __attribute__((format(printf,6,7)));
AP_DECLARE(void) ap_log_rerror(const char *file, int line, int level,
                               apr_status_t status, const request_rec *r,
                               const char *fmt, ...)
                               __attribute__((format(printf,6,7)));
AP_DECLARE(void) ap_log_cerror(const char *file, int line, int level,
                               apr_status_t status, const conn_rec *c,
                               const char *fmt, ...)
                               __attribute__((format(printf,6,7)));
```

The normal practice is to use macros for the first three arguments. In fact, the single macro APLOG_MARK gives us both of the first two arguments, so the logger can report the location where the message arose:

```
#define APLOG_MARK    __FILE__,__LINE__
```

The level argument is a classic log level based on syslog. From high to low priority (though ascending numeric order), log level values are

```
#define APLOG_EMERG     LOG_EMERG    /* system is unusable */
#define APLOG_ALERT     LOG_ALERT    /* action must be taken immediately*/
#define APLOG_CRIT      LOG_CRIT     /* critical conditions */
#define APLOG_ERR       LOG_ERR      /* error conditions */
#define APLOG_WARNING   LOG_WARNING  /* warning conditions */
#define APLOG_NOTICE    LOG_NOTICE   /* normal but significant condition */
#define APLOG_INFO      LOG_INFO     /* informational */
#define APLOG_DEBUG     LOG_DEBUG    /* debug-level messages */
```

System administrators can determine which messages will be logged by using the LogLevel configuration directive. Only messages having priority at least that of the LogLevel configured will be logged; other messages will be discarded. The default log level is warning.

Some additional flags can be ORed with these log level values, the most interesting of which is APLOG_TOCLIENT. It is valid only in ap_log_rerror, and causes the logger to set an entry in the request notes. Thus a handler can retrieve an error message using

```
    errmsg = apr_table_get(r->notes, "error-notes");
```

and report the exact error message back to the browser. (Note that errmsg must be escaped if it appears in an HTML or XML response.)

The behavior of LogLevel is *not* consistent across the four logging calls, because it is set in the server configuration hierarchy. As a consequence, configured LogLevel values are valid only when the relevant server_rec is available. That is, of course, always the case with ap_log_error and ap_log_rerror. It is not true for ap_log_cerror in the presence of name virtual hosts in the configuration (making it unusable in general), nor ever for ap_log_perror.

The fourth argument to the logging functions is an APR error code. For messages that are not reporting an error returned by an APR/APU function, use an argument of 0, and it will be duly ignored. The fifth argument is a descriptor object: the server, pool, connection, or request.

The remaining arguments are those of `printf`: a C format string, followed by arguments whose number and types depend on the format string.

The following example demonstrates one way to handle the possible failure to open a file. It is typical of the error logging we've been using throughout this book, and could appear anywhere in request processing:

```
rv = apr_file_open(&file, r->filename, APR_FOPEN_READ|APR_SHARELOCK,
          APR_FPROT_OS_DEFAULT, r->pool) ;
if (rv != APR_SUCCESS) {
 ap_log_rerror(APLOG_MARK, APLOG_ERR, rv, r,
          "Failed to open file %s", r->filename) ;
 return HTTP_FILE_NOT_FOUND;
}
```

12.1.2 Debugging

Now that we've seen the Apache error log, it's pretty easy to see how we can use it for debugging. We can add logging statements to generate a trace of program execution through critical parts of our module, as well as the values of relevant data and expressions. Where debug output might be relevant to end users, we can even leave debug output with level `APLOG_DEBUG` permanently in place, so that system administrators can generate it at will. We can also enclose some of our debug statements in `#ifdef DEBUG` or similar constructs.

Debugging Assistance for System Administrators

Where module configuration may be nontrivial, we can and should use error logging to generate information that might help system administrators to debug their setups. The appropriate level for events that are perfectly normal but useful for the user to know is usually `APLOG_INFO`.

At the extreme end of complexity, `mod_rewrite` implements its own log, which remains entirely separate from the standard error log. A more typical example is `mod_proxy_html`,[1] an output filter that supports markup-aware rewriting of certain strings, specifically URLs, in HTML pages. Rule sets for markup rewriting can be quite complex, particularly when extended mode is enabled so that URLs embedded in Javascript and CSS stylesheets are also rewritten. `mod_proxy_html`

---

1. `http://apache.webthing.com/mod_proxy_html/`

provides system administrators with the option of reporting every match-and-replace encountered with statements like

```
     while ( ! ap_regexec(m->from.r, ctx->buf+offs,
             nmatch, pmatch, 0) ) {
   match = pmatch[0].rm_so ;
   s_from = pmatch[0].rm_eo - match ;
   subs = ap_pregsub(ctx->f->r->pool, m->to, ctx->buf+offs,
           nmatch, pmatch) ;
   s_to = strlen(subs) ;
   len = strlen(ctx->buf) ;
   offs += match ;
   if ( verbose ) {
     const char* f = apr_pstrndup(ctx->f->r->pool,
           ctx->buf + offs , s_from ) ;
     ap_log_rerror(APLOG_MARK, APLOG_INFO, 0, ctx->f->r,
           "C/RX: match at %s, substituting %s", f, subs) ;
   }
 /* Substitution code deleted for brevity */

   offs += s_to ;
 }
```

The logging at log level APLOG_INFO here shows a regular expression match-and-replacement encountered in a CDATA section (C/RX) of the markup. The user can infer from this exactly how his or her current rule set is performing. Note that the use of the verbose variable means it needs *both* mod_proxy_html running in verbose mode *and* LogLevel set to Info (or Debug) to generate this output.

12.2 Running Apache Under a Debugger

The debugger is the regular workhorse of the programmer in many fields, and Apache is certainly one of them. Apache is written in ANSI C, which is well supported across platforms and environments. The fact that Apache has no GUI helps simplify the job, as nothing competes with the debugger for your attention. On the negative side, you must deal with Apache's complex start-up, with multiple processes and threads, and with the dynamic loading of modules and libraries.

What you can do with Apache in a debugger will, of course, vary across different debuggers and environments. For the purposes of this discussion, we'll look at the most widely available and widely used debugger, gdb. There's no uniquely correct way to run Apache under gdb; the discussion here simply covers how this author normally uses it.

When we run Apache under a debugger, we are running it as a real system user, with a login account and a shell. That means important elements of normal Apache security are disabled, so we should always ensure that the debug machine is protected from the outside world—for example, by a firewall. This consideration is particularly important if, against all standard security advice and practice, we debug as root.

Another consequence of running as a different user is that errors arising from trouble with system privileges will differ from normal use, particularly if our operational environment includes strong security such as chroot. Errors arising from this cause will occur in the course of APR system calls, so we'll see them in the error log rather than the debugger.

To run Apache under gdb, we use the -X option to prevent Apache from detaching itself, forking children, and going into daemon mode. Here's a typical start-up, using the Worker MPM on Linux:

```
$ gdb bin/httpd
GNU gdb 6.4
Copyright 2005 Free Software Foundation, Inc.
GDB is free software, covered by the GNU General Public License, and you are
welcome to change it and/or distribute copies of it under certain conditions.
Type "show copying" to see the conditions.
There is absolutely no warranty for GDB. Type "show warranty" for details.
This GDB was configured as "i686-pc-linux-gnu"...Using host libthread_db library
"/lib/libthread_db.so.1".

(gdb) r -X
Starting program: /usr/local/apache2/bin/httpd -X
[Thread debugging using libthread_db enabled]
[New Thread 16384 (LWP 14117)]
[New Thread 32769 (LWP 14122)]
[New Thread 16386 (LWP 14123)]
[New Thread 32771 (LWP 14124)]
... and many more threads
```

Now Apache is in operational mode, and is blocked while waiting for incoming connections. All modules are loaded, and the configuration is active. If we leave it there, the webserver is basically up and running and will service incoming requests. We can interrupt it with Ctrl-C to return to the debugger:

```
Program received signal SIGINT, Interrupt.
[Switching to Thread 16384 (LWP 14117)]
0xb717612b in sigsuspend () from /lib/libc.so.6
(gdb)
```

Because all modules are loaded, we can now set breakpoints on any functions in which we are interested. Those locations could be something generic, such as `ap_process_request` (the core function from which the request processing hooks are called), or they could be functions from our own module. Depending on the gdb version and build, we may need to use the `shared` command to load symbols from dynamically loaded modules. After setting breakpoints (and anything else appropriate) in the debugger, we continue program execution, which returns Apache to a state of waiting for connections:

```
(gdb) b my_handler
Breakpoint 1 at 0xb6ddfd5e: file my_module.c, line 252.
(gdb) c
Continuing.
```

Now you can use an HTTP client such as a browser to request a URL from your server, selecting a URL designed to test the execution path of interest. Lynx is often a good choice for this purpose: It doesn't (by default) time out a request, so we can spend as long as we need in the debugger yet still complete a request.

```
[in another terminal window]
$ lynx -dump -source http://127.0.0.1/path/to/test/my-handler
```

Now the server will hit our breakpoint in gdb:

```
[Switching to Thread 32771 (LWP 14124)]

Breakpoint 1, my_handler (r=0x81e3570) at my_module.c:252
252          int rv = 0;
(gdb)
```

Now we are where we need to be. We can debug at will: step through the program, examine variables and the stack, and so forth. Go ahead and debug!

12.2.1 Server Start-up and Debugging

Functions in the server start-up phase (configuration, pre-configuration, post-configuration, and `child_init`) are a little more elusive from the debugger's perspective. To run a function under the debugger, we need to set the breakpoint before the function is called. But we cannot set the breakpoint before the module is loaded, unless the debugger supports provisional breakpoints (as recent versions of gdb do).

A workaround in this situation is to set a breakpoint on a core function near the function we are interested in. The traceback for a command handler function usually takes the following form:

```
(gdb) bt
#0  foo_cmd (cmd=0xbffff100, cfg=0x0, val=0xbffff100 "foobar") at mod_foo.c:70
#1  0x08075315 in invoke_cmd (cmd=0xb6cf6020, parms=0xbffff100, mconfig=0x0,
    args=0x812d7ae "") at config.c:735
#2  0x08075f8a in ap_walk_config_sub (current=0x812d788, parms=0xbffff100,
    section_vector=0x80dd600) at config.c:1141
#3  0x08076023 in ap_walk_config (current=0x812d788, parms=0xbffff100,
    section_vector=0x80dd600) at config.c:1174
#4  0x08076da6 in ap_process_config_tree (s=0xb6cf6020, conftree=0x0,
    p=0x80aae28, ptemp=0x0) at config.c:1743
#5  0x080620d2 in main (argc=2, argv=0xbffff214) at main.c:616
```

In principle, the nearest we can come to the function of interest is a breakpoint on invoke_cmd. However, that function is called a huge number of times for a typical configuration, so it's not particularly useful for our purposes here. Another option is to walk through ap_walk_config.

Alternatively, we can break on load_module (from mod_so) and set breakpoints on our module's functions as soon as the module is loaded. This approach works best if we load the module being debugged ahead of other modules, so we don't have to step through a lot of other modules loading before we reach ours.

Here is the standard traceback for load_module:

```
(gdb) bt
#0  load_module (cmd=0xbfffef90, dummy=0x80deb20,
    modname=0x80deb10 "foo_module", filename=0x80deb20 "modules/mod_foo.so")
    at mod_so.c:158
#1  0x08075425 in invoke_cmd (cmd=0x8099f00, parms=0xbfffef90,
    mconfig=0xbfffee20, args=0x80e1f28 "") at config.c:778
#2  0x0807654a in execute_now (cmd_line=0x80deab0 "LoadModule",
    args=0x80e1f0b "foo_module modules/mod_foo.so", parms=0xbfffef90,
    p=0x80aae28, ptemp=0x80daee8, sub_tree=0xbfffee20, parent=0x0)
    at config.c:1419
#3  0x08075cef in ap_build_config_sub (p=0x80aae28, temp_pool=0x80daee8,
    l=0x8099f00 "$\235\t\b\220B\b\b", parms=0xbfffef90, current=0xbfffee64,
    curr_parent=0xbfffee68, conftree=0x80a0ab4) at config.c:990
#4  0x080760e8 in ap_build_config (parms=0xbfffef90, p=0x80aae28,
    temp_pool=0x80daee8, conftree=0x80a0ab4) at config.c:1202
#5  0x080769b0 in process_resource_config_nofnmatch (s=0x80b06c8,
    fname=0x80dd9c8 "/usr/local/apache/conf/httpd.conf", conftree=0x80a0ab4,
    p=0x80aae28, ptemp=0x80daee8, depth=0) at config.c:1612
#6  0x08076a85 in ap_process_resource_config (s=0x80b06c8,
    fname=0x80dd9c8 "/usr/local/apache/conf/httpd.conf", conftree=0x80a0ab4,
    p=0x80aae28, ptemp=0x80daee8) at config.c:1644
```

```
#7  0x080774c2 in ap_read_config (process=0x80deb20, ptemp=0x80daee8,
    filename=0x8090b6f "conf/httpd.conf", conftree=0x80a0ab4) at config.c:2002
#8  0x08062085 in main (argc=2, argv=0xbffff214) at main.c:605
```

12.2.2 Debugging and MPMs

Occasionally, we may have to debug a problem that affects some MPMs but not others, which constrains the choice of MPM for debugging. In most cases, however, the issues we are using the debugger to investigate are no different between different MPMs, so we are free to select an MPM that works best with our debugger. There is no one "best" MPM for all cases, so you may want to try out a variety of choices if you have a lot of debugging to do. In any case, there are a few differences worth bearing in mind.

The main choice is whether to use a threaded or a nonthreaded MPM. Running the Prefork MPM (nonthreaded) with the -X flag means we are running on a single-process, single-thread basis, so we can process only one request at a time. This precludes some operations, such as debugging Apache running as a proxy and using the server as its own origin server. With the Worker MPM or other multithreaded MPM, the proxy will run in one thread, and another thread will serve as the origin server. However, if we have any breakpoints or watchpoints that apply to both proxy and origin requests, gdb will switch contexts between the threads, so it benefits from a front end that separates the threads into different displays.

12.2.3 Tracing a Crash

From a debugging point of view, two kinds of crashes exist: those that we can reliably reproduce and those that occur apparently at random. The former are well suited to identifying with gdb:

```
$ gdb bin/httpd
(gdb) r -X
```

Now use a browser to submit a request that generates the crash. Because Apache is running under the debugger, it will hand control back to us:

```
Program received signal SIGSEGV, Segmentation fault.
[Switching to Thread 32771 (LWP 10084)]
0x08063b93 in ap_strcmp_match (str=0x8108ec0 "test", expected=0x0)
    at util.c:179
179             if ((!str[x]) && (expected[y] != '*'))
(gdb)
```

At this point, we can use the debugger to get information about the crash, including getting and stepping through a traceback, and displaying variables on the stack. Sometimes this investigation suffices to identify the problem. For example, if the error was one of dereferencing a null or junk pointer, we can identify it, determine where it originates in the calling stack, and focus on that function. At worst, knowing when and where the system crashed will enable us to set a breakpoint somewhere before it in the code we are debugging; we can then examine the data and step through to the crash.

Our example crashed in a string-matching function, where a null pointer is being dereferenced. We've reduced the problem to figuring out why it's getting passed a null pointer:

```
(gdb) up
#1  0xb6cfd782 in test_filter_init (f=0x81e86e8, b=0x81e1540)
    at mod_test_filter.c:141
141         if (!ap_strcmp_match(str, cfg->basestr)) {
(gdb) p cfg->basestr
$1 = 0x0
(gdb)
```

That's pretty clear: We're using a NULL string that should have been initialized. A suitable fix would be to ensure that this string always has a valid default value.

12.2.4 Debugging a Core Dump

If we have an intermittent crash we cannot figure out and that cannot be reproduced in the debugger, we may need to debug a core dump. To get a core dump, apply the CoredumpDirectory directive in httpd.conf to somewhere the server has permission to write, and ensure the operating system doesn't prevent core dumps (e.g., through ulimit). Because the core dump directory must be writable by Apache, you should secure it. In particular, you should mount it with noexec if the server is exposed to untrusted traffic from the Web. Mounting this directory on a separate partition is good practice for a second reason: It shields you from the danger of a disk filled with core dumps adversely affecting the server.

Once you have a core dump, you can load it with gdb. This gives us a full traceback of the program at the point where it crashed, and it may reveal data such as bad pointers or buffer overflows that are likely to be implicated in the crash.

Note that a threaded MPM will generate a separate traceback for each thread. If you just ask gdb for a traceback, you'll probably get a trace headed by

```
__read_nocancel ()
ap_mpm_pod_check()
```

That's an inactive thread waiting for input—it has nothing to do with the crash! You need to find the guilty thread:

```
(gdb) thread apply all bt 5
```

This traceback provides five lines of backtrace for each thread. You can now find which thread got killed and attach to it:

```
(gdb) thread <number>
(gdb) bt
```

12.3 Special-Purpose Hooks and Modules

A few modules exist specifically to enable a developer or administrator to obtain information on the state of Apache and to prevent bad things happening. These modules include mod_info, mod_status, mod_backtrace, mod_whatkilledus, mod_backdoor, mod_watchdog, and mod_diagnostics. Some of them will reveal server information via HTTP. This information has potential security implications, so the modules should be configured to allow access only to authorized users, typically using the Order, Allow, and Deny directives.

12.3.1 Standard Modules

The standard Apache distribution includes two introspection modules: mod_info and mod_status.

12.3.1.1 mod_info

mod_info provides information on Apache's configuration and modules, or subsets thereof. The basic information displayed by default is the configuration tree, comprising a complete list of active modules, the configuration directives that apply to them, and the hooks they are attached to. This response can be filtered to reduce information overload.

12.3.1.2 mod_status

mod_status provides information on server activity and performance. It returns an HTML page that gives the current server statistics in an easily readable form. If necessary, this page can be made to automatically refresh (given a compatible browser). Another page gives a simple machine-readable list of the current server state.

The following details are available:

- The number of workers serving requests

- The number of idle workers

- The status of each worker, the number of requests that worker has performed, and the total number of bytes served by the worker

- The total number of accesses and byte counts served

- The time when the server was started/restarted and the time for which it has been running

- The average number of requests per second, the average number of bytes served per second, and the average number of bytes per request

- The current percentage of the CPU used by each worker and in total by Apache

- The current hosts and requests being processed

12.3.1.3 The Scoreboard

The information mod_status presents consists of a shared memory segment called the scoreboard. It is created at server start-up and can hold an entry for each active process and worker, according to the MPM in use and its configuration. Each worker is responsible for maintaining its own information in the scoreboard.

The scoreboard is defined in scoreboard.h:

```
typedef struct {
    global_score *global;
    process_score *parent;
    worker_score **servers;
    lb_score     *balancers;
} scoreboard;
```

The global_score entry contains primarily information from the MPM. It determines the number of process and worker scores and balancers required through the server_limit, thread_limit, and lb_limit fields.

The `process_score` entry is a vector comprising one entry for each child process and having space for the maximum number of children allowed in the configuration. It includes the PID of the process, plus a flag that indicates whether the process is terminating.

The `worker_score` entry contains useful status/debugging information. In general, it is an array of arrays; that is, there is an array for each child process, which in turn contains an array for each worker thread. The actual size depends on the MPM and configuration. For example, the Prefork MPM will have a maximum of one worker per process, while threaded MPMs may be configured to have only one process. In all cases, the array must be big enough to hold entries for the configured maximum numbers of processes and workers.

The definition of `worker_score` is

```
struct worker_score {
    int thread_num;
#if APR_HAS_THREADS
    apr_os_thread_t tid;
#endif
    /* With some MPMs (e.g., Worker), a worker_score can represent
     * a thread in a terminating process that is no longer
     * represented by the corresponding process_score. These MPMs
     * should set pid and generation fields in the worker_score.
     */
    pid_t pid;
    ap_generation_t generation;
    unsigned char status;
    unsigned long access_count;
    apr_off_t      bytes_served;
    unsigned long my_access_count;
    apr_off_t      my_bytes_served;
    apr_off_t      conn_bytes;
    unsigned short conn_count;
    apr_time_t start_time;
    apr_time_t stop_time;
#ifdef HAVE_TIMES
    struct tms times;
#endif
    apr_time_t last_used;
    char client[32];          /* Keep 'em small... */
    char request[64];         /* We just want an idea... */
    char vhost[32];           /* Which virtual host is being accessed? */
};
```

Finally, the `lb_scores` are owned by the proxy balancer and are relevant only when that balancer is in use. These entries are unlikely to be relevant to debugging.

12.3.2 Fatal Exception Modules

The fatal exception hook (ap_hook_fatal_exception) in Apache enables modules to hook a function into a server crash. Two modules that use this ability to provide information on a crash are mod_backtrace and mod_whatkilledus, both of which are available from Jeff Trawick's page at apache.org.[2] The fatal exception hook is a compile-time option in Apache. To use it, you will need the -enable-exception-hook configuration option to Apache 2.0.49 or later.

12.3.2.1 mod_backtrace

mod_backtrace is an experimental module for Apache httpd 2.x that collects backtraces when a child process crashes. Currently, it is implemented only on Linux and FreeBSD, but other platforms could be supported in the future. You should verify that it works reasonably well on your system before putting it in production.

mod_backtrace implements a fatal exception hook that will be called when a child process crashes. In the exception hook, it uses system library routines to obtain information about the call stack, and then it writes the call stack to a log file or the webserver error log. The backtrace is a crucial piece of information when you need to determine which failing software component caused the crash. Note that the backtrace written by mod_backtrace may not offer as much information as a debugger can display from a core dump.

12.3.2.2 mod_whatkilledus

mod_whatkilledus is an experimental module for Apache httpd 2.x that tracks the current request and logs a report of the active request when a child process crashes. The information logged includes the complete HTTP request, which you can use to reproduce a request that triggered a crash in your test environment. You should verify that this module works reasonably on your system before putting it in production.

mod_whatkilledus is called during request processing to save information about the current request. It also implements a fatal exception hook that will be called when a child process crashes.

---

2. http://people.apache.org/~trawick/

12.3.3 Modules to Deal with Abnormal Running

12.3.3.1 mod_backdoor

mod_backdoor is another module from Jeff Trawick's page. Its main purpose is to provide a relatively fail-safe way to send requests to the webserver when overall there are serious webserver problems. mod_backdoor represents a kind of "Plan B" when something is wrong with the webserver but a request for mod_status or any test request is not being processed.

Perhaps all of your webserver threads are blocked while waiting for an application server to respond? Sneak in through the back door, get a mod_status report, and see if that is the case. (Check the URLs and look for W as the state.)

Perhaps something very fundamental, such as an accept mutex, has broken, and all of your webserver threads are idle with no work to do? Sneak in through the back door, get a mod_status report, and see if that could be the case. (Check for a diminishing number of active connections.)

mod_backdoor also supports a simple module/core server debugging environment alongside the processes and threads created by the normal MPM. If you send a request through the back door, there is no question which process/thread will handle it, because mod_backdoor has only one, and you can have your debugger waiting. Also, because the mod_backdoor daemon process is not threaded, any problems your platform experiences while debugging threaded processes will no longer be a problem. And if this system is being actively accessed, controlling the mod_backdoor daemon process with a debugger won't affect threads in the real MPM processes.

12.3.3.2 The Monitor Hook

The monitor hook ap_hook_monitor enables a module to hook a function into the Apache parent (root) process, so that it can run regularly in a loop. This hook can be used to watch the scoreboard for workers that could be in trouble (e.g., a worker stuck in any busy state) and to take action such as logging a diagnostic message, alerting an external agent, or even killing the worker. At the time of writing, no open-source module implements this functionality.

Monitor functions are called every 10 seconds, so functions that are required less frequently should maintain a counter or timer. Because the parent is a single nonthreaded process, it is important that monitor functions have a small footprint. For example, a function that could block would be serious trouble.

When using the monitor hook, you should be aware that the pool is never destroyed, so any usage of it is likely to create a memory leak. Modules that need to make regular use of a pool should create a subpool and perform garbage collection from time to time.

On the positive side, monitor functions do not have to be concerned with threading issues. They can also use static or global variables where other modules must use the configuration vectors.

12.4 Filter Debugging

Filter debugging involves all the same processes as any other debugging: tracing program execution, watching variables, and so forth. But sometimes we encounter bugs where the code simply "doesn't work" or "takes a long, long time," yet it doesn't crash or manifest any other obvious problem.

Fortunately, we have a higher-level debugging tool at our disposal in such cases. The purpose of a filter is to manipulate streamed data, and we can watch this data stream as it passes down the chain. Specifically, we can readily check the progression of buckets and brigades through our filters and identify any anomalies. At best, this effort leads us directly to the bug; in other cases, it simply tells us where to look with the debugger.

12.4.1 mod_diagnostics

mod_diagnostics[3] is a debugging and diagnostic tool for filter modules. It can be inserted anywhere in the Apache filter chain—input or output—and logs traffic (buckets and brigades) passing through. It is a purely passive watcher, meaning that it will never modify the data or metadata passing through the filter.

For the output filter chain, mod_filter provides a similar function. It is slightly less flexible, in that it will only watch data coming into a filter, and will automatically be removed (along with the filter) when processing an HTTP error.

To understand working with mod_diagnostics, we'll look at two examples from the author's own experience.

---

3. http://apache.webthing.com/mod_diagnostics/

12.4.1.1 Example: Strange Delays and Broken Connections in Some Browsers

As part of an update to mod_xml, a new bug was introduced. It was not immediately obvious, but in some browsers the request would hang and then time out. The effect was observed only when using the XSLT output filter with Xalan-C, and it happened only with HTTP/1.1 browsers, not with HTTP/1.0. Furthermore, clicking "Cancel" before the timeout in an HTTP/1.1 browser would cause the page to display correctly!

We can reproduce this problem with a tiny, static XML file and XSLT stylesheet, and a version of mod_transform hacked to introduce the same bug:

test.xml

```
<?xml version="1.0"?>
<?xml-stylesheet type="text/xsl" href="test.xsl"?>
<!-- We're not debugging XML or XSLT, so there's no reason to do
     anything interesting here
-->
<html>
<title>A title for the page</title>
<body>
<h1>A heading</h1>
<p>Some text</p>
<insertion />
</body>
</html>
```

test.xsl

```
<?xml version="1.0"?>
<xsl:stylesheet version="1.0"
        xmlns:xsl="http://www.w3.org/1999/XSL/Transform">
<xsl:output method="html" doctype-public="-//W3C//DTD HTML 4.01//EN"/>
<xsl:template match="*">
<xsl:choose>
<xsl:when test="node() != 'insertion'">
<xsl:copy>
<xsl:apply-templates select="@*|*|text()"/>
</xsl:copy>
</xsl:when>
<xsl:otherwise>
<p>This paragraph is inserted by the stylesheet!</p>
</xsl:otherwise>
</xsl:choose>
</xsl:template>
</xsl:stylesheet>
```

Inserting `mod_diagnostics` before and after the offending filter, the bug becomes immediately obvious. We configure our trivial documents with diagnostic filters before and after the transform operation:

```
<Files test.xml>
    SetOutputFilter o-resource-1;bad-xslt;o-resource-2
</Files>
```

Here's the error log as it processes the request:

```
[Tue Jan 10 22:10:49 2006] [notice] o-resource-1
[Tue Jan 10 22:10:49 2006] [notice]   o-resource-1 FILE: 312 bytes
[Tue Jan 10 22:10:49 2006] [notice]   o-resource-1 EOS: 0 bytes
[Tue Jan 10 22:10:49 2006] [notice] o-resource-2
[Tue Jan 10 22:10:49 2006] [notice]   o-resource-2 HEAP: 206 bytes
```

From our configuration, `o-resource-1` is the diagnostic filter before our XSLT, while `o-resource-2` comes after it. The first entry of each filter represents a brigade, while the indented entries with more detail report a bucket within the brigade. Because the document is tiny both before and after the transform, it goes into a single brigade, and we see the crucial error: The EOS bucket is missing after the transform. It worked with an HTTP/1.0 browser because Apache was following the default behavior of closing the connection in HTTP/1.0, so all that really mattered was that the data had been sent. In HTTP/1.1, the connection is kept open by default, so the response isn't flushed until the EOS or until the browser closes the connection.

Having made this diagnosis, the fix is now trivial.

12.4.1.2 Example: Obscure Bug in a Third-Party Library

A user of `mod_proxy_html` reported serious performance problems when parsing an 8MB HTML file. When he profiled the problem, he discovered that the entire processing time derived from the final call to `htmlParseChunk` in libxml2.

The author of this book investigated this report by inserting `mod_diagnostics` before and after `mod_proxy_html`, and running it with the largest HTML document I had available (a MySQL manual, about 2.6MB). I was able to confirm that nothing was passed down the chain until the final call: Thus, not only was the module slow, but it had also broken Apache pipelining.

To refine the diagnosis, I added a flush in each call to the filter in `mod_proxy_html`. Now `mod_diagnostics` showed a small amount of data (less than 1K) coming through during the first call to the filter, but nothing else until the end. Further investigation revealed that the data stopped coming when the first HTML comment was encountered in the source.

At this point, I ran the module under gdb, looking for the comment handling. I found that it was failing to find the end of the comment. The problem was resolved only in the last call to `htmlParseChunk`, which didn't go through the buggy code. When I disabled the buggy code, I found that it was now working correctly, with approximately the same amount of input and output data in each call to the `mod_proxy_html` filter—so pipelining was now fixed. My correspondent reported total processing time for his 8MB file was reduced from 30 minutes to 9 seconds (on late-1990s hardware).

The bug was reported to the libxml team, who fixed it in libxml2.5.10.

12.5 Summary

This chapter examined a number of techniques for debugging modules in Apache. It did not venture into high-level or application-oriented areas such as test plans or test suites, but rather focused on low-level debugging techniques that complement the programming subjects discussed elsewhere in this book.

Specifically, we looked at the following topics:

- The logging API
- Logging to support system administrators
- Logging for debugging purposes
- Running Apache interactively under a debugger
- Tracing the causes of a crash: core dumps and special-purpose modules
- Introspection
- Filter debugging with `mod_diagnostics`

Apache License

Apache License
Version 2.0, January 2004
http://www.apache.org/licenses/

TERMS AND CONDITIONS FOR USE, REPRODUCTION, AND DISTRIBUTION

1. Definitions.

"License" shall mean the terms and conditions for use, reproduction, and distribution as defined by Sections 1 through 9 of this document.

"Licensor" shall mean the copyright owner or entity authorized by the copyright owner that is granting the License.

"Legal Entity" shall mean the union of the acting entity and all other entities that control, are controlled by, or are under common control with that entity. For the

343

purposes of this definition, "control" means (i) the power, direct or indirect, to cause the direction or management of such entity, whether by contract or otherwise, or (ii) ownership of fifty percent (50%) or more of the outstanding shares, or (iii) beneficial ownership of such entity.

"You" (or "Your") shall mean an individual or Legal Entity exercising permissions granted by this License.

"Source" form shall mean the preferred form for making modifications, including but not limited to software source code, documentation source, and configuration files.

"Object" form shall mean any form resulting from mechanical transformation or translation of a Source form, including but not limited to compiled object code, generated documentation, and conversions to other media types.

"Work" shall mean the work of authorship, whether in Source or Object form, made available under the License, as indicated by a copyright notice that is included in or attached to the work (an example is provided in the Appendix below).

"Derivative Works" shall mean any work, whether in Source or Object form, that is based on (or derived from) the Work and for which the editorial revisions, annotations, elaborations, or other modifications represent, as a whole, an original work of authorship. For the purposes of this License, Derivative Works shall not include works that remain separable from, or merely link (or bind by name) to the interfaces of, the Work and Derivative Works thereof.

"Contribution" shall mean any work of authorship, including the original version of the Work and any modifications or additions to that Work or Derivative Works thereof, that is intentionally submitted to Licensor for inclusion in the Work by the copyright owner or by an individual or Legal Entity authorized to submit on behalf of the copyright owner. For the purposes of this definition, "submitted" means any form of electronic, verbal, or written communication sent to the Licensor or its representatives, including but not limited to communication on electronic mailing lists, source code control systems, and issue tracking systems that are managed by, or on behalf of, the Licensor for the purpose of discussing and improving the Work, but excluding communication that is conspicuously marked or otherwise designated in writing by the copyright owner as "Not a Contribution."

"Contributor" shall mean Licensor and any individual or Legal Entity on behalf of whom a Contribution has been received by Licensor and subsequently incorporated within the Work.

2. Grant of Copyright License. Subject to the terms and conditions of this License, each Contributor hereby grants to You a perpetual, worldwide, non-exclusive, no-charge, royalty-free, irrevocable copyright license to reproduce, prepare Derivative Works of, publicly display, publicly perform, sublicense, and distribute the Work and such Derivative Works in Source or Object form.

3. Grant of Patent License. Subject to the terms and conditions of this License, each Contributor hereby grants to You a perpetual, worldwide, non-exclusive, no-charge, royalty-free, irrevocable (except as stated in this section) patent license to make, have made, use, offer to sell, sell, import, and otherwise transfer the Work, where such license applies only to those patent claims licensable by such Contributor that are necessarily infringed by their Contribution(s) alone or by combination of their Contribution(s) with the Work to which such Contribution(s) was submitted. If You institute patent litigation against any entity (including a cross-claim or coun-terclaim in a lawsuit) alleging that the Work or a Contribution incorporated within the Work constitutes direct or contributory patent infringement, then any patent licenses granted to You under this License for that Work shall terminate as of the date such litigation is filed.

4. Redistribution. You may reproduce and distribute copies of the Work or Derivative Works thereof in any medium, with or without modifications, and in Source or Object form, provided that You meet the following conditions:

(a) You must give any other recipients of the Work or Derivative Works a copy of this License; and

(b) You must cause any modified files to carry prominent notices stating that You changed the files; and

(c) You must retain, in the Source form of any Derivative Works that You dis-tribute, all copyright, patent, trademark, and attribution notices from the Source form of the Work, excluding those notices that do not pertain to any part of the Derivative Works; and

(d) If the Work includes a "NOTICE" text file as part of its distribution, then any Derivative Works that You distribute must include a readable copy of the attribution notices contained within such NOTICE file, excluding those notices that do not pertain to any part of the Derivative Works, in at least one of the following places: within a NOTICE text file distributed as part of the Derivative Works; within the Source form or documentation, if provided along with the Derivative Works; or, within a display generated by the Derivative Works, if and wherever such third-party notices normally appear. The contents of the NOTICE file are for informational purposes only and do not modify the License. You may add Your own attribution notices within Derivative Works that You distribute, alongside or as an addendum to the NOTICE text from the Work, provided that such additional attribution notices cannot be construed as modifying the License.

You may add Your own copyright statement to Your modifications and may provide additional or different license terms and conditions for use, reproduction, or distribution of Your modifications, or for any such Derivative Works as a whole, provided Your use, reproduction, and distribution of the Work otherwise complies with the conditions stated in this License.

5. Submission of Contributions. Unless You explicitly state otherwise, any Contribution intentionally submitted for inclusion in the Work by You to the Licensor shall be under the terms and conditions of this License, without any additional terms or conditions. Notwithstanding the above, nothing herein shall supersede or modify the terms of any separate license agreement you may have executed with Licensor regarding such Contributions.

6. Trademarks. This License does not grant permission to use the trade names, trademarks, service marks, or product names of the Licensor, except as required for reasonable and customary use in describing the origin of the Work and reproducing the content of the NOTICE file.

7. Disclaimer of Warranty. Unless required by applicable law or agreed to in writing, Licensor provides the Work (and each Contributor provides its Contributions) on an "AS IS" BASIS, WITHOUT WARRANTIES OR CONDITIONS OF ANY KIND, either express or implied, including, without limitation, any warranties or conditions of TITLE, NON-INFRINGEMENT, MERCHANTABILITY, or FITNESS FOR A PARTICULAR PURPOSE. You are

solely responsible for determining the appropriateness of using or redistributing the Work and assume any risks associated with Your exercise of permissions under this License.

8. Limitation of Liability. In no event and under no legal theory, whether in tort (including negligence), contract, or otherwise, unless required by applicable law (such as deliberate and grossly negligent acts) or agreed to in writing, shall any Contributor be liable to You for damages, including any direct, indirect, special, incidental, or consequential damages of any character arising as a result of this License or out of the use or inability to use the Work (including but not limited to damages for loss of goodwill, work stoppage, computer failure or malfunction, or any and all other commercial damages or losses), even if such Contributor has been advised of the possibility of such damages.

9. Accepting Warranty or Additional Liability. While redistributing the Work or Derivative Works thereof, You may choose to offer, and charge a fee for, acceptance of support, warranty, indemnity, or other liability obligations and/or rights consistent with this License. However, in accepting such obligations, You may act only on Your own behalf and on Your sole responsibility, not on behalf of any other Contributor, and only if You agree to indemnify, defend, and hold each Contributor harmless for any liability incurred by, or claims asserted against, such Contributor by reason of your accepting any such warranty or additional liability.

END OF TERMS AND CONDITIONS

APPENDIX: How to apply the Apache License to your work.

To apply the Apache License to your work, attach the following boilerplate notice, with the fields enclosed by brackets "[]" replaced with your own identifying information. (Don't include the brackets!) The text should be enclosed in the appropriate comment syntax for the file format. We also recommend that a file or class name and description of purpose be included on the same "printed page" as the copyright notice for easier identification within third-party archives.

Copyright [yyyy] [name of copyright owner]

Licensed under the Apache License, Version 2.0 (the "License"); you may not use this file except in compliance with the License.

You may obtain a copy of the License at

http://www.apache.org/licenses/LICENSE-2.0

Unless required by applicable law or agreed to in writing, software distributed under the License is distributed on an "AS IS" BASIS, WITHOUT WARRANTIES OR CONDITIONS OF ANY KIND, either express or implied. See the License for the specific language governing permissions and limitations under the License.

B

Contributor License Agreements

There are two standard Contributor License Agreements. The Individual CLA is signed by every committer. The Corporate CLA is signed by companies or other institutions contributing to Apache, or having rights over an individual contributor's work as (for example) the contributor's employer or client.

Individual CLA

The Apache Software Foundation
Individual Contributor License Agreement ("Agreement") V2.0
http://www.apache.org/licenses/

Thank you for your interest in The Apache Software Foundation (the "Foundation"). In order to clarify the intellectual property license granted with Contributions from any person or entity, the Foundation must have a Contributor

License Agreement ("CLA") on file that has been signed by each Contributor, indicating agreement to the license terms below. This license is for your protection as a Contributor as well as the protection of the Foundation and its users; it does not change your rights to use your own Contributions for any other purpose. If you have not already done so, please complete and send an original signed Agreement to The Apache Software Foundation, 1901 Munsey Drive, Forest Hill, MD 21050-2747, U.S.A. If necessary, you may send it by facsimile to the Foundation at +1-410-803-2258. Please read this document carefully before signing and keep a copy for your records.

Full name: _____   E-Mail: _____

Mailing Address: _____   Telephone: _____

_____   Facsimile: _____

_____   Country: _____

You accept and agree to the following terms and conditions for Your present and future Contributions submitted to the Foundation. In return, the Foundation shall not use Your Contributions in a way that is contrary to the public benefit or inconsistent with its nonprofit status and bylaws in effect at the time of the Contribution. Except for the license granted herein to the Foundation and recipients of software distributed by the Foundation, You reserve all right, title, and interest in and to Your Contributions.

1. Definitions.

"You" (or "Your") shall mean the copyright owner or legal entity authorized by the copyright owner that is making this Agreement with the Foundation. For legal entities, the entity making a Contribution and all other entities that control, are controlled by, or are under common control with that entity are considered to be a single Contributor. For the purposes of this definition, "control" means (i) the power, direct or indirect, to cause the direction or management of such entity, whether by contract or otherwise, or (ii) ownership of fifty percent (50%) or more of the outstanding shares, or (iii) beneficial ownership of such entity.

"Contribution" shall mean any original work of authorship, including any modifications or additions to an existing work, that is intentionally submitted by You to the Foundation for inclusion in, or documentation of, any of the products owned or managed by the Foundation (the "Work"). For the purposes of this definition, "submitted" means any form of electronic, verbal, or written communication sent to the Foundation or its representatives, including but not limited to communication on electronic mailing lists, source code control systems, and issue tracking systems that are managed by, or on behalf of, the Foundation for the purpose of discussing and improving the Work, but excluding communication that is conspicuously marked or otherwise designated in writing by You as "Not a Contribution."

2. Grant of Copyright License. Subject to the terms and conditions of this Agreement, You hereby grant to the Foundation and to recipients of software distributed by the Foundation a perpetual, worldwide, non-exclusive, no-charge, royalty-free, irrevocable copyright license to reproduce, prepare derivative works of, publicly display, publicly perform, sublicense, and distribute Your Contributions and such derivative works.

3. Grant of Patent License. Subject to the terms and conditions of this Agreement, You hereby grant to the Foundation and to recipients of software distributed by the Foundation a perpetual, worldwide, non-exclusive, no-charge, royalty-free, irrevocable (except as stated in this section) patent license to make, have made, use, offer to sell, sell, import, and otherwise transfer the Work, where such license applies only to those patent claims licensable by You that are necessarily infringed by Your Contribution(s) alone or by combination of Your Contribution(s) with the Work to which such Contribution(s) was submitted. If any entity institutes patent litigation against You or any other entity (including a cross-claim or counterclaim in a lawsuit) alleging that your Contribution, or the Work to which you have contributed, constitutes direct or contributory patent infringement, then any patent licenses granted to that entity under this Agreement for that Contribution or Work shall terminate as of the date such litigation is filed.

4. You represent that you are legally entitled to grant the above license. If your employer(s) has rights to intellectual property that you create that includes your Contributions, you represent that you have received permission to make Contributions on behalf of that employer, that your employer has waived such rights for your Contributions to the Foundation, or that your employer has executed a separate Corporate CLA with the Foundation.

5. You represent that each of Your Contributions is Your original creation (see section 7 for submissions on behalf of others). You represent that Your Contribution submissions include complete details of any third-party license or other restriction

(including, but not limited to, related patents and trademarks) of which you are personally aware and which are associated with any part of Your Contributions.

6. You are not expected to provide support for Your Contributions, except to the extent You desire to provide support. You may provide support for free, for a fee, or not at all. Unless required by applicable law or agreed to in writing, You provide Your Contributions on an "AS IS" BASIS, WITHOUT WARRANTIES OR CONDITIONS OF ANY KIND, either express or implied, including, without limitation, any warranties or conditions of TITLE, NON-INFRINGEMENT, MERCHANTABILITY, or FITNESS FOR A PARTICULAR PURPOSE.

7. Should You wish to submit work that is not Your original creation, You may submit it to the Foundation separately from any Contribution, identifying the complete details of its source and of any license or other restriction (including, but not limited to, related patents, trademarks, and license agreements) of which you are personally aware, and conspicuously marking the work as "Submitted on behalf of a third-party: [named here]".

8. You agree to notify the Foundation of any facts or circumstances of which you become aware that would make these representations inaccurate in any respect.

Please sign: _____ Date: _____

Corporate CLA

The Apache Software Foundation
Software Grant and Corporate Contributor License Agreement ("Agreement")
http://www.apache.org/licenses/
(v r190612)

Thank you for your interest in The Apache Software Foundation (the "Foundation"). In order to clarify the intellectual property license granted with Contributions from any person or entity, the Foundation must have a Contributor License Agreement (CLA) on file that has been signed by each Contributor, indicating agreement to the license terms below. This license is for your protection as a Contributor as well as the protection of the Foundation and its users; it does not change your rights to use your own Contributions for any other purpose.

This version of the Agreement allows an entity (the "Corporation") to submit Contributions to the Foundation, to authorize Contributions submitted by its designated employees to the Foundation, and to grant copyright and patent licenses thereto.

If you have not already done so, please complete and send an original signed Agreement to The Apache Software Foundation, 1901 Munsey Drive, Forest Hill, MD 21050-2747, U.S.A. If necessary, you may send it by facsimile to the Foundation at +1-410-803-2258. Please read this document carefully before signing and keep a copy for your records.

Corporation name: _____

Corporation address: _____

_____

_____

Point of Contact: _____

E-Mail: _____

Telephone: _____ Fax: _____

You accept and agree to the following terms and conditions for Your present and future Contributions submitted to the Foundation. In return, the Foundation shall not use Your Contributions in a way that is contrary to the public benefit or inconsistent with its nonprofit status and bylaws in effect at the time of the Contribution. Except for the license granted herein to the Foundation and recipients of software distributed by the Foundation, You reserve all right, title, and interest in and to Your Contributions.

1. Definitions.

"You" (or "Your") shall mean the copyright owner or legal entity authorized by the copyright owner that is making this Agreement with the Foundation. For legal entities, the entity making a Contribution and all other entities that control, are controlled by, or are under common control with that entity are considered to be a single Contributor. For the purposes of this definition, "control" means (i) the power, direct or indirect, to cause the direction or management of such entity, whether by contract or otherwise, or (ii) ownership of fifty percent (50%) or more of the outstanding shares, or (iii) beneficial ownership of such entity.

"Contribution" shall mean the code, documentation, or other original works of authorship expressly identified in Schedule B, as well as any original work of authorship, including any modifications or additions to an existing work, that is intentionally submitted by You to the Foundation for inclusion in, or documentation of, any of the products owned or managed by the Foundation (the "Work"). For the purposes of this definition, "submitted" means any form of electronic, verbal, or written communication sent to the Foundation or its representatives, including but not limited to communication on electronic mailing lists, source code control systems, and issue tracking systems that are managed by, or on behalf of, the Foundation for the purpose of discussing and improving the Work, but excluding communication that is conspicuously marked or otherwise designated in writing by You as "Not a Contribution."

2. Grant of Copyright License. Subject to the terms and conditions of this Agreement, You hereby grant to the Foundation and to recipients of software distributed by the Foundation a perpetual, worldwide, non-exclusive, no-charge, royalty-free, irrevocable copyright license to reproduce, prepare derivative works of, publicly display, publicly perform, sublicense, and distribute Your Contributions and such derivative works.

3. Grant of Patent License. Subject to the terms and conditions of this Agreement, You hereby grant to the Foundation and to recipients of software distributed by the Foundation a perpetual, worldwide, non-exclusive, no-charge, royalty-free, irrevocable (except as stated in this section) patent license to make, have made, use, offer to sell, sell, import, and otherwise transfer the Work, where such license applies only to those patent claims licensable by You that are necessarily infringed by Your Contribution(s) alone or by combination of Your Contribution(s) with the Work to which such Contribution(s) were submitted. If any entity institutes patent litigation against You or any other entity (including a cross-claim or counterclaim in a lawsuit) alleging that your Contribution, or the Work to which you have contributed, constitutes direct or contributory patent infringement, then any patent licenses granted to that entity under this Agreement for that Contribution or Work shall terminate as of the date such litigation is filed.

4. You represent that You are legally entitled to grant the above license. You represent further that each employee of the Corporation designated on Schedule A below (or in a subsequent written modification to that Schedule) is authorized to submit Contributions on behalf of the Corporation.

5. You represent that each of Your Contributions is Your original creation (see section 7 for submissions on behalf of others).

6. You are not expected to provide support for Your Contributions, except to the extent You desire to provide support. You may provide support for free, for a fee, or not at all. Unless required by applicable law or agreed to in writing, You provide Your Contributions on an "AS IS" BASIS, WITHOUT WARRANTIES OR CONDITIONS OF ANY KIND, either express or implied, including, without limitation, any warranties or conditions of TITLE, NON-INFRINGEMENT, MERCHANTABILITY, or FITNESS FOR A PARTICULAR PURPOSE.

7. Should You wish to submit work that is not Your original creation, You may submit it to the Foundation separately from any Contribution, identifying the complete details of its source and of any license or other restriction (including, but not limited to, related patents, trademarks, and license agreements) of which you are personally aware, and conspicuously marking the work as "Submitted on behalf of a third-party: [named here]".

8. It is your responsibility to notify the Foundation when any change is required to the list of designated employees authorized to submit Contributions on behalf of the Corporation, or to the Corporation's Point of Contact with the Foundation.

Please sign: _____ Date: _____

Title: _____

Corporation: _____

Schedule A

[Initial list of designated employees. N.B.: authorization is not tied to particular Contributions.]

Schedule B

[Identification of optional concurrent software grant. Would be left blank or omitted if there is no concurrent software grant.]

C

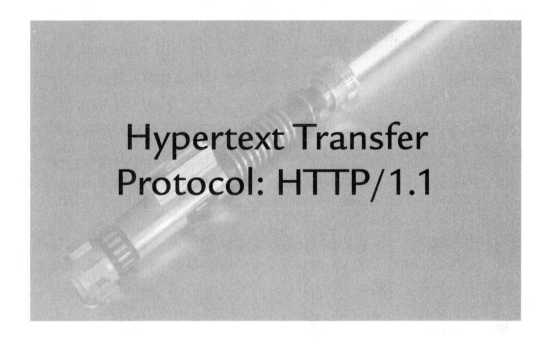

Hypertext Transfer Protocol: HTTP/1.1

Network Working Group
Request for Comments: 2616
Obsoletes: 2068
Category: Standards Track

R. Fielding, UC Irvine
J. Gettys, Compaq/W3C
J. Mogul, Compaq
H. Frystyk, W3C/MIT
L. Masinter, Xerox
P. Leach, Microsoft
T. Berners-Lee, W3C/MIT
June 1999

Status of This Memo

This document specifies an Internet standards track protocol for the Internet community, and requests discussion and suggestions for improvements. Please refer to the current edition of the "Internet Official Protocol Standards" (STD 1) for the standardization state and status of this protocol. Distribution of this memo is unlimited.

Copyright Notice

Abstract

The Hypertext Transfer Protocol (HTTP) is an application-level protocol for distributed, collaborative, hypermedia information systems. It is a generic, stateless, protocol which can be used for many tasks beyond its use for hypertext, such as name servers and distributed object management systems, through extension of its request methods, error codes, and headers [47]. A feature of HTTP is the typing and negotiation of data representation, allowing systems to be built independently of the data being transferred.

HTTP has been in use by the World-Wide Web global information initiative since 1990. This specification defines the protocol referred to as "HTTP/1.1" and is an update to RFC 2068 [33].

1 Introduction

1.1 Purpose

The Hypertext Transfer Protocol (HTTP) is an application-level protocol for distributed, collaborative, hypermedia information systems. HTTP has been in use by the World-Wide Web global information initiative since 1990. The first version of HTTP, referred to as HTTP/0.9, was a simple protocol for raw data transfer across the Internet. HTTP/1.0, as defined by RFC 1945 [6], improved the protocol by allowing messages to be in the format of MIME-like messages, containing meta-information about the data transferred and modifiers on the request/response semantics. However, HTTP/1.0 does not sufficiently take into consideration the effects of hierarchical proxies, caching, the need for persistent connections, or virtual hosts. In addition, the proliferation of incompletely implemented applications calling themselves "HTTP/1.0" has necessitated a protocol version change in order for two communicating applications to determine each other's true capabilities.

This specification defines the protocol referred to as "HTTP/1.1." This protocol includes more stringent requirements than HTTP/1.0 in order to ensure reliable implementation of its features.

Practical information systems require more functionality than simple retrieval, including search, front-end update, and annotation. HTTP allows an open-ended set of methods and headers that indicate the purpose of a request [47]. It builds on the discipline of reference provided by the Uniform Resource Identifier (URI) [3], as a location (URL) [4] or name (URN) [20], for indicating the resource to which a method is to be applied. Messages are passed in a format similar to that used by Internet mail [9] as defined by the Multipurpose Internet Mail Extensions (MIME) [7].

HTTP is also used as a generic protocol for communication between user agents and proxies/gateways to other Internet systems, including those supported by the SMTP [16], NNTP [13], FTP [18], Gopher [2], and WAIS [10] protocols. In this way, HTTP allows basic hypermedia access to resources available from diverse applications.

1.2 Requirements

The key words "MUST," "MUST NOT," "REQUIRED," "SHALL," "SHALL NOT," "SHOULD," "SHOULD NOT," "RECOMMENDED," "MAY," and "OPTIONAL" in this document are to be interpreted as described in RFC 2119 [34].

An implementation is not compliant if it fails to satisfy one or more of the MUST or REQUIRED level requirements for the protocols it implements. An implementation that satisfies all the MUST or REQUIRED level and all the SHOULD level requirements for its protocols is said to be "unconditionally compliant"; one that satisfies all the MUST level requirements but not all the SHOULD level requirements for its protocols is said to be "conditionally compliant."

1.3 Terminology

This specification uses a number of terms to refer to the roles played by participants in, and objects of, the HTTP communication.

connection

A transport layer virtual circuit established between two programs for the purpose of communication.

message

The basic unit of HTTP communication, consisting of a structured sequence of octets matching the syntax defined in section 4 and transmitted via the connection.

request

An HTTP request message, as defined in section 5.

response

An HTTP response message, as defined in section 6.

resource

A network data object or service that can be identified by a URI, as defined in section 3.2. Resources may be available in multiple representations (e.g., multiple languages, data formats, size, and resolutions) or vary in other ways.

entity

The information transferred as the payload of a request or response. An entity consists of metainformation in the form of entity-header fields and content in the form of an entity-body, as described in section 7.

representation

An entity included with a response that is subject to content negotiation, as described in section 12. There may exist multiple representations associated with a particular response status.

content negotiation

The mechanism for selecting the appropriate representation when servicing a request, as described in section 12. The representation of entities in any response can be negotiated (including error responses).

variant

A resource may have one, or more than one, representation(s) associated with it at any given instant. Each of these representations is termed a "variant." Use of the term "variant" does not necessarily imply that the resource is subject to content negotiation.

client

A program that establishes connections for the purpose of sending requests.

user agent

The client which initiates a request. These are often browsers, editors, spiders (web-traversing robots), or other end user tools.

server

An application program that accepts connections in order to service requests by sending back responses. Any given program may be capable of being both a client and a server; our use of these terms refers only to the role being performed by the program for a particular connection, rather than to the program's capabilities in general. Likewise, any server may act as an origin server, proxy, gateway, or tunnel, switching behavior based on the nature of each request.

origin server

The server on which a given resource resides or is to be created.

proxy

An intermediary program which acts as both a server and a client for the purpose of making requests on behalf of other clients. Requests are serviced internally or by passing them on, with possible translation, to other servers. A proxy MUST implement both the client and server requirements of this specification. A "transparent proxy" is a proxy that does not modify the request or response beyond what is required for proxy authentication and identification. A "non-transparent proxy" is a proxy that modifies the request or response in order to provide some added service to the user agent, such as group annotation services, media type transformation, protocol reduction, or anonymity filtering. Except where either transparent or non-transparent behavior is explicitly stated, the HTTP proxy requirements apply to both types of proxies.

gateway

A server which acts as an intermediary for some other server. Unlike a proxy, a gateway receives requests as if it were the origin server for the requested resource; the requesting client may not be aware that it is communicating with a gateway.

tunnel

An intermediary program which is acting as a blind relay between two connections. Once active, a tunnel is not considered a party to the HTTP communication, though the tunnel may have been initiated by an HTTP request. The tunnel ceases to exist when both ends of the relayed connections are closed.

cache

A program's local store of response messages and the subsystem that controls its message storage, retrieval, and deletion. A cache stores cacheable responses in order to reduce the response time and network bandwidth consumption on future, equivalent requests. Any client or server may include a cache, though a cache cannot be used by a server that is acting as a tunnel.

cacheable

A response is cacheable if a cache is allowed to store a copy of the response message for use in answering subsequent requests. The rules for determining the cacheability of HTTP responses are defined in section 13. Even if a resource is cacheable, there may be additional constraints on whether a cache can use the cached copy for a particular request.

first-hand

A response is first-hand if it comes directly and without unnecessary delay from the origin server, perhaps via one or more proxies. A response is also first-hand if its validity has just been checked directly with the origin server.

explicit expiration time

The time at which the origin server intends that an entity should no longer be returned by a cache without further validation.

heuristic expiration time

An expiration time assigned by a cache when no explicit expiration time is available.

age

The age of a response is the time since it was sent by, or successfully validated with, the origin server.

freshness lifetime

The length of time between the generation of a response and its expiration time.

fresh

A response is fresh if its age has not yet exceeded its freshness lifetime.

stale

A response is stale if its age has passed its freshness lifetime.

semantically transparent

A cache behaves in a "semantically transparent" manner, with respect to a particular response, when its use affects neither the requesting client nor the origin server, except to improve performance. When a cache is semantically transparent, the client receives exactly the same response (except for hop-by-hop headers) that it would have received had its request been handled directly by the origin server.

validator

A protocol element (e.g., an entity tag or a Last-Modified time) that is used to find out whether a cache entry is an equivalent copy of an entity.

upstream/downstream

Upstream and downstream describe the flow of a message: all messages flow from upstream to downstream.

inbound/outbound

Inbound and outbound refer to the request and response paths for messages: "inbound" means "traveling toward the origin server," and "outbound" means "traveling toward the user agent."

1.4 Overall Operation

The HTTP protocol is a request/response protocol. A client sends a request to the server in the form of a request method, URI, and protocol version, followed by a MIME-like message containing request modifiers, client information, and possible body content over a connection with a server. The server responds with a status line, including the message's protocol version and a success or error code, followed by a MIME-like message containing server information, entity metainformation, and possible entity-body content. The relationship between HTTP and MIME is described in appendix 19.4.

Most HTTP communication is initiated by a user agent and consists of a request to be applied to a resource on some origin server. In the simplest case, this may be accomplished via a single connection (v) between the user agent (UA) and the origin server (O).

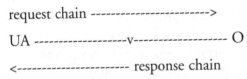

```
       request chain ----------------------->
       UA ------------------v------------------ O
       <---------------------- response chain
```

A more complicated situation occurs when one or more intermediaries are present in the request/response chain. There are three common forms of intermediary: proxy, gateway, and tunnel. A proxy is a forwarding agent, receiving requests for a URI in its absolute form, rewriting all or part of the message, and forwarding the reformatted request toward the server identified by the URI. A gateway is a receiving agent, acting as a layer above some other server(s) and, if necessary, translating the requests to the underlying server's protocol. A tunnel acts as a relay point between two connections without changing the messages; tunnels are used when the communication needs to pass through an intermediary (such as a firewall) even when the intermediary cannot understand the contents of the messages.

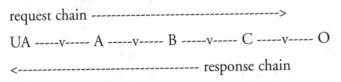

```
       request chain -------------------------------------->
       UA -----v----- A -----v----- B -----v----- C -----v----- O
       <------------------------------------- response chain
```

The figure above shows three intermediaries (A, B, and C) between the user agent and origin server. A request or response message that travels the whole chain will pass through four separate connections. This distinction is important because some HTTP communication options may apply only to the connection with the nearest, non-tunnel neighbor, only to the end-points of the chain, or to all connections along the chain. Although the diagram is linear, each participant may be engaged in multiple, simultaneous communications. For example, B may be receiving requests from many clients other than A, and/or forwarding requests to servers other than C, at the same time that it is handling A's request.

Any party to the communication which is not acting as a tunnel may employ an internal cache for handling requests. The effect of a cache is that the request/response chain is shortened if one of the participants along the chain has a cached response applicable to that request. The following illustrates the resulting chain if B has a cached copy of an earlier response from O (via C) for a request which has not been cached by UA or A.

```
request chain ---------->
UA -----v----- A -----v----- B - - - - - - C - - - - - - O
<--------- response chain
```

Not all responses are usefully cacheable, and some requests may contain modifiers which place special requirements on cache behavior. HTTP requirements for cache behavior and cacheable responses are defined in section 13.

In fact, there are a wide variety of architectures and configurations of caches and proxies currently being experimented with or deployed across the World Wide Web. These systems include national hierarchies of proxy caches to save transoceanic bandwidth, systems that broadcast or multicast cache entries, organizations that distribute subsets of cached data via CD-ROM, and so on. HTTP systems are used in corporate intranets over high-bandwidth links, and for access via PDAs with low-power radio links and intermittent connectivity. The goal of HTTP/1.1 is to support the wide diversity of configurations already deployed while introducing protocol constructs that meet the needs of those who build web applications that require high reliability and, failing that, at least reliable indications of failure.

HTTP communication usually takes place over TCP/IP connections. The default port is TCP 80 [19], but other ports can be used. This does not preclude HTTP from being implemented on top of any other protocol on the Internet, or on other networks. HTTP only presumes a reliable transport; any protocol that provides such guarantees can be used; the mapping of the HTTP/1.1 request and response structures onto the transport data units of the protocol in question is outside the scope of this specification.

In HTTP/1.0, most implementations used a new connection for each request/ response exchange. In HTTP/1.1, a connection may be used for one or more request/response exchanges, although connections may be closed for a variety of reasons (see section 8.1).

2 Notational Conventions and Generic Grammar

2.1 Augmented BNF

All of the mechanisms specified in this document are described in both prose and an augmented Backus-Naur Form (BNF) similar to that used by RFC 822 [9]. Implementers will need to be familiar with the notation in order to understand this specification. The augmented BNF includes the following constructs:

name = definition

The name of a rule is simply the name itself (without any enclosing "<" and ">") and is separated from its definition by the equal "=" character. White space is only significant in that indentation of continuation lines is used to indicate a rule definition that spans more than one line. Certain basic rules are in uppercase, such as SP, LWS, HT, CRLF, DIGIT, ALPHA, etc. Angle brackets are used within definitions whenever their presence will facilitate discerning the use of rule names.

"literal"

Quotation marks surround literal text. Unless stated otherwise, the text is case-insensitive.

rule1 | rule2

Elements separated by a bar ("|") are alternatives, e.g., "yes | no" will accept yes or no.

(rule1 rule2)

Elements enclosed in parentheses are treated as a single element. Thus, "(elem (foo | bar) elem)" allows the token sequences "elem foo elem" and "elem bar elem."

*rule

The character "*" preceding an element indicates repetition. The full form is "<n>*<m>element" indicating at least <n> and at most <m> occurrences of element. Default values are 0 and infinity so that "*(element)" allows any number, including zero; "1*element" requires at least one; and "1*2element" allows one or two.

[rule]

Square brackets enclose optional elements; "[foo bar]" is equivalent to "*1(foo bar)."

N rule

Specific repetition: "<n>(element)" is equivalent to "<n>*<n>(element)"; that is, exactly <n> occurrences of (element). Thus 2DIGIT is a 2-digit number, and 3ALPHA is a string of three alphabetic characters.

#rule

A construct "#" is defined, similar to "*", for defining lists of elements. The full form is "<n>#<m>element" indicating at least <n> and at most <m> elements, each separated by one or more commas (",") and OPTIONAL linear white space (LWS). This makes the usual form of lists very easy; a rule such as

```
( *LWS element *( *LWS "," *LWS element ))
```

can be shown as

```
1#element
```

Wherever this construct is used, null elements are allowed, but do not contribute to the count of elements present. That is, "(element), , (element) " is permitted, but counts as only two elements. Therefore, where at least one element is required, at least one non-null element MUST be present. Default values are 0 and infinity so that "#element" allows any number, including zero; "1#element" requires at least one; and "1#2element" allows one or two.

; comment

A semi-colon, set off some distance to the right of rule text, starts a comment that continues to the end of line. This is a simple way of including useful notes in parallel with the specifications.

implied *LWS

The grammar described by this specification is word-based. Except where noted otherwise, linear white space (LWS) can be included between any two adjacent words (token or quoted-string), and between adjacent words and separators, without changing the interpretation of a field. At least one delimiter (LWS and/or separators) MUST exist between any two tokens (for the definition of "token" below), since they would otherwise be interpreted as a single token.

2.2 Basic Rules

The following rules are used throughout this specification to describe basic parsing constructs. The US-ASCII coded character set is defined by ANSI X3.4-1986 [21].

```
OCTET    = <any 8-bit sequence of data>
CHAR     = <any US-ASCII character (octets 0 - 127)>
UPALPHA  = <any US-ASCII uppercase letter "A".."Z">
LOALPHA  = <any US-ASCII lowercase letter "a".."z">
ALPHA    = UPALPHA | LOALPHA
DIGIT    = <any US-ASCII digit "0".."9">
CTL      = <any US-ASCII control character
           (octets 0 - 31) and DEL (127)>
CR       = <US-ASCII CR, carriage return (13)>
LF       = <US-ASCII LF, linefeed (10)>
SP       = <US-ASCII SP, space (32)>
HT       = <US-ASCII HT, horizontal-tab (9)>
<">      = <US-ASCII double-quote mark (34)>
```

HTTP/1.1 defines the sequence CR LF as the end-of-line marker for all protocol elements except the entity-body (see appendix 19.3 for tolerant applications). The end-of-line marker within an entity-body is defined by its associated media type, as described in section 3.7.

```
CRLF     = CR LF
```

HTTP/1.1 header field values can be folded onto multiple lines if the continuation line begins with a space or horizontal tab. All linear white space, including folding, has the same semantics as SP. A recipient MAY replace any linear white space with a single SP before interpreting the field value or forwarding the message down-stream.

```
LWS      = [CRLF] 1*( SP | HT )
```

The TEXT rule is only used for descriptive field contents and values that are not intended to be interpreted by the message parser. Words of *TEXT MAY contain characters from character sets other than ISO-8859-1 [22] only when encoded according to the rules of RFC 2047[14].

```
TEXT     = <any OCTET except CTLs, but including LWS>
```

A CRLF is allowed in the definition of TEXT only as part of a header field contin-uation. It is expected that the folding LWS will be replaced with a single SP before interpretation of the TEXT value.

Hexadecimal numeric characters are used in several protocol elements.

```
HEX      = "A" | "B" | "C" | "D" | "E" | "F" | "a" | "b" | "c" | "d" | "e" |
           "f" | DIGIT
```

Many HTTP/1.1 header field values consist of words separated by LWS or special characters. These special characters MUST be in a quoted string to be used within a parameter value (as defined in section 3.6).

```
token      = 1*<any CHAR except CTLs or separators>
separators = "(" | ")" | "<" | ">" | "@" | "," | ";" | ":"
           | "\" | <"> | "/" | "[" | "]" | "?" | "="
           | "{" | "}" | SP | HT
```

Comments can be included in some HTTP header fields by surrounding the com-ment text with parentheses. Comments are only allowed in fields containing "comment" as part of their field value definition. In all other fields, parentheses are considered part of the field value.

```
comment  = "(" *( ctext | quoted-pair | comment ) ")"
ctext    = <any TEXT excluding "(" and ")">
```

A string of text is parsed as a single word if it is quoted using double-quote marks.

```
quoted-string = ( <"> *(qdtext | quoted-pair ) <"> )
qdtext        = <any TEXT except <">>
```

The backslash character ("\") MAY be used as a single-character quoting mechanism only within quoted-string and comment constructs.

```
quoted-pair  = "\" CHAR
```

3 Protocol Parameters

3.1 HTTP Version

HTTP uses a "<major>.<minor>" numbering scheme to indicate versions of the protocol. The protocol versioning policy is intended to allow the sender to indicate the format of a message and its capacity for understanding further HTTP communication, rather than the features obtained via that communication. No change is made to the version number for the addition of message components which do not affect communication behavior or which only add to extensible field values. The <minor> number is incremented when the changes made to the protocol add features which do not change the general message parsing algorithm, but which may add to the message semantics and imply additional capabilities of the sender. The <major> number is incremented when the format of a message within the protocol is changed. See RFC 2145 [36] for a fuller explanation.

The version of an HTTP message is indicated by an HTTP-Version field in the first line of the message.

```
HTTP-Version = "HTTP" "/" 1*DIGIT "." 1*DIGIT
```

Note that the major and minor numbers MUST be treated as separate integers and that each MAY be incremented higher than a single digit. Thus, HTTP/2.4 is a lower version than HTTP/2.13, which in turn is lower than HTTP/12.3. Leading zeros MUST be ignored by recipients and MUST NOT be sent.

An application that sends a request or response message that includes HTTP-Version of "HTTP/1.1" MUST be at least conditionally compliant with this specification. Applications that are at least conditionally compliant with this specification SHOULD use an HTTP-Version of "HTTP/1.1" in their messages, and MUST do so for any message that is not compatible with HTTP/1.0. For more details on when to send specific HTTP-Version values, see RFC 2145 [36].

The HTTP version of an application is the highest HTTP version for which the application is at least conditionally compliant.

Proxy and gateway applications need to be careful when forwarding messages in protocol versions different from that of the application. Since the protocol version indicates the protocol capability of the sender, a proxy/gateway MUST NOT send a message with a version indicator which is greater than its actual version. If a higher version request is received, the proxy/gateway MUST either downgrade the request version, or respond with an error, or switch to tunnel behavior.

Due to interoperability problems with HTTP/1.0 proxies discovered since the publication of RFC 2068 [33], caching proxies MUST, gateways MAY, and tunnels MUST NOT upgrade the request to the highest version they support. The proxy/gateway's response to that request MUST be in the same major version as the request.

> **Note:** Converting between versions of HTTP may involve modification of header fields required or forbidden by the versions involved.

3.2 Uniform Resource Identifiers

URIs have been known by many names: WWW addresses, Universal Document Identifiers, Universal Resource Identifiers [3], and finally the combination of Uniform Resource Locators (URL) [4] and Names (URN) [20]. As far as HTTP is concerned, Uniform Resource Identifiers are simply formatted strings which identify—via name, location, or any other characteristic—a resource.

3.2.1 General Syntax

URIs in HTTP can be represented in absolute form or relative to some known base URI [11], depending upon the context of their use. The two forms are differentiated by the fact that absolute URIs always begin with a scheme name followed by a colon. For definitive information on URL syntax and semantics, see "Uniform Resource Identifiers (URI): Generic Syntax and Semantics," RFC 2396 [42] (which replaces RFCs 1738 [4] and RFC 1808 [11]). This specification adopts the definitions of "URI-reference," "absoluteURI," "relativeURI," "port," "host,""abs_path," "rel_path," and "authority" from that specification.

The HTTP protocol does not place any a priori limit on the length of a URI. Servers MUST be able to handle the URI of any resource they serve, and SHOULD be able to handle URIs of unbounded length if they provide GET-based forms that could generate such URIs. A server SHOULD return 414 (Request-URI Too Long) status if a URI is longer than the server can handle (see section 10.4.15).

Note: Servers ought to be cautious about depending on URI lengths above 255 bytes, because some older client or proxy implementations might not properly support these lengths.

3.2.2 http URL

The "http" scheme is used to locate network resources via the HTTP protocol. This section defines the scheme-specific syntax and semantics for http URLs.

```
http_URL = "http:" "//" host [ ":" port ] [ abs_path [ "?" query ]]
```

If the port is empty or not given, port 80 is assumed. The semantics are that the identified resource is located at the server listening for TCP connections on that port of that host, and the Request-URI for the resource is abs_path (section 5.1.2). The use of IP addresses in URLs SHOULD be avoided whenever possible (see RFC 1900 [24]). If the abs_path is not present in the URL, it MUST be given as "/" when used as a Request-URI for a resource (section 5.1.2). If a proxy receives a host name which is not a fully qualified domain name, it MAY add its domain to the host name it received. If a proxy receives a fully qualified domain name, the proxy MUST NOT change the host name.

3.2.3 URI Comparison

When comparing two URIs to decide if they match or not, a client SHOULD use a case-sensitive octet-by-octet comparison of the entire URIs, with these exceptions:

- A port that is empty or not given is equivalent to the default port for that URI-reference;

- Comparisons of host names MUST be case-insensitive;

- Comparisons of scheme names MUST be case-insensitive;

- An empty abs_path is equivalent to an abs_path of "/".

Characters other than those in the "reserved" and "unsafe" sets (see RFC 2396 [42]) are equivalent to their ""%" HEX HEX" encoding.

For example, the following three URIs are equivalent:

```
http://abc.com:80/~smith/home.html
http://ABC.com/%7Esmith/home.html
http://ABC.com:/%7esmith/home.html
```

3.3 Date/Time Formats

3.3.1 Full Date

HTTP applications have historically allowed three different formats for the representation of date/time stamps:

```
Sun, 06 Nov 1994 08:49:37 GMT  ; RFC 822, updated by RFC 1123
Sunday, 06-Nov-94 08:49:37 GMT ; RFC 850, obsoleted by RFC 1036
Sun Nov 6 08:49:37 1994        ; ANSI C's asctime() format
```

The first format is preferred as an Internet standard and represents a fixed-length subset of that defined by RFC 1123 [8] (an update to RFC 822 [9]). The second format is in common use, but is based on the obsolete RFC 850 [12] date format and lacks a four-digit year. HTTP/1.1 clients and servers that parse the date value MUST accept all three formats (for compatibility with HTTP/1.0), though they MUST only generate the RFC 1123 format for representing HTTP-date values in header fields. See section 19.3 for further information.

> **Note:** Recipients of date values are encouraged to be robust in accepting date values that may have been sent by non-HTTP applications, as is sometimes the case when retrieving or posting messages via proxies/gateways to SMTP or NNTP.

All HTTP date/time stamps MUST be represented in Greenwich Mean Time (GMT), without exception. For the purposes of HTTP, GMT is exactly equal to UTC (Coordinated Universal Time). This is indicated in the first two formats by the inclusion of "GMT" as the three-letter abbreviation for time zone, and MUST be assumed when reading the asctime format. HTTP-date is case-sensitive and MUST NOT include additional LWS beyond that specifically included as SP in the grammar.

```
HTTP-date   = rfc1123-date | rfc850-date | asctime-date
rfc1123-date = wkday "," SP date1 SP time SP "GMT"
rfc850-date = weekday "," SP date2 SP time SP "GMT"
asctime-date = wkday SP date3 SP time SP 4DIGIT
date1     = 2DIGIT SP month SP 4DIGIT
          ; day month year (e.g., 02 Jun 1982)
date2     = 2DIGIT "-" month "-" 2DIGIT
          ; day-month-year (e.g., 02-Jun-82)
date3     = month SP ( 2DIGIT | ( SP 1DIGIT ))
          ; month day (e.g., Jun 2)
time      = 2DIGIT ":" 2DIGIT ":" 2DIGIT
          ; 00:00:00 - 23:59:59
wkday     = "Mon" | "Tue" | "Wed"
          | "Thu" | "Fri" | "Sat" | "Sun"
weekday   = "Monday" | "Tuesday" | "Wednesday"
          | "Thursday" | "Friday" | "Saturday" | "Sunday"
```

```
month    = "Jan" | "Feb" | "Mar" | "Apr"
       | "May" | "Jun" | "Jul" | "Aug"
       | "Sep" | "Oct" | "Nov" | "Dec"
```

Note: HTTP requirements for the date/time stamp format apply only to their usage within the protocol stream. Clients and servers are not required to use these formats for user presentation, request logging, etc.

3.3.2 Delta Seconds

Some HTTP header fields allow a time value to be specified as an integer number of seconds, represented in decimal, after the time that the message was received.

```
delta-seconds = 1*DIGIT
```

3.4 Character Sets

HTTP uses the same definition of the term "character set" as that described for MIME: The term "character set" is used in this document to refer to a method used with one or more tables to convert a sequence of octets into a sequence of characters. Note that unconditional conversion in the other direction is not required, in that not all characters may be available in a given character set and a character set may provide more than one sequence of octets to represent a particular character. This definition is intended to allow various kinds of character encoding, from simple single-table mappings such as US-ASCII to complex table switching methods such as those that use ISO-2022's techniques. However, the definition associated with a MIME character set name MUST fully specify the mapping to be performed from octets to characters. In particular, use of external profiling information to determine the exact mapping is not permitted.

Note: This use of the term "character set" is more commonly referred to as a "character encoding." However, since HTTP and MIME share the same registry, it is important that the terminology also be shared.

HTTP character sets are identified by case-insensitive tokens. The complete set of tokens is defined by the IANA Character Set registry [19].

```
charset = token
```

Although HTTP allows an arbitrary token to be used as a charset value, any token that has a predefined value within the IANA Character Set registry [19] MUST represent the character set defined by that registry. Applications SHOULD limit their use of character sets to those defined by the IANA registry.

Implementers should be aware of IETF character set requirements [38] [41].

3.4.1 Missing Charset

Some HTTP/1.0 software has interpreted a Content-Type header without charset parameter incorrectly to mean "recipient should guess." Senders wishing to defeat this behavior MAY include a charset parameter even when the charset is ISO-8859-1 and SHOULD do so when it is known that it will not confuse the recipient.

Unfortunately, some older HTTP/1.0 clients did not deal properly with an explicit charset parameter. HTTP/1.1 recipients MUST respect the charset label provided by the sender; and those user agents that have a provision to "guess" a charset MUST use the charset from the content-type field if they support that charset, rather than the recipient's preference, when initially displaying a document. See section 3.7.1.

3.5 Content Codings

Content coding values indicate an encoding transformation that has been or can be applied to an entity. Content codings are primarily used to allow a document to be compressed or otherwise usefully transformed without losing the identity of its underlying media type and without loss of information. Frequently, the entity is stored in coded form, transmitted directly, and only decoded by the recipient.

```
content-coding = token
```

All content-coding values are case-insensitive. HTTP/1.1 uses content-coding values in the Accept-Encoding (section 14.3) and Content-Encoding (section 14.11) header fields. Although the value describes the content-coding, what is more important is that it indicates what decoding mechanism will be required to remove the encoding.

The Internet Assigned Numbers Authority (IANA) acts as a registry for content-coding value tokens. Initially, the registry contains the following tokens:

gzip

An encoding format produced by the file compression program "gzip" (GNU zip) as described in RFC 1952 [25]. This format is a Lempel-Ziv coding (LZ77) with a 32 bit CRC.

compress

The encoding format produced by the common UNIX file compression program "compress." This format is an adaptive Lempel-Ziv-Welch coding (LZW). Use of program names for the identification of encoding formats is not desirable and is discouraged for future encodings. Their use here is representative of historical practice, not good design. For compatibility with previous implementations of HTTP, applications SHOULD consider "x-gzip" and "x-compress" to be equivalent to "gzip" and "compress," respectively.

deflate

The "zlib" format defined in RFC 1950 [31] in combination with the "deflate" compression mechanism described in RFC 1951 [29].

identity

The default (identity) encoding; the use of no transformation whatsoever. This content-coding is used only in the Accept-Encoding header, and SHOULD NOT be used in the Content-Encoding header.

New content-coding value tokens SHOULD be registered; to allow interoperability between clients and servers, specifications of the content coding algorithms needed to implement a new value SHOULD be publicly available and adequate for independent implementation, and conform to the purpose of content coding defined in this section.

3.6 Transfer Codings

Transfer-coding values are used to indicate an encoding transformation that has been, can be, or may need to be applied to an entity-body in order to ensure "safe transport" through the network. This differs from a content-coding in that the transfer-coding is a property of the message, not of the original entity.

```
transfer-coding     = "chunked" | transfer-extension
transfer-extension  = token *( ";" parameter )
```

Parameters are in the form of attribute/value pairs.

```
parameter   = attribute "=" value
attribute   = token
value       = token | quoted-string
```

All transfer-coding values are case-insensitive. HTTP/1.1 uses transfer-coding values in the TE header field (section 14.39) and in the Transfer-Encoding header field (section 14.41).

Whenever a transfer-coding is applied to a message-body, the set of transfer-codings MUST include "chunked," unless the message is terminated by closing the connection. When the "chunked" transfer-coding is used, it MUST be the last transfer-coding applied to the message-body. The "chunked" transfer-coding MUST NOT be applied more than once to a message-body. These rules allow the recipient to determine the transfer-length of the message (section 4.4).

Transfer-codings are analogous to the Content-Transfer-Encoding values of MIME [7], which were designed to enable safe transport of binary data over a 7-bit transport service. However, safe transport has a different focus for an 8-bit-clean transfer protocol. In HTTP, the only unsafe characteristic of message-bodies is the difficulty in determining the exact body length (section 7.2.2), or the desire to encrypt data over a shared transport.

The Internet Assigned Numbers Authority (IANA) acts as a registry for transfer-coding value tokens. Initially, the registry contains the following tokens: "chunked" (section 3.6.1), "identity" (section 3.6.2), "gzip" (section 3.5), "compress" (section 3.5), and "deflate" (section 3.5).

New transfer-coding value tokens SHOULD be registered in the same way as new content-coding value tokens (section 3.5).

A server which receives an entity-body with a transfer-coding it does not understand SHOULD return 501 (Unimplemented), and close the connection. A server MUST NOT send transfer-codings to an HTTP/1.0 client.

3.6.1 Chunked Transfer Coding

The chunked encoding modifies the body of a message in order to transfer it as a series of chunks, each with its own size indicator, followed by an OPTIONAL trailer containing entity-header fields. This allows dynamically produced content to be transferred along with the information necessary for the recipient to verify that it has received the full message.

```
Chunked-Body  = *chunk
        last-chunk
        trailer
        CRLF
```

```
chunk      = chunk-size [ chunk-extension ] CRLF
           chunk-data CRLF
chunk-size   = 1*HEX
last-chunk   = 1*("0") [ chunk-extension ] CRLF
chunk-extension= *( ";" chunk-ext-name [ "=" chunk-ext-val ] )
chunk-ext-name = token
chunk-ext-val = token | quoted-string
chunk-data   = chunk-size(OCTET)
trailer     = *(entity-header CRLF)
```

The chunk-size field is a string of hex digits indicating the size of the chunk. The chunked encoding is ended by any chunk whose size is zero, followed by the trailer, which is terminated by an empty line.

The trailer allows the sender to include additional HTTP header fields at the end of the message. The Trailer header field can be used to indicate which header fields are included in a trailer (see section 14.40).

A server using chunked transfer-coding in a response MUST NOT use the trailer for any header fields unless at least one of the following is true:

(a)   The request included a TE header field that indicates "trailers" is acceptable in the transfer-coding of the response, as described in section 14.39; or,

(b)   The server is the origin server for the response, the trailer fields consist entirely of optional metadata, and the recipient could use the message (in a manner acceptable to the origin server) without receiving this metadata. In other words, the origin server is willing to accept the possibility that the trailer fields might be silently discarded along the path to the client.

This requirement prevents an interoperability failure when the message is being received by an HTTP/1.1 (or later) proxy and forwarded to an HTTP/1.0 recipient. It avoids a situation where compliance with the protocol would have necessitated a possibly infinite buffer on the proxy.

An example process for decoding a Chunked-Body is presented in appendix 19.4.6.

All HTTP/1.1 applications MUST be able to receive and decode the "chunked" transfer-coding, and MUST ignore chunk-extension extensions they do not understand.

3.7 Media Types

HTTP uses Internet Media Types [17] in the Content-Type (section 14.17) and Accept (section 14.1) header fields in order to provide open and extensible data typing and type negotiation.

```
media-type      = type "/" subtype *( ";" parameter )
type            = token
subtype         = token
```

Parameters MAY follow the type/subtype in the form of attribute/value pairs (as defined in section 3.6).

The type, subtype, and parameter attribute names are case-insensitive. Parameter values might or might not be case-sensitive, depending on the semantics of the parameter name. Linear white space (LWS) MUST NOT be used between the type and subtype, nor between an attribute and its value. The presence or absence of a parameter might be significant to the processing of a media-type, depending on its definition within the media type registry.

Note that some older HTTP applications do not recognize media type parameters. When sending data to older HTTP applications, implementations SHOULD only use media type parameters when they are required by that type/subtype definition.

Media-type values are registered with the Internet Assigned Number Authority (IANA [19]). The media type registration process is outlined in RFC 1590 [17]. Use of nonregistered media types is discouraged.

3.7.1 Canonicalization and Text Defaults

Internet media types are registered with a canonical form. An entity-body transferred via HTTP messages MUST be represented in the appropriate canonical form prior to its transmission except for "text" types, as defined in the next paragraph.

When in canonical form, media subtypes of the "text" type use CRLF as the text line break. HTTP relaxes this requirement and allows the transport of text media with plain CR or LF alone representing a line break when it is done consistently for an entire entity-body. HTTP applications MUST accept CRLF, bare CR, and bare

LF as being representative of a line break in text media received via HTTP. In addition, if the text is represented in a character set that does not use octets 13 and 10 for CR and LF respectively, as is the case for some multi-byte character sets, HTTP allows the use of whatever octet sequences are defined by that character set to represent the equivalent of CR and LF for line breaks. This flexibility regarding line breaks applies only to text media in the entity-body; a bare CR or LF MUST NOT be substituted for CRLF within any of the HTTP control structures (such as header fields and multipart boundaries).

If an entity-body is encoded with a content-coding, the underlying data MUST be in a form defined above prior to being encoded.

The "charset" parameter is used with some media types to define the character set (section 3.4) of the data. When no explicit charset parameter is provided by the sender, media subtypes of the "text" type are defined to have a default charset value of "ISO-8859-1" when received via HTTP. Data in character sets other than "ISO-8859-1" or its subsets MUST be labeled with an appropriate charset value. See section 3.4.1 for compatibility problems.

3.7.2 Multipart Types

MIME provides for a number of "multipart" types—encapsulations of one or more entities within a single message-body. All multipart types share a common syntax, as defined in section 5.1.1 of RFC 2046 [40], and MUST include a boundary parameter as part of the media type value. The message body is itself a protocol element and MUST therefore use only CRLF to represent line breaks between body-parts. Unlike in RFC 2046, the epilogue of any multipart message MUST be empty; HTTP applications MUST NOT transmit the epilogue (even if the original multipart contains an epilogue). These restrictions exist in order to preserve the self-delimiting nature of a multipart message-body, wherein the "end" of the message-body is indicated by the ending multipart boundary.

In general, HTTP treats a multipart message-body no differently than any other media type: strictly as payload. The one exception is the "multipart/byteranges" type (appendix 19.2) when it appears in a 206 (Partial Content) response, which will be interpreted by some HTTP caching mechanisms as described in sections 13.5.4 and 14.16. In all other cases, an HTTP user agent SHOULD follow the same or similar behavior as a MIME user agent would upon receipt of a multipart type. The MIME header fields within each body-part of a multipart message-body do not have any significance to HTTP beyond that defined by their MIME semantics.

In general, an HTTP user agent SHOULD follow the same or similar behavior as a MIME user agent would upon receipt of a multipart type. If an application receives an unrecognized multipart subtype, the application MUST treat it as being equivalent to "multipart/mixed."

> **Note:** The "multipart/form-data" type has been specifically defined for carrying form data suitable for processing via the POST request method, as described in RFC 1867 [15].

3.8 Product Tokens

Product tokens are used to allow communicating applications to identify themselves by software name and version. Most fields using product tokens also allow sub-products which form a significant part of the application to be listed, separated by white space. By convention, the products are listed in order of their significance for identifying the application.

```
product         = token ["/" product-version]
product-version = token
```

Examples:

```
User-Agent: CERN-LineMode/2.15 libwww/2.17b3
Server: Apache/0.8.4
```

Product tokens SHOULD be short and to the point. They MUST NOT be used for advertising or other non-essential information. Although any token character MAY appear in a product-version, this token SHOULD only be used for a version identifier (i.e., successive versions of the same product SHOULD only differ in the product-version portion of the product value).

3.9 Quality Values

HTTP content negotiation (section 12) uses short "floating point" numbers to indicate the relative importance ("weight") of various negotiable parameters. A weight is normalized to a real number in the range 0 through 1, where 0 is the minimum and 1 the maximum value. If a parameter has a quality value of 0, then content with this parameter is "not acceptable" for the client. HTTP/1.1 applications MUST NOT generate more than three digits after the decimal point. User configuration of these values SHOULD also be limited in this fashion.

$$qvalue = (\text{"0"} [\text{"."} 0*3DIGIT])$$
$$| (\text{"1"} [\text{"."} 0*3(\text{"0"})])$$

"Quality values" is a misnomer, since these values merely represent relative degradation in desired quality.

3.10 Language Tags

A language tag identifies a natural language spoken, written, or otherwise conveyed by human beings for communication of information to other human beings. Computer languages are explicitly excluded. HTTP uses language tags within the Accept-Language and Content-Language fields.

The syntax and registry of HTTP language tags is the same as that defined by RFC 1766 [1]. In summary, a language tag is composed of 1 or more parts: A primary language tag and a possibly empty series of subtags:

```
language-tag = primary-tag *( "-" subtag )
primary-tag  = 1*8ALPHA
subtag       = 1*8ALPHA
```

White space is not allowed within the tag and all tags are case-insensitive. The name space of language tags is administered by the IANA. Example tags include

```
en, en-US, en-cockney, i-cherokee, x-pig-latin
```

where any two-letter primary-tag is an ISO-639 language abbreviation and any two-letter initial subtag is an ISO-3166 country code. (The last three tags above are not registered tags; all but the last are examples of tags which could be registered in future.)

3.11 Entity Tags

Entity tags are used for comparing two or more entities from the same requested resource. HTTP/1.1 uses entity tags in the ETag (section 14.19), If-Match (section 14.24), If-None-Match (section 14.26), and If-Range (section 14.27) header fields. The definition of how they are used and compared as cache validators is in section 13.3.3. An entity tag consists of an opaque quoted string, possibly prefixed by a weakness indicator.

```
entity-tag = [ weak ] opaque-tag
weak       = "W/"
opaque-tag = quoted-string
```

A "strong entity tag" MAY be shared by two entities of a resource only if they are equivalent by octet equality.

A "weak entity tag," indicated by the "W/" prefix, MAY be shared by two entities of a resource only if the entities are equivalent and could be substituted for each other with no significant change in semantics. A weak entity tag can only be used for weak comparison.

An entity tag MUST be unique across all versions of all entities associated with a particular resource. A given entity tag value MAY be used for entities obtained by requests on different URIs. The use of the same entity tag value in conjunction with entities obtained by requests on different URIs does not imply the equivalence of those entities.

3.12 Range Units

HTTP/1.1 allows a client to request that only part (a range of) the response entity be included within the response. HTTP/1.1 uses range units in the Range (section 14.35) and Content-Range (section 14.16) header fields. An entity can be broken down into subranges according to various structural units.

```
range-unit     = bytes-unit | other-range-unit
bytes-unit     = "bytes"
other-range-unit = token
```

The only range unit defined by HTTP/1.1 is "bytes." HTTP/1.1 implementations MAY ignore ranges specified using other units.

HTTP/1.1 has been designed to allow implementations of applications that do not depend on knowledge of ranges.

4 HTTP Message

4.1 Message Types

HTTP messages consist of requests from client to server and responses from server to client.

```
HTTP-message  = Request | Response   ; HTTP/1.1 messages
```

Request (section 5) and Response (section 6) messages use the generic message format of RFC 822 [9] for transferring entities (the payload of the message). Both types of message consist of a start-line, zero or more header fields (also known as "headers"), an empty line (i.e., a line with nothing preceding the CRLF) indicating the end of the header fields, and possibly a message-body.

```
generic-message = start-line
          *(message-header CRLF)
          CRLF
          [ message-body ]
start-line   = Request-Line | Status-Line
```

In the interest of robustness, servers SHOULD ignore any empty line(s) received where a Request-Line is expected. In other words, if the server is reading the protocol stream at the beginning of a message and receives a CRLF first, it should ignore the CRLF.

Certain buggy HTTP/1.0 client implementations generate extra CRLFs after a POST request. To restate what is explicitly forbidden by the BNF, an HTTP/1.1 client MUST NOT preface or follow a request with an extra CRLF.

4.2 Message Headers

HTTP header fields, which include general-header (section 4.5), request-header (section 5.3), response-header (section 6.2), and entity-header (section 7.1) fields, follow the same generic format as that given in Section 3.1 of RFC 822 [9]. Each header field consists of a name followed by a colon (":") and the field value. Field names are case-insensitive. The field value MAY be preceded by any amount of LWS, though a single SP is preferred. Header fields can be extended over multiple lines by preceding each extra line with at least one SP or HT. Applications ought to follow "common form," where one is known or indicated, when generating HTTP constructs, since there might exist some implementations that fail to accept anything beyond the common forms.

```
message-header = field-name ":" [ field-value ]
field-name   = token
field-value  = *( field-content | LWS )
field-content = <the OCTETs making up the field-value and
        consisting of either *TEXT or combinations of
            token, separators, and quoted-string>
```

The field-content does not include any leading or trailing LWS: linear white space occurring before the first non-whitespace character of the field-value or after the last non-whitespace character of the field-value. Such leading or trailing LWS MAY be removed without changing the semantics of the field value. Any LWS that occurs between field-content MAY be replaced with a single SP before interpreting the field value or forwarding the message downstream.

The order in which header fields with differing field names are received is not significant. However, it is "good practice" to send general-header fields first, followed by request-header or response-header fields, and end with the entity-header fields.

Multiple message-header fields with the same field-name MAY be present in a message if and only if the entire field-value for that header field is defined as a comma-separated list [i.e., #(values)]. It MUST be possible to combine the multiple header fields into one "field-name: field-value" pair, without changing the semantics of the message, by appending each subsequent field-value to the first, each separated by a comma. The order in which header fields with the same field-name are received is therefore significant to the interpretation of the combined field value, and thus a proxy MUST NOT change the order of these field values when a message is forwarded.

4.3 Message Body

The message-body (if any) of an HTTP message is used to carry the entity-body associated with the request or response. The message-body differs from the entity-body only when a transfer-coding has been applied, as indicated by the Transfer-Encoding header field (section 14.41).

```
message-body = entity-body
             | <entity-body encoded as per Transfer-Encoding>
```

Transfer-Encoding MUST be used to indicate any transfer-codings applied by an application to ensure safe and proper transfer of the message. Transfer-Encoding is a property of the message, not of the entity, and thus MAY be added or removed by any application along the request/response chain. (However, section 3.6 places restrictions on when certain transfer-codings may be used.)

The rules for when a message-body is allowed in a message differ for requests and responses.

The presence of a message-body in a request is signaled by the inclusion of a Content-Length or Transfer-Encoding header field in the request's message-headers. A message-body MUST NOT be included in a request if the specification of the request method (section 5.1.1) does not allow sending an entity-body in requests. A server SHOULD read and forward a message-body on any request; if the request method does not include defined semantics for an entity-body, then the message-body SHOULD be ignored when handling the request.

For response messages, whether or not a message-body is included with a message is dependent on both the request method and the response status code (section 6.1.1). All responses to the HEAD request method MUST NOT include a message-body, even though the presence of entity-header fields might lead one to believe they do. All 1xx (informational), 204 (no content), and 304 (not modified) responses MUST NOT include a message-body. All other responses do include a message-body, although it MAY be of zero length.

4.4 Message Length

The transfer-length of a message is the length of the message-body as it appears in the message; that is, after any transfer-codings have been applied. When a message-body is included with a message, the transfer-length of that body is determined by one of the following (in order of precedence):

1. Any response message which "MUST NOT" include a message-body (such as the 1xx, 204, and 304 responses and any response to a HEAD request) is always terminated by the first empty line after the header fields, regardless of the entity-header fields present in the message.

2. If a Transfer-Encoding header field (section 14.41) is present and has any value other than "identity," then the transfer-length is defined by use of the "chunked" transfer-coding (section 3.6), unless the message is terminated by closing the connection.

3. If a Content-Length header field (section 14.13) is present, its decimal value in OCTETs represents both the entity-length and the transfer-length. The Content-Length header field MUST NOT be sent if these two lengths are different (i.e., if a Transfer-Encoding header field is present). If a message is received with both a Transfer-Encoding header field and a Content-Length header field, the latter MUST be ignored.

4. If the message uses the media type "multipart/byteranges," and the Transfer-length is not otherwise specified, then this self-limiting media type defines the transfer-length. This media type MUST NOT be used unless the sender knows that the recipient can parse it; the presence in a request of a Range header with multiple byte-range specifiers from a 1.1 client implies that the client can parse multipart/byteranges responses.

A range header might be forwarded by a 1.0 proxy that does not understand multipart/byteranges; in this case the server MUST delimit the message using methods defined in item 1, 3, or 5 of this section.

5. By the server closing the connection. (Closing the connection cannot be used to indicate the end of a request body, since that would leave no possibility for the server to send back a response.)

For compatibility with HTTP/1.0 applications, HTTP/1.1 requests containing a message-body MUST include a valid Content-Length header field unless the server is known to be HTTP/1.1 compliant. If a request contains a message-body and a Content-Length is not given, the server SHOULD respond with 400 (bad request) if it cannot determine the length of the message, or with 411 (length required) if it wishes to insist on receiving a valid Content-Length.

All HTTP/1.1 applications that receive entities MUST accept the "chunked" transfer-coding (section 3.6), thus allowing this mechanism to be used for messages when the message length cannot be determined in advance.

Messages MUST NOT include both a Content-Length header field and a non-identity transfer-coding. If the message does include a non-identity transfer-coding, the Content-Length MUST be ignored.

When a Content-Length is given in a message where a message-body is allowed, its field value MUST exactly match the number of OCTETs in the message-body. HTTP/1.1 user agents MUST notify the user when an invalid length is received and detected.

4.5 General Header Fields

There are a few header fields which have general applicability for both request and response messages, but which do not apply to the entity being transferred. These header fields apply only to the message being transmitted.

```
general-header = Cache-Control      ; Section 14.9
             | Connection           ; Section 14.10
             | Date                 ; Section 14.18
             | Pragma               ; Section 14.32
             | Trailer              ; Section 14.40
             | Transfer-Encoding    ; Section 14.41
             | Upgrade              ; Section 14.42
             | Via                  ; Section 14.45
             | Warning              ; Section 14.46
```

General-header field names can be extended reliably only in combination with a change in the protocol version. However, new or experimental header fields may be given the semantics of general-header fields if all parties in the communication recognize them to be general-header fields. Unrecognized header fields are treated as entity-header fields.

5 Request

A request message from a client to a server includes, within the first line of that message, the method to be applied to the resource, the identifier of the resource, and the protocol version in use.

```
Request    = Request-Line          ; Section 5.1
        *(( general-header          ; Section 4.5
        | request-header            ; Section 5.3
        | entity-header ) CRLF)     ; Section 7.1
        CRLF
        [ message-body ]            ; Section 4.3
```

5.1 Request-Line

The Request-Line begins with a method token, followed by the Request-URI and the protocol version, and ending with CRLF. The elements are separated by SP characters. No CR or LF is allowed except in the final CRLF sequence.

```
Request-Line  = Method SP Request-URI SP HTTP-Version CRLF
```

5.1.1 Method

The Method token indicates the method to be performed on the resource identified by the Request-URI. The method is case-sensitive.

```
Method      = "OPTIONS"             ; Section 9.2
        | "GET"                     ; Section 9.3
        | "HEAD"                    ; Section 9.4
        | "POST"                    ; Section 9.5
        | "PUT"                     ; Section 9.6
        | "DELETE"                  ; Section 9.7
        | "TRACE"                   ; Section 9.8
        | "CONNECT"                 ; Section 9.9
        | extension-method
    extension-method = token
```

The list of methods allowed by a resource can be specified in an Allow header field (section 14.7). The return code of the response always notifies the client whether a method is currently allowed on a resource, since the set of allowed methods can change dynamically. An origin server SHOULD return the status code 405 (Method Not Allowed) if the method is known by the origin server but not allowed for the requested resource, and 501 (Not Implemented) if the method is unrecognized or not implemented by the origin server. The methods GET and HEAD MUST be supported by all general-purpose servers. All other methods are OPTIONAL; however, if the above methods are implemented, they MUST be implemented with the same semantics as those specified in section 9.

5.1.2 Request-URI

The Request-URI is a Uniform Resource Identifier (section 3.2) and identifies the resource upon which to apply the request.

```
Request-URI  = "*" | absoluteURI | abs_path | authority
```

The four options for Request-URI are dependent on the nature of the request. The asterisk "*" means that the request does not apply to a particular resource, but to the server itself, and is only allowed when the method used does not necessarily apply to a resource. One example would be

```
OPTIONS * HTTP/1.1
```

The absoluteURI form is REQUIRED when the request is being made to a proxy. The proxy is requested to forward the request or service it from a valid cache, and return the response. Note that the proxy MAY forward the request on to another proxy or directly to the server specified by the absoluteURI. In order to avoid request loops, a proxy MUST be able to recognize all of its server names, including any aliases, local variations, and the numeric IP address. An example Request-Line would be

```
GET http://www.w3.org/pub/WWW/TheProject.html HTTP/1.1
```

To allow for transition to absoluteURIs in all requests in future versions of HTTP, all HTTP/1.1 servers MUST accept the absoluteURI form in requests, even though HTTP/1.1 clients will only generate them in requests to proxies.

The authority form is only used by the CONNECT method (section 9.9).

The most common form of Request-URI is that used to identify a resource on an origin server or gateway. In this case the absolute path of the URI MUST be transmitted (see section 3.2.1, abs_path) as the Request-URI, and the network location of the URI (authority) MUST be transmitted in a Host header field. For example, a client wishing to retrieve the resource above directly from the origin server would create a TCP connection to port 80 of the host "www.w3.org" and send the lines

```
GET /pub/WWW/TheProject.html HTTP/1.1
Host: www.w3.org
```

followed by the remainder of the Request. Note that the absolute path cannot be empty; if none is present in the original URI, it MUST be given as "/" (the server root).

The Request-URI is transmitted in the format specified in section 3.2.1. If the Request-URI is encoded using the "% HEX HEX" encoding [42], the origin server MUST decode the Request-URI in order to properly interpret the request. Servers SHOULD respond to invalid Request-URIs with an appropriate status code.

A transparent proxy MUST NOT rewrite the "abs_path" part of the received Request-URI when forwarding it to the next inbound server, except as noted above to replace a null abs_path with "/".

> **Note:** The "no rewrite" rule prevents the proxy from changing the meaning of the request when the origin server is improperly using a nonreserved URI character for a reserved purpose. Implementers should be aware that some pre-HTTP/1.1 proxies have been known to rewrite the Request-URI.

5.2 The Resource Identified by a Request

The exact resource identified by an Internet request is determined by examining both the Request-URI and the Host header field.

An origin server that does not allow resources to differ by the requested host MAY ignore the Host header field value when determining the resource identified by an HTTP/1.1 request. (But see section 19.6.1.1 for other requirements on Host support in HTTP/1.1.)

An origin server that does differentiate resources based on the host requested (sometimes referred to as virtual hosts or vanity host names) MUST use the following rules for determining the requested resource on an HTTP/1.1 request:

1. If Request-URI is an absoluteURI, the host is part of the Request-URI. Any Host header field value in the request MUST be ignored.

2. If the Request-URI is not an absoluteURI, and the request includes a Host header field, the host is determined by the Host header field value.

3. If the host as determined by rule 1 or 2 is not a valid host on the server, the response MUST be a 400 (Bad Request) error message.

Recipients of an HTTP/1.0 request that lacks a Host header field MAY attempt to use heuristics (e.g., examination of the URI path for something unique to a particular host) in order to determine what exact resource is being requested.

5.3 Request Header Fields

The request-header fields allow the client to pass additional information about the request, and about the client itself, to the server. These fields act as request modifiers, with semantics equivalent to the parameters on a programming language method invocation.

```
request-header = Accept              ; Section 14.1
       | Accept-Charset              ; Section 14.2
       | Accept-Encoding             ; Section 14.3
       | Accept-Language             ; Section 14.4
       | Authorization               ; Section 14.8
       | Expect                      ; Section 14.20
       | From                        ; Section 14.22
       | Host                        ; Section 14.23
       | If-Match                    ; Section 14.24
       | If-Modified-Since           ; Section 14.25
       | If-None-Match               ; Section 14.26
       | If-Range                    ; Section 14.27
       | If-Unmodified-Since         ; Section 14.28
       | Max-Forwards                ; Section 14.31
       | Proxy-Authorization         ; Section 14.34
       | Range                       ; Section 14.35
       | Referer                     ; Section 14.36
       | TE                          ; Section 14.39
       | User-Agent                  ; Section 14.43
```

Request-header field names can be extended reliably only in combination with a change in the protocol version. However, new or experimental header fields MAY be given the semantics of request-header fields if all parties in the communication recognize them to be request-header fields. Unrecognized header fields are treated as entity-header fields.

6 Response

After receiving and interpreting a request message, a server responds with an HTTP response message.

```
Response   = Status-Line        ; Section 6.1
           *(( general-header    ; Section 4.5
            | response-header    ; Section 6.2
            | entity-header ) CRLF) ; Section 7.1
           CRLF
           [ message-body ]      ; Section 7.2
```

6.1 Status-Line

The first line of a Response message is the Status-Line, consisting of the protocol version followed by a numeric status code and its associated textual phrase, with each element separated by SP characters. No CR or LF is allowed except in the final CRLF sequence.

```
Status-Line = HTTP-Version SP Status-Code SP Reason-Phrase CRLF
```

6.1.1 Status Code and Reason Phrase

The Status-Code element is a 3-digit integer result code of the attempt to understand and satisfy the request. These codes are fully defined in section 10. The Reason-Phrase is intended to give a short textual description of the Status-Code. The Status-Code is intended for use by automata and the Reason-Phrase is intended for the human user. The client is not required to examine or display the Reason-Phrase.

The first digit of the Status-Code defines the class of response. The last two digits do not have any categorization role. There are 5 values for the first digit:

1xx: Informational—Request received, continuing process

2xx: Success—The action was successfully received, understood, and accepted

3xx: Redirection—Further action must be taken in order to complete the request

4xx: Client Error—The request contains bad syntax or cannot be fulfilled

5xx: Server Error—The server failed to fulfill an apparently valid request

The individual values of the numeric status codes defined for HTTP/1.1, and an example set of corresponding Reason-Phrases, are presented below. The reason phrases listed here are only recommendations—they MAY be replaced by local equivalents without affecting the protocol.

```
Status-Code  =
    "100" ; Section 10.1.1: Continue
  | "101" ; Section 10.1.2: Switching Protocols
  | "200" ; Section 10.2.1: OK
  | "201" ; Section 10.2.2: Created
  | "202" ; Section 10.2.3: Accepted
  | "203" ; Section 10.2.4: Non-Authoritative Information
  | "204" ; Section 10.2.5: No Content
  | "205" ; Section 10.2.6: Reset Content
  | "206" ; Section 10.2.7: Partial Content
  | "300" ; Section 10.3.1: Multiple Choices
  | "301" ; Section 10.3.2: Moved Permanently
  | "302" ; Section 10.3.3: Found
  | "303" ; Section 10.3.4: See Other
  | "304" ; Section 10.3.5: Not Modified
  | "305" ; Section 10.3.6: Use Proxy
  | "307" ; Section 10.3.8: Temporary Redirect
  | "400" ; Section 10.4.1: Bad Request
  | "401" ; Section 10.4.2: Unauthorized
  | "402" ; Section 10.4.3: Payment Required
  | "403" ; Section 10.4.4: Forbidden
  | "404" ; Section 10.4.5: Not Found
  | "405" ; Section 10.4.6: Method Not Allowed
  | "406" ; Section 10.4.7: Not Acceptable
  | "407" ; Section 10.4.8: Proxy Authentication Required
  | "408" ; Section 10.4.9: Request Time-out
  | "409" ; Section 10.4.10: Conflict
  | "410" ; Section 10.4.11: Gone
  | "411" ; Section 10.4.12: Length Required
  | "412" ; Section 10.4.13: Precondition Failed
  | "413" ; Section 10.4.14: Request Entity Too Large
  | "414" ; Section 10.4.15: Request-URI Too Large
  | "415" ; Section 10.4.16: Unsupported Media Type
  | "416" ; Section 10.4.17: Requested range not satisfiable
  | "417" ; Section 10.4.18: Expectation Failed
  | "500" ; Section 10.5.1: Internal Server Error
  | "501" ; Section 10.5.2: Not Implemented
  | "502" ; Section 10.5.3: Bad Gateway
  | "503" ; Section 10.5.4: Service Unavailable
  | "504" ; Section 10.5.5: Gateway Time-out
  | "505" ; Section 10.5.6: HTTP Version not supported
  | extension-code

extension-code = 3DIGIT
Reason-Phrase = *<TEXT, excluding CR, LF>
```

HTTP status codes are extensible. HTTP applications are not required to understand the meaning of all registered status codes, though such understanding is obviously desirable. However, applications MUST understand the class of any status code, as indicated by the first digit, and treat any unrecognized response as being equivalent to the x00 status code of that class, with the exception that an unrecognized response MUST NOT be cached. For example, if an unrecognized status code of 431 is received by the client, it can safely assume that there was something wrong with its request and treat the response as if it had received a 400 status code. In such cases, user agents SHOULD present to the user the entity returned with the response, since that entity is likely to include human-readable information which will explain the unusual status.

6.2 Response Header Fields

The response-header fields allow the server to pass additional information about the response which cannot be placed in the Status-Line. These header fields give information about the server and about further access to the resource identified by the Request-URI.

```
response-header = Accept-Ranges      ; Section 14.5
          | Age                      ; Section 14.6
          | ETag                     ; Section 14.19
          | Location                 ; Section 14.30
          | Proxy-Authenticate       ; Section 14.33
          | Retry-After              ; Section 14.37
          | Server                   ; Section 14.38
          | Vary                     ; Section 14.44
          | WWW-Authenticate         ; Section 14.47
```

Response-header field names can be extended reliably only in combination with a change in the protocol version. However, new or experimental header fields MAY be given the semantics of response-header fields if all parties in the communication recognize them to be response-header fields. Unrecognized header fields are treated as entity-header fields.

7 Entity

Request and Response messages MAY transfer an entity if not otherwise restricted by the request method or response status code. An entity consists of entity-header fields and an entity-body, although some responses will only include the entity-headers.

In this section, both sender and recipient refer to either the client or the server, depending on who sends and who receives the entity.

7.1 Entity Header Fields

Entity-header fields define metainformation about the entity-body or, if no body is present, about the resource identified by the request. Some of this metainformation is OPTIONAL; some might be REQUIRED by portions of this specification.

```
entity-header = Allow                ; Section 14.7
        | Content-Encoding           ; Section 14.11
        | Content-Language           ; Section 14.12
        | Content-Length             ; Section 14.13
        | Content-Location           ; Section 14.14
        | Content-MD5                ; Section 14.15
        | Content-Range              ; Section 14.16
        | Content-Type               ; Section 14.17
        | Expires                    ; Section 14.21
        | Last-Modified              ; Section 14.29
        | extension-header
extension-header = message-header
```

The extension-header mechanism allows additional entity-header fields to be defined without changing the protocol, but these fields cannot be assumed to be recognizable by the recipient. Unrecognized header fields SHOULD be ignored by the recipient and MUST be forwarded by transparent proxies.

7.2 Entity Body

The entity-body (if any) sent with an HTTP request or response is in a format and encoding defined by the entity-header fields.

```
entity-body  = *OCTET
```

An entity-body is only present in a message when a message-body is present, as described in section 4.3. The entity-body is obtained from the message-body by decoding any Transfer-Encoding that might have been applied to ensure safe and proper transfer of the message.

7.2.1 Type

When an entity-body is included with a message, the data type of that body is determined via the header fields Content-Type and Content-Encoding. These define a two-layer, ordered encoding model:

```
entity-body := Content-Encoding( Content-Type( data ) )
```

Content-Type specifies the media type of the underlying data.

Content-Encoding may be used to indicate any additional content-codings applied to the data, usually for the purpose of data compression, that are a property of the requested resource. There is no default encoding.

Any HTTP/1.1 message containing an entity-body SHOULD include a Content-Type header field defining the media type of that body. If and only if the media type is not given by a Content-Type field, the recipient MAY attempt to guess the media type via inspection of its content and/or the name extension(s) of the URI used to identify the resource. If the media type remains unknown, the recipient SHOULD treat it as type "application/octet-stream."

7.2.2 Entity Length

The entity-length of a message is the length of the message-body before any transfer-codings have been applied. Section 4.4 defines how the transfer-length of a message-body is determined.

8 Connections

8.1 Persistent Connections

8.1.1 Purpose

Prior to persistent connections, a separate TCP connection was established to fetch each URL, increasing the load on HTTP servers and causing congestion on the Internet. The use of inline images and other associated data often require a client to make multiple requests of the same server in a short amount of time. Analysis of these performance problems and results from a prototype implementation are available [26] [30]. Implementation experience and measurements of actual HTTP/1.1 (RFC 2068) implementations show good results [39]. Alternatives have also been explored—for example, T/TCP [27].

Persistent HTTP connections have a number of advantages:

- By opening and closing fewer TCP connections, CPU time is saved in routers and hosts (clients, servers, proxies, gateways, tunnels, or caches), and memory used for TCP protocol control blocks can be saved in hosts.

- HTTP requests and responses can be pipelined on a connection. Pipelining allows a client to make multiple requests without waiting for each response, allowing a single TCP connection to be used much more efficiently, with much lower elapsed time.

- Network congestion is reduced by reducing the number of packets caused by TCP opens, and by allowing TCP sufficient time to determine the congestion state of the network.

- Latency on subsequent requests is reduced since there is no time spent in TCP's connection opening handshake.

- HTTP can evolve more gracefully, since errors can be reported without the penalty of closing the TCP connection. Clients using future versions of HTTP might optimistically try a new feature, but if communicating with an older server, retry with old semantics after an error is reported.

HTTP implementations SHOULD implement persistent connections.

8.1.2 Overall Operation

A significant difference between HTTP/1.1 and earlier versions of HTTP is that persistent connections are the default behavior of any HTTP connection. That is, unless otherwise indicated, the client SHOULD assume that the server will maintain a persistent connection, even after error responses from the server.

Persistent connections provide a mechanism by which a client and a server can signal the close of a TCP connection. This signaling takes place using the Connection header field (section 14.10). Once a close has been signaled, the client MUST NOT send any more requests on that connection.

8.1.2.1 Negotiation

An HTTP/1.1 server MAY assume that a HTTP/1.1 client intends to maintain a persistent connection unless a Connection header including the connection-token "close" was sent in the request. If the server chooses to close the connection immediately after sending the response, it SHOULD send a Connection header including the connection-token close.

An HTTP/1.1 client MAY expect a connection to remain open, but would decide to keep it open based on whether the response from a server contains a Connection header with the connection-token close. In case the client does not want to maintain a connection for more than that request, it SHOULD send a Connection header including the connection-token close.

If either the client or the server sends the close token in the Connection header, that request becomes the last one for the connection.

Clients and servers SHOULD NOT assume that a persistent connection is maintained for HTTP versions less than 1.1 unless it is explicitly signaled. See section 19.6.2 for more information on backward compatibility with HTTP/1.0 clients.

In order to remain persistent, all messages on the connection MUST have a self-defined message length (i.e., one not defined by closure of the connection), as described in section 4.4.

8.1.2.2 Pipelining

A client that supports persistent connections MAY "pipeline" its requests (i.e., send multiple requests without waiting for each response). A server MUST send its responses to those requests in the same order that the requests were received.

Clients which assume persistent connections and pipeline immediately after connection establishment SHOULD be prepared to retry their connection if the first pipelined attempt fails. If a client does such a retry, it MUST NOT pipeline before it knows the connection is persistent. Clients MUST also be prepared to resend their requests if the server closes the connection before sending all of the corresponding responses.

Clients SHOULD NOT pipeline requests using non-idempotent methods or non-idempotent sequences of methods (see section 9.1.2). Otherwise, a premature termination of the transport connection could lead to indeterminate results. A client wishing to send a non-idempotent request SHOULD wait to send that request until it has received the response status for the previous request.

8.1.3 Proxy Servers

It is especially important that proxies correctly implement the properties of the Connection header field as specified in section 14.10.

The proxy server MUST signal persistent connections separately with its clients and the origin servers (or other proxy servers) that it connects to. Each persistent connection applies to only one transport link.

A proxy server MUST NOT establish a HTTP/1.1 persistent connection with an HTTP/1.0 client (but see RFC 2068 [33] for information and discussion of the problems with the Keep-Alive header implemented by many HTTP/1.0 clients).

8.1.4 Practical Considerations

Servers will usually have some time-out value beyond which they will no longer maintain an inactive connection. Proxy servers might make this a higher value since it is likely that the client will be making more connections through the same server. The use of persistent connections places no requirements on the length (or existence) of this time-out for either the client or the server.

When a client or server wishes to time-out it SHOULD issue a graceful close on the transport connection. Clients and servers SHOULD both constantly watch for the other side of the transport close, and respond to it as appropriate. If a client or server does not detect the other side's close promptly it could cause unnecessary resource drain on the network.

A client, server, or proxy MAY close the transport connection at any time. For example, a client might have started to send a new request at the same time that the server has decided to close the "idle" connection. From the server's point of view, the connection is being closed while it was idle, but from the client's point of view, a request is in progress.

This means that clients, servers, and proxies MUST be able to recover from asynchronous close events. Client software SHOULD reopen the transport connection and retransmit the aborted sequence of requests without user interaction so long as the request sequence is idempotent (see section 9.1.2). Non-idempotent methods or sequences MUST NOT be automatically retried, although user agents MAY offer a human operator the choice of retrying the request(s). Confirmation by user agent software with semantic understanding of the application MAY substitute for user confirmation. The automatic retry SHOULD NOT be repeated if the second sequence of requests fails.

Servers SHOULD always respond to at least one request per connection, if at all possible. Servers SHOULD NOT close a connection in the middle of transmitting a response, unless a network or client failure is suspected.

Clients that use persistent connections SHOULD limit the number of simultaneous connections that they maintain to a given server. A single-user client SHOULD NOT maintain more than 2 connections with any server or proxy. A proxy SHOULD use up to 2*N connections to another server or proxy, where N is the number of simultaneously active users. These guidelines are intended to improve HTTP response times and avoid congestion.

8.2 Message Transmission Requirements

8.2.1 Persistent Connections and Flow Control

HTTP/1.1 servers SHOULD maintain persistent connections and use TCP's flow control mechanisms to resolve temporary overloads, rather than terminating connections with the expectation that clients will retry. The latter technique can exacerbate network congestion.

8.2.2 Monitoring Connections for Error Status Messages

An HTTP/1.1 (or later) client sending a message-body SHOULD monitor the network connection for an error status while it is transmitting the request. If the client sees an error status, it SHOULD immediately cease transmitting the body. If the body is being sent using a "chunked" encoding (section 3.6), a zero-length chunk and empty trailer MAY be used to prematurely mark the end of the message. If the body was preceded by a Content-Length header, the client MUST close the connection.

8.2.3 Use of the 100 (Continue) Status

The purpose of the 100 (Continue) status (see section 10.1.1) is to allow a client that is sending a request message with a request body to determine if the origin server is willing to accept the request (based on the request headers) before the client sends the request body. In some cases, it might either be inappropriate or highly inefficient for the client to send the body if the server will reject the message without looking at the body.

Requirements for HTTP/1.1 clients:

- If a client will wait for a 100 (Continue) response before sending the request body, it MUST send an Expect request-header field (section 14.20) with the "100-continue" expectation.

- A client MUST NOT send an Expect request-header field (section 14.20) with the "100-continue" expectation if it does not intend to send a request body.

Because of the presence of older implementations, the protocol allows ambiguous situations in which a client may send "Expect: 100-continue" without receiving either a 417 (Expectation Failed) status or a 100 (Continue) status. Therefore, when a client sends this header field to an origin server (possibly via a proxy) from which it has never seen a 100 (Continue) status, the client SHOULD NOT wait for an indefinite period before sending the request body.

Requirements for HTTP/1.1 origin servers:

- Upon receiving a request which includes an Expect request-header field with the "100-continue" expectation, an origin server MUST either respond with 100 (Continue) status and continue to read from the input stream, or respond with a final status code. The origin server MUST NOT wait for the request body before sending the 100 (Continue) response. If it responds with a final status code, it MAY close the transport connection or it MAY continue to read and discard the rest of the request. It MUST NOT perform the requested method if it returns a final status code.

- An origin server SHOULD NOT send a 100 (Continue) response if the request message does not include an Expect request-header field with the "100-continue" expectation, and MUST NOT send a 100 (Continue) response if such a request comes from an HTTP/1.0 (or earlier) client. There is an exception to this rule: For compatibility with RFC 2068, a server MAY send a 100 (Continue) status in response to an HTTP/1.1 PUT or POST request that does not include an Expect request-header field with the "100-continue" expectation. This exception, the purpose of which is to minimize any client processing delays associated with an undeclared wait for 100 (Continue) status, applies only to HTTP/1.1 requests, and not to requests with any other HTTP-version value.

- An origin server MAY omit a 100 (Continue) response if it has already received some or all of the request body for the corresponding request.

- An origin server that sends a 100 (Continue) response MUST ultimately send a final status code, once the request body is received and processed, unless it terminates the transport connection prematurely.

- If an origin server receives a request that does not include an Expect request-header field with the "100-continue" expectation, the request includes a request body, and the server responds with a final status code before reading the entire request body from the transport connection, then the server SHOULD NOT close the transport connection until it has read the entire request, or until the client closes the connection. Otherwise, the client might not reliably receive the response message. However, this requirement is not be construed as preventing a server from defending itself against denial of service attacks, or from badly broken client implementations.

Requirements for HTTP/1.1 proxies:

- If a proxy receives a request that includes an Expect request-header field with the "100-continue" expectation, and the proxy either knows that the next-hop server complies with HTTP/1.1 or higher, or does not know the HTTP version of the next-hop server, it MUST forward the request, including the Expect header field.

- If the proxy knows that the version of the next-hop server is HTTP/1.0 or lower, it MUST NOT forward the request, and it MUST respond with a 417 (Expectation Failed) status.

- Proxies SHOULD maintain a cache recording the HTTP version numbers received from recently referenced next-hop servers.

- A proxy MUST NOT forward a 100 (Continue) response if the request message was received from an HTTP/1.0 (or earlier) client and did not include an Expect request-header field with the "100-continue" expectation. This requirement overrides the general rule for forwarding of 1xx responses (see section 10.1).

8.2.4 Client Behavior if Server Prematurely Closes Connection

If an HTTP/1.1 client sends a request which includes a request body, but which does not include an Expect request-header field with the "100-continue" expectation, and if the client is not directly connected to an HTTP/1.1 origin server, and if the client sees the connection close before receiving any status from the server, the client SHOULD retry the request. If the client does retry this request, it MAY use the following "binary exponential backoff" algorithm to be assured of obtaining a reliable response:

1. Initiate a new connection to the server.

2. Transmit the request-headers.

3. Initialize a variable R to the estimated round-trip time to the server (e.g., based on the time it took to establish the connection), or to a constant value of 5 seconds if the round-trip time is not available.

4. Compute T = R * (2**N), where N is the number of previous retries of this request.

5. Wait either for an error response from the server, or for T seconds (whichever comes first).

6. If no error response is received, after T seconds transmit the body of the request.

7. If client sees that the connection is closed prematurely, repeat from step 1 until the request is accepted, an error response is received, or the user becomes impatient and terminates the retry process.

If at any point an error status is received, the client

- SHOULD NOT continue and

- SHOULD close the connection if it has not completed sending the request message.

9 Method Definitions

The set of common methods for HTTP/1.1 is defined below. Although this set can be expanded, additional methods cannot be assumed to share the same semantics for separately extended clients and servers.

The Host request-header field (section 14.23) MUST accompany all HTTP/1.1 requests.

9.1 Safe and Idempotent Methods

9.1.1 Safe Methods

Implementers should be aware that the software represents the user in their interactions over the Internet, and should be careful to allow the user to be aware of any actions they might take which may have an unexpected significance to themselves or others.

In particular, the convention has been established that the GET and HEAD methods SHOULD NOT have the significance of taking an action other than retrieval. These methods ought to be considered "safe." This allows user agents to represent other methods, such as POST, PUT and DELETE, in a special way, so that the user is made aware of the fact that a possibly unsafe action is being requested.

Naturally, it is not possible to ensure that the server does not generate side effects as a result of performing a GET request; in fact, some dynamic resources consider that a feature. The important distinction here is that the user did not request the side effects, so therefore cannot be held accountable for them.

9.1.2 Idempotent Methods

Methods can also have the property of "idempotence" in that (aside from error or expiration issues) the side effects of N > 0 identical requests are the same as for a single request. The methods GET, HEAD, PUT, and DELETE share this property. Also, the methods OPTIONS and TRACE SHOULD NOT have side effects, and so are inherently idempotent.

However, it is possible that a sequence of several requests is non-idempotent, even if all of the methods executed in that sequence are idempotent. (A sequence is idempotent if a single execution of the entire sequence always yields a result that is not changed by a reexecution of all, or part, of that sequence.) For example, a sequence is non-idempotent if its result depends on a value that is later modified in the same sequence.

A sequence that never has side effects is idempotent, by definition (provided that no concurrent operations are being executed on the same set of resources).

9.2 OPTIONS

The OPTIONS method represents a request for information about the communication options available on the request/response chain identified by the Request-URI. This method allows the client to determine the options and/or requirements associated with a resource, or the capabilities of a server, without implying a resource action or initiating a resource retrieval.

Responses to this method are not cacheable.

If the OPTIONS request includes an entity-body (as indicated by the presence of Content-Length or Transfer-Encoding), then the media type MUST be indicated by a Content-Type field. Although this specification does not define any use for such a body, future extensions to HTTP might use the OPTIONS body to make more detailed queries on the server. A server that does not support such an extension MAY discard the request body.

If the Request-URI is an asterisk ("*"), the OPTIONS request is intended to apply to the server in general rather than to a specific resource. Since a server's communication options typically depend on the resource, the "*" request is only useful as a "ping" or "no-op" type of method; it does nothing beyond allowing the client to test the capabilities of the server. For example, this can be used to test a proxy for HTTP/1.1 compliance (or lack thereof).

If the Request-URI is not an asterisk, the OPTIONS request applies only to the options that are available when communicating with that resource.

A 200 response SHOULD include any header fields that indicate optional features implemented by the server and applicable to that resource (e.g., Allow), possibly including extensions not defined by this specification. The response body, if any, SHOULD also include information about the communication options. The format for such a body is not defined by this specification, but might be defined by future extensions to HTTP. Content negotiation MAY be used to select the appropriate response format. If no response body is included, the response MUST include a Content-Length field with a field-value of "0".

The Max-Forwards request-header field MAY be used to target a specific proxy in the request chain. When a proxy receives an OPTIONS request on an absoluteURI for which request forwarding is permitted, the proxy MUST check for a Max-Forwards field. If the Max-Forwards field-value is zero ("0"), the proxy MUST NOT forward the message; instead, the proxy SHOULD respond with its own communication options. If the Max-Forwards field-value is an integer greater than zero, the proxy MUST decrement the field-value when it forwards the request. If no Max-Forwards field is present in the request, then the forwarded request MUST NOT include a Max-Forwards field.

9.3 GET

The GET method means retrieve whatever information (in the form of an entity) is identified by the Request-URI. If the Request-URI refers to a data-producing process, it is the produced data which shall be returned as the entity in the response and not the source text of the process, unless that text happens to be the output of the process.

The semantics of the GET method change to a "conditional GET" if the request message includes an If-Modified-Since, If-Unmodified-Since, If-Match, If-None-Match, or If-Range header field. A conditional GET method requests that the entity be transferred only under the circumstances described by the conditional header field(s). The conditional GET method is intended to reduce unnecessary network usage by allowing cached entities to be refreshed without requiring multiple requests or transferring data already held by the client.

The semantics of the GET method change to a "partial GET" if the request message includes a Range header field. A partial GET requests that only part of the entity be transferred, as described in section 14.35. The partial GET method is intended to reduce unnecessary network usage by allowing partially retrieved entities to be completed without transferring data already held by the client.

The response to a GET request is cacheable if and only if it meets the requirements for HTTP caching described in section 13.

See section 15.1.3 for security considerations when used for forms.

9.4 HEAD

The HEAD method is identical to GET except that the server MUST NOT return a message-body in the response. The metainformation contained in the HTTP headers in response to a HEAD request SHOULD be identical to the information sent in response to a GET request. This method can be used for obtaining metainformation about the entity implied by the request without transferring the entity-body itself. This method is often used for testing hypertext links for validity, accessibility, and recent modification.

The response to a HEAD request MAY be cacheable in the sense that the information contained in the response MAY be used to update a previously cached entity from that resource. If the new field values indicate that the cached entity differs from the current entity (as would be indicated by a change in Content-Length, Content-MD5, ETag or Last-Modified), then the cache MUST treat the cache entry as stale.

9.5 POST

The POST method is used to request that the origin server accept the entity enclosed in the request as a new subordinate of the resource identified by the Request-URI in the Request-Line. POST is designed to allow a uniform method to cover the following functions:

- Annotation of existing resources;

- Posting a message to a bulletin board, newsgroup, mailing list, or similar group of articles;

- Providing a block of data, such as the result of submitting a form, to a data-handling process;

- Extending a database through an append operation.

The actual function performed by the POST method is determined by the server and is usually dependent on the Request-URI. The posted entity is subordinate to that URI in the same way that a file is subordinate to a directory containing it, a news article is subordinate to a newsgroup to which it is posted, or a record is subordinate to a database.

The action performed by the POST method might not result in a resource that can be identified by a URI. In this case, either 200 (OK) or 204 (No Content) is the appropriate response status, depending on whether or not the response includes an entity that describes the result.

If a resource has been created on the origin server, the response SHOULD be 201 (Created) and contain an entity which describes the status of the request and refers to the new resource, and a Location header (see section 14.30).

Responses to this method are not cacheable, unless the response includes appropriate Cache-Control or Expires header fields. However, the 303 (See Other) response can be used to direct the user agent to retrieve a cacheable resource.

POST requests MUST obey the message transmission requirements set out in section 8.2.

See section 15.1.3 for security considerations.

9.6 PUT

The PUT method requests that the enclosed entity be stored under the supplied Request-URI. If the Request-URI refers to an already existing resource, the enclosed entity SHOULD be considered as a modified version of the one residing on the origin server. If the Request-URI does not point to an existing resource, and that URI is capable of being defined as a new resource by the requesting user agent, the origin server can create the resource with that URI. If a new resource is created, the origin server MUST inform the user agent via the 201 (Created) response. If an existing resource is modified, either the 200 (OK) or 204 (No Content) response code SHOULD be sent to indicate successful completion of the request. If the resource could not be created or modified with the Request-URI, an appropriate error response SHOULD be given that reflects the nature of the problem. The recipient of the entity MUST NOT ignore any Content-* (e.g., Content-Range) headers that it does not understand or implement and MUST return a 501 (Not Implemented) response in such cases.

If the request passes through a cache and the Request-URI identifies one or more currently cached entities, those entries SHOULD be treated as stale. Responses to this method are not cacheable.

The fundamental difference between the POST and PUT requests is reflected in the different meaning of the Request-URI. The URI in a POST request identifies the resource that will handle the enclosed entity. That resource might be a data-accepting process, a gateway to some other protocol, or a separate entity that accepts annotations. In contrast, the URI in a PUT request identifies the entity enclosed with the request—the user agent knows what URI is intended and the server MUST NOT attempt to apply the request to some other resource. If the server desires that the request be applied to a different URI, it MUST send a 301 (Moved Permanently) response; the user agent MAY then make its own decision regarding whether or not to redirect the request.

A single resource MAY be identified by many different URIs. For example, an article might have a URI for identifying "the current version" which is separate from the URI identifying each particular version. In this case, a PUT request on a general URI might result in several other URIs being defined by the origin server.

HTTP/1.1 does not define how a PUT method affects the state of an origin server.

PUT requests MUST obey the message transmission requirements set out in section 8.2.

Unless otherwise specified for a particular entity-header, the entity-headers in the PUT request SHOULD be applied to the resource created or modified by the PUT.

9.7 DELETE

The DELETE method requests that the origin server delete the resource identified by the Request-URI. This method MAY be overridden by human intervention (or other means) on the origin server. The client cannot be guaranteed that the operation has been carried out, even if the status code returned from the origin server indicates that the action has been completed successfully. However, the server SHOULD NOT indicate success unless, at the time the response is given, it intends to delete the resource or move it to an inaccessible location.

A successful response SHOULD be 200 (OK) if the response includes an entity describing the status, 202 (Accepted) if the action has not yet been enacted, or 204 (No Content) if the action has been enacted but the response does not include an entity.

If the request passes through a cache and the Request-URI identifies one or more currently cached entities, those entries SHOULD be treated as stale. Responses to this method are not cacheable.

9.8 TRACE

The TRACE method is used to invoke a remote, application-layer loopback of the request message. The final recipient of the request SHOULD reflect the message received back to the client as the entity-body of a 200 (OK) response. The final recipient is either the origin server or the first proxy or gateway to receive a Max-Forwards value of zero (0) in the request (see section 14.31). A TRACE request MUST NOT include an entity.

TRACE allows the client to see what is being received at the other end of the request chain and use that data for testing or diagnostic information. The value of the Via header field (section 14.45) is of particular interest, since it acts as a trace of the request chain. Use of the Max-Forwards header field allows the client to limit the length of the request chain, which is useful for testing a chain of proxies forwarding messages in an infinite loop.

If the request is valid, the response SHOULD contain the entire request message in the entity-body, with a Content-Type of "message/http." Responses to this method MUST NOT be cached.

9.9 CONNECT

This specification reserves the method name CONNECT for use with a proxy that can dynamically switch to being a tunnel (e.g., SSL tunneling [44]).

10 Status Code Definitions

Each Status-Code is described below, including a description of which method(s) it can follow and any metainformation required in the response.

10.1 Informational 1xx

This class of status code indicates a provisional response, consisting only of the Status-Line and optional headers, and is terminated by an empty line. There are no required headers for this class of status code. Since HTTP/1.0 did not define any 1xx status codes, servers MUST NOT send a 1xx response to an HTTP/1.0 client except under experimental conditions.

A client MUST be prepared to accept one or more 1xx status responses prior to a regular response, even if the client does not expect a 100 (Continue) status message. Unexpected 1xx status responses MAY be ignored by a user agent.

Proxies MUST forward 1xx responses, unless the connection between the proxy and its client has been closed, or unless the proxy itself requested the generation of the 1xx response. [For example, if a proxy adds an "Expect: 100-continue" field when it forwards a request, then it need not forward the corresponding 100 (Continue) response(s).]

10.1.1 100 Continue

The client SHOULD continue with its request. This interim response is used to inform the client that the initial part of the request has been received and has not yet been rejected by the server. The client SHOULD continue by sending the remainder of the request or, if the request has already been completed, ignore this response.

The server MUST send a final response after the request has been completed. See section 8.2.3 for detailed discussion of the use and handling of this status code.

10.1.2 101 Switching Protocols

The server understands and is willing to comply with the client's request, via the Upgrade message header field (section 14.42), for a change in the application protocol being used on this connection. The server will switch protocols to those defined by the response's Upgrade header field immediately after the empty line which terminates the 101 response.

The protocol SHOULD be switched only when it is advantageous to do so. For example, switching to a newer version of HTTP is advantageous over older versions, and switching to a real-time, synchronous protocol might be advantageous when delivering resources that use such features.

10.2 Successful 2xx

This class of status code indicates that the client's request was successfully received, understood, and accepted.

10.2.1 200 OK

The request has succeeded. The information returned with the response is dependent on the method used in the request, for example:

- **GET:** an entity corresponding to the requested resource is sent in the response;
- **HEAD:** the entity-header fields corresponding to the requested resource are sent in the response without any message-body;
- **POST:** an entity describing or containing the result of the action;
- **TRACE:** an entity containing the request message as received by the end server.

10.2.2 201 Created

The request has been fulfilled and resulted in a new resource being created. The newly created resource can be referenced by the URI(s) returned in the entity of the response, with the most specific URI for the resource given by a Location header field. The response SHOULD include an entity containing a list of resource characteristics and location(s) from which the user or user agent can choose the one most appropriate. The entity format is specified by the media type given in the Content-Type header field. The origin server MUST create the resource before returning the 201 status code. If the action cannot be carried out immediately, the server SHOULD respond with 202 (Accepted) response instead.

A 201 response MAY contain an ETag response header field indicating the current value of the entity tag for the requested variant just created, see section 14.19.

10.2.3 202 Accepted

The request has been accepted for processing, but the processing has not been completed. The request might or might not eventually be acted upon, as it might be disallowed when processing actually takes place. There is no facility for resending a status code from an asynchronous operation such as this.

The 202 response is intentionally noncommittal. Its purpose is to allow a server to accept a request for some other process (perhaps a batch-oriented process that is only run once per day) without requiring that the user agent's connection to the server persist until the process is completed. The entity returned with this response SHOULD include an indication of the request's current status and either a pointer to a status monitor or some estimate of when the user can expect the request to be fulfilled.

10.2.4 203 Non-authoritative Information

The returned metainformation in the entity-header is not the definitive set as available from the origin server, but is gathered from a local or a third-party copy. The set presented MAY be a subset or superset of the original version. For example, including local annotation information about the resource might result in a superset of the metainformation known by the origin server. Use of this response code is not required and is only appropriate when the response would otherwise be 200 (OK).

10.2.5 204 No Content

The server has fulfilled the request but does not need to return an entity-body, and might want to return updated metainformation. The response MAY include new or updated metainformation in the form of entity-headers, which if present SHOULD be associated with the requested variant.

If the client is a user agent, it SHOULD NOT change its document view from that which caused the request to be sent. This response is primarily intended to allow input for actions to take place without causing a change to the user agent's active document view, although any new or updated metainformation SHOULD be applied to the document currently in the user agent's active view.

The 204 response MUST NOT include a message-body, and thus is always terminated by the first empty line after the header fields.

10.2.6 205 Reset Content

The server has fulfilled the request and the user agent SHOULD reset the document view which caused the request to be sent. This response is primarily intended to allow input for actions to take place via user input, followed by a clearing of the form in which the input is given so that the user can easily initiate another input action. The response MUST NOT include an entity.

10.2.7 206 Partial Content

The server has fulfilled the partial GET request for the resource. The request MUST have included a Range header field (section 14.35) indicating the desired range, and MAY have included an If-Range header field (section 14.27) to make the request conditional.

The response MUST include the following header fields:

- Either a Content-Range header field (section 14.16) indicating the range included with this response, or a multipart/byteranges Content-Type including Content-Range fields for each part. If a Content-Length header field is present in the response, its value MUST match the actual number of OCTETs transmitted in the message-body.

- Date.

- ETag and/or Content-Location, if the header would have been sent in a 200 response to the same request.

- Expires, Cache-Control, and/or Vary, if the field-value might differ from that sent in any previous response for the same variant.

If the 206 response is the result of an If-Range request that used a strong cache validator (see section 13.3.3), the response SHOULD NOT include other entity-headers. If the response is the result of an If-Range request that used a weak validator, the response MUST NOT include other entity-headers; this prevents inconsistencies between cached entity-bodies and updated headers. Otherwise, the response MUST include all of the entity-headers that would have been returned with a 200 (OK) response to the same request.

A cache MUST NOT combine a 206 response with other previously cached content if the ETag or Last-Modified headers do not match exactly; see section 13.5.4.

A cache that does not support the Range and Content-Range headers MUST NOT cache 206 (Partial) responses.

10.3 Redirection 3xx

This class of status code indicates that further action needs to be taken by the user agent in order to fulfill the request. The action required MAY be carried out by the user agent without interaction with the user if and only if the method used in the second request is GET or HEAD. A client SHOULD detect infinite redirection loops, since such loops generate network traffic for each redirection.

> **Note:** Previous versions of this specification recommended a maximum of five redirections. Content developers should be aware that there might be clients that implement such a fixed limitation.

10.3.1 300 Multiple Choices

The requested resource corresponds to any one of a set of representations, each with its own specific location, and agent-driven negotiation information (section 12) is being provided so that the user (or user agent) can select a preferred representation and redirect its request to that location.

Unless it was a HEAD request, the response SHOULD include an entity containing a list of resource characteristics and location(s) from which the user or user agent can choose the one most appropriate. The entity format is specified by the media type given in the Content-Type header field. Depending upon the format and the capabilities of the user agent, selection of the most appropriate choice MAY be performed automatically. However, this specification does not define any standard for such automatic selection.

If the server has a preferred choice of representation, it SHOULD include the specific URI for that representation in the Location field; user agents MAY use the Location field value for automatic redirection. This response is cacheable unless indicated otherwise.

10.3.2 301 Moved Permanently

The requested resource has been assigned a new permanent URI and any future references to this resource SHOULD use one of the returned URIs. Clients with link editing capabilities ought to automatically relink references to the Request-URI to one or more of the new references returned by the server, where possible. This response is cacheable unless indicated otherwise.

The new permanent URI SHOULD be given by the Location field in the response. Unless the request method was HEAD, the entity of the response SHOULD contain a short hypertext note with a hyperlink to the new URI(s).

If the 301 status code is received in response to a request other than GET or HEAD, the user agent MUST NOT automatically redirect the request unless it can be confirmed by the user, since this might change the conditions under which the request was issued.

> **Note:** When automatically redirecting a POST request after receiving a 301 status code, some existing HTTP/1.0 user agents will erroneously change it into a GET request.

10.3.3 302 Found

The requested resource resides temporarily under a different URI. Since the redirection might be altered on occasion, the client SHOULD continue to use the Request-URI for future requests. This response is only cacheable if indicated by a Cache-Control or Expires header field.

The temporary URI SHOULD be given by the Location field in the response. Unless the request method was HEAD, the entity of the response SHOULD contain a short hypertext note with a hyperlink to the new URI(s).

If the 302 status code is received in response to a request other than GET or HEAD, the user agent MUST NOT automatically redirect the request unless it can be confirmed by the user, since this might change the conditions under which the request was issued.

> **Note:** RFC 1945 and RFC 2068 specify that the client is not allowed to change the method on the redirected request. However, most existing user agent implementations treat 302 as if it were a 303 response, performing a GET on the Location field-value regardless of the original request method. The status codes 303 and 307 have been added for servers that wish to make unambiguously clear which kind of reaction is expected of the client.

10.3.4 303 See Other

The response to the request can be found under a different URI and SHOULD be retrieved using a GET method on that resource. This method exists primarily to allow the output of a POST-activated script to redirect the user agent to a selected resource. The new URI is not a substitute reference for the originally requested resource. The 303 response MUST NOT be cached, but the response to the second (redirected) request might be cacheable.

The different URI SHOULD be given by the Location field in the response. Unless the request method was HEAD, the entity of the response SHOULD contain a short hypertext note with a hyperlink to the new URI(s).

> **Note:** Many pre-HTTP/1.1 user agents do not understand the 303 status. When interoperability with such clients is a concern, the 302 status code may be used instead, since most user agents react to a 302 response as described here for 303.

10.3.5 304 Not Modified

If the client has performed a conditional GET request and access is allowed, but the document has not been modified, the server SHOULD respond with this status code. The 304 response MUST NOT contain a message-body, and thus is always terminated by the first empty line after the header fields.

The response MUST include the following header fields:

- Date, unless its omission is required by section 14.18.1

If a clockless origin server obeys these rules, and proxies and clients add their own Date to any response received without one (as already specified by [RFC 2068], section 14.19), caches will operate correctly.

- ETag and/or Content-Location, if the header would have been sent in a 200 response to the same request

- Expires, Cache-Control, and/or Vary, if the field-value might differ from that sent in any previous response for the same variant

If the conditional GET used a strong cache validator (see section 13.3.3), the response SHOULD NOT include other entity-headers. Otherwise (i.e., the conditional GET used a weak validator), the response MUST NOT include other entity-headers; this prevents inconsistencies between cached entity-bodies and updated headers.

If a 304 response indicates an entity not currently cached, then the cache MUST disregard the response and repeat the request without the conditional.

If a cache uses a received 304 response to update a cache entry, the cache MUST update the entry to reflect any new field values given in the response.

10.3.6 305 Use Proxy

The requested resource MUST be accessed through the proxy given by the Location field. The Location field gives the URI of the proxy. The recipient is expected to repeat this single request via the proxy. 305 responses MUST only be generated by origin servers.

> **Note:** RFC 2068 was not clear that 305 was intended to redirect a single request, and to be generated by origin servers only. Not observing these limitations has significant security consequences.

10.3.7 306 (Unused)

The 306 status code was used in a previous version of the specification, but is no longer used, and the code is reserved.

10.3.8 307 Temporary Redirect

The requested resource resides temporarily under a different URI. Since the redirection MAY be altered on occasion, the client SHOULD continue to use the Request-URI for future requests. This response is only cacheable if indicated by a Cache-Control or Expires header field.

The temporary URI SHOULD be given by the Location field in the response. Unless the request method was HEAD, the entity of the response SHOULD contain a short hypertext note with a hyperlink to the new URI(s) , since many pre-HTTP/1.1 user agents do not understand the 307 status. Therefore, the note SHOULD contain the information necessary for a user to repeat the original request on the new URI.

If the 307 status code is received in response to a request other than GET or HEAD, the user agent MUST NOT automatically redirect the request unless it can be confirmed by the user, since this might change the conditions under which the request was issued.

10.4 Client Error 4xx

The 4xx class of status code is intended for cases in which the client seems to have erred. Except when responding to a HEAD request, the server SHOULD include an entity containing an explanation of the error situation, and whether it is a temporary or permanent condition. These status codes are applicable to any request method. User agents SHOULD display any included entity to the user.

If the client is sending data, a server implementation using TCP SHOULD be careful to ensure that the client acknowledges receipt of the packet(s) containing the response, before the server closes the input connection. If the client continues sending data to the server after the close, the server's TCP stack will send a reset packet to the client, which may erase the client's unacknowledged input buffers before they can be read and interpreted by the HTTP application.

10.4.1 400 Bad Request

The request could not be understood by the server due to malformed syntax. The client SHOULD NOT repeat the request without modifications.

10.4.2 401 Unauthorized

The request requires user authentication. The response MUST include a WWW-Authenticate header field (section 14.47) containing a challenge applicable to the requested resource. The client MAY repeat the request with a suitable Authorization header field (section 14.8). If the request already included Authorization credentials, then the 401 response indicates that authorization has been refused for those credentials. If the 401 response contains the same challenge as the prior response, and the user agent has already attempted authentication at least once, then the user SHOULD be presented the entity that was given in the response, since that entity might include relevant diagnostic information. HTTP access authentication is explained in "HTTP Authentication: Basic and Digest Access Authentication" [43].

10.4.3 402 Payment Required

This code is reserved for future use.

10.4.4 403 Forbidden

The server understood the request, but is refusing to fulfill it. Authorization will not help and the request SHOULD NOT be repeated. If the request method was not HEAD and the server wishes to make public why the request has not been fulfilled, it SHOULD describe the reason for the refusal in the entity. If the server does not wish to make this information available to the client, the status code 404 (Not Found) can be used instead.

10.4.5 404 Not Found

The server has not found anything matching the Request-URI. No indication is given of whether the condition is temporary or permanent. The 410 (Gone) status code SHOULD be used if the server knows, through some internally configurable mechanism, that an old resource is permanently unavailable and has no forwarding address. This status code is commonly used when the server does not wish to reveal exactly why the request has been refused, or when no other response is applicable.

10.4.6 405 Method Not Allowed

The method specified in the Request-Line is not allowed for the resource identified by the Request-URI. The response MUST include an Allow header containing a list of valid methods for the requested resource.

10.4.7 406 Not Acceptable

The resource identified by the request is only capable of generating response entities which have content characteristics not acceptable according to the accept headers sent in the request.

Unless it was a HEAD request, the response SHOULD include an entity containing a list of available entity characteristics and location(s) from which the user or user agent can choose the one most appropriate. The entity format is specified by the media type given in the Content-Type header field. Depending upon the format and the capabilities of the user agent, selection of the most appropriate choice MAY be performed automatically. However, this specification does not define any standard for such automatic selection.

> **Note:** HTTP/1.1 servers are allowed to return responses which are not acceptable according to the accept headers sent in the request. In some cases, this may even be preferable to sending a 406 response. User agents are encouraged to inspect the headers of an incoming response to determine if it is acceptable.

If the response could be unacceptable, a user agent SHOULD temporarily stop receipt of more data and query the user for a decision on further actions.

10.4.8 407 Proxy Authentication Required

This code is similar to 401 (Unauthorized), but indicates that the client must first authenticate itself with the proxy. The proxy MUST return a Proxy-Authenticate header field (section 14.33) containing a challenge applicable to the proxy for the requested resource. The client MAY repeat the request with a suitable Proxy-Authorization header field (section 14.34). HTTP access authentication is explained in "HTTP Authentication: Basic and Digest Access Authentication" [43].

10.4.9 408 Request Timeout

The client did not produce a request within the time that the server was prepared to wait. The client MAY repeat the request without modifications at any later time.

10.4.10 409 Conflict

The request could not be completed due to a conflict with the current state of the resource. This code is only allowed in situations where it is expected that the user might be able to resolve the conflict and resubmit the request. The response body SHOULD include enough information for the user to recognize the source of the conflict. Ideally, the response entity would include enough information for the user or user agent to fix the problem; however, that might not be possible and is not required.

Conflicts are most likely to occur in response to a PUT request. For example, if versioning were being used and the entity being PUT included changes to a resource which conflict with those made by an earlier (third-party) request, the server might use the 409 response to indicate that it can't complete the request. In this case, the response entity would likely contain a list of the differences between the two versions in a format defined by the response Content-Type.

10.4.11 410 Gone

The requested resource is no longer available at the server and no forwarding address is known. This condition is expected to be considered permanent. Clients with link editing capabilities SHOULD delete references to the Request-URI after user approval. If the server does not know, or has no facility to determine, whether or not the condition is permanent, the status code 404 (Not Found) SHOULD be used instead. This response is cacheable unless indicated otherwise.

The 410 response is primarily intended to assist the task of web maintenance by notifying the recipient that the resource is intentionally unavailable and that the server owners desire that remote links to that resource be removed. Such an event is common for limited-time, promotional services and for resources belonging to individuals no longer working at the server's site. It is not necessary to mark all permanently unavailable resources as "gone" or to keep the mark for any length of time—that is left to the discretion of the server owner.

10.4.12 411 Length Required

The server refuses to accept the request without a defined Content-Length. The client MAY repeat the request if it adds a valid Content-Length header field containing the length of the message-body in the request message.

10.4.13 412 Precondition Failed

The precondition given in one or more of the request-header fields evaluated to false when it was tested on the server. This response code allows the client to place preconditions on the current resource metainformation (header field data) and thus prevent the requested method from being applied to a resource other than the one intended.

10.4.14 413 Request Entity Too Large

The server is refusing to process a request because the request entity is larger than the server is willing or able to process. The server MAY close the connection to prevent the client from continuing the request.

If the condition is temporary, the server SHOULD include a Retry-After header field to indicate that it is temporary and after what time the client MAY try again.

10.4.15 414 Request-URI Too Long

The server is refusing to service the request because the Request-URI is longer than the server is willing to interpret. This rare condition is only likely to occur when a client has improperly converted a POST request to a GET request with long query information, when the client has descended into a URI "black hole" of redirection (e.g., a redirected URI prefix that points to a suffix of itself), or when the server is under attack by a client attempting to exploit security holes present in some servers using fixed-length buffers for reading or manipulating the Request-URI.

10.4.16 415 Unsupported Media Type

The server is refusing to service the request because the entity of the request is in a format not supported by the requested resource for the requested method.

10.4.17 416 Requested Range Not Satisfiable

A server SHOULD return a response with this status code if a request included a Range request-header field (section 14.35), and none of the range-specifier values in this field overlap the current extent of the selected resource, and the request did not include an If-Range request-header field. (For byte ranges, this means that the first-byte-pos of all of the byte-range-spec values were greater than the current length of the selected resource.)

When this status code is returned for a byte-range request, the response SHOULD include a Content-Range entity-header field specifying the current length of the selected resource (see section 14.16). This response MUST NOT use the multipart/byteranges content-type.

10.4.18 417 Expectation Failed

The expectation given in an Expect request-header field (see section 14.20) could not be met by this server, or, if the server is a proxy, the server has unambiguous evidence that the request could not be met by the next-hop server.

10.5 Server Error 5xx

Response status codes beginning with the digit "5" indicate cases in which the server is aware that it has erred or is incapable of performing the request. Except when responding to a HEAD request, the server SHOULD include an entity containing an explanation of the error situation, and whether it is a temporary or permanent condition. User agents SHOULD display any included entity to the user. These response codes are applicable to any request method.

10.5.1 500 Internal Server Error

The server encountered an unexpected condition which prevented it from fulfilling the request.

10.5.2 501 Not Implemented

The server does not support the functionality required to fulfill the request. This is the appropriate response when the server does not recognize the request method and is not capable of supporting it for any resource.

10.5.3 502 Bad Gateway

The server, while acting as a gateway or proxy, received an invalid response from the upstream server it accessed in attempting to fulfill the request.

10.5.4 503 Service Unavailable

The server is currently unable to handle the request due to a temporary overloading or maintenance of the server. The implication is that this is a temporary condition which will be alleviated after some delay. If known, the length of the delay MAY be indicated in a Retry-After header. If no Retry-After is given, the client SHOULD handle the response as it would for a 500 response.

Note: The existence of the 503 status code does not imply that a server must use it when becoming overloaded. Some servers may wish to simply refuse the connection.

10.5.5 504 Gateway Timeout

The server, while acting as a gateway or proxy, did not receive a timely response from the upstream server specified by the URI (e.g., HTTP, FTP, LDAP) or some other auxiliary server (e.g., DNS) it needed to access in attempting to complete the request.

Note to implementers: Some deployed proxies are known to return 400 or 500 when DNS lookups time out.

10.5.6 505 HTTP Version Not Supported

The server does not support, or refuses to support, the HTTP protocol version that was used in the request message. The server is indicating that it is unable or unwilling to complete the request using the same major version as the client, as described in section 3.1, other than with this error message. The response SHOULD contain an entity describing why that version is not supported and what other protocols are supported by that server.

11 Access Authentication

HTTP provides several OPTIONAL challenge-response authentication mechanisms which can be used by a server to challenge a client request and by a client to provide authentication information. The general framework for access authentication, and the specification of "basic" and "digest" authentication, are specified in "HTTP Authentication: Basic and Digest Access Authentication" [43]. This specification adopts the definitions of "challenge" and "credentials" from that specification.

12 Content Negotiation

Most HTTP responses include an entity which contains information for interpretation by a human user. Naturally, it is desirable to supply the user with the "best available" entity corresponding to the request. Unfortunately for servers and caches, not all users have the same preferences for what is "best," and not all user agents are equally capable of rendering all entity types. For that reason, HTTP has provisions for several mechanisms for "content negotiation"—the process of selecting the best representation for a given response when there are multiple representations available.

> **Note:** This is not called "format negotiation" because the alternate representations may be of the same media type, but use different capabilities of that type, be in different languages, etc. Any response containing an entity-body MAY be subject to negotiation, including error responses.

There are two kinds of content negotiation which are possible in HTTP: server-driven and agent-driven negotiation. These two kinds of negotiation are orthogonal and thus may be used separately or in combination. One method of combination, referred to as transparent negotiation, occurs when a cache uses the agent-driven negotiation information provided by the origin server in order to provide server-driven negotiation for subsequent requests.

12.1 Server-Driven Negotiation

If the selection of the best representation for a response is made by an algorithm located at the server, it is called server-driven negotiation. Selection is based on the available representations of the response (the dimensions over which it can vary; e.g. language, content-coding, etc.) and the contents of particular header fields in the request message or on other information pertaining to the request (such as the network address of the client).

Server-driven negotiation is advantageous when the algorithm for selecting from among the available representations is difficult to describe to the user agent, or when the server desires to send its "best guess" to the client along with the first response (hoping to avoid the round-trip delay of a subsequent request if the "best guess" is good enough for the user). In order to improve the server's guess, the user agent MAY include request header fields (Accept, Accept-Language, Accept-Encoding, etc.) which describe its preferences for such a response.

Server-driven negotiation has disadvantages:

1. It is impossible for the server to accurately determine what might be "best" for any given user, since that would require complete knowledge of both the capabilities of the user agent and the intended use for the response (e.g., does the user want to view it on screen or print it on paper?).

2. Having the user agent describe its capabilities in every request can be both very inefficient (given that only a small percentage of responses have multiple representations) and a potential violation of the user's privacy.

3. It complicates the implementation of an origin server and the algorithms for generating responses to a request.

4. It may limit a public cache's ability to use the same response for multiple user's requests.

HTTP/1.1 includes the following request-header fields for enabling server-driven negotiation through description of user agent capabilities and user preferences: Accept (section 14.1), Accept-Charset (section 14.2), Accept-Encoding (section 14.3), Accept-Language (section 14.4), and User-Agent (section 14.43). However, an origin server is not limited to these dimensions and MAY vary the response based on any aspect of the request, including information outside the request-header fields or within extension header fields not defined by this specification.

The Vary header field can be used to express the parameters the server uses to select a representation that is subject to server-driven negotiation. See section 13.6 for use of the Vary header field by caches and section 14.44 for use of the Vary header field by servers.

12.2 Agent-Driven Negotiation

With agent-driven negotiation, selection of the best representation for a response is performed by the user agent after receiving an initial response from the origin server. Selection is based on a list of the available representations of the response included within the header fields or entity-body of the initial response, with each representation identified by its own URI. Selection from among the representations may be performed automatically (if the user agent is capable of doing so) or manually by the user selecting from a generated (possibly hypertext) menu.

Agent-driven negotiation is advantageous when the response would vary over commonly used dimensions (such as type, language, or encoding), when the origin server is unable to determine a user agent's capabilities from examining the request, and generally when public caches are used to distribute server load and reduce network usage.

Agent-driven negotiation suffers from the disadvantage of needing a second request to obtain the best alternate representation. This second request is only efficient when caching is used. In addition, this specification does not define any mechanism for supporting automatic selection, though it also does not prevent any such mechanism from being developed as an extension and used within HTTP/1.1.

HTTP/1.1 defines the 300 (Multiple Choices) and 406 (Not Acceptable) status codes for enabling agent-driven negotiation when the server is unwilling or unable to provide a varying response using server-driven negotiation.

12.3 Transparent Negotiation

Transparent negotiation is a combination of both server-driven and agent-driven negotiation. When a cache is supplied with a form of the list of available representations of the response (as in agent-driven negotiation) and the dimensions of variance are completely understood by the cache, then the cache becomes capable of performing server-driven negotiation on behalf of the origin server for subsequent requests on that resource.

Transparent negotiation has the advantage of distributing the negotiation work that would otherwise be required of the origin server and also removing the second request delay of agent-driven negotiation when the cache is able to correctly guess the right response.

This specification does not define any mechanism for transparent negotiation, though it also does not prevent any such mechanism from being developed as an extension that could be used within HTTP/1.1.

13 Caching in HTTP

HTTP is typically used for distributed information systems, where performance can be improved by the use of response caches. The HTTP/1.1 protocol includes a number of elements intended to make caching work as well as possible. Because these elements are inextricable from other aspects of the protocol, and because they interact with each other, it is useful to describe the basic caching design of HTTP separately from the detailed descriptions of methods, headers, response codes, etc.

Caching would be useless if it did not significantly improve performance. The goal of caching in HTTP/1.1 is to eliminate the need to send requests in many cases, and to eliminate the need to send full responses in many other cases. The former reduces the number of network round-trips required for many operations; we use an "expiration" mechanism for this purpose (see section 13.2). The latter reduces network bandwidth requirements; we use a "validation" mechanism for this purpose (see section 13.3).

Requirements for performance, availability, and disconnected operation require us to be able to relax the goal of semantic transparency. The HTTP/1.1 protocol allows origin servers, caches, and clients to explicitly reduce transparency when necessary. However, because non-transparent operation may confuse non-expert users, and might be incompatible with certain server applications (such as those for ordering merchandise), the protocol requires that transparency be relaxed

- Only by an explicit protocol-level request when relaxed by client or origin server

- Only with an explicit warning to the end user when relaxed by cache or client

Therefore, the HTTP/1.1 protocol provides these important elements:

1. Protocol features that provide full semantic transparency when this is required by all parties.

2. Protocol features that allow an origin server or user agent to explicitly request and control non-transparent operation.

3. Protocol features that allow a cache to attach warnings to responses that do not preserve the requested approximation of semantic transparency.

A basic principle is that it must be possible for the clients to detect any potential relaxation of semantic transparency.

> **Note:** The server, cache, or client implementer might be faced with design decisions not explicitly discussed in this specification. If a decision might affect semantic transparency, the implementer ought to err on the side of maintaining transparency unless a careful and complete analysis shows significant benefits in breaking transparency.

13.1.1 Cache Correctness

A correct cache MUST respond to a request with the most up-to-date response held by the cache that is appropriate to the request (see sections 13.2.5, 13.2.6, and 13.12) which meets one of the following conditions:

1. It has been checked for equivalence with what the origin server would have returned by revalidating the response with the origin server (section 13.3).

2. It is "fresh enough" (see section 13.2). In the default case, this means it meets the least restrictive freshness requirement of the client, origin server, and cache (see section 14.9); if the origin server so specifies, it is the freshness requirement of the origin server alone.

3. If a stored response is not "fresh enough" by the most restrictive freshness requirement of both the client and the origin server, in carefully considered circumstances the cache MAY still return the response with the appropriate Warning header (see section 13.1.5 and 14.46), unless such a response is prohibited (e.g., by a "no-store" cache-directive or "no-cache" cache-request-directive; see section 14.9).

4. It is an appropriate 304 (Not Modified), 305 (Proxy Redirect), or error (4xx or 5xx) response message.

If the cache can not communicate with the origin server, then a correct cache SHOULD respond as above if the response can be correctly served from the cache; if not, it MUST return an error or warning indicating that there was a communication failure.

If a cache receives a response (either an entire response or a 304 (Not Modified) response) that it would normally forward to the requesting client, and the received response is no longer fresh, the cache SHOULD forward it to the requesting client without adding a new Warning (but without removing any existing Warning headers). A cache SHOULD NOT attempt to revalidate a response simply because that response became stale in transit; this might lead to an infinite loop. A user agent that receives a stale response without a Warning MAY display a warning indication to the user.

13.1.2 Warnings

Whenever a cache returns a response that is neither first-hand nor "fresh enough" (in the sense of condition 2 in section 13.1.1), it MUST attach a warning to that effect, using a Warning general-header. The Warning header and the currently defined warnings are described in section 14.46. The warning allows clients to take appropriate action.

Warnings MAY be used for other purposes, both cache-related and otherwise. The use of a warning, rather than an error status code, distinguishes these responses from true failures.

Warnings are assigned three-digit warn-codes. The first digit indicates whether the Warning MUST or MUST NOT be deleted from a stored cache entry after a successful revalidation:

- **1xx:** Warnings that describe the freshness or revalidation status of the response, and so MUST be deleted after a successful revalidation. 1xx warn-codes MAY be generated by a cache only when validating a cached entry. It MUST NOT be generated by clients.

- **2xx:** Warnings that describe some aspect of the entity body or entity headers that is not rectified by a revalidation (for example, a lossy compression of the entity bodies) and which MUST NOT be deleted after a successful revalidation.

See section 14.46 for the definitions of the codes themselves.

HTTP/1.0 caches will cache all Warnings in responses, without deleting the ones in the first category. Warnings in responses that are passed to HTTP/1.0 caches carry an extra warning-date field, which prevents a future HTTP/1.1 recipient from believing an erroneously cached Warning.

Warnings also carry a warning text. The text MAY be in any appropriate natural language (perhaps based on the client's Accept headers) and include an OPTIONAL indication of what character set is used.

Multiple warnings MAY be attached to a response (either by the origin server or by a cache), including multiple warnings with the same code number. For example, a server might provide the same warning with texts in both English and Basque.

When multiple warnings are attached to a response, it might not be practical or reasonable to display all of them to the user. This version of HTTP does not specify strict priority rules for deciding which warnings to display and in what order, but does suggest some heuristics.

13.1.3 Cache-Control Mechanisms

The basic cache mechanisms in HTTP/1.1 (server-specified expiration times and validators) are implicit directives to caches. In some cases, a server or client might need to provide explicit directives to the HTTP caches. We use the Cache-Control header for this purpose.

The Cache-Control header allows a client or server to transmit a variety of directives in either requests or responses. These directives typically override the default caching algorithms. As a general rule, if there is any apparent conflict between header values, the most restrictive interpretation is applied (that is, the one that is most likely to preserve semantic transparency). However, in some cases, cache-control directives are explicitly specified as weakening the approximation of semantic transparency (for example, "max-stale" or "public").

The cache-control directives are described in detail in section 14.9.

13.1.4 Explicit User Agent Warnings

Many user agents make it possible for users to override the basic caching mechanisms. For example, the user agent might allow the user to specify that cached entities (even explicitly stale ones) are never validated, or the user agent might habitually add "Cache-Control: max-stale=3600" to every request. The user agent SHOULD NOT default to either non-transparent behavior, or behavior that results in abnormally ineffective caching, but MAY be explicitly configured to do so by an explicit action of the user.

If the user has overridden the basic caching mechanisms, the user agent SHOULD explicitly indicate to the user whenever this results in the display of information that might not meet the server's transparency requirements (in particular, if the displayed entity is known to be stale). Since the protocol normally allows the user agent to determine if responses are stale or not, this indication need only be displayed when this actually happens. The indication need not be a dialog box; it could be an icon (for example, a picture of a rotting fish) or some other indicator.

If the user has overridden the caching mechanisms in a way that would abnormally reduce the effectiveness of caches, the user agent SHOULD continually indicate this state to the user (for example, by a display of a picture of currency in flames) so that the user does not inadvertently consume excess resources or suffer from excessive latency.

13.1.5 Exceptions to the Rules and Warnings

In some cases, the operator of a cache MAY choose to configure it to return stale responses even when not requested by clients. This decision ought not be made lightly, but may be necessary for reasons of availability or performance, especially when the cache is poorly connected to the origin server. Whenever a cache returns a stale response, it MUST mark it as such (using a Warning header), enabling the client software to alert the user that there might be a potential problem.

It also allows the user agent to take steps to obtain a first-hand or fresh response. For this reason, a cache SHOULD NOT return a stale response if the client explicitly requests a first-hand or fresh one, unless it is impossible to comply with this request for technical or policy reasons.

13.1.6 Client-Controlled Behavior

While the origin server (and to a lesser extent, intermediate caches, by their contribution to the age of a response) is the primary source of expiration information, in some cases the client might need to control a cache's decision about whether to return a cached response without validating it. Clients do this using several directives of the Cache-Control header.

A client's request MAY specify the maximum age it is willing to accept of an unvalidated response; specifying a value of zero forces the cache(s) to revalidate all responses. A client MAY also specify the minimum time remaining before a response expires. Both of these options increase constraints on the behavior of caches, and so cannot further relax the cache's approximation of semantic transparency.

A client MAY also specify that it will accept stale responses, up to some maximum amount of staleness. This loosens the constraints on the caches, and so might violate the origin server's specified constraints on semantic transparency, but might be necessary to support disconnected operation, or high availability in the face of poor connectivity.

13.2 Expiration Model

13.2.1 Server-Specified Expiration

HTTP caching works best when caches can entirely avoid making requests to the origin server. The primary mechanism for avoiding requests is for an origin server to provide an explicit expiration time in the future, indicating that a response MAY be used to satisfy subsequent requests. In other words, a cache can return a fresh response without first contacting the server.

Our expectation is that servers will assign future explicit expiration times to responses in the belief that the entity is not likely to change, in a semantically significant way, before the expiration time is reached. This normally preserves semantic transparency, as long as the server's expiration times are carefully chosen.

The expiration mechanism applies only to responses taken from a cache and not to first-hand responses forwarded immediately to the requesting client.

If an origin server wishes to force a semantically transparent cache to validate every request, it MAY assign an explicit expiration time in the past. This means that the response is always stale, and so the cache SHOULD validate it before using it for subsequent requests. See section 14.9.4 for a more restrictive way to force revalidation.

If an origin server wishes to force any HTTP/1.1 cache, no matter how it is configured, to validate every request, it SHOULD use the "must-revalidate" cache-control directive (see section 14.9).

Servers specify explicit expiration times using either the Expires header or the max-age directive of the Cache-Control header.

An expiration time cannot be used to force a user agent to refresh its display or reload a resource; its semantics apply only to caching mechanisms, and such mechanisms need only check a resource's expiration status when a new request for that resource is initiated. See section 13.13 for an explanation of the difference between caches and history mechanisms.

13.2.2 Heuristic Expiration

Since origin servers do not always provide explicit expiration times, HTTP caches typically assign heuristic expiration times, employing algorithms that use other header values (such as the Last-Modified time) to estimate a plausible expiration time. The HTTP/1.1 specification does not provide specific algorithms, but does impose worst-case constraints on their results. Since heuristic expiration times might compromise semantic transparency, they ought to be used cautiously, and we encourage origin servers to provide explicit expiration times as much as possible.

13.2.3 Age Calculations

In order to know if a cached entry is fresh, a cache needs to know if its age exceeds its freshness lifetime. We discuss how to calculate the latter in section 13.2.4; this section describes how to calculate the age of a response or cache entry.

In this discussion, we use the term "now" to mean "the current value of the clock at the host performing the calculation." Hosts that use HTTP, but especially hosts running origin servers and caches, SHOULD use NTP [28] or some similar protocol to synchronize their clocks to a globally accurate time standard.

HTTP/1.1 requires origin servers to send a Date header, if possible, with every response, giving the time at which the response was generated (see section 14.18). We use the term "date_value" to denote the value of the Date header, in a form appropriate for arithmetic operations.

HTTP/1.1 uses the Age response-header to convey the estimated age of the response message when obtained from a cache. The Age field value is the cache's estimate of the amount of time since the response was generated or revalidated by the origin server.

In essence, the Age value is the sum of the time that the response has been resident in each of the caches along the path from the origin server, plus the amount of time it has been in transit along network paths.

We use the term "age_value" to denote the value of the Age header, in a form appropriate for arithmetic operations.

A response's age can be calculated in two entirely independent ways:

1. now minus date_value, if the local clock is reasonably well synchronized to the origin server's clock. If the result is negative, the result is replaced by zero.

2. age_value, if all of the caches along the response path implement HTTP/1.1.

Given that we have two independent ways to compute the age of a response when it is received, we can combine these as

```
corrected_received_age = max(now - date_value, age_value)
```

and as long as we have either nearly synchronized clocks or all-HTTP/1.1 paths, one gets a reliable (conservative) result.

Because of network-imposed delays, some significant interval might pass between the time that a server generates a response and the time that it is received at the next outbound cache or client. If uncorrected, this delay could result in improperly low ages.

Because the request that resulted in the returned Age value must have been initiated prior to that Age value's generation, we can correct for delays imposed by the network by recording the time at which the request was initiated. Then, when an Age value is received, it MUST be interpreted relative to the time the request was initiated, not the time that the response was received. This algorithm results in conservative behavior no matter how much delay is experienced. So, we compute

```
corrected_initial_age = corrected_received_age + (now - request_time)
```

where "request_time" is the time (according to the local clock) when the request that elicited this response was sent.

Summary of age calculation algorithm, when a cache receives a response:

```
/*
 * age_value
 *    is the value of Age: header received by the cache with
 *        this response.
 * date_value
 *    is the value of the origin server's Date: header
 * request_time
 *    is the (local) time when the cache made the request
 *        that resulted in this cached response
 * response_time
 *    is the (local) time when the cache received the
 *        response
 * now
 *    is the current (local) time
 */

apparent_age = max(0, response_time - date_value);
corrected_received_age = max(apparent_age, age_value);
response_delay = response_time - request_time;
corrected_initial_age = corrected_received_age + response_delay;
resident_time = now - response_time;
current_age  = corrected_initial_age + resident_time;
```

The current_age of a cache entry is calculated by adding the amount of time (in seconds) since the cache entry was last validated by the origin server to the corrected_initial_age. When a response is generated from a cache entry, the cache MUST include a single Age header field in the response with a value equal to the cache entry's current_age.

The presence of an Age header field in a response implies that a response is not first-hand. However, the converse is not true, since the lack of an Age header field in a response does not imply that the response is first-hand unless all caches along the request path are compliant with HTTP/1.1 (i.e., older HTTP caches did not implement the Age header field).

13.2.4 Expiration Calculations

In order to decide whether a response is fresh or stale, we need to compare its freshness lifetime to its age. The age is calculated as described in section 13.2.3; this section describes how to calculate the freshness lifetime, and to determine if a response has expired. In the discussion below, the values can be represented in any form appropriate for arithmetic operations.

We use the term "expires_value" to denote the value of the Expires header. We use the term "max_age_value" to denote an appropriate value of the number of seconds carried by the "max-age" directive of the Cache-Control header in a response (see section 14.9.3).

The max-age directive takes priority over Expires, so if max-age is present in a response, the calculation is simply

```
freshness_lifetime = max_age_value
```

Otherwise, if Expires is present in the response, the calculation is

```
freshness_lifetime = expires_value - date_value
```

Note that neither of these calculations is vulnerable to clock skew, since all of the information comes from the origin server.

If none of Expires, Cache-Control: max-age, or Cache-Control: s-maxage (see section 14.9.3) appears in the response, and the response does not include other restrictions on caching, the cache MAY compute a freshness lifetime using a heuristic. The cache MUST attach Warning 113 to any response whose age is more than 24 hours if such a warning has not already been added.

Also, if the response does have a Last-Modified time, the heuristic expiration value SHOULD be no more than some fraction of the interval since that time. A typical setting of this fraction might be 10%.

The calculation to determine if a response has expired is quite simple:

```
response_is_fresh = (freshness_lifetime > current_age)
```

13.2.5 Disambiguating Expiration Values

Because expiration values are assigned optimistically, it is possible for two caches to contain fresh values for the same resource that are different.

If a client performing a retrieval receives a non-first-hand response for a request that was already fresh in its own cache, and the Date header in its existing cache entry is newer than the Date on the new response, then the client MAY ignore the response. If so, it MAY retry the request with a "Cache-Control: max-age=0" directive (see section 14.9), to force a check with the origin server.

If a cache has two fresh responses for the same representation with different validators, it MUST use the one with the more recent Date header. This situation might arise because the cache is pooling responses from other caches, or because a client has asked for a reload or a revalidation of an apparently fresh cache entry.

13.2.6 Disambiguating Multiple Responses

Because a client might be receiving responses via multiple paths, so that some responses flow through one set of caches and other responses flow through a different set of caches, a client might receive responses in an order different from that in which the origin server sent them. We would like the client to use the most recently generated response, even if older responses are still apparently fresh.

Neither the entity tag nor the expiration value can impose an ordering on responses, since it is possible that a later response intentionally carries an earlier expiration time. The Date values are ordered to a granularity of one second.

When a client tries to revalidate a cache entry, and the response it receives contains a Date header that appears to be older than the one for the existing entry, then the client SHOULD repeat the request unconditionally, and include

```
Cache-Control: max-age=0
```

to force any intermediate caches to validate their copies directly with the origin server, or

```
Cache-Control: no-cache
```

to force any intermediate caches to obtain a new copy from the origin server.

If the Date values are equal, then the client MAY use either response (or MAY, if it is being extremely prudent, request a new response). Servers MUST NOT depend on clients being able to choose deterministically between responses generated during the same second, if their expiration times overlap.

13.3 Validation Model

When a cache has a stale entry that it would like to use as a response to a client's request, it first has to check with the origin server (or possibly an intermediate cache with a fresh response) to see if its cached entry is still usable. We call this "validating" the cache entry. Since we do not want to have to pay the overhead of retransmitting the full response if the cached entry is good, and we do not want to pay the overhead of an extra round-trip if the cached entry is invalid, the HTTP/1.1 protocol supports the use of conditional methods.

The key protocol features for supporting conditional methods are those concerned with "cache validators." When an origin server generates a full response, it attaches some sort of validator to it, which is kept with the cache entry. When a client (user agent or proxy cache) makes a conditional request for a resource for which it has a cache entry, it includes the associated validator in the request.

The server then checks that validator against the current validator for the entity, and, if they match (see section 13.3.3), it responds with a special status code [usually, 304 (Not Modified)] and no entity-body. Otherwise, it returns a full response (including an entity-body). Thus, we avoid transmitting the full response if the validator matches, and we avoid an extra round-trip if it does not match.

In HTTP/1.1, a conditional request looks exactly the same as a normal request for the same resource, except that it carries a special header (which includes the validator) that implicitly turns the method (usually, GET) into a conditional.

The protocol includes both positive and negative senses of cache-validating conditions. That is, it is possible to request either that a method be performed if and only if a validator matches or if and only if no validators match.

> **Note:** A response that lacks a validator may still be cached, and served from cache until it expires, unless this is explicitly prohibited by a cache-control directive. However, a cache cannot do a conditional retrieval if it does not have a validator for the entity, which means it will not be refreshable after it expires.

13.3.1 Last-Modified Dates

The Last-Modified entity-header field value is often used as a cache validator. In simple terms, a cache entry is considered to be valid if the entity has not been modified since the Last-Modified value.

13.3.2 Entity Tag Cache Validators

The ETag response-header field value, an entity tag, provides for an "opaque" cache validator. This might allow more reliable validation in situations where it is inconvenient to store modification dates, where the one-second resolution of HTTP date values is not sufficient, or where the origin server wishes to avoid certain paradoxes that might arise from the use of modification dates.

Entity Tags are described in section 3.11. The headers used with entity tags are described in sections 14.19, 14.24, 14.26 and 14.44.

13.3.3 Weak and Strong Validators

Since both origin servers and caches will compare two validators to decide if they represent the same or different entities, one normally would expect that if the entity (the entity-body or any entity-headers) changes in any way, then the associated validator would change as well. If this is true, then we call this validator a "strong validator."

However, there might be cases when a server prefers to change the validator only on semantically significant changes, and not when insignificant aspects of the entity change. A validator that does not always change when the resource changes is a "weak validator."

Entity tags are normally "strong validators," but the protocol provides a mechanism to tag an entity tag as "weak." One can think of a strong validator as one that changes whenever the bits of an entity changes, while a weak value changes whenever the meaning of an entity changes. Alternatively, one can think of a strong validator as part of an identifier for a specific entity, while a weak validator is part of an identifier for a set of semantically equivalent entities.

> **Note:** One example of a strong validator is an integer that is incremented in stable storage every time an entity is changed.
>
> An entity's modification time, if represented with one-second resolution, could be a weak validator, since it is possible that the resource might be modified twice during a single second.
>
> Support for weak validators is optional. However, weak validators allow for more efficient caching of equivalent objects; for example, a hit counter on a site is probably good enough if it is updated every few days or weeks, and any value during that period is likely "good enough" to be equivalent.

A "use" of a validator is either when a client generates a request and includes the validator in a validating header field, or when a server compares two validators.

Strong validators are usable in any context. Weak validators are only usable in contexts that do not depend on exact equality of an entity. For example, either kind is usable for a conditional GET of a full entity. However, only a strong validator is usable for a subrange retrieval, since otherwise the client might end up with an internally inconsistent entity.

Clients MAY issue simple (non-subrange) GET requests with either weak validators or strong validators. Clients MUST NOT use weak validators in other forms of request.

The only function that the HTTP/1.1 protocol defines on validators is comparison. There are two validator comparison functions, depending on whether the comparison context allows the use of weak validators or not:

- The strong comparison function: In order to be considered equal, both validators MUST be identical in every way, and both MUST NOT be weak.

- The weak comparison function: In order to be considered equal, both validators MUST be identical in every way, but either or both of them MAY be tagged as "weak" without affecting the result.

An entity tag is strong unless it is explicitly tagged as weak. Section 3.11 gives the syntax for entity tags.

A Last-Modified time, when used as a validator in a request, is implicitly weak unless it is possible to deduce that it is strong, using the following rules:

- The validator is being compared by an origin server to the actual current validator for the entity, and

- That origin server reliably knows that the associated entity did not change twice during the second covered by the presented validator.

or

- The validator is about to be used by a client in an If-Modified-Since or If-Unmodified-Since header, because the client has a cache entry for the associated entity, and

- That cache entry includes a Date value, which gives the time when the origin server sent the original response, and

- The presented Last-Modified time is at least 60 seconds before the Date value.

or

- The validator is being compared by an intermediate cache to the validator stored in its cache entry for the entity, and

- That cache entry includes a Date value, which gives the time when the origin server sent the original response, and

- The presented Last-Modified time is at least 60 seconds before the Date value.

This method relies on the fact that if two different responses were sent by the origin server during the same second, but both had the same Last-Modified time, then at least one of those responses would have a Date value equal to its Last-Modified time. The arbitrary 60-second limit guards against the possibility that the Date and Last-Modified values are generated from different clocks, or at somewhat different times during the preparation of the response. An implementation MAY use a value larger than 60 seconds, if it is believed that 60 seconds is too short.

If a client wishes to perform a subrange retrieval on a value for which it has only a Last-Modified time and no opaque validator, it MAY do this only if the Last-Modified time is strong in the sense described here.

A cache or origin server receiving a conditional request, other than a full-body GET request, MUST use the strong comparison function to evaluate the condition.

These rules allow HTTP/1.1 caches and clients to safely perform subrange retrievals on values that have been obtained from HTTP/1.0 servers.

13.3.4 Rules for When to Use Entity Tags and Last-Modified Dates

We adopt a set of rules and recommendations for origin servers, clients, and caches regarding when various validator types ought to be used, and for what purposes.

HTTP/1.1 origin servers

- SHOULD send an entity tag validator unless it is not feasible to generate one.

- MAY send a weak entity tag instead of a strong entity tag, if performance considerations support the use of weak entity tags, or if it is unfeasible to send a strong entity tag.

- SHOULD send a Last-Modified value if it is feasible to send one, unless the risk of a breakdown in semantic transparency that could result from using this date in an If-Modified-Since header would lead to serious problems.

In other words, the preferred behavior for an HTTP/1.1 origin server is to send both a strong entity tag and a Last-Modified value.

In order to be legal, a strong entity tag MUST change whenever the associated entity value changes in any way. A weak entity tag SHOULD change whenever the associated entity changes in a semantically significant way.

> **Note:** In order to provide semantically transparent caching, an origin server must avoid reusing a specific strong entity tag value for two different entities, or reusing a specific weak entity tag value for two semantically different entities. Cache entries might persist for arbitrarily long periods, regardless of

expiration times, so it might be inappropriate to expect that a cache will never again attempt to validate an entry using a validator that it obtained at some point in the past.

HTTP/1.1 clients

- If an entity tag has been provided by the origin server, MUST use that entity tag in any cache-conditional request (using If-Match or If-None-Match).

- If only a Last-Modified value has been provided by the origin server, SHOULD use that value in non-subrange cache-conditional requests (using If-Modified-Since).

- If only a Last-Modified value has been provided by an HTTP/1.0 origin server, MAY use that value in subrange cache-conditional requests (using If-Unmodified-Since). The user agent SHOULD provide a way to disable this, in case of difficulty.

- If both an entity tag and a Last-Modified value have been provided by the origin server, SHOULD use both validators in cache-conditional requests. This allows both HTTP/1.0 and HTTP/1.1 caches to respond appropriately.

An HTTP/1.1 origin server, upon receiving a conditional request that includes both a Last-Modified date (e.g., in an If-Modified-Since or If-Unmodified-Since header field) and one or more entity tags (e.g., in an If-Match, If-None-Match, or If-Range header field) as cache validators, MUST NOT return a response status of 304 (Not Modified) unless doing so is consistent with all of the conditional header fields in the request.

An HTTP/1.1 caching proxy, upon receiving a conditional request that includes both a Last-Modified date and one or more entity tags as cache validators, MUST NOT return a locally cached response to the client unless that cached response is consistent with all of the conditional header fields in the request.

> **Note:** The general principle behind these rules is that HTTP/1.1 servers and clients should transmit as much nonredundant information as is available in their responses and requests. HTTP/1.1 systems receiving this information will make the most conservative assumptions about the validators they receive.

HTTP/1.0 clients and caches will ignore entity tags. Generally, last-modified values received or used by these systems will support transparent and efficient caching, and so HTTP/1.1 origin servers should provide Last-Modified values. In those rare cases where the use of a Last-Modified value as a validator by an HTTP/1.0 system could result in a serious problem, then HTTP/1.1 origin servers should not provide one.

13.3.5 Nonvalidating Conditionals

The principle behind entity tags is that only the service author knows the semantics of a resource well enough to select an appropriate cache validation mechanism, and the specification of any validator comparison function more complex than byte-equality would open up a can of worms. Thus, comparisons of any other headers (except Last-Modified, for compatibility with HTTP/1.0) are never used for purposes of validating a cache entry.

13.4 Response Cacheability

Unless specifically constrained by a cache-control (section 14.9) directive, a caching system MAY always store a successful response (see section 13.8) as a cache entry, MAY return it without validation if it is fresh, and MAY return it after successful validation. If there is neither a cache validator nor an explicit expiration time associated with a response, we do not expect it to be cached, but certain caches MAY violate this expectation (for example, when little or no network connectivity is available). A client can usually detect that such a response was taken from a cache by comparing the Date header to the current time.

> **Note:** Some HTTP/1.0 caches are known to violate this expectation without providing any Warning.

However, in some cases it might be inappropriate for a cache to retain an entity, or to return it in response to a subsequent request. This might be because absolute semantic transparency is deemed necessary by the service author, or because of security or privacy considerations. Certain cache-control directives are therefore provided so that the server can indicate that certain resource entities, or portions thereof, are not to be cached regardless of other considerations.

Note that section 14.8 normally prevents a shared cache from saving and returning a response to a previous request if that request included an Authorization header.

A response received with a status code of 200, 203, 206, 300, 301, or 410 MAY be stored by a cache and used in reply to a subsequent request, subject to the expiration mechanism, unless a cache-control directive prohibits caching. However, a cache that does not support the Range and Content-Range headers MUST NOT cache 206 (Partial Content) responses.

A response received with any other status code (e.g., status codes 302 and 307) MUST NOT be returned in a reply to a subsequent request unless there are cache-control directives or other headers that explicitly allow it. For example, these include the following: an Expires header (section 14.21); a "max-age," "s-maxage," "must-revalidate," "proxy-revalidate," "public" or "private" cache-control directive (section 14.9).

13.5 Constructing Responses from Caches

The purpose of an HTTP cache is to store information received in response to requests for use in responding to future requests. In many cases, a cache simply returns the appropriate parts of a response to the requester. However, if the cache holds a cache entry based on a previous response, it might have to combine parts of a new response with what is held in the cache entry.

13.5.1 End-to-End and Hop-by-Hop Headers

For the purpose of defining the behavior of caches and noncaching proxies, we divide HTTP headers into two categories:

- End-to-end headers, which are transmitted to the ultimate recipient of a request or response. End-to-end headers in responses MUST be stored as part of a cache entry and MUST be transmitted in any response formed from a cache entry.

- Hop-by-hop headers, which are meaningful only for a single transport-level connection, and are not stored by caches or forwarded by proxies.

The following HTTP/1.1 headers are hop-by-hop headers:

- Connection
- Keep-Alive
- Proxy-Authenticate
- Proxy-Authorization
- TE

- Trailers
- Transfer-Encoding
- Upgrade

All other headers defined by HTTP/1.1 are end-to-end headers.

Other hop-by-hop headers MUST be listed in a Connection header (section 14.10) to be introduced into HTTP/1.1 (or later).

13.5.2 Nonmodifiable Headers

Some features of the HTTP/1.1 protocol, such as Digest Authentication, depend on the value of certain end-to-end headers. A transparent proxy SHOULD NOT modify an end-to-end header unless the definition of that header requires or specifically allows that.

A transparent proxy MUST NOT modify any of the following fields in a request or response, and it MUST NOT add any of these fields if not already present:

- Content-Location
- Content-MD5
- ETag
- Last-Modified

A transparent proxy MUST NOT modify the following field in a response:

- Expires

It MAY add this field if not already present. If an Expires header is added, it MUST be given a field-value identical to that of the Date header in that response.

A proxy MUST NOT modify or add any of the following fields in a message that contains the no-transform cache-control directive, or in any request:

- Content-Encoding
- Content-Range
- Content-Type

A non-transparent proxy MAY modify or add these fields to a message that does not include no-transform, but if it does so, it MUST add a Warning 214 (Transformation applied) if one does not already appear in the message (see section 14.46).

> Warning: Unnecessary modification of end-to-end headers might cause authentication failures if stronger authentication mechanisms are introduced in later versions of HTTP. Such authentication mechanisms MAY rely on the values of header fields not listed here.

The Content-Length field of a request or response is added or deleted according to the rules in section 4.4. A transparent proxy MUST preserve the entity-length (section 7.2.2) of the entity-body, although it MAY change the transfer-length (section 4.4).

13.5.3 Combining Headers

When a cache makes a validating request to a server, and the server provides a 304 (Not Modified) response or a 206 (Partial Content) response, the cache then constructs a response to send to the requesting client.

If the status code is 304 (Not Modified), the cache uses the entity-body stored in the cache entry as the entity-body of this outgoing response. If the status code is 206 (Partial Content) and the ETag or Last-Modified headers match exactly, the cache MAY combine the contents stored in the cache entry with the new contents received in the response and use the result as the entity-body of this outgoing response (see 13.5.4).

The end-to-end headers stored in the cache entry are used for the constructed response, except that

- any stored Warning headers with warn-code 1xx (see section 14.46) MUST be deleted from the cache entry and the forwarded response.

- any stored Warning headers with warn-code 2xx MUST be retained in the cache entry and the forwarded response.

- any end-to-end headers provided in the 304 or 206 response MUST replace the corresponding headers from the cache entry.

Unless the cache decides to remove the cache entry, it MUST also replace the end-to-end headers stored with the cache entry with corresponding headers received in the incoming response, except for Warning headers as described immediately above. If a header field-name in the incoming response matches more than one header in the cache entry, all such old headers MUST be replaced.

In other words, the set of end-to-end headers received in the incoming response overrides all corresponding end-to-end headers stored with the cache entry (except for stored Warning headers with warn-code 1xx, which are deleted even if not over-ridden).

> **Note:** This rule allows an origin server to use a 304 (Not Modified) or a 206 (Partial Content) response to update any header associated with a previous response for the same entity or subranges thereof, although it might not always be meaningful or correct to do so. This rule does not allow an origin server to use a 304 (Not Modified) or a 206 (Partial Content) response to entirely delete a header that it had provided with a previous response.

13.5.4 Combining Byte Ranges

A response might transfer only a subrange of the bytes of an entity-body, either because the request included one or more Range specifications, or because a connection was broken prematurely. After several such transfers, a cache might have received several ranges of the same entity-body.

If a cache has a stored non-empty set of subranges for an entity, and an incoming response transfers another subrange, the cache MAY combine the new subrange with the existing set if both the following conditions are met:

- Both the incoming response and the cache entry have a cache validator.

- The two cache validators match using the strong comparison function (see section 13.3.3).

If either requirement is not met, the cache MUST use only the most recent partial response (based on the Date values transmitted with every response, and using the incoming response if these values are equal or missing), and MUST discard the other partial information.

13.6 Caching Negotiated Responses

Use of server-driven content negotiation (section 12.1), as indicated by the presence of a Vary header field in a response, alters the conditions and procedure by which a cache can use the response for subsequent requests. See section 14.44 for use of the Vary header field by servers.

A server SHOULD use the Vary header field to inform a cache of what request-header fields were used to select among multiple representations of a cacheable response subject to server-driven negotiation. The set of header fields named by the Vary field value is known as the "selecting" request-headers.

When the cache receives a subsequent request whose Request-URI specifies one or more cache entries including a Vary header field, the cache MUST NOT use such a cache entry to construct a response to the new request unless all of the selecting request-headers present in the new request match the corresponding stored request-headers in the original request.

The selecting request-headers from two requests are defined to match if and only if the selecting request-headers in the first request can be transformed to the selecting request-headers in the second request by adding or removing linear white space (LWS) at places where this is allowed by the corresponding BNF, and/or combining multiple message-header fields with the same field name following the rules about message headers in section 4.2.

A Vary header field-value of "*" always fails to match and subsequent requests on that resource can only be properly interpreted by the origin server.

If the selecting request header fields for the cached entry do not match the selecting request header fields of the new request, then the cache MUST NOT use a cached entry to satisfy the request unless it first relays the new request to the origin server in a conditional request and the server responds with 304 (Not Modified), including an entity tag or Content-Location that indicates the entity to be used.

If an entity tag was assigned to a cached representation, the forwarded request SHOULD be conditional and include the entity tags in an If-None-Match header field from all its cache entries for the resource. This conveys to the server the set of entities currently held by the cache, so that if any one of these entities matches the requested entity, the server can use the ETag header field in its 304 (Not Modified) response to tell the cache which entry is appropriate. If the entity-tag of the new response matches that of an existing entry, the new response SHOULD be used to update the header fields of the existing entry, and the result MUST be returned to the client.

If any of the existing cache entries contains only partial content for the associated entity, its entity-tag SHOULD NOT be included in the If-None-Match header field unless the request is for a range that would be fully satisfied by that entry.

If a cache receives a successful response whose Content-Location field matches that of an existing cache entry for the same Request-URI, whose entity-tag differs from that of the existing entry, and whose Date is more recent than that of the existing entry, the existing entry SHOULD NOT be returned in response to future requests and SHOULD be deleted from the cache.

13.7 Shared and Non-shared Caches

For reasons of security and privacy, it is necessary to make a distinction between "shared" and "non-shared" caches. A non-shared cache is one that is accessible only to a single user. Accessibility in this case SHOULD be enforced by appropriate security mechanisms. All other caches are considered to be "shared." Other sections of this specification place certain constraints on the operation of shared caches in order to prevent loss of privacy or failure of access controls.

13.8 Errors or Incomplete Response Cache Behavior

A cache that receives an incomplete response (for example, with fewer bytes of data than specified in a Content-Length header) MAY store the response. However, the cache MUST treat this as a partial response. Partial responses MAY be combined as described in section 13.5.4; the result might be a full response or might still be partial. A cache MUST NOT return a partial response to a client without explicitly marking it as such, using the 206 (Partial Content) status code. A cache MUST NOT return a partial response using a status code of 200 (OK).

If a cache receives a 5xx response while attempting to revalidate an entry, it MAY either forward this response to the requesting client or act as if the server failed to respond. In the latter case, it MAY return a previously received response unless the cached entry includes the "must-revalidate" cache-control directive (see section 14.9).

13.9 Side Effects of GET and HEAD

Unless the origin server explicitly prohibits the caching of their responses, the application of GET and HEAD methods to any resources SHOULD NOT have side effects that would lead to erroneous behavior if these responses are taken from a cache. They MAY still have side effects, but a cache is not required to consider such side effects in its caching decisions. Caches are always expected to observe an origin server's explicit restrictions on caching.

We note one exception to this rule: Since some applications have traditionally used GETs and HEADs with query URLs (those containing a "?" in the rel_path part) to perform operations with significant side effects, caches MUST NOT treat responses to such URIs as fresh unless the server provides an explicit expiration time. This specifically means that responses from HTTP/1.0 servers for such URIs SHOULD NOT be taken from a cache. See section 9.1.1 for related information.

13.10 Invalidation After Updates or Deletions

The effect of certain methods performed on a resource at the origin server might cause one or more existing cache entries to become non-transparently invalid. That is, although they might continue to be "fresh," they do not accurately reflect what the origin server would return for a new request on that resource.

There is no way for the HTTP protocol to guarantee that all such cache entries are marked invalid. For example, the request that caused the change at the origin server might not have gone through the proxy where a cache entry is stored. However, several rules help reduce the likelihood of erroneous behavior.

In this section, the phrase "invalidate an entity" means that the cache will either remove all instances of that entity from its storage or will mark these as "invalid" and in need of a mandatory revalidation before they can be returned in response to a subsequent request.

Some HTTP methods MUST cause a cache to invalidate an entity. This is either the entity referred to by the Request-URI or by the Location or Content-Location headers (if present). These methods are

- PUT

- DELETE

- POST

In order to prevent denial of service attacks, an invalidation based on the URI in a Location or Content-Location header MUST only be performed if the host part is the same as in the Request-URI.

A cache that passes through requests for methods it does not understand SHOULD invalidate any entities referred to by the Request-URI.

13.11 Write-Through Mandatory

All methods that might be expected to cause modifications to the origin server's resources MUST be written through to the origin server. This currently includes all methods except for GET and HEAD. A cache MUST NOT reply to such a request from a client before having transmitted the request to the inbound server, and having received a corresponding response from the inbound server. This does not prevent a proxy cache from sending a 100 (Continue) response before the inbound server has sent its final reply. The alternative (known as "write-back" or "copy-back" caching) is not allowed in HTTP/1.1, due to the difficulty of providing consistent updates and the problems arising from server, cache, or network failure prior to write-back.

13.12 Cache Replacement

If a new cacheable (see sections 14.9.2, 13.2.5, 13.2.6, and 13.8) response is received from a resource while any existing responses for the same resource are cached, the cache SHOULD use the new response to reply to the current request. It MAY insert it into cache storage and MAY, if it meets all other requirements, use it to respond to any future requests that would previously have caused the old response to be returned. If it inserts the new response into cache storage the rules in section 13.5.3 apply.

> **Note:** A new response that has an older Date header value than existing cached responses is not cacheable.

13.13 History Lists

User agents often have history mechanisms, such as "Back" buttons and history lists, which can be used to redisplay an entity retrieved earlier in a session.

History mechanisms and caches are different. In particular, history mechanisms SHOULD NOT try to show a semantically transparent view of the current state of a resource. Rather, a history mechanism is meant to show exactly what the user saw at the time when the resource was retrieved.

By default, an expiration time does not apply to history mechanisms. If the entity is still in storage, a history mechanism SHOULD display it even if the entity has expired, unless the user has specifically configured the agent to refresh expired history documents.

This is not to be construed to prohibit the history mechanism from telling the user that a view might be stale.

> **Note:** If history list mechanisms unnecessarily prevent users from viewing stale resources, this will tend to force service authors to avoid using HTTP expiration controls and cache controls when they would otherwise like to. Service authors may consider it important that users not be presented with error messages or warning messages when they use navigation controls (such as BACK) to view previously fetched resources. Even though sometimes such resources ought not to be cached, or ought to expire quickly, user interface considerations may force service authors to resort to other means of preventing caching (e.g., "once-only" URLs) in order not to suffer the effects of improperly functioning history mechanisms.

14 Header Field Definitions

This section defines the syntax and semantics of all standard HTTP/1.1 header fields. For entity-header fields, both sender and recipient refer to either the client or the server, depending on who sends and who receives the entity.

14.1 Accept

The Accept request-header field can be used to specify certain media types which are acceptable for the response. Accept headers can be used to indicate that the request is specifically limited to a small set of desired types, as in the case of a request for an inline image.

```
Accept      = "Accept" ":"
              #( media-range [ accept-params ] )
media-range = ( "*/*"
              | ( type "/" "*" )
              | ( type "/" subtype )
              ) *( ";" parameter )
accept-params = ";" "q" "=" qvalue *( accept-extension )
accept-extension = ";" token [ "=" ( token | quoted-string ) ]
```

The asterisk "*" character is used to group media types into ranges, with "*/*" indicating all media types and "type/*" indicating all subtypes of that type. The media-range MAY include media type parameters that are applicable to that range.

Each media-range MAY be followed by one or more accept-params, beginning with the "q" parameter for indicating a relative quality factor. The first "q" parameter (if any) separates the media-range parameter(s) from the accept-params. Quality factors allow the user or user agent to indicate the relative degree of preference for that media-range, using the qvalue scale from 0 to 1 (section 3.9). The default value is q=1.

> **Note:** Use of the "q" parameter name to separate media type parameters from Accept extension parameters is due to historical practice. Although this prevents any media type parameter named "q" from being used with a media range, such an event is believed to be unlikely given the lack of any "q" parameters in the IANA media type registry and the rare usage of any media type parameters in Accept. Future media types are discouraged from registering any parameter named "q".

The example

```
Accept: audio/*; q=0.2, audio/basic
```

SHOULD be interpreted as "I prefer audio/basic, but send me any audio type if it is the best available after an 80% markdown in quality."

If no Accept header field is present, then it is assumed that the client accepts all media types. If an Accept header field is present, and if the server cannot send a response which is acceptable according to the combined Accept field value, then the server SHOULD send a 406 (not acceptable) response.

A more elaborate example is

```
Accept: text/plain; q=0.5, text/html, text/x-dvi; q=0.8, text/x-c
```

Verbally, this would be interpreted as "text/html and text/x-c are the preferred media types, but if they do not exist, then send the text/x-dvi entity, and if that does not exist, send the text/plain entity."

Media ranges can be overridden by more specific media ranges or specific media types. If more than one media range applies to a given type, the most specific reference has precedence. For example,

```
Accept: text/*, text/html, text/html;level=1, */*
```

have the following precedence:

1. text/html;level=1

2. text/html

3. text/*

4. */*

The media type quality factor associated with a given type is determined by finding the media range with the highest precedence which matches that type. For example,

```
Accept: text/*;q=0.3, text/html;q=0.7, text/html;level=1,
    text/html;level=2;q=0.4, */*;q=0.5
```

would cause the following values to be associated:

text/html;level=1 = 1

text/html   = 0.7

text/plain   = 0.3

image/jpeg   = 0.5

text/html;level=2 = 0.4

text/html;level=3 = 0.7

Note: A user agent might be provided with a default set of quality values for certain media ranges. However, unless the user agent is a closed system which cannot interact with other rendering agents, this default set ought to be configurable by the user.

14.2 Accept-Charset

The Accept-Charset request-header field can be used to indicate what character sets are acceptable for the response. This field allows clients capable of understanding more comprehensive or special-purpose character sets to signal that capability to a server which is capable of representing documents in those character sets.

```
Accept-Charset = "Accept-Charset" ":" 1#( ( charset | "*" )[ ";" "q" "=" qvalue ] )
```

Character set values are described in section 3.4. Each charset MAY be given an associated quality value which represents the user's preference for that charset. The default value is q=1. An example is

```
Accept-Charset: iso-8859-5, unicode-1-1;q=0.8
```

The special value "*", if present in the Accept-Charset field, matches every character set (including ISO-8859-1) which is not mentioned elsewhere in the Accept-Charset field. If no "*" is present in an Accept-Charset field, then all character sets not explicitly mentioned get a quality value of 0, except for ISO-8859-1, which gets a quality value of 1 if not explicitly mentioned.

If no Accept-Charset header is present, the default is that any character set is acceptable. If an Accept-Charset header is present, and if the server cannot send a response which is acceptable according to the Accept-Charset header, then the server SHOULD send an error response with the 406 (not acceptable) status code, though the sending of an unacceptable response is also allowed.

14.3 Accept-Encoding

The Accept-Encoding request-header field is similar to Accept, but restricts the content-codings (section 3.5) that are acceptable in the response.

```
Accept-Encoding = "Accept-Encoding" ":"
                  1#( codings [ ";" "q" "=" qvalue ] )
codings         = ( content-coding | "*" )
```

Examples of its use are:

```
Accept-Encoding: compress, gzip
Accept-Encoding:
Accept-Encoding: *
Accept-Encoding: compress;q=0.5, gzip;q=1.0
Accept-Encoding: gzip;q=1.0, identity; q=0.5, *;q=0
```

A server tests whether a content-coding is acceptable, according to an Accept-Encoding field, using these rules:

1. If the content-coding is one of the content-codings listed in the Accept-Encoding field, then it is acceptable, unless it is accompanied by a qvalue of 0. (As defined in section 3.9, a qvalue of 0 means "not acceptable.")

2. The special "*" symbol in an Accept-Encoding field matches any available content-coding not explicitly listed in the header field.

3. If multiple content-codings are acceptable, then the acceptable content-coding with the highest non-zero qvalue is preferred.

4. The "identity" content-coding is always acceptable, unless specifically refused because the Accept-Encoding field includes "identity;q=0", or because the field includes "*;q=0" and does not explicitly include the "identity" content-coding. If the Accept-Encoding field-value is empty, then only the "identity" encoding is acceptable.

If an Accept-Encoding field is present in a request, and if the server cannot send a response which is acceptable according to the Accept-Encoding header, then the server SHOULD send an error response with the 406 (Not Acceptable) status code.

If no Accept-Encoding field is present in a request, the server MAY assume that the client will accept any content coding. In this case, if "identity" is one of the available content-codings, then the server SHOULD use the "identity" content-coding, unless it has additional information that a different content-coding is meaningful to the client.

> **Note:** If the request does not include an Accept-Encoding field, and if the "identity" content-coding is unavailable, then content-codings commonly understood by HTTP/1.0 clients (i.e., "gzip" and "compress") are preferred; some older clients improperly display messages sent with other content-codings. The server might also make this decision based on information about the particular user agent or client.

> **Note:** Most HTTP/1.0 applications do not recognize or obey qvalues associated with content-codings. This means that qvalues will not work and are not permitted with x-gzip or x-compress.

14.4 Accept-Language

The Accept-Language request-header field is similar to Accept, but restricts the set of natural languages that are preferred as a response to the request. Language tags are defined in section 3.10.

```
Accept-Language = "Accept-Language" ":"
         1#( language-range [ ";" "q" "=" qvalue ] )
language-range = ( ( 1*8ALPHA *( "-" 1*8ALPHA ) ) | "*" )
```

Each language-range MAY be given an associated quality value which represents an estimate of the user's preference for the languages specified by that range. The quality value defaults to "q=1". For example,

```
Accept-Language: da, en-gb;q=0.8, en;q=0.7
```

would mean: "I prefer Danish, but will accept British English and other types of English." A language-range matches a language-tag if it exactly equals the tag, or if it exactly equals a prefix of the tag such that the first tag character following the prefix is "-". The special range "*", if present in the Accept-Language field, matches every tag not matched by any other range present in the Accept-Language field.

> **Note:** This use of a prefix matching rule does not imply that language tags are assigned to languages in such a way that it is always true that if a user understands a language with a certain tag, then this user will also understand all languages with tags for which this tag is a prefix. The prefix rule simply allows the use of prefix tags if this is the case.

The language quality factor assigned to a language-tag by the Accept-Language field is the quality value of the longest language-range in the field that matches the language-tag. If no language-range in the field matches the tag, the language quality factor assigned is 0. If no Accept-Language header is present in the request, the server SHOULD assume that all languages are equally acceptable. If an Accept-Language header is present, then all languages which are assigned a quality factor greater than 0 are acceptable.

It might be contrary to the privacy expectations of the user to send an Accept-Language header with the complete linguistic preferences of the user in every request. For a discussion of this issue, see section 15.1.4.

As intelligibility is highly dependent on the individual user, it is recommended that client applications make the choice of linguistic preference available to the user. If the choice is not made available, then the Accept-Language header field MUST NOT be given in the request.

> **Note:** When making the choice of linguistic preference available to the user, we remind implementers of the fact that users are not familiar with the details of language matching as described above, so they should provide appropriate guidance. As an example, users might assume that on selecting "en-gb", they will be served any kind of English document if British English is not available. A user agent might suggest in such a case to add "en" to get the best matching behavior.

14.5 Accept-Ranges

The Accept-Ranges response-header field allows the server to indicate its acceptance of range requests for a resource:

```
Accept-Ranges    = "Accept-Ranges" ":" acceptable-ranges
acceptable-ranges = 1#range-unit | "none"
```

Origin servers that accept byte-range requests MAY send

```
Accept-Ranges: bytes
```

but are not required to do so. Clients MAY generate byte-range requests without having received this header for the resource involved. Range units are defined in section 3.12.

Servers that do not accept any kind of range request for a resource MAY send

```
Accept-Ranges: none
```

to advise the client not to attempt a range request.

14.6 Age

The Age response-header field conveys the sender's estimate of the amount of time since the response (or its revalidation) was generated at the origin server. A cached response is "fresh" if its age does not exceed its freshness lifetime. Age values are calculated as specified in section 13.2.3.

```
Age = "Age" ":" age-value
age-value = delta-seconds
```

Age values are non-negative decimal integers, representing time in seconds.

If a cache receives a value larger than the largest positive integer it can represent, or if any of its age calculations overflows, it MUST transmit an Age header with a value of 2147483648 (2^{31}). An HTTP/1.1 server that includes a cache MUST include an Age header field in every response generated from its own cache. Caches SHOULD use an arithmetic type of at least 31 bits of range.

14.7 Allow

The Allow entity-header field lists the set of methods supported by the resource identified by the Request-URI. The purpose of this field is strictly to inform the recipient of valid methods associated with the resource. An Allow header field MUST be present in a 405 (Method Not Allowed) response.

```
Allow  = "Allow" ":" #Method
```

Example of use:

```
Allow: GET, HEAD, PUT
```

This field cannot prevent a client from trying other methods. However, the indications given by the Allow header field-value SHOULD be followed. The actual set of allowed methods is defined by the origin server at the time of each request.

The Allow header field MAY be provided with a PUT request to recommend the methods to be supported by the new or modified resource. The server is not required to support these methods and SHOULD include an Allow header in the response giving the actual supported methods.

A proxy MUST NOT modify the Allow header field even if it does not understand all the methods specified, since the user agent might have other means of communicating with the origin server.

14.8 Authorization

A user agent that wishes to authenticate itself with a server—usually, but not necessarily, after receiving a 401 response—does so by including an Authorization request-header field with the request. The Authorization field value consists of credentials containing the authentication information of the user agent for the realm of the resource being requested.

```
Authorization = "Authorization" ":" credentials
```

HTTP access authentication is described in "HTTP Authentication: Basic and Digest Access Authentication" [43]. If a request is authenticated and a realm specified, the same credentials SHOULD be valid for all other requests within this realm (assuming that the authentication scheme itself does not require otherwise, such as credentials that vary according to a challenge value or using synchronized clocks).

When a shared cache (see section 13.7) receives a request containing an Authorization field, it MUST NOT return the corresponding response as a reply to any other request, unless one of the following specific exceptions holds:

1. If the response includes the "s-maxage" cache-control directive, the cache MAY use that response in replying to a subsequent request. But (if the specified maximum age has passed) a proxy cache MUST first revalidate it with the origin server, using the request-headers from the new request to allow the origin server to authenticate the new request. (This is the defined behavior for s-maxage.) If the response includes "s-maxage=0", the proxy MUST always revalidate it before reusing it.

2. If the response includes the "must-revalidate" cache-control directive, the cache MAY use that response in replying to a subsequent request. But if the response is stale, all caches MUST first revalidate it with the origin server, using the request-headers from the new request to allow the origin server to authenticate the new request.

3. If the response includes the "public" cache-control directive, it MAY be returned in reply to any subsequent request.

14.9 Cache-Control

The Cache-Control general-header field is used to specify directives that MUST be obeyed by all caching mechanisms along the request/response chain. The directives specify behavior intended to prevent caches from adversely interfering with the request or response. These directives typically override the default caching algorithms. Cache directives are unidirectional in that the presence of a directive in a request does not imply that the same directive is to be given in the response.

> Note that HTTP/1.0 caches might not implement Cache-Control and might only implement Pragma: no-cache (see section 14.32).

Cache directives MUST be passed through by a proxy or gateway application, regardless of their significance to that application, since the directives might be applicable to all recipients along the request/response chain. It is not possible to specify a cache-directive for a specific cache.

```
Cache-Control  = "Cache-Control" ":" 1#cache-directive

cache-directive = cache-request-directive
   | cache-response-directive
```

```
cache-request-directive =
    "no-cache"                              ; Section 14.9.1
  | "no-store"                              ; Section 14.9.2
  | "max-age" "=" delta-seconds            ; Section 14.9.3, 14.9.4
  | "max-stale" [ "=" delta-seconds ]      ; Section 14.9.3
  | "min-fresh" "=" delta-seconds          ; Section 14.9.3
  | "no-transform"                          ; Section 14.9.5
  | "only-if-cached"                        ; Section 14.9.4
  | cache-extension                         ; Section 14.9.6

cache-response-directive =
    "public"                                ; Section 14.9.1
  | "private" [ "=" <"> 1#field-name <"> ] ; Section 14.9.1
  | "no-cache" [ "=" <"> 1#field-name <"> ]; Section 14.9.1
  | "no-store"                              ; Section 14.9.2
  | "no-transform"                          ; Section 14.9.5
  | "must-revalidate"                       ; Section 14.9.4
  | "proxy-revalidate"                      ; Section 14.9.4
  | "max-age" "=" delta-seconds            ; Section 14.9.3
  | "s-maxage" "=" delta-seconds           ; Section 14.9.3
  | cache-extension                         ; Section 14.9.6

cache-extension = token [ "=" ( token | quoted-string ) ]
```

When a directive appears without any 1#field-name parameter, the directive applies to the entire request or response. When such a directive appears with a 1#field-name parameter, it applies only to the named field or fields, and not to the rest of the request or response. This mechanism supports extensibility; implementations of future versions of the HTTP protocol might apply these directives to header fields not defined in HTTP/1.1.

The cache-control directives can be broken down into these general categories:

- Restrictions on what are cacheable; these may only be imposed by the origin server.

- Restrictions on what may be stored by a cache; these may be imposed by either the origin server or the user agent.

- Modifications of the basic expiration mechanism; these may be imposed by either the origin server or the user agent.

- Controls over cache revalidation and reload; these may only be imposed by a user agent.

- Control over transformation of entities.

- Extensions to the caching system.

14.9.1 What Is Cacheable

By default, a response is cacheable if the requirements of the request method, request header fields, and the response status indicate that it is cacheable. Section 13.4 summarizes these defaults for cacheability. The following Cache-Control response directives allow an origin server to override the default cacheability of a response.

public

Indicates that the response MAY be cached by any cache, even if it would normally be non-cacheable or cacheable only within a non-shared cache. (See also Authorization, section 14.8, for additional details.)

private

Indicates that all or part of the response message is intended for a single user and MUST NOT be cached by a shared cache. This allows an origin server to state that the specified parts of the response are intended for only one user and are not a valid response for requests by other users. A private (non-shared) cache MAY cache the response.

> **Note:** This usage of the word "private" only controls where the response may be cached, and cannot ensure the privacy of the message content.

no-cache

If the no-cache directive does not specify a field-name, then a cache MUST NOT use the response to satisfy a subsequent request without successful revalidation with the origin server. This allows an origin server to prevent caching even by caches that have been configured to return stale responses to client requests.

If the no-cache directive does specify one or more field-names, then a cache MAY use the response to satisfy a subsequent request, subject to any other restrictions on caching. However, the specified field-name(s) MUST NOT be sent in the response to a subsequent request without successful revalidation with the origin server. This allows an origin server to prevent the reuse of certain header fields in a response, while still allowing caching of the rest of the response.

> **Note:** Most HTTP/1.0 caches will not recognize or obey this directive.

14.9.2 What May Be Stored by Caches

no-store

The purpose of the no-store directive is to prevent the inadvertent release or retention of sensitive information (for example, on backup tapes). The no-store directive applies to the entire message and MAY be sent either in a response or in a request. If sent in a request, a cache MUST NOT store any part of either this request or any response to it. If sent in a response, a cache MUST NOT store any part of either this response or the request that elicited it. This directive applies to both non-shared and shared caches. "MUST NOT store" in this context means that the cache MUST NOT intentionally store the information in nonvolatile storage, and MUST make a best-effort attempt to remove the information from volatile storage as promptly as possible after forwarding it.

Even when this directive is associated with a response, users might explicitly store such a response outside of the caching system (e.g., with a "Save As" dialog). History buffers MAY store such responses as part of their normal operation.

The purpose of this directive is to meet the stated requirements of certain users and service authors who are concerned about accidental releases of information via unanticipated accesses to cache data structures. While the use of this directive might improve privacy in some cases, we caution that it is NOT in any way a reliable or sufficient mechanism for ensuring privacy. In particular, malicious or compromised caches might not recognize or obey this directive, and communications networks might be vulnerable to eavesdropping.

14.9.3 Modifications of the Basic Expiration Mechanism

The expiration time of an entity MAY be specified by the origin server using the Expires header (see section 14.21). Alternatively, it MAY be specified using the max-age directive in a response. When the max-age cache-control directive is present in a cached response, the response is stale if its current age is greater than the age value given (in seconds) at the time of a new request for that resource. The max-age directive on a response implies that the response is cacheable (i.e., "public") unless some other, more restrictive cache directive is also present.

If a response includes both an Expires header and a max-age directive, the max-age directive overrides the Expires header, even if the Expires header is more restrictive. This rule allows an origin server to provide, for a given response, a longer expiration time to an HTTP/1.1 (or later) cache than to an HTTP/1.0 cache. This might be useful if certain HTTP/1.0 caches improperly calculate ages or expiration times, perhaps due to desynchronized clocks.

Many HTTP/1.0 cache implementations will treat an Expires value that is less than or equal to the response Date value as being equivalent to the Cache-Control response directive "no-cache." If an HTTP/1.1 cache receives such a response, and the response does not include a Cache-Control header field, it SHOULD consider the response to be non-cacheable in order to retain compatibility with HTTP/1.0 servers.

> **Note:** An origin server might wish to use a relatively new HTTP cache control feature, such as the "private" directive, on a network including older caches that do not understand that feature. The origin server will need to combine the new feature with an Expires field whose value is less than or equal to the Date value. This will prevent older caches from improperly caching the response.

s-maxage

If a response includes an s-maxage directive, then for a shared cache (but not for a private cache), the maximum age specified by this directive overrides the maximum age specified by either the max-age directive or the Expires header. The s-maxage directive also implies the semantics of the proxy-revalidate directive (see section 14.9.4)—i.e., that the shared cache must not use the entry after it becomes stale to respond to a subsequent request without first revalidating it with the origin server. The s-maxage directive is always ignored by a private cache.

Note that most older caches, not compliant with this specification, do not implement any cache-control directives. An origin server wishing to use a cache-control directive that restricts, but does not prevent, caching by an HTTP/1.1-compliant cache MAY exploit the requirement that the max-age directive overrides the Expires header, and the fact that pre-HTTP/1.1-compliant caches do not observe the max-age directive.

Other directives allow a user agent to modify the basic expiration mechanism. These directives MAY be specified on a request:

max-age

Indicates that the client is willing to accept a response whose age is no greater than the specified time in seconds. Unless the max-stale directive is also included, the client is not willing to accept a stale response.

min-fresh

Indicates that the client is willing to accept a response whose freshness lifetime is no less than its current age plus the specified time in seconds. That is, the client wants a response that will still be fresh for at least the specified number of seconds.

max-stale

Indicates that the client is willing to accept a response that has exceeded its expiration time. If max-stale is assigned a value, then the client is willing to accept a response that has exceeded its expiration time by no more than the specified number of seconds. If no value is assigned to max-stale, then the client is willing to accept a stale response of any age.

If a cache returns a stale response, either because of a max-stale directive on a request, or because the cache is configured to override the expiration time of a response, the cache MUST attach a Warning header to the stale response, using Warning 110 (Response is stale).

A cache MAY be configured to return stale responses without validation, but only if this does not conflict with any "MUST"-level requirements concerning cache validation (e.g., a "must-revalidate" cache-control directive).

If both the new request and the cached entry include "max-age" directives, then the lesser of the two values is used for determining the freshness of the cached entry for that request.

14.9.4 Cache Revalidation and Reload Controls

Sometimes a user agent might want or need to insist that a cache revalidate its cache entry with the origin server (and not just with the next cache along the path to the origin server), or to reload its cache entry from the origin server. End-to-end revalidation might be necessary if either the cache or the origin server has overestimated the expiration time of the cached response. End-to-end reload may be necessary if the cache entry has become corrupted for some reason.

End-to-end revalidation may be requested either when the client does not have its own local cached copy, in which case we call it "unspecified end-to-end revalidation," or when the client does have a local cached copy, in which case we call it "specific end-to-end revalidation."

The client can specify these three kinds of action using Cache-Control request directives:

End-to-end reload

The request includes a "no-cache" cache-control directive or, for compatibility with HTTP/1.0 clients, "Pragma: no-cache." Field names MUST NOT be included with the no-cache directive in a request. The server MUST NOT use a cached copy when responding to such a request.

Specific end-to-end revalidation

The request includes a "max-age=0" cache-control directive, which forces each cache along the path to the origin server to revalidate its own entry, if any, with the next cache or server. The initial request includes a cache-validating conditional with the client's current validator.

Unspecified end-to-end revalidation

The request includes a "max-age=0" cache-control directive, which forces each cache along the path to the origin server to revalidate its own entry, if any, with the next cache or server. The initial request does not include a cache-validating conditional; the first cache along the path (if any) that holds a cache entry for this resource includes a cache-validating conditional with its current validator.

max-age

When an intermediate cache is forced, by means of a max-age=0 directive, to revalidate its own cache entry, and the client has supplied its own validator in the request, the supplied validator might differ from the validator currently stored with the cache entry. In this case, the cache MAY use either validator in making its own request without affecting semantic transparency.

However, the choice of validator might affect performance. The best approach is for the intermediate cache to use its own validator when making its request. If the server replies with 304 (Not Modified), then the cache can return its now validated copy to the client with a 200 (OK) response. If the server replies with a new entity and cache validator, however, the intermediate cache can compare the returned validator with the one provided in the client's request, using the strong comparison function. If the client's validator is equal to the origin server's, then the intermediate cache simply returns 304 (Not Modified). Otherwise, it returns the new entity with a 200 (OK) response.

If a request includes the no-cache directive, it SHOULD NOT include min-fresh, max-stale, or max-age.

only-if-cached

In some cases, such as times of extremely poor network connectivity, a client may want a cache to return only those responses that it currently has stored, and not to reload or revalidate with the origin server. To do this, the client may include the only-if-cached directive in a request. If it receives this directive, a cache SHOULD either respond using a cached entry that is consistent with the other constraints of the request, or respond with a 504 (Gateway Timeout) status. However, if a group of caches is being operated as a unified system with good internal connectivity, such a request MAY be forwarded within that group of caches.

must-revalidate

Because a cache MAY be configured to ignore a server's specified expiration time, and because a client request MAY include a max-stale directive (which has a similar effect), the protocol also includes a mechanism for the origin server to require revalidation of a cache entry on any subsequent use. When the must-revalidate directive is present in a response received by a cache, that cache MUST NOT use the entry after it becomes stale to respond to a subsequent request without first revalidating it with the origin server (i.e., the cache MUST do an end-to-end revalidation every time, if, based solely on the origin server's Expires or max-age value, the cached response is stale).

The must-revalidate directive is necessary to support reliable operation for certain protocol features. In all circumstances, an HTTP/1.1 cache MUST obey the must-revalidate directive; in particular, if the cache cannot reach the origin server for any reason, it MUST generate a 504 (Gateway Timeout) response.

Servers SHOULD send the must-revalidate directive if and only if failure to revalidate a request on the entity could result in incorrect operation, such as a silently unexecuted financial transaction. Recipients MUST NOT take any automated action that violates this directive, and MUST NOT automatically provide an unvalidated copy of the entity if revalidation fails.

Although this is not recommended, user agents operating under severe connectivity constraints MAY violate this directive but, if so, MUST explicitly warn the user that an unvalidated response has been provided. The warning MUST be provided on each unvalidated access, and SHOULD require explicit user confirmation.

proxy-revalidate

The proxy-revalidate directive has the same meaning as the must-revalidate directive, except that it does not apply to non-shared user agent caches. It can be used on a response to an authenticated request to permit the user's cache to store and later return the response without needing to revalidate it (since it has already been authenticated once by that user), while still requiring proxies that service many users to revalidate each time (in order to make sure that each user has been authenticated). Note that such authenticated responses also need the public cache control directive in order to allow them to be cached at all.

14.9.5 No-Transform Directive

no-transform

Implementers of intermediate caches (proxies) have found it useful to convert the media type of certain entity bodies. A non-transparent proxy might, for example, convert between image formats in order to save cache space or to reduce the amount of traffic on a slow link.

Serious operational problems occur, however, when these transformations are applied to entity bodies intended for certain kinds of applications. For example, applications for medical imaging, scientific data analysis, and those using end-to-end authentication all depend on receiving an entity body that is bit-for-bit identical to the original entity-body.

Therefore, if a message includes the no-transform directive, an intermediate cache or proxy MUST NOT change those headers that are listed in section 13.5.2 as being subject to the no-transform directive. This implies that the cache or proxy MUST NOT change any aspect of the entity-body that is specified by these headers, including the value of the entity-body itself.

14.9.6 Cache Control Extensions

The Cache-Control header field can be extended through the use of one or more cache-extension tokens, each with an optional assigned value. Informational extensions (those which do not require a change in cache behavior) MAY be added without changing the semantics of other directives. Behavioral extensions are designed to work by acting as modifiers to the existing base of cache directives. Both the new directive and the standard directive are supplied, such that applications which do not understand the new directive will default to the behavior specified by the standard directive, and those that understand the new directive will recognize it as modifying the requirements associated with the standard directive. In this way, extensions to the cache-control directives can be made without requiring changes to the base protocol.

This extension mechanism depends on an HTTP cache obeying all of the cache-control directives defined for its native HTTP-version, obeying certain extensions, and ignoring all directives that it does not understand.

For example, consider a hypothetical new response directive called community which acts as a modifier to the private directive. We define this new directive to mean that, in addition to any non-shared cache, any cache which is shared only by members of the community named within its value may cache the response. An origin server wishing to allow the UCI community to use an otherwise private response in their shared cache(s) could do so by including

```
Cache-Control: private, community="UCI"
```

A cache seeing this header field will act correctly even if the cache does not understand the community cache-extension, since it will also see and understand the private directive and thus default to the safe behavior.

Unrecognized cache-directives MUST be ignored; it is assumed that any cache-directive likely to be unrecognized by an HTTP/1.1 cache will be combined with standard directives (or the response's default cacheability) such that the cache behavior will remain minimally correct even if the cache does not understand the extension(s).

14.10 Connection

The Connection general-header field allows the sender to specify options that are desired for that particular connection and MUST NOT be communicated by proxies over further connections.

The Connection header has the following grammar:

```
Connection = "Connection" ":" 1#(connection-token)
connection-token = token
```

HTTP/1.1 proxies MUST parse the Connection header field before a message is forwarded and, for each connection-token in this field, remove any header field(s) from the message with the same name as the connection-token. Connection options are signaled by the presence of a connection-token in the Connection header field, not by any corresponding additional header field(s), since the additional header field may not be sent if there are no parameters associated with that connection option.

Message headers listed in the Connection header MUST NOT include end-to-end headers, such as Cache-Control.

HTTP/1.1 defines the "close" connection option for the sender to signal that the connection will be closed after completion of the response. For example,

```
Connection: close
```

in either the request or the response header fields indicates that the connection SHOULD NOT be considered "persistent" (section 8.1) after the current request/response is complete.

HTTP/1.1 applications that do not support persistent connections MUST include the "close" connection option in every message.

A system receiving an HTTP/1.0 (or lower-version) message that includes a Connection header MUST, for each connection-token in this field, remove and ignore any header field(s) from the message with the same name as the connection-token. This protects against mistaken forwarding of such header fields by pre-HTTP/1.1 proxies. See section 19.6.2.

14.11 Content-Encoding

The Content-Encoding entity-header field is used as a modifier to the media-type. When present, its value indicates what additional content-codings have been applied to the entity-body, and thus what decoding mechanisms must be applied in order to obtain the media-type referenced by the Content-Type header field. Content-Encoding is primarily used to allow a document to be compressed without losing the identity of its underlying media type.

```
Content-Encoding = "Content-Encoding" ":" 1#content-coding
```

Content-codings are defined in section 3.5. An example of its use is

```
Content-Encoding: gzip
```

The content-coding is a characteristic of the entity identified by the Request-URI. Typically, the entity-body is stored with this encoding and is only decoded before rendering or analogous usage. However, a non-transparent proxy MAY modify the content-coding if the new coding is known to be acceptable to the recipient, unless the "no-transform" cache-control directive is present in the message.

If the content-coding of an entity is not "identity," then the response MUST include a Content-Encoding entity-header (section 14.11) that lists the non-identity content-coding(s) used.

If the content-coding of an entity in a request message is not acceptable to the origin server, the server SHOULD respond with a status code of 415 (Unsupported Media Type).

If multiple encodings have been applied to an entity, the content codings MUST be listed in the order in which they were applied. Additional information about the encoding parameters MAY be provided by other entity-header fields not defined by this specification.

14.12 Content-Language

The Content-Language entity-header field describes the natural language(s) of the intended audience for the enclosed entity. Note that this might not be equivalent to all the languages used within the entity-body.

```
Content-Language = "Content-Language" ":" 1#language-tag
```

Language tags are defined in section 3.10. The primary purpose of Content-Language is to allow a user to identify and differentiate entities according to the user's own preferred language. Thus, if the body content is intended only for a Danish-literate audience, the appropriate field is

```
Content-Language: da
```

If no Content-Language is specified, the default is that the content is intended for all language audiences. This might mean that the sender does not consider it to be specific to any natural language, or that the sender does not know for which language it is intended.

Multiple languages MAY be listed for content that is intended for multiple audiences. For example, a rendition of the "Treaty of Waitangi," presented simultaneously in the original Maori and English versions, would call for

```
Content-Language: mi, en
```

However, just because multiple languages are present within an entity does not mean that it is intended for multiple linguistic audiences. An example would be a beginner's language primer, such as "A First Lesson in Latin," which is clearly intended to be used by an English-literate audience. In this case, the Content-Language would properly only include "en."

Content-Language MAY be applied to any media type—it is not limited to textual documents.

14.13 Content-Length

The Content-Length entity-header field indicates the size of the entity-body, in a decimal number of OCTETs, sent to the recipient or, in the case of the HEAD method, the size of the entity-body that would have been sent had the request been a GET.

```
Content-Length  = "Content-Length" ":" 1*DIGIT
```

An example is

```
Content-Length: 3495
```

Applications SHOULD use this field to indicate the transfer-length of the message-body, unless this is prohibited by the rules in section 4.4.

Any Content-Length greater than or equal to zero is a valid value. Section 4.4 describes how to determine the length of a message-body if a Content-Length is not given.

> Note that the meaning of this field is significantly different from the corresponding definition in MIME, where it is an optional field used within the "message/external-body" content-type. In HTTP, it SHOULD be sent whenever the message's length can be determined prior to being transferred, unless this is prohibited by the rules in section 4.4.

14.14 Content-Location

The Content-Location entity-header field MAY be used to supply the resource location for the entity enclosed in the message when that entity is accessible from a location separate from the requested resource's URI. A server SHOULD provide a Content-Location for the variant corresponding to the response entity; especially in the case where a resource has multiple entities associated with it, and those entities actually have separate locations by which they might be individually accessed, the server SHOULD provide a Content-Location for the particular variant which is returned.

```
Content-Location = "Content-Location" ":"
          ( absoluteURI | relativeURI )
```

The value of Content-Location also defines the base URI for the entity.

The Content-Location value is not a replacement for the original requested URI; it is only a statement of the location of the resource corresponding to this particular entity at the time of the request. Future requests MAY specify the Content-Location URI as the request-URI if the desire is to identify the source of that particular entity.

A cache cannot assume that an entity with a Content-Location different from the URI used to retrieve it can be used to respond to later requests on that Content-Location URI. However, the Content-Location can be used to differentiate between multiple entities retrieved from a single requested resource, as described in section 13.6.

If the Content-Location is a relative URI, the relative URI is interpreted relative to the Request-URI.

The meaning of the Content-Location header in PUT or POST requests is undefined; servers are free to ignore it in those cases.

14.15 Content-MD5

The Content-MD5 entity-header field, as defined in RFC 1864 [23], is an MD5 digest of the entity-body for the purpose of providing an end-to-end message integrity check (MIC) of the entity-body. (Note: A MIC is good for detecting accidental modification of the entity-body in transit, but is not proof against malicious attacks.)

```
Content-MD5  = "Content-MD5" ":" md5-digest
md5-digest  = <base64 of 128 bit MD5 digest as per RFC 1864>
```

The Content-MD5 header field MAY be generated by an origin server or client to function as an integrity check of the entity-body. Only origin servers or clients MAY generate the Content-MD5 header field; proxies and gateways MUST NOT generate it, as this would defeat its value as an end-to-end integrity check. Any recipient of the entity-body, including gateways and proxies, MAY check that the digest value in this header field matches that of the entity-body as received.

The MD5 digest is computed based on the content of the entity-body, including any content-coding that has been applied, but not including any transfer-encoding applied to the message-body. If the message is received with a transfer-encoding, that encoding MUST be removed prior to checking the Content-MD5 value against the received entity.

This has the result that the digest is computed on the octets of the entity-body exactly as, and in the order that, they would be sent if no transfer-encoding were being applied.

HTTP extends RFC 1864 to permit the digest to be computed for MIME composite media-types (e.g., multipart/* and message/rfc822), but this does not change how the digest is computed as defined in the preceding paragraph.

There are several consequences of this. The entity-body for composite types MAY contain many body-parts, each with its own MIME and HTTP headers (including Content-MD5, Content-Transfer-Encoding, and Content-Encoding headers). If a body-part has a Content-Transfer-Encoding or Content-Encoding header, it is assumed that the content of the body-part has had the encoding applied, and the body-part is included in the Content-MD5 digest as is—i.e., after the application. The Transfer-Encoding header field is not allowed within body-parts.

Conversion of all line breaks to CRLF MUST NOT be done before computing or checking the digest: The line break convention used in the text actually transmitted MUST be left unaltered when computing the digest.

> **Note:** While the definition of Content-MD5 is exactly the same for HTTP as in RFC 1864 for MIME entity-bodies, there are several ways in which the application of Content-MD5 to HTTP entity-bodies differs from its application to MIME entity-bodies. One is that HTTP, unlike MIME, does not use Content-Transfer-Encoding, and does use Transfer-Encoding and

Content-Encoding. Another is that HTTP more frequently uses binary content types than MIME, so it is worth noting that, in such cases, the byte order used to compute the digest is the transmission byte order defined for the type. Lastly, HTTP allows transmission of text types with any of several line break conventions and not just the canonical form using CRLF.

14.16 Content-Range

The Content-Range entity-header is sent with a partial entity-body to specify where in the full entity-body the partial body should be applied. Range units are defined in section 3.12.

```
Content-Range = "Content-Range" ":" content-range-spec

content-range-spec      = byte-content-range-spec
byte-content-range-spec = bytes-unit SP
                          byte-range-resp-spec "/"
                          ( instance-length | "*" )

byte-range-resp-spec = (first-byte-pos "-" last-byte-pos)
                     | "*"
instance-length         = 1*DIGIT
```

The header SHOULD indicate the total length of the full entity-body, unless this length is unknown or difficult to determine. The asterisk "*" character means that the instance-length is unknown at the time when the response was generated.

Unlike byte-ranges-specifier values (see section 14.35.1), a byte-range-resp-spec MUST only specify one range, and MUST contain absolute byte positions for both the first and last byte of the range.

A byte-content-range-spec with a byte-range-resp-spec whose last-byte-pos value is less than its first-byte-pos value, or whose instance-length value is less than or equal to its last-byte-pos value, is invalid. The recipient of an invalid byte-content-range-spec MUST ignore it and any content transferred along with it.

A server sending a response with status code 416 (Requested range not satisfiable) SHOULD include a Content-Range field with a byte-range-resp-spec of "*". The instance-length specifies the current length of the selected resource. A response with status code 206 (Partial Content) MUST NOT include a Content-Range field with a byte-range-resp-spec of "*".

Examples of byte-content-range-spec values, assuming that the entity contains a total of 1234 bytes:

- The first 500 bytes:

  `bytes 0-499/1234`

- The second 500 bytes:

  `bytes 500-999/1234`

- All except for the first 500 bytes:

  `bytes 500-1233/1234`

- The last 500 bytes:

  `bytes 734-1233/1234`

When an HTTP message includes the content of a single range (for example, a response to a request for a single range or a request for a set of ranges that overlap without any holes), this content is transmitted with a Content-Range header, and a Content-Length header showing the number of bytes actually transferred. For example,

```
HTTP/1.1 206 Partial content
Date: Wed, 15 Nov 1995 06:25:24 GMT
Last-Modified: Wed, 15 Nov 1995 04:58:08 GMT
Content-Range: bytes 21010-47021/47022
Content-Length: 26012
Content-Type: image/gif
```

When an HTTP message includes the content of multiple ranges (for example, a response to a request for multiple non-overlapping ranges), these are transmitted as a multipart message. The multipart media type used for this purpose is "multipart/byteranges" as defined in appendix 19.2. See appendix 19.6.3 for a compatibility issue.

A response to a request for a single range MUST NOT be sent using the multipart/byteranges media type. A response to a request for multiple ranges, whose result is a single range, MAY be sent as a multipart/byteranges media type with one part. A client that cannot decode a multipart/byteranges message MUST NOT ask for multiple byte ranges in a single request.

When a client requests multiple byte ranges in one request, the server SHOULD return them in the order that they appeared in the request. If the server ignores a byte-range-spec because it is syntactically invalid, the server SHOULD treat the request as if the invalid Range header field did not exist. (Normally, this means return a 200 response containing the full entity).

If the server receives a request (other than one including an If-Range request-header field) with an unsatisfiable Range request-header field (that is, all of whose byte-range-spec values have a first-byte-pos value greater than the current length of the selected resource), it SHOULD return a response code of 416 (Requested range not satisfiable) (section 10.4.17).

> **Note:** Clients cannot depend on servers to send a 416 (Requested range not satisfiable) response instead of a 200 (OK) response for an unsatisfiable Range request-header, since not all servers implement this request-header.

14.17 Content-Type

The Content-Type entity-header field indicates the media type of the entity-body sent to the recipient or, in the case of the HEAD method, the media type that would have been sent had the request been a GET.

```
Content-Type  = "Content-Type" ":" media-type
```

Media types are defined in section 3.7. An example of the field is

```
Content-Type: text/html; charset=ISO-8859-4
```

Further discussion of methods for identifying the media type of an entity is provided in section 7.2.1.

14.18 Date

The Date general-header field represents the date and time at which the message originated, having the same semantics as orig-date in RFC 822. The field value is an HTTP-date, as described in section 3.3.1; it MUST be sent in RFC 1123 [8]-date format.

```
Date = "Date" ":" HTTP-date
```

An example is

```
Date: Tue, 15 Nov 1994 08:12:31 GMT
```

Origin servers MUST include a Date header field in all responses, except in these cases:

1. If the response status code is 100 (Continue) or 101 (Switching Protocols), the response MAY include a Date header field, at the server's option.

2. If the response status code conveys a server error—e.g., 500 (Internal Server Error) or 503 (Service Unavailable)—and it is inconvenient or impossible to generate a valid Date.

3. If the server does not have a clock that can provide a reasonable approximation of the current time, its responses MUST NOT include a Date header field. In this case, the rules in section 14.18.1 MUST be followed.

A received message that does not have a Date header field MUST be assigned one by the recipient if the message will be cached by that recipient or gatewayed via a protocol which requires a Date. An HTTP implementation without a clock MUST NOT cache responses without revalidating them on every use. An HTTP cache, especially a shared cache, SHOULD use a mechanism, such as NTP [28], to synchronize its clock with a reliable external standard.

Clients SHOULD only send a Date header field in messages that include an entity-body, as in the case of the PUT and POST requests, and even then it is optional. A client without a clock MUST NOT send a Date header field in a request.

The HTTP-date sent in a Date header SHOULD NOT represent a date and time subsequent to the generation of the message. It SHOULD represent the best available approximation of the date and time of message generation, unless the implementation has no means of generating a reasonably accurate date and time. In theory, the date ought to represent the moment just before the entity is generated. In practice, the date can be generated at any time during the message origination without affecting its semantic value.

14.18.1 Clockless Origin Server Operation

Some origin server implementations might not have a clock available. An origin server without a clock MUST NOT assign Expires or Last-Modified values to a response, unless these values were associated with the resource by a system or user with a reliable clock. It MAY assign an Expires value that is known, at or before server configuration time, to be in the past (this allows "pre-expiration" of responses without storing separate Expires values for each resource).

14.19 ETag

The ETag response-header field provides the current value of the entity tag for the requested variant. The headers used with entity tags are described in sections 14.24, 14.26, and 14.44. The entity tag MAY be used for comparison with other entities from the same resource (see section 13.3.3).

```
ETag = "ETag" ":" entity-tag
```

Examples:

```
ETag: "xyzzy"
ETag: W/"xyzzy"
ETag: ""
```

14.20 Expect

The Expect request-header field is used to indicate that particular server behaviors are required by the client.

```
Expect     = "Expect" ":" 1#expectation

expectation = "100-continue" | expectation-extension
expectation-extension = token [ "=" ( token | quoted-string )
             *expect-params ]
expect-params = ";" token [ "=" ( token | quoted-string ) ]
```

A server that does not understand or is unable to comply with any of the expectation values in the Expect field of a request MUST respond with appropriate error status. The server MUST respond with a 417 (Expectation Failed) status if any of the expectations cannot be met or, if there are other problems with the request, some other 4xx status.

This header field is defined with extensible syntax to allow for future extensions. If a server receives a request containing an Expect field that includes an expectation-extension that it does not support, it MUST respond with a 417 (Expectation Failed) status.

Comparison of expectation values is case-insensitive for unquoted tokens (including the 100-continue token), and is case-sensitive for quoted-string expectation-extensions.

The Expect mechanism is hop-by-hop; that is, an HTTP/1.1 proxy MUST return a 417 (Expectation Failed) status if it receives a request with an expectation that it cannot meet. However, the Expect request-header itself is end-to-end; it MUST be forwarded if the request is forwarded.

Many older HTTP/1.0 and HTTP/1.1 applications do not understand the Expect header.

See section 8.2.3 for the use of the 100 (Continue) status.

14.21 Expires

The Expires entity-header field gives the date/time after which the response is considered stale. A stale cache entry may not normally be returned by a cache (either a proxy cache or a user agent cache) unless it is first validated with the origin server (or with an intermediate cache that has a fresh copy of the entity). See section 13.2 for further discussion of the expiration model.

The presence of an Expires field does not imply that the original resource will change or cease to exist at, before, or after that time.

The format is an absolute date and time as defined by HTTP-date in section 3.3.1; it MUST be in RFC 1123 date format:

```
Expires = "Expires" ":" HTTP-date
```

An example of its use is

```
Expires: Thu, 01 Dec 1994 16:00:00 GMT
```

Note: If a response includes a Cache-Control field with the max-age directive (see section 14.9.3), that directive overrides the Expires field.

HTTP/1.1 clients and caches MUST treat other invalid date formats, especially including the value "0", as in the past (i.e., "already expired").

To mark a response as "already expired," an origin server sends an Expires date that is equal to the Date header value. (See the rules for expiration calculations in section 13.2.4.)

To mark a response as "never expires," an origin server sends an Expires date approximately one year from the time the response is sent. HTTP/1.1 servers SHOULD NOT send Expires dates more than one year in the future.

The presence of an Expires header field with a date value of some time in the future on a response that otherwise would by default be non-cacheable indicates that the response is cacheable, unless indicated otherwise by a Cache-Control header field (section 14.9).

14.22 From

The From request-header field, if given, SHOULD contain an Internet e-mail address for the human user who controls the requesting user agent. The address SHOULD be machine-usable, as defined by "mailbox" in RFC 822 [9] as updated by RFC 1123 [8]:

```
From  = "From" ":" mailbox
```

An example is

```
From: webmaster@w3.org
```

This header field MAY be used for logging purposes and as a means for identifying the source of invalid or unwanted requests. It SHOULD NOT be used as an insecure form of access protection. The interpretation of this field is that the request is being performed on behalf of the person given, who accepts responsibility for the method performed. In particular, robot agents SHOULD include this header so that the person responsible for running the robot can be contacted if problems occur on the receiving end.

The Internet e-mail address in this field MAY be separate from the Internet host which issued the request. For example, when a request is passed through a proxy, the original issuer's address SHOULD be used.

The client SHOULD NOT send the From header field without the user's approval, as it might conflict with the user's privacy interests or their site's security policy. It is strongly recommended that the user be able to disable, enable, and modify the value of this field at any time prior to a request.

14.23 Host

The Host request-header field specifies the Internet host and port number of the resource being requested, as obtained from the original URI given by the user or referring resource (generally an HTTP URL, as described in section 3.2.2). The Host field value MUST represent the naming authority of the origin server or gateway given by the original URL. This allows the origin server or gateway to differentiate between internally ambiguous URLs, such as the root "/" URL of a server for multiple host names on a single IP address.

```
Host = "Host" ":" host [ ":" port ] ; Section 3.2.2
```

A "host" without any trailing port information implies the default port for the service requested (e.g., "80" for an HTTP URL). For example, a request on the origin server for <http://www.w3.org/pub/WWW/> would properly include

```
GET /pub/WWW/ HTTP/1.1
Host: www.w3.org
```

A client MUST include a Host header field in all HTTP/1.1 request messages. If the requested URI does not include an Internet host name for the service being requested, then the Host header field MUST be given with an empty value. An HTTP/1.1 proxy MUST ensure that any request message it forwards does contain an appropriate Host header field that identifies the service being requested by the proxy. All Internet-based HTTP/1.1 servers MUST respond with a 400 (Bad Request) status code to any HTTP/1.1 request message which lacks a Host header field.

See sections 5.2 and 19.6.1.1 for other requirements relating to Host.

14.24 If-Match

The If-Match request-header field is used with a method to make it conditional. A client that has one or more entities previously obtained from the resource can verify that one of those entities is current by including a list of their associated entity tags in the If-Match header field. Entity tags are defined in section 3.11. The purpose of this feature is to allow efficient updates of cached information with a minimum amount of transaction overhead. It is also used, on updating requests, to prevent inadvertent modification of the wrong version of a resource. As a special case, the value "*" matches any current entity of the resource.

```
If-Match = "If-Match" ":" ( "*" | 1#entity-tag )
```

If any of the entity tags match the entity tag of the entity that would have been returned in the response to a similar GET request (without the If-Match header) on that resource, or if "*" is given and any current entity exists for that resource, then the server MAY perform the requested method as if the If-Match header field did not exist.

A server MUST use the strong comparison function (see section 13.3.3) to compare the entity tags in If-Match.

If none of the entity tags match, or if "*" is given and no current entity exists, the server MUST NOT perform the requested method, and MUST return a 412 (Precondition Failed) response. This behavior is most useful when the client wants to prevent an updating method, such as PUT, from modifying a resource that has changed since the client last retrieved it.

If the request would, without the If-Match header field, result in anything other than a 2xx or 412 status, then the If-Match header MUST be ignored.

The meaning of "If-Match: *" is that the method SHOULD be performed if the representation selected by the origin server (or by a cache, possibly using the Vary mechanism; see section 14.44) exists, and MUST NOT be performed if the representation does not exist.

A request intended to update a resource (e.g., a PUT) MAY include an If-Match header field to signal that the request method MUST NOT be applied if the entity corresponding to the If-Match value (a single entity tag) is no longer a representation of that resource. This allows the user to indicate that they do not wish the request to be successful if the resource has been changed without their knowledge. Examples:

```
If-Match: "xyzzy"
If-Match: "xyzzy", "r2d2xxxx", "c3piozzzz"
If-Match: *
```

The result of a request having both an If-Match header field and either an If-None-Match or an If-Modified-Since header field is undefined by this specification.

14.25 If-Modified-Since

The If-Modified-Since request-header field is used with a method to make it conditional: If the requested variant has not been modified since the time specified in this field, an entity will not be returned from the server; instead, a 304 (not modified) response will be returned without any message-body.

```
If-Modified-Since = "If-Modified-Since" ":" HTTP-date
```

An example of the field is

```
If-Modified-Since: Sat, 29 Oct 1994 19:43:31 GMT
```

A GET method with an If-Modified-Since header and no Range header requests that the identified entity be transferred only if it has been modified since the date given by the If-Modified-Since header. The algorithm for determining this includes the following cases:

(a) If the request would normally result in anything other than a 200 (OK) status, or if the passed If-Modified-Since date is invalid, the response is exactly the same as for a normal GET. A date which is later than the server's current time is invalid.

(b) If the variant has been modified since the If-Modified-Since date, the response is exactly the same as for a normal GET.

(c) If the variant has not been modified since a valid If-Modified-Since date, the server SHOULD return a 304 (Not Modified) response.

The purpose of this feature is to allow efficient updates of cached information with a minimum amount of transaction overhead.

> **Note:** The Range request-header field modifies the meaning of If-Modified-Since; see section 14.35 for full details.

> **Note:** If-Modified-Since times are interpreted by the server, whose clock might not be synchronized with the client.

> **Note:** When handling an If-Modified-Since header field, some servers will use an exact date comparison function, rather than a less-than function, for deciding whether to send a 304 (Not Modified) response. To get the best results when sending an If-Modified-Since header field for cache validation, clients are advised to use the exact date string received in a previous Last-Modified header field whenever possible.

> **Note:** If a client uses an arbitrary date in the If-Modified-Since header instead of a date taken from the Last-Modified header for the same request, the client should be aware of the fact that this date is interpreted in the server's understanding of time. The client should consider unsynchronized clocks and rounding problems due to the different encodings of time between the client and server. This includes the possibility of race conditions if the document has changed between the time it was first requested and the If-Modified-Since date of a subsequent request, and the possibility of clock-skew-related problems if the If-Modified-Since date is derived from the client's clock without correction

to the server's clock. Corrections for different time bases between client and server are at best approximate due to network latency.

The result of a request having both an If-Modified-Since header field and either an If-Match or an If-Unmodified-Since header field is undefined by this specification.

14.26 If-None-Match

The If-None-Match request-header field is used with a method to make it conditional. A client that has one or more entities previously obtained from the resource can verify that none of those entities is current by including a list of their associated entity tags in the If-None-Match header field. The purpose of this feature is to allow efficient updates of cached information with a minimum amount of transaction overhead. It is also used to prevent a method (e.g., PUT) from inadvertently modifying an existing resource when the client believes that the resource does not exist.

As a special case, the value "*" matches any current entity of the resource.

```
If-None-Match = "If-None-Match" ":" ( "*" | 1#entity-tag )
```

If any of the entity tags match the entity tag of the entity that would have been returned in the response to a similar GET request (without the If-None-Match header) on that resource, or if "*" is given and any current entity exists for that resource, then the server MUST NOT perform the requested method, unless required to do so because the resource's modification date fails to match that supplied in an If-Modified-Since header field in the request. Instead, if the request method was GET or HEAD, the server SHOULD respond with a 304 (Not Modified) response, including the cache-related header fields (particularly ETag) of one of the entities that matched. For all other request methods, the server MUST respond with a status of 412 (Precondition Failed).

See section 13.3.3 for rules on how to determine if two entities tags match. The weak comparison function can only be used with GET or HEAD requests.

If none of the entity tags match, then the server MAY perform the requested method as if the If-None-Match header field did not exist, but MUST also ignore any If-Modified-Since header field(s) in the request. That is, if no entity tags match, then the server MUST NOT return a 304 (Not Modified) response.

If the request would, without the If-None-Match header field, result in anything other than a 2xx or 304 status, then the If-None-Match header MUST be ignored.

(See section 13.3.4 for a discussion of server behavior when both If-Modified-Since and If-None-Match appear in the same request.)

The meaning of "If-None-Match: *" is that the method MUST NOT be performed if the representation selected by the origin server (or by a cache, possibly using the Vary mechanism; see section 14.44) exists, and SHOULD be performed if the representation does not exist. This feature is intended to be useful in preventing races between PUT operations.

Examples:

```
If-None-Match: "xyzzy"
If-None-Match: W/"xyzzy"
If-None-Match: "xyzzy", "r2d2xxxx", "c3piozzzz"
If-None-Match: W/"xyzzy", W/"r2d2xxxx", W/"c3piozzzz"
If-None-Match: *
```

The result of a request having both an If-None-Match header field and either an If-Match or an If-Unmodified-Since header field is undefined by this specification.

14.27 If-Range

If a client has a partial copy of an entity in its cache, and wishes to have an up-to-date copy of the entire entity in its cache, it could use the Range request-header with a conditional GET (using either or both of If-Unmodified-Since and If-Match.) However, if the condition fails because the entity has been modified, the client would then have to make a second request to obtain the entire current entity-body.

The If-Range header allows a client to "short-circuit" the second request. Informally, its meaning is "If the entity is unchanged, send me the part(s) that I am missing; otherwise, send me the entire new entity."

```
If-Range = "If-Range" ":" ( entity-tag | HTTP-date )
```

If the client has no entity tag for an entity but does have a Last-Modified date, it MAY use that date in an If-Range header. (The server can distinguish between a valid HTTP-date and any form of entity-tag by examining no more than two characters.) The If-Range header SHOULD only be used together with a Range header, and MUST be ignored if the request does not include a Range header or if the server does not support the subrange operation.

If the entity tag given in the If-Range header matches the current entity tag for the entity, then the server SHOULD provide the specified subrange of the entity using a 206 (Partial content) response. If the entity tag does not match, then the server SHOULD return the entire entity using a 200 (OK) response.

14.28 If-Unmodified-Since

The If-Unmodified-Since request-header field is used with a method to make it conditional. If the requested resource has not been modified since the time specified in this field, the server SHOULD perform the requested operation as if the If-Unmodified-Since header were not present.

If the requested variant has been modified since the specified time, the server MUST NOT perform the requested operation, and MUST return a 412 (Precondition Failed).

```
If-Unmodified-Since = "If-Unmodified-Since" ":" HTTP-date
```

An example of the field is

```
If-Unmodified-Since: Sat, 29 Oct 1994 19:43:31 GMT
```

If the request normally (i.e., without the If-Unmodified-Since header) would result in anything other than a 2xx or 412 status, the If-Unmodified-Since header SHOULD be ignored.

If the specified date is invalid, the header is ignored.

The result of a request having both an If-Unmodified-Since header field and either an If-None-Match or an If-Modified-Since header field is undefined by this specification.

14.29 Last-Modified

The Last-Modified entity-header field indicates the date and time at which the origin server believes the variant was last modified.

```
Last-Modified = "Last-Modified" ":" HTTP-date
```

An example of its use is

```
Last-Modified: Tue, 15 Nov 1994 12:45:26 GMT
```

The exact meaning of this header field depends on the implementation of the origin server and the nature of the original resource. For files, it may be just the file system last-modified time. For entities with dynamically included parts, it may be the most recent of the set of last-modify times for its component parts. For database gateways, it may be the last-update time stamp of the record. For virtual objects, it may be the last time the internal state changed.

An origin server MUST NOT send a Last-Modified date which is later than the server's time of message origination. In such cases, where the resource's last modification would indicate some time in the future, the server MUST replace that date with the message origination date.

An origin server SHOULD obtain the Last-Modified value of the entity as close as possible to the time that it generates the Date value of its response. This allows a recipient to make an accurate assessment of the entity's modification time, especially if the entity changes near the time that the response is generated.

HTTP/1.1 servers SHOULD send Last-Modified whenever feasible.

14.30 Location

The Location response-header field is used to redirect the recipient to a location other than the Request-URI for completion of the request or identification of a new resource. For 201 (Created) responses, the Location is that of the new resource which was created by the request. For 3xx responses, the location SHOULD indicate the server's preferred URI for automatic redirection to the resource. The field value consists of a single absolute URI.

```
Location    = "Location" ":" absoluteURI
```

An example is

```
Location: http://www.w3.org/pub/WWW/People.html
```

> **Note:** The Content-Location header field (section 14.14) differs from Location in that the Content-Location identifies the original location of the entity enclosed in the request. It is therefore possible for a response to contain header fields for both Location and Content-Location. Also see section 13.10 for cache requirements of some methods.

14.31 Max-Forwards

The Max-Forwards request-header field provides a mechanism with the TRACE (section 9.8) and OPTIONS (section 9.2) methods to limit the number of proxies or gateways that can forward the request to the next inbound server. This can be useful when the client is attempting to trace a request chain which appears to be failing or looping in mid-chain.

```
Max-Forwards   = "Max-Forwards" ":" 1*DIGIT
```

The Max-Forwards value is a decimal integer indicating the remaining number of times this request message may be forwarded.

Each proxy or gateway recipient of a TRACE or OPTIONS request containing a Max-Forwards header field MUST check and update its value prior to forwarding the request. If the received value is zero (0), the recipient MUST NOT forward the request; instead, it MUST respond as the final recipient. If the received Max-Forwards value is greater than zero, then the forwarded message MUST contain an updated Max-Forwards field with a value decremented by one (1).

The Max-Forwards header field MAY be ignored for all other methods defined by this specification and for any extension methods for which it is not explicitly referred to as part of that method definition.

14.32 Pragma

The Pragma general-header field is used to include implementation-specific directives that might apply to any recipient along the request/response chain. All pragma directives specify optional behavior from the viewpoint of the protocol; however, some systems MAY require that behavior be consistent with the directives.

```
Pragma         = "Pragma" ":" 1#pragma-directive
pragma-directive = "no-cache" | extension-pragma
extension-pragma = token [ "=" ( token | quoted-string ) ]
```

When the no-cache directive is present in a request message, an application SHOULD forward the request toward the origin server even if it has a cached copy of what is being requested. This pragma directive has the same semantics as the no-cache cache-directive (see section 14.9) and is defined here for backward compatibility with HTTP/1.0. Clients SHOULD include both header fields when a no-cache request is sent to a server not known to be HTTP/1.1 compliant.

Pragma directives MUST be passed through by a proxy or gateway application, regardless of their significance to that application, since the directives might be applicable to all recipients along the request/response chain. It is not possible to specify a pragma for a specific recipient; however, any pragma directive not relevant to a recipient SHOULD be ignored by that recipient.

HTTP/1.1 caches SHOULD treat "Pragma: no-cache" as if the client had sent "Cache-Control: no-cache." No new Pragma directives will be defined in HTTP.

> **Note:** Because the meaning of "Pragma: no-cache" as a response header field is not actually specified, it does not provide a reliable replacement for "Cache-Control: no-cache" in a response.

14.33 Proxy-Authenticate

The Proxy-Authenticate response-header field MUST be included as part of a 407 (Proxy Authentication Required) response. The field value consists of a challenge that indicates the authentication scheme and parameters applicable to the proxy for this Request-URI.

```
Proxy-Authenticate = "Proxy-Authenticate" ":" 1#challenge
```

The HTTP access authentication process is described in "HTTP Authentication: Basic and Digest Access Authentication" [43]. Unlike WWW-Authenticate, the Proxy-Authenticate header field applies only to the current connection and SHOULD NOT be passed on to downstream clients. However, an intermediate proxy might need to obtain its own credentials by requesting them from the downstream client, which in some circumstances will appear as if the proxy is forwarding the Proxy-Authenticate header field.

14.34 Proxy-Authorization

The Proxy-Authorization request-header field allows the client to identify itself (or its user) to a proxy which requires authentication. The Proxy-Authorization field value consists of credentials containing the authentication information of the user agent for the proxy and/or realm of the resource being requested.

```
Proxy-Authorization   = "Proxy-Authorization" ":" credentials
```

The HTTP access authentication process is described in "HTTP Authentication: Basic and Digest Access Authentication" [43]. Unlike Authorization, the Proxy-Authorization header field applies only to the next outbound proxy that demanded authentication using the Proxy-Authenticate field. When multiple proxies are used in a chain, the Proxy-Authorization header field is consumed by the first outbound proxy that was expecting to receive credentials. A proxy MAY relay the credentials from the client request to the next proxy if that is the mechanism by which the proxies cooperatively authenticate a given request.

14.35 Range

14.35.1 Byte Ranges

Since all HTTP entities are represented in HTTP messages as sequences of bytes, the concept of a byte range is meaningful for any HTTP entity. (However, not all clients and servers need to support byte-range operations.)

Byte-range specifications in HTTP apply to the sequence of bytes in the entity-body (not necessarily the same as the message-body).

A byte-range operation MAY specify a single range of bytes, or a set of ranges within a single entity.

```
ranges-specifier = byte-ranges-specifier
byte-ranges-specifier = bytes-unit "=" byte-range-set
byte-range-set = 1#( byte-range-spec | suffix-byte-range-spec )
byte-range-spec = first-byte-pos "-" [last-byte-pos]
first-byte-pos = 1*DIGIT
last-byte-pos  = 1*DIGIT
```

The first-byte-pos value in a byte-range-spec gives the byte offset of the first byte in a range. The last-byte-pos value gives the byte offset of the last byte in the range; that is, the byte positions specified are inclusive. Byte offsets start at zero.

If the last-byte-pos value is present, it MUST be greater than or equal to the first-byte-pos in that byte-range-spec, or the byte-range-spec is syntactically invalid. The recipient of a byte-range-set that includes one or more syntactically invalid byte-range-spec values MUST ignore the header field that includes that byte-range-set.

If the last-byte-pos value is absent, or if the value is greater than or equal to the current length of the entity-body, the last-byte-pos is taken to be equal to one less than the current length of the entity-body in bytes.

By its choice of last-byte-pos, a client can limit the number of bytes retrieved without knowing the size of the entity.

```
suffix-byte-range-spec = "-" suffix-length
suffix-length = 1*DIGIT
```

A suffix-byte-range-spec is used to specify the suffix of the entity-body, of a length given by the suffix-length value. (That is, this form specifies the last N bytes of an entity-body.) If the entity is shorter than the specified suffix-length, the entire entity-body is used.

If a syntactically valid byte-range-set includes at least one byte-range-spec whose first-byte-pos is less than the current length of the entity-body, or at least one suffix-byte-range-spec with a non-zero suffix-length, then the byte-range-set is satisfiable. Otherwise, the byte-range-set is unsatisfiable. If the byte-range-set is unsatisfiable, the server SHOULD return a response with a status of 416 (Requested range not satisfiable). Otherwise, the server SHOULD return a response with a status of 206 (Partial Content) containing the satisfiable ranges of the entity-body.

Examples of byte-ranges-specifier values (assuming an entity-body of length 10000):

- The first 500 bytes (byte offsets 0-499, inclusive): bytes=0-499

- The second 500 bytes (byte offsets 500-999, inclusive): bytes=500-999

- The final 500 bytes (byte offsets 9500-9999, inclusive): bytes=-500

- Or bytes=9500-

- The first and last bytes only (bytes 0 and 9999): bytes=0-0,-1

- Several legal but not canonical specifications of the second 500 bytes (byte offsets 500-999, inclusive):

```
bytes=500-600,601-999
bytes=500-700,601-999
```

14.35.2 Range Retrieval Requests

HTTP retrieval requests using conditional or unconditional GET methods MAY request one or more subranges of the entity, instead of the entire entity, using the Range request header, which applies to the entity returned as the result of the request:

```
Range = "Range" ":" ranges-specifier
```

A server MAY ignore the Range header. However, HTTP/1.1 origin servers and intermediate caches ought to support byte ranges when possible, since Range supports efficient recovery from partially failed transfers and supports efficient partial retrieval of large entities.

If the server supports the Range header and the specified range or ranges are appropriate for the entity:

- The presence of a Range header in an unconditional GET modifies what is returned if the GET is otherwise successful. In other words, the response carries a status code of 206 (Partial Content) instead of 200 (OK).

- The presence of a Range header in a conditional GET (a request using one or both of If-Modified-Since and If-None-Match, or one or both of If-Unmodified-Since and If-Match) modifies what is returned if the GET is otherwise successful and the condition is true. It does not affect the 304 (Not Modified) response returned if the conditional is false.

In some cases, it might be more appropriate to use the If-Range header (see section 14.27) in addition to the Range header.

If a proxy that supports ranges receives a Range request, forwards the request to an inbound server, and receives an entire entity in reply, it SHOULD only return the requested range to its client. It SHOULD store the entire received response in its cache if that is consistent with its cache allocation policies.

14.36 Referer

The Referer [sic] request-header field allows the client to specify, for the server's benefit, the address (URI) of the resource from which the Request-URI was obtained (the "referrer," although the header field is misspelled.) The Referer request-header allows a server to generate lists of back-links to resources for interest, logging, optimized caching, etc. It also allows obsolete or mistyped links to be traced for maintenance. The Referer field MUST NOT be sent if the Request-URI was obtained from a source that does not have its own URI, such as input from the user keyboard.

```
Referer    = "Referer" ":" ( absoluteURI | relativeURI )
```

Example:

```
Referer: http://www.w3.org/hypertext/DataSources/Overview.html
```

If the field value is a relative URI, it SHOULD be interpreted relative to the Request-URI. The URI MUST NOT include a fragment. See section 15.1.3 for security considerations.

14.37 Retry-After

The Retry-After response-header field can be used with a 503 (Service Unavailable) response to indicate how long the service is expected to be unavailable to the requesting client. This field MAY also be used with any 3xx (Redirection) response to indicate the minimum time the user agent is asked wait before issuing the redirected request. The value of this field can be either an HTTP-date or an integer number of seconds (in decimal) after the time of the response.

```
Retry-After = "Retry-After" ":" ( HTTP-date | delta-seconds )
```

Two examples of its use are

```
Retry-After: Fri, 31 Dec 1999 23:59:59 GMT
Retry-After: 120
```

In the latter example, the delay is 2 minutes.

14.38 Server

The Server response-header field contains information about the software used by the origin server to handle the request. The field can contain multiple product tokens (section 3.8) and comments identifying the server and any significant subproducts. The product tokens are listed in order of their significance for identifying the application.

```
Server     = "Server" ":" 1*( product | comment )
```

Example:

```
Server: CERN/3.0 libwww/2.17
```

If the response is being forwarded through a proxy, the proxy application MUST NOT modify the Server response-header. Instead, it SHOULD include a Via field (as described in section 14.45).

> **Note:** Revealing the specific software version of the server might allow the server machine to become more vulnerable to attacks against software that is known to contain security holes. Server implementers are encouraged to make this field a configurable option.

14.39 TE

The TE request-header field indicates what extension transfer-codings it is willing to accept in the response and whether or not it is willing to accept trailer fields in a chunked transfer-coding. Its value may consist of the keyword "trailers" and/or a comma-separated list of extension transfer-coding names with optional accept parameters (as described in section 3.6).

```
TE    = "TE" ":" #( t-codings )
t-codings = "trailers" | ( transfer-extension [ accept-params ] )
```

The presence of the keyword "trailers" indicates that the client is willing to accept trailer fields in a chunked transfer-coding, as defined in section 3.6.1. This keyword is reserved for use with transfer-coding values even though it does not itself represent a transfer-coding.

Examples of its use are

```
TE: deflate
TE:
TE: trailers, deflate;q=0.5
```

The TE header field only applies to the immediate connection. Therefore, the keyword MUST be supplied within a Connection header field (section 14.10) whenever TE is present in an HTTP/1.1 message.

A server tests whether a transfer-coding is acceptable, according to a TE field, using these rules:

1. The "chunked" transfer-coding is always acceptable. If the keyword "trailers" is listed, the client indicates that it is willing to accept trailer fields in the chunked response on behalf of itself and any downstream clients. The implication is that, if given, the client is stating that either all downstream clients are willing to accept trailer fields in the forwarded response, or that it will attempt to buffer the response on behalf of downstream recipients.

    Note: HTTP/1.1 does not define any means to limit the size of a chunked response such that a client can be assured of buffering the entire response.

2. If the transfer-coding being tested is one of the transfer-codings listed in the TE field, then it is acceptable unless it is accompanied by a qvalue of 0. (As defined in section 3.9, a qvalue of 0 means "not acceptable.")

3. If multiple transfer-codings are acceptable, then the acceptable transfer-coding with the highest non-zero qvalue is preferred. The "chunked" transfer-coding always has a qvalue of 1.

If the TE field-value is empty or if no TE field is present, the only transfer-coding is "chunked." A message with no transfer-coding is always acceptable.

14.40 Trailer

The Trailer general field value indicates that the given set of header fields is present in the trailer of a message encoded with chunked transfer-coding.

```
Trailer = "Trailer" ":" 1#field-name
```

An HTTP/1.1 message SHOULD include a Trailer header field in a message using chunked transfer-coding with a non-empty trailer. Doing so allows the recipient to know which header fields to expect in the trailer.

If no Trailer header field is present, the trailer SHOULD NOT include any header fields. See section 3.6.1 for restrictions on the use of trailer fields in a "chunked" transfer-coding.

Message header fields listed in the Trailer header field MUST NOT include the following header fields:

- Transfer-Encoding
- Content-Length
- Trailer

14.41 Transfer-Encoding

The Transfer-Encoding general-header field indicates what (if any) type of transformation has been applied to the message body in order to safely transfer it between the sender and the recipient. This differs from the content-coding in that the transfer-coding is a property of the message, not of the entity.

```
Transfer-Encoding    = "Transfer-Encoding" ":" 1#transfer-coding
```

Transfer-codings are defined in section 3.6. An example is

```
Transfer-Encoding: chunked
```

If multiple encodings have been applied to an entity, the transfer-codings MUST be listed in the order in which they were applied. Additional information about the encoding parameters MAY be provided by other entity-header fields not defined by this specification.

Many older HTTP/1.0 applications do not understand the Transfer-Encoding header.

14.42 Upgrade

The Upgrade general-header allows the client to specify what additional communication protocols it supports and would like to use if the server finds it appropriate to switch protocols. The server MUST use the Upgrade header field within a 101 (Switching Protocols) response to indicate which protocol(s) are being switched.

```
Upgrade    = "Upgrade" ":" 1#product
```

Example:

```
Upgrade: HTTP/2.0, SHTTP/1.3, IRC/6.9, RTA/x11
```

The Upgrade header field is intended to provide a simple mechanism for transition from HTTP/1.1 to some other, incompatible protocol. It does so by allowing the client to advertise its desire to use another protocol, such as a later version of HTTP with a higher major version number, even though the current request has been made using HTTP/1.1. This eases the difficult transition between incompatible protocols by allowing the client to initiate a request in the more commonly supported protocol while indicating to the server that it would like to use a "better" protocol if available (where "better" is determined by the server, possibly according to the nature of the method and/or resource being requested).

The Upgrade header field only applies to switching application-layer protocols upon the existing transport-layer connection. Upgrade cannot be used to insist on a protocol change; its acceptance and use by the server is optional. The capabilities and nature of the application-layer communication after the protocol change are entirely dependent upon the new protocol chosen, although the first action after changing the protocol MUST be a response to the initial HTTP request containing the Upgrade header field.

The Upgrade header field only applies to the immediate connection. Therefore, the upgrade keyword MUST be supplied within a Connection header field (section 14.10) whenever Upgrade is present in an HTTP/1.1 message.

The Upgrade header field cannot be used to indicate a switch to a protocol on a different connection. For that purpose, it is more appropriate to use a 301, 302, 303, or 305 redirection response.

This specification only defines the protocol name "HTTP" for use by the family of Hypertext Transfer Protocols, as defined by the HTTP version rules of section 3.1

and future updates to this specification. Any token can be used as a protocol name; however, it will only be useful if both the client and the server associate the name with the same protocol.

14.43 User-Agent

The User-Agent request-header field contains information about the user agent originating the request. This is for statistical purposes, the tracing of protocol violations, and automated recognition of user agents for the sake of tailoring responses to avoid particular user agent limitations. User agents SHOULD include this field with requests. The field can contain multiple product tokens (section 3.8) and comments identifying the agent and any subproducts which form a significant part of the user agent. By convention, the product tokens are listed in order of their significance for identifying the application.

```
User-Agent   = "User-Agent" ":" 1*( product | comment )
```

Example:

```
User-Agent: CERN-LineMode/2.15 libwww/2.17b3
```

14.44 Vary

The Vary field value indicates the set of request-header fields that fully determines, while the response is fresh, whether a cache is permitted to use the response to reply to a subsequent request without revalidation. For non-cacheable or stale responses, the Vary field value advises the user agent about the criteria that were used to select the representation. A Vary field value of "*" implies that a cache cannot determine from the request headers of a subsequent request whether this response is the appropriate representation. See section 13.6 for use of the Vary header field by caches.

```
Vary = "Vary" ":" ( "*" | 1#field-name )
```

An HTTP/1.1 server SHOULD include a Vary header field with any cacheable response that is subject to server-driven negotiation. Doing so allows a cache to properly interpret future requests on that resource and informs the user agent about the presence of negotiation on that resource. A server MAY include a Vary header field with a non-cacheable response that is subject to server-driven negotiation, since this might provide the user agent with useful information about the dimensions over which the response varies at the time of the response.

A Vary field value consisting of a list of field-names signals that the representation selected for the response is based on a selection algorithm which considers ONLY the listed request-header field values in selecting the most appropriate representation. A cache MAY assume that the same selection will be made for future requests with the same values for the listed field-names, for the duration of time for which the response is fresh.

The field-names given are not limited to the set of standard request-header fields defined by this specification. Field-names are case-insensitive.

A Vary field value of "*" signals that unspecified parameters not limited to the request-headers (e.g., the network address of the client) play a role in the selection of the response representation. The "*" value MUST NOT be generated by a proxy server; it may only be generated by an origin server.

14.45 Via

The Via general-header field MUST be used by gateways and proxies to indicate the intermediate protocols and recipients between the user agent and the server on requests, and between the origin server and the client on responses. It is analogous to the "Received" field of RFC 822 [9] and is intended to be used for tracking message forwards, avoiding request loops, and identifying the protocol capabilities of all senders along the request/response chain.

```
Via = "Via" ":" 1#( received-protocol received-by [ comment ] )
received-protocol = [ protocol-name "/" ] protocol-version
protocol-name   = token
protocol-version = token
received-by     = ( host [ ":" port ] ) | pseudonym
pseudonym       = token
```

The received-protocol indicates the protocol version of the message received by the server or client along each segment of the request/response chain. The received-protocol version is appended to the Via field value when the message is forwarded so that information about the protocol capabilities of upstream applications remains visible to all recipients.

The protocol-name is optional if and only if it would be "HTTP." The received-by field is normally the host and optional port number of a recipient server or client that subsequently forwarded the message. However, if the real host is considered to be sensitive information, it MAY be replaced by a pseudonym. If the port is not given, it MAY be assumed to be the default port of the received-protocol.

Multiple Via field values represent each proxy or gateway that has forwarded the message. Each recipient MUST append its information such that the end result is ordered according to the sequence of forwarding applications.

Comments MAY be used in the Via header field to identify the software of the recipient proxy or gateway, analogous to the User-Agent and Server header fields. However, all comments in the Via field are optional and MAY be removed by any recipient prior to forwarding the message.

For example, a request message could be sent from an HTTP/1.0 user agent to an internal proxy code-named "fred," which uses HTTP/1.1 to forward the request to a public proxy at nowhere.com, which completes the request by forwarding it to the origin server at www.ics.uci.edu. The request received by www.ics.uci.edu would then have the following Via header field:

```
Via: 1.0 fred, 1.1 nowhere.com (Apache/1.1)
```

Proxies and gateways used as a portal through a network firewall SHOULD NOT, by default, forward the names and ports of hosts within the firewall region. This information SHOULD only be propagated if explicitly enabled. If not enabled, the received-by host of any host behind the firewall SHOULD be replaced by an appropriate pseudonym for that host.

For organizations that have strong privacy requirements for hiding internal structures, a proxy MAY combine an ordered subsequence of Via header field entries with identical received-protocol values into a single such entry. For example,

```
Via: 1.0 ricky, 1.1 ethel, 1.1 fred, 1.0 lucy
```

could be collapsed to

```
Via: 1.0 ricky, 1.1 mertz, 1.0 lucy
```

Applications SHOULD NOT combine multiple entries unless they are all under the same organizational control and the hosts have already been replaced by pseudonyms. Applications MUST NOT combine entries which have different received-protocol values.

14.46 Warning

The Warning general-header field is used to carry additional information about the status or transformation of a message which might not be reflected in the message. This information is typically used to warn about a possible lack of semantic transparency from caching operations or transformations applied to the entity body of the message.

Warning headers are sent with responses using

```
Warning     = "Warning" ":" 1#warning-value
warning-value = warn-code SP warn-agent SP warn-text [SP warn-date]
warn-code = 3DIGIT
warn-agent = ( host [ ":" port ] ) | pseudonym
        ; the name or pseudonym of the server adding
        ; the Warning header, for use in debugging
warn-text = quoted-string
warn-date = <"> HTTP-date <">
```

A response MAY carry more than one Warning header.

The warn-text SHOULD be in a natural language and character set that is most likely to be intelligible to the human user receiving the response. This decision MAY be based on any available knowledge, such as the location of the cache or user, the Accept-Language field in a request, the Content-Language field in a response, etc. The default language is English and the default character set is ISO-8859-1.

If a character set other than ISO-8859-1 is used, it MUST be encoded in the warn-text using the method described in RFC 2047 [14].

Warning headers can in general be applied to any message; however, some specific warn-codes are specific to caches and can only be applied to response messages. New Warning headers SHOULD be added after any existing Warning headers. A cache MUST NOT delete any Warning header that it received with a message. However, if a cache successfully validates a cache entry, it SHOULD remove any Warning headers previously attached to that entry except as specified for specific Warning codes. It MUST then add any Warning headers received in the validating response. In other words, Warning headers are those that would be attached to the most recent relevant response.

When multiple Warning headers are attached to a response, the user agent ought to inform the user of as many of them as possible, in the order that they appear in the response. If it is not possible to inform the user of all of the warnings, the user agent SHOULD follow these heuristics:

- Warnings that appear early in the response take priority over those appearing later in the response.

- Warnings in the user's preferred character set take priority over warnings in other character sets but with identical warn-codes and warn-agents.

Systems that generate multiple Warning headers SHOULD order them with this user agent behavior in mind.

Requirements for the behavior of caches with respect to Warnings are stated in section 13.1.2.

This is a list of the currently defined warn-codes, each with a recommended warn-text in English, and a description of its meaning:

110 Response is stale

MUST be included whenever the returned response is stale.

111 Revalidation failed

MUST be included if a cache returns a stale response because an attempt to revalidate the response failed, due to an inability to reach the server.

112 Disconnected operation

SHOULD be included if the cache is intentionally disconnected from the rest of the network for a period of time.

113 Heuristic expiration

MUST be included if the cache heuristically chose a freshness lifetime greater than 24 hours and the response's age is greater than 24 hours.

199 Miscellaneous warning

The warning text MAY include arbitrary information to be presented to a human user, or logged. A system receiving this warning MUST NOT take any automated action, besides presenting the warning to the user.

214 Transformation applied

MUST be added by an intermediate cache or proxy if it applies any transformation changing the content-coding (as specified in the Content-Encoding header) or media-type (as specified in the Content-Type header) of the response, or the entity-body of the response, unless this Warning code already appears in the response.

299 Miscellaneous persistent warning

The warning text MAY include arbitrary information to be presented to a human user, or logged. A system receiving this warning MUST NOT take any automated action.

If an implementation sends a message with one or more Warning headers whose version is HTTP/1.0 or lower, then the sender MUST include in each warning-value a warn-date that matches the date in the response.

If an implementation receives a message with a warning-value that includes a warn-date, and that warn-date is different from the Date value in the response, then that warning-value MUST be deleted from the message before storing, forwarding, or using it. (This prevents bad consequences of naive caching of Warning header fields.) If all of the warning-values are deleted for this reason, the Warning header MUST be deleted as well.

14.47 WWW-Authenticate

The WWW-Authenticate response-header field MUST be included in 401 (Unauthorized) response messages. The field value consists of at least one challenge that indicates the authentication scheme(s) and parameters applicable to the Request-URI.

```
WWW-Authenticate = "WWW-Authenticate" ":" 1#challenge
```

The HTTP access authentication process is described in "HTTP Authentication: Basic and Digest Access Authentication" [43]. User agents are advised to take special care in parsing the WWW-Authenticate field value as it might contain more than one challenge, or if more than one WWW-Authenticate header field is provided, the contents of a challenge itself can contain a comma-separated list of authentication parameters.

15 Security Considerations

This section is meant to inform application developers, information providers, and users of the security limitations in HTTP/1.1 as described by this document. The discussion does not include definitive solutions to the problems revealed, though it does make some suggestions for reducing security risks.

15.1 Personal Information

HTTP clients are often privy to large amounts of personal information (e.g., the user's name, location, mail address, passwords, encryption keys), and SHOULD be very careful to prevent unintentional leakage of this information via the HTTP protocol to other sources. We very strongly recommend that a convenient interface be provided for the user to control dissemination of such information, and that designers and implementers be particularly careful in this area. History shows that errors in this area often create serious security and/or privacy problems and generate highly adverse publicity for the implementer's company.

15.1.1 Abuse of Server Log Information

A server is in the position to save personal data about a user's requests which might identify their reading patterns or subjects of interest. This information is clearly confidential in nature and its handling can be constrained by law in certain countries. People using the HTTP protocol to provide data are responsible for ensuring that such material is not distributed without the permission of any individuals that are identifiable by the published results.

15.1.2 Transfer of Sensitive Information

Like any generic data transfer protocol, HTTP cannot regulate the content of the data that is transferred, nor is there any a priori method of determining the sensitivity of any particular piece of information within the context of any given request. Therefore, applications SHOULD supply as much control over this information as possible to the provider of that information. Four header fields are worth special mention in this context: Server, Via, Referer, and From.

Revealing the specific software version of the server might allow the server machine to become more vulnerable to attacks against software that is known to contain security holes. Implementers SHOULD make the Server header field a configurable option.

Proxies that serve as a portal through a network firewall SHOULD take special precautions regarding the transfer of header information that identifies the hosts behind the firewall. In particular, they SHOULD remove, or replace with sanitized versions, any Via fields generated behind the firewall.

The Referer header allows reading patterns to be studied and reverse links drawn. Although it can be very useful, its power can be abused if user details are not separated from the information contained in the Referer. Even when the personal information has been removed, the Referer header might indicate a private document's URI whose publication would be inappropriate.

The information sent in the From field might conflict with the user's privacy interests or their site's security policy, and hence it SHOULD NOT be transmitted without the user being able to disable, enable, and modify the contents of the field. The user MUST be able to set the contents of this field within a user preference or application defaults configuration.

We suggest, though do not require, that a convenient toggle interface be provided for the user to enable or disable the sending of From and Referer information.

The User-Agent (section 14.43) and Server (section 14.38) header fields can sometimes be used to determine that a specific client or server have a particular security hole which might be exploited. Unfortunately, this same information is often used for other valuable purposes for which HTTP currently has no better mechanism.

15.1.3 Encoding Sensitive Information in URIs

Because the source of a link might be private information or might reveal an otherwise private information source, it is strongly recommended that the user be able to select whether or not the Referer field is sent. For example, a browser client could have a toggle switch for browsing openly/anonymously, which would respectively enable/disable the sending of Referer and From information.

Clients SHOULD NOT include a Referer header field in a (non-secure) HTTP request if the referring page was transferred with a secure protocol.

Authors of services which use the HTTP protocol SHOULD NOT use GET-based forms for the submission of sensitive data, because this will cause this data to be encoded in the Request-URI. Many existing servers, proxies, and user agents will log the request URI in some place where it might be visible to third parties. Servers can use POST-based form submission instead

15.1.4 Privacy Issues Connected to Accept Headers

Accept request-headers can reveal information about the user to all servers which are accessed. The Accept-Language header in particular can reveal information the user would consider to be of a private nature, because the understanding of particular languages is often strongly correlated to the membership of a particular ethnic group. User agents that offer the option to configure the contents of an Accept-Language header to be sent in every request are strongly encouraged to let the configuration process include a message which makes the user aware of the loss of privacy involved.

An approach that limits the loss of privacy would be for a user agent to omit the sending of Accept-Language headers by default, and to ask the user whether or not to start sending Accept-Language headers to a server if it detects, by looking for any Vary response-header fields generated by the server indicating that such sending could improve the quality of service.

Elaborate user-customized accept header fields sent in every request—in particular, if they include quality values—can be used by servers as relatively reliable and long-lived user identifiers. Such user identifiers would allow content providers to do click-trail tracking, and would allow collaborating content providers to match cross-server click-trails or form submissions of individual users. Note that for many users not behind a proxy, the network address of the host running the user agent will also serve as a long-lived user identifier. In environments where proxies are used to enhance privacy, user agents ought to be conservative in offering accept header configuration options to end users. As an extreme privacy measure, proxies could filter the accept headers in relayed requests. General-purpose user agents that provide a high degree of header configurability SHOULD warn users about the loss of privacy which can be involved.

15.2 Attacks Based on File and Path Names

Implementations of HTTP origin servers SHOULD be careful to restrict the documents returned by HTTP requests to only those that were intended by the server administrators. If an HTTP server translates HTTP URIs directly into file system calls, the server MUST take special care not to serve files that were not intended to be delivered to HTTP clients. For example, UNIX, Microsoft Windows, and other operating systems use ".." as a path component to indicate a directory level above the current one. On such a system, an HTTP server MUST disallow any such construct in the Request-URI if it would otherwise allow access to a resource outside those intended to be accessible via the HTTP server. Similarly, files intended for reference only internally to the server (such as access control files, configuration files, and script code) MUST be protected from inappropriate retrieval, since they might contain sensitive information. Experience has shown that minor bugs in such HTTP server implementations have turned into security risks.

15.3 DNS Spoofing

Clients using HTTP rely heavily on the Domain Name Service, and are thus generally prone to security attacks based on the deliberate mis-association of IP addresses and DNS names. Clients need to be cautious in assuming the continuing validity of an IP number/DNS name association.

In particular, HTTP clients SHOULD rely on their name resolver for confirmation of an IP number/DNS name association, rather than caching the result of previous host name lookups. Many platforms already can cache host name lookups locally when appropriate, and they SHOULD be configured to do so. It is proper for these lookups to be cached, however, only when the TTL (Time to Live) information reported by the name server makes it likely that the cached information will remain useful.

If HTTP clients cache the results of host name lookups in order to achieve a performance improvement, they MUST observe the TTL information reported by DNS.

If HTTP clients do not observe this rule, they could be spoofed when a previously accessed server's IP address changes. As network renumbering is expected to become increasingly common [24], the possibility of this form of attack will grow. Observing this requirement thus reduces this potential security vulnerability.

This requirement also improves the load-balancing behavior of clients for replicated servers using the same DNS name and reduces the likelihood of a user's experiencing failure in accessing sites which use that strategy.

15.4 Location Headers and Spoofing

If a single server supports multiple organizations that do not trust one another, then it MUST check the values of Location and Content-Location headers in responses that are generated under control of said organizations to make sure that they do not attempt to invalidate resources over which they have no authority.

15.5 Content-Disposition Issues

RFC 1806 [35], from which the often implemented Content-Disposition (see section 19.5.1) header in HTTP is derived, has a number of very serious security considerations. Content-Disposition is not part of the HTTP standard, but since it is widely implemented, we are documenting its use and risks for implementers. See RFC 2183 [49] (which updates RFC 1806) for details.

15.6 Authentication Credentials and Idle Clients

Existing HTTP clients and user agents typically retain authentication information indefinitely. HTTP/1.1 does not provide a method for a server to direct clients to discard these cached credentials. This is a significant defect that requires further extensions to HTTP. Circumstances under which credential caching can interfere with the application's security model include but are not limited to:

- Clients that have been idle for an extended period following which the server might wish to cause the client to reprompt the user for credentials.

- Applications that include a session termination indication (such as a "logout" or "commit" button on a page) after which the server side of the application "knows" that there is no further reason for the client to retain the credentials.

This is currently under separate study. There are a number of work-arounds to parts of this problem, and we encourage the use of password protection in screen savers, idle time-outs, and other methods which mitigate the security problems inherent in this problem. In particular, user agents which cache credentials are encouraged to provide a readily accessible mechanism for discarding cached credentials under user control.

15.7 Proxies and Caching

By their very nature, HTTP proxies are men-in-the-middle, and represent an opportunity for man-in-the-middle attacks. Compromise of the systems on which the proxies run can result in serious security and privacy problems. Proxies have access to security-related information, personal information about individual users and organizations, and proprietary information belonging to users and content providers. A compromised proxy, or a proxy implemented or configured without regard to security and privacy considerations, might be used in the commission of a wide range of potential attacks.

Proxy operators should protect the systems on which proxies run as they would protect any system that contains or transports sensitive information. In particular, log information gathered at proxies often contains highly sensitive personal information and/or information about organizations. Log information should be carefully guarded, and appropriate guidelines for use developed and followed (see section 15.1.1).

Caching proxies provide additional potential vulnerabilities, since the contents of the cache represent an attractive target for malicious exploitation. Because cache contents persist after an HTTP request is complete, an attack on the cache can reveal information long after a user believes that the information has been removed from the network. Therefore, cache contents should be protected as sensitive information.

Proxy implementers should consider the privacy and security implications of their design and coding decisions, and of the configuration options they provide to proxy operators (especially the default configuration).

Users of a proxy need to be aware that they are no more trustworthy than the people who run the proxy; HTTP itself cannot solve this problem.

The judicious use of cryptography, when appropriate, may suffice to protect against a broad range of security and privacy attacks. Such cryptography is beyond the scope of the HTTP/1.1 specification.

15.7.1 Denial of Service Attacks on Proxies

They exist. They are hard to defend against. Research continues. Beware.

16 Acknowledgments

This specification makes heavy use of the augmented BNF and generic constructs defined by David H. Crocker for RFC 822 [9]. Similarly, it reuses many of the definitions provided by Nathaniel Borenstein and Ned Freed for MIME [7]. We hope that their inclusion in this specification will help reduce past confusion over the relationship between HTTP and Internet mail message formats.

The HTTP protocol has evolved considerably over the years. It has benefited from a large and active developer community—the many people who have participated on the www-talk mailing list—and it is that community which has been most responsible for the success of HTTP and of the World-Wide Web in general. Marc Andreessen, Robert Cailliau, Daniel W. Connolly, Bob Denny, John Franks, Jean-Francois Groff, Phillip M. Hallam-Baker, Hakon W. Lie, Ari Luotonen, Rob McCool, Lou Montulli, Dave Raggett, Tony Sanders, and Marc VanHeyningen deserve special recognition for their efforts in defining early aspects of the protocol.

This document has benefited greatly from the comments of all those participating in the HTTP-WG. In addition to those already mentioned, the following individuals have contributed to this specification:

Gary Adams	Paul J. Leach
Harald Tveit Alvestrand	Albert Lunde
Keith Ball	John C. Mallery
Brian Behlendorf	Jean-Philippe Martin-Flatin
Paul Burchard	Mitra
Maurizio Codogno	David Morris
Josh Cohen	Gavin Nicol
Mike Cowlishaw	Ross Patterson
Roman Czyborra	Bill Perry
Michael A. Dolan	Jeffrey Perry
Daniel DuBois	Scott Powers
David J. Fiander	Owen Rees
Alan Freier	Luigi Rizzo
Marc Hedlund	David Robinson
Greg Herlihy	Marc Salomon
Koen Holtman	Rich Salz
Alex Hopmann	Allan M. Schiffman
Bob Jernigan	Jim Seidman
Shel Kaphan	Chuck Shotton
Rohit Khare	Eric W. Sink
John Klensin	Simon E. Spero
Martijn Koster	Richard N. Taylor
Alexei Kosut	Robert S. Thau
David M. Kristol	Bill (BearHeart) Weinman
Daniel LaLiberte	Francois Yergeau
Ben Laurie	Mary Ellen Zurko

Much of the content and presentation of the caching design is due to suggestions and comments from individuals including Shel Kaphan, Paul Leach, Koen Holtman, David Morris, and Larry Masinter.

Most of the specification of ranges is based on work originally done by Ari Luotonen and John Franks, with additional input from Steve Zilles.

Thanks to the "cave men" of Palo Alto. You know who you are.

Jim Gettys (the current editor of this document) wishes particularly to thank Roy Fielding, the previous editor of this document, along with John Klensin, Jeff Mogul, Paul Leach, Dave Kristol, Koen Holtman, John Franks, Josh Cohen, Alex Hopmann, Scott Lawrence, and Larry Masinter for their help. And thanks go particularly to Jeff Mogul and Scott Lawrence for performing the "MUST/MAY/SHOULD" audit.

The Apache Group; Anselm Baird-Smith, author of Jigsaw; and Henrik Frystyk implemented RFC 2068 early, and we wish to thank them for the discovery of many of the problems that this document attempts to rectify.

17 References

[1] Alvestrand, H., "Tags for the Identification of Languages," RFC 1766, March 1995.

[2] Anklesaria, F., McCahill, M., Lindner, P., Johnson, D., Torrey, D., and Alberti, B., "The Internet Gopher Protocol (a distributed document search and retrieval protocol)," RFC 1436, March 1993.

[3] Berners-Lee, T., "Universal Resource Identifiers in WWW," RFC 1630, June 1994.

[4] Berners-Lee, T., Masinter, L., and McCahill, M., "Uniform Resource Locators (URL)," RFC 1738, December 1994.

[5] Berners-Lee, T., and Connolly, D., "Hypertext Markup Language—2.0," RFC 1866, November 1995.

[6] Berners-Lee, T., Fielding, R., and Frystyk, H., "Hypertext Transfer Protocol—HTTP/1.0," RFC 1945, May 1996.

[7] Freed, N., and Borenstein, N., "Multipurpose Internet Mail Extensions (MIME) Part One: Format of Internet Message Bodies," RFC 2045, November 1996.

[8] Braden, R., "Requirements for Internet Hosts—Communication Layers," STD 3, RFC 1123, October 1989.

[9] Crocker, D., "Standard for the Format of ARPA Internet Text Messages," STD 11, RFC 822, August 1982.

[10] Davis, F., Kahle, B., Morris, H., Salem, J., Shen, T., Wang, R., Sui, J., and Grinbaum, M., "WAIS Interface Protocol Prototype Functional Specification (v1.5)," Thinking Machines Corporation, April 1990.

[11] Fielding, R., "Relative Uniform Resource Locators," RFC 1808, June 1995.

[12] Horton, M., and Adams, R., "Standard for Interchange of USENET Messages," RFC 1036, December 1987.

[13] Kantor, B., and Lapsley, P., "Network News Transfer Protocol," RFC 977, February 1986.

[14] Moore, K., "MIME (Multipurpose Internet Mail Extensions) Part Three: Message Header Extensions for Non-ASCII Text," RFC 2047, November 1996.

[15] Nebel, E., and Masinter, L., "Form-based File Upload in HTML," RFC 1867, November 1995.

[16] Postel, J., "Simple Mail Transfer Protocol," STD 10, RFC 821, August 1982.

[17] Postel, J., "Media Type Registration Procedure," RFC 1590, November 1996.

[18] Postel, J., and Reynolds, J., "File Transfer Protocol," STD 9, RFC 959, October 1985.

[19] Reynolds, J., and Postel, J., "Assigned Numbers," STD 2, RFC 1700, October 1994.

[20] Sollins, K., and Masinter, L., "Functional Requirements for Uniform Resource Names," RFC 1737, December 1994.

[21] US-ASCII. Coded Character Set—7-Bit American Standard Code for Information Interchange. Standard ANSI X3.4-1986, ANSI, 1986.

[22] ISO-8859. International Standard—Information Processing—

8-Bit Single-Byte Coded Graphic Character Sets—

Part 1: Latin Alphabet No. 1, ISO-8859-1:1987.

Part 2: Latin Alphabet No. 2, ISO-8859-2, 1987.

Part 3: Latin Alphabet No. 3, ISO-8859-3, 1988.

Part 4: Latin alphabet No. 4, ISO-8859-4, 1988.

Part 5: Latin/Cyrillic Alphabet, ISO-8859-5, 1988.

Part 6: Latin/Arabic Alphabet, ISO-8859-6, 1987.

Part 7: Latin/Greek Alphabet, ISO-8859-7, 1987.

Part 8: Latin/Hebrew Alphabet, ISO-8859-8, 1988.

Part 9: Latin Alphabet No. 5, ISO-8859-9, 1990.

[23] Meyers, J., and Rose, M., "The Content-MD5 Header Field," RFC 1864, October 1995.

[24] Carpenter, B., and Rekhter, Y., "Renumbering Needs Work," RFC 1900, February 1996.

[25] Deutsch, P., "GZIP File Format Specification Version 4.3," RFC 1952, May 1996.

[26] Padmanabhan, V. N., and Mogul, J. C., "Improving HTTP Latency," Computer Networks and ISDN Systems, v. 28, pp. 25–35, December 1995. Slightly revised version of paper in Proc. 2nd International WWW Conference '94: Mosaic and the Web, October 1994, which is available at http://www.ncsa.uiuc.edu/SDG/IT94/Proceedings/DDay/mogul/HTTPLatency.html.

[27] Touch, J., Heidemann, J., and Obraczka, K., "Analysis of HTTP Performance," <URL: http://www.isi.edu/touch/pubs/http-perf96/>, ISI Research Report ISI/RR-98-463, (original report dated August 1996), USC/Information Sciences Institute, August 1998.

[28] Mills, D., "Network Time Protocol (Version 3) Specification, Implementation and Analysis," RFC 1305, March 1992.

[29] Deutsch, P., "DEFLATE Compressed Data Format Specification Version 1.3," RFC 1951, May 1996.

[30] Spero, S., "Analysis of HTTP Performance Problems," http://sunsite.unc.edu/mdma-release/http-prob.html.

[31] Deutsch, P., and Gailly, J., "ZLIB Compressed Data Format Specification Version 3.3," RFC 1950, May 1996.

[32] Franks, J., Hallam-Baker, P., Hostetler, J., Leach, P., Luotonen, A., Sink, E., and Stewart, L., "An Extension to HTTP: Digest Access Authentication," RFC 2069, January 1997.

[33] Fielding, R., Gettys, J., Mogul, J., Frystyk, H., and Berners-Lee, T., "Hypertext Transfer Protocol—HTTP/1.1," RFC 2068, January 1997.

[34] Bradner, S., "Key Words for Use in RFCs to Indicate Requirement Levels," BCP 14, RFC 2119, March 1997.

[35] Troost, R., and Dorner, S., "Communicating Presentation Information in Internet Messages: The Content-Disposition Header," RFC 1806, June 1995.

[36] Mogul, J., Fielding, R., Gettys, J., and Frystyk, H., "Use and Interpretation of HTTP Version Numbers," RFC 2145, May 1997. [jg639]

[37] Palme, J., "Common Internet Message Headers," RFC 2076, February 1997. [jg640]

[38] Yergeau, F., "UTF-8, a Transformation Format of Unicode and ISO-10646," RFC 2279, January 1998. [jg641]

[39] Nielsen, H. F., Gettys, J., Baird-Smith, A., Prud'hommeaux, E., Lie, H., and Lilley, C., "Network Performance Effects of HTTP/1.1, CSS1, and PNG," Proceedings of ACM SIGCOMM '97, Cannes France, September 1997. [jg642]

[40] Freed, N., and Borenstein, N., "Multipurpose Internet Mail Extensions (MIME) Part Two: Media Types," RFC 2046, November 1996. [jg643]

[41] Alvestrand, H., "IETF Policy on Character Sets and Languages," BCP 18, RFC 2277, January 1998. [jg644]

[42] Berners-Lee, T., Fielding, R., and Masinter, L., "Uniform Resource Identifiers (URI): Generic Syntax and Semantics," RFC 2396, August 1998. [jg645]

[43] Franks, J., Hallam-Baker, P., Hostetler, J., Lawrence, S., Leach, P., Luotonen, A., Sink, E., and Stewart, L., "HTTP Authentication: Basic and Digest Access Authentication," RFC 2617, June 1999. [jg646]

[44] Luotonen, A., "Tunneling TCP-based Protocols through Web Proxy Servers," Work in Progress. [jg647]

[45] Palme, J., and Hopmann, A., "MIME E-mail Encapsulation of Aggregate Documents, such as HTML (MHTML)," RFC 2110, March 1997.

[46] Bradner, S., "The Internet Standards Process—Revision 3," BCP 9, RFC 2026, October 1996.

[47] Masinter, L., "Hyper Text Coffee Pot Control Protocol (HTCPCP/1.0)," RFC 2324, 1 April 1998.

[48] Freed, N., and Borenstein, N., "Multipurpose Internet Mail Extensions (MIME) Part Five: Conformance Criteria and Examples," RFC 2049, November 1996.

[49] Troost, R., Dorner, S., and Moore, K., "Communicating Presentation Information in Internet Messages: The Content-Disposition Header Field," RFC 2183, August 1997.

18 Authors' Addresses

Roy T. Fielding
Information and Computer Science
University of California, Irvine
Irvine, CA 92697-3425, USA
Fax: +1 (949) 824-1715
EMail: fielding@ics.uci.edu

James Gettys
World Wide Web Consortium
MIT Laboratory for Computer Science
545 Technology Square
Cambridge, MA 02139, USA
Fax: +1 (617) 258 8682
EMail: jg@w3.org

Jeffrey C. Mogul
Western Research Laboratory
Compaq Computer Corporation
250 University Avenue
Palo Alto, California, 94305, USA
EMail: mogul@wrl.dec.com

Henrik Frystyk Nielsen
World Wide Web Consortium
MIT Laboratory for Computer Science
545 Technology Square
Cambridge, MA 02139, USA
Fax: +1 (617) 258 8682
EMail: frystyk@w3.org

Larry Masinter
Xerox Corporation
3333 Coyote Hill Road
Palo Alto, CA 94034, USA
EMail: masinter@parc.xerox.com

Paul J. Leach
Microsoft Corporation
1 Microsoft Way
Redmond, WA 98052, USA
EMail: paulle@microsoft.com

Tim Berners-Lee
Director, World Wide Web Consortium
MIT Laboratory for Computer Science
545 Technology Square
Cambridge, MA 02139, USA
Fax: +1 (617) 258 8682
EMail: timbl@w3.org

19 Appendices

19.1 Internet Media Type message/http and application/http

In addition to defining the HTTP/1.1 protocol, this document serves as the specification for the Internet media type "message/http" and "application/http." The message/http type can be used to enclose a single HTTP request or response message, provided that it obeys the MIME restrictions for all "message" types regarding line length and encodings. The application/http type can be used to enclose a pipeline of one or more HTTP request or response messages (not intermixed). The following is to be registered with IANA [17].

> Media Type name: message
>
> Media subtype name: http
>
> Required parameters: none
>
> Optional parameters: version, msgtype
>
> version: The HTTP-Version number of the enclosed message (e.g., "1.1"). If not present, the version can be determined from the first line of the body.
>
> msgtype: The message type—"request" or "response." If not present, the type can be determined from the first line of the body.
>
> Encoding considerations: only "7bit," "8bit," or "binary" are permitted
>
> Security considerations: none
>
>
> Media Type name: application
>
> Media subtype name: http

Required parameters: none

Optional parameters: version, msgtype

version: The HTTP-Version number of the enclosed messages (e.g., "1.1"). If not present, the version can be determined from the first line of the body.

msgtype: The message type—"request" or "response." If not present, the type can be determined from the first line of the body.

Encoding considerations: HTTP messages enclosed by this type are in "binary" format; use of an appropriate Content-Transfer-Encoding is required when transmitted via E-mail.

Security considerations: none

19.2 Internet Media Type multipart/byteranges

When an HTTP 206 (Partial Content) response message includes the content of multiple ranges (a response to a request for multiple non-overlapping ranges), these are transmitted as a multipart message-body. The media type for this purpose is called "multipart/byteranges."

The multipart/byteranges media type includes two or more parts, each with its own Content-Type and Content-Range fields. The required boundary parameter specifies the boundary string used to separate each body-part.

Media Type name: multipart

Media subtype name: byteranges

Required parameters: boundary

Optional parameters: none

Encoding considerations: only "7bit," "8bit," or "binary" are permitted

Security considerations: none

For example:

```
HTTP/1.1 206 Partial Content
Date: Wed, 15 Nov 1995 06:25:24 GMT
Last-Modified: Wed, 15 Nov 1995 04:58:08 GMT
Content-type: multipart/byteranges; boundary=THIS_STRING_SEPARATES
```

```
--THIS_STRING_SEPARATES
Content-type: application/pdf
Content-range: bytes 500-999/8000

...the first range...
--THIS_STRING_SEPARATES
Content-type: application/pdf
Content-range: bytes 7000-7999/8000

...the second range
--THIS_STRING_SEPARATES--
```

Notes:

1. Additional CRLFs may precede the first boundary string in the entity.

2. Although RFC 2046 [40] permits the boundary string to be quoted, some existing implementations handle a quoted boundary string incorrectly.

3. A number of browsers and servers were coded to an early draft of the byte-ranges specification to use a media type of multipart/x-byteranges, which is almost, but not quite compatible with the version documented in HTTP/1.1.

19.3 Tolerant Applications

Although this document specifies the requirements for the generation of HTTP/1.1 messages, not all applications will be correct in their implementation. We therefore recommend that operational applications be tolerant of deviations whenever those deviations can be interpreted unambiguously.

Clients SHOULD be tolerant in parsing the Status-Line and servers tolerant when parsing the Request-Line. In particular, they SHOULD accept any amount of SP or HT characters between fields, even though only a single SP is required.

The line terminator for message-header fields is the sequence CRLF. However, we recommend that applications, when parsing such headers, recognize a single LF as a line terminator and ignore the leading CR.

The character set of an entity-body SHOULD be labeled as the lowest common denominator of the character codes used within that body, with the exception that not labeling the entity is preferred over labeling the entity with the labels US-ASCII or ISO-8859-1. See section 3.7.1 and 3.4.1.

Additional rules for requirements on parsing and encoding of dates and other potential problems with date encodings include:

- HTTP/1.1 clients and caches SHOULD assume that an RFC 850 date which appears to be more than 50 years in the future is in fact in the past (this helps solve the "year 2000" problem).

- An HTTP/1.1 implementation MAY internally represent a parsed Expires date as earlier than the proper value, but MUST NOT internally represent a parsed Expires date as later than the proper value.

- All expiration-related calculations MUST be done in GMT. The local time zone MUST NOT influence the calculation or comparison of an age or expiration time.

- If an HTTP header incorrectly carries a date value with a time zone other than GMT, it MUST be converted into GMT using the most conservative possible conversion.

19.4 Differences Between HTTP Entities and RFC 2045 Entities

HTTP/1.1 uses many of the constructs defined for Internet Mail (RFC 822 [9]) and the Multipurpose Internet Mail Extensions (MIME [7]) to allow entities to be transmitted in an open variety of representations and with extensible mechanisms. However, RFC 2045 discusses mail, and HTTP has a few features that are different from those described in RFC 2045. These differences were carefully chosen to optimize performance over binary connections, to allow greater freedom in the use of new media types, to make date comparisons easier, and to acknowledge the practice of some early HTTP servers and clients.

This appendix describes specific areas where HTTP differs from RFC 2045. Proxies and gateways to strict MIME environments SHOULD be aware of these differences and provide the appropriate conversions where necessary. Proxies and gateways from MIME environments to HTTP also need to be aware of the differences because some conversions might be required.

19.4.1 MIME-Version

HTTP is not a MIME-compliant protocol. However, HTTP/1.1 messages MAY include a single MIME-Version general-header field to indicate what version of the

MIME protocol was used to construct the message. Use of the MIME-Version header field indicates that the message is in full compliance with the MIME protocol (as defined in RFC 2045 [7]). Proxies/gateways are responsible for ensuring full compliance (where possible) when exporting HTTP messages to strict MIME environments.

```
MIME-Version   = "MIME-Version" ":" 1*DIGIT "." 1*DIGIT
```

MIME version "1.0" is the default for use in HTTP/1.1. However, HTTP/1.1 message parsing and semantics are defined by this document and not the MIME specification.

19.4.2 Conversion to Canonical Form

RFC 2045 [7] requires that an Internet mail entity be converted to canonical form prior to being transferred, as described in section 4 of RFC 2049 [48]. Section 3.7.1 of this document describes the forms allowed for subtypes of the "text" media type when transmitted over HTTP. RFC 2046 requires that content with a type of "text" represent line breaks as CRLF and forbids the use of CR or LF outside of line break sequences. HTTP allows CRLF, bare CR, and bare LF to indicate a line break within text content when a message is transmitted over HTTP.

Where it is possible, a proxy or gateway from HTTP to a strict MIME environment SHOULD translate all line breaks within the text media types described in section 3.7.1 of this document to the RFC 2049 canonical form of CRLF. Note, however, that this might be complicated by the presence of a Content-Encoding and by the fact that HTTP allows the use of some character sets which do not use octets 13 and 10 to represent CR and LF, as is the case for some multi-byte character sets.

Implementers should note that conversion will break any cryptographic checksums applied to the original content unless the original content is already in canonical form. Therefore, the canonical form is recommended for any content that uses such checksums in HTTP.

19.4.3 Conversion of Date Formats

HTTP/1.1 uses a restricted set of date formats (section 3.3.1) to simplify the process of date comparison. Proxies and gateways from other protocols SHOULD ensure that any Date header field present in a message conforms to one of the HTTP/1.1 formats and rewrite the date if necessary.

19.4.4 Introduction of Content-Encoding

RFC 2045 does not include any concept equivalent to HTTP/1.1's Content-Encoding header field. Since this acts as a modifier on the media type, proxies and gateways from HTTP to MIME-compliant protocols MUST either change the value of the Content-Type header field or decode the entity-body before forwarding the message. (Some experimental applications of Content-Type for Internet mail have used a media-type parameter of ";conversions=<content-coding>" to perform a function equivalent to Content-Encoding. However, this parameter is not part of RFC 2045.)

19.4.5 No Content-Transfer-Encoding

HTTP does not use the Content-Transfer-Encoding (CTE) field of RFC 2045. Proxies and gateways from MIME-compliant protocols to HTTP MUST remove any non-identity CTE ("quoted-printable" or "base64") encoding prior to delivering the response message to an HTTP client.

Proxies and gateways from HTTP to MIME-compliant protocols are responsible for ensuring that the message is in the correct format and encoding for safe transport on that protocol, where "safe transport" is defined by the limitations of the protocol being used. Such a proxy or gateway SHOULD label the data with an appropriate Content-Transfer-Encoding if doing so will improve the likelihood of safe transport over the destination protocol.

19.4.6 Introduction of Transfer-Encoding

HTTP/1.1 introduces the Transfer-Encoding header field (section 14.41). Proxies/gateways MUST remove any transfer-coding prior to forwarding a message via a MIME-compliant protocol.

A process for decoding the "chunked" transfer-coding (section 3.6) can be represented in pseudocode as

```
length := 0
read chunk-size, chunk-extension (if any) and CRLF
while (chunk-size > 0) {
 read chunk-data and CRLF
 append chunk-data to entity-body
 length := length + chunk-size
 read chunk-size and CRLF
}
read entity-header
```

```
while (entity-header not empty) {
 append entity-header to existing header fields
 read entity-header
}
Content-Length := length
Remove "chunked" from Transfer-Encoding
```

19.4.7 MHTML and Line Length Limitations

HTTP implementations which share code with MHTML [45] implementations need to be aware of MIME line-length limitations. Since HTTP does not have this limitation, HTTP does not fold long lines. MHTML messages being transported by HTTP follow all conventions of MHTML, including line-length limitations and folding, canonicalization, etc., since HTTP transports all message-bodies as payload (see section 3.7.2) and does not interpret the content or any MIME header lines that might be contained therein.

19.5 Additional Features

RFC 1945 and RFC 2068 document protocol elements used by some existing HTTP implementations, but not consistently and correctly across most HTTP/1.1 applications. Implementers are advised to be aware of these features, but cannot rely upon their presence in, or interoperability with, other HTTP/1.1 applications. Some of these describe proposed experimental features, and some describe features that experimental deployment found lacking that are now addressed in the base HTTP/1.1 specification.

A number of other headers, such as Content-Disposition and Title, from SMTP and MIME are also often implemented (see RFC 2076 [37]).

19.5.1 Content-Disposition

The Content-Disposition response-header field has been proposed as a means for the origin server to suggest a default filename if the user requests that the content is saved to a file. This usage is derived from the definition of Content-Disposition in RFC 1806 [35].

```
content-disposition = "Content-Disposition" ":"
          disposition-type *( ";" disposition-parm )
disposition-type = "attachment" | disp-extension-token
disposition-parm = filename-parm | disp-extension-parm
filename-parm = "filename" "=" quoted-string
disp-extension-token = token
disp-extension-parm = token "=" ( token | quoted-string )
```

An example is

```
Content-Disposition: attachment; filename="fname.ext"
```

The receiving user agent SHOULD NOT respect any directory path information present in the filename-parm parameter, which is the only parameter believed to apply to HTTP implementations at this time. The filename SHOULD be treated as a terminal component only.

If this header is used in a response with the application/octet-stream content-type, the implied suggestion is that the user agent should not display the response, but directly enter a "save response as..." dialog.

See section 15.5 for Content-Disposition security issues.

19.6 Compatibility with Previous Versions

It is beyond the scope of a protocol specification to mandate compliance with previous versions. HTTP/1.1 was deliberately designed, however, to make supporting previous versions easy. It is worth noting that, at the time of composing this specification (1996), we would expect commercial HTTP/1.1 servers to

- Recognize the format of the Request-Line for HTTP/0.9, 1.0, and 1.1 requests;

- Understand any valid request in the format of HTTP/0.9, 1.0, or 1.1; and

- Respond appropriately with a message in the same major version used by the client.

And we would expect HTTP/1.1 clients to

- Recognize the format of the Status-Line for HTTP/1.0 and 1.1 responses; and

- Understand any valid response in the format of HTTP/0.9, 1.0, or 1.1.

For most implementations of HTTP/1.0, each connection is established by the client prior to the request and closed by the server after sending the response. Some implementations implement the Keep-Alive version of persistent connections described in section 19.7.1 of RFC 2068 [33].

19.6.1 Changes from HTTP/1.0

This section summarizes major differences between versions HTTP/1.0 and HTTP/1.1.

19.6.1.1 Changes to Simplify Multi-homed Web Servers and Conserve IP Addresses

The requirements that clients and servers support the Host request-header, report an error if the Host request-header (section 14.23) is missing from an HTTP/1.1 request, and accept absolute URIs (section 5.1.2) are among the most important changes defined by this specification.

Older HTTP/1.0 clients assumed a one-to-one relationship of IP addresses and servers; there was no other established mechanism for distinguishing the intended server of a request from the IP address to which that request was directed. The changes outlined above will allow the Internet, once older HTTP clients are no longer common, to support multiple Web sites from a single IP address, greatly simplifying large operational Web servers, where allocation of many IP addresses to a single host has created serious problems. The Internet will also be able to recover the IP addresses that have been allocated for the sole purpose of allowing special-purpose domain names to be used in root-level HTTP URLs. Given the rate of growth of the Web and the number of servers already deployed, it is extremely important that all implementations of HTTP (including updates to existing HTTP/1.0 applications) correctly implement these requirements:

- Both clients and servers MUST support the Host request-header.

- A client that sends an HTTP/1.1 request MUST send a Host header.

- Servers MUST report a 400 (Bad Request) error if an HTTP/1.1 request does not include a Host request-header.

- Servers MUST accept absolute URIs.

19.6.2 Compatibility with HTTP/1.0 Persistent Connections

Some clients and servers might wish to be compatible with some previous implementations of persistent connections in HTTP/1.0 clients and servers. Persistent connections in HTTP/1.0 are explicitly negotiated as they are not the default behavior. HTTP/1.0 experimental implementations of persistent connections are faulty, and the new facilities in HTTP/1.1 are designed to rectify these problems. The problem was that some existing 1.0 clients may be sending Keep-Alive to a proxy server that doesn't understand Connection, which would then erroneously forward it to the next inbound server, which would establish the Keep-Alive connection and result in a hung HTTP/1.0 proxy waiting for the close on the response.

The result is that HTTP/1.0 clients must be prevented from using Keep-Alive when talking to proxies. However, talking to proxies is the most important use of persistent connections, so that prohibition is clearly unacceptable. Therefore, we need some other mechanism for indicating a persistent connection is desired, which is safe to use even when talking to an old proxy that ignores Connection. Persistent connections are the default for HTTP/1.1 messages; we introduce a new keyword (Connection: close) for declaring non-persistence. See section 14.10.

The original HTTP/1.0 form of persistent connections (the Connection: Keep-Alive and Keep-Alive header) is documented in RFC 2068 [33].

19.6.3 Changes from RFC 2068

This specification has been carefully audited to correct and disambiguate key word usage; RFC 2068 had many problems in respect to the conventions laid out in RFC 2119 [34].

It clarified which error code should be used for inbound server failures (e.g., DNS failures). (Section 10.5.5)

CREATE had a race that required an ETag be sent when a resource is first created. (Section 10.2.2).

Content-Base was deleted from the specification: It was not implemented widely, and there is no simple, safe way to introduce it without a robust extension mechanism. In addition, it is used in a similar, but not identical fashion in MHTML [45].

Transfer-coding and message lengths all interact in ways that required fixing exactly when chunked encoding is used (to allow for transfer encoding that may not be self-delimiting); it was important to straighten out exactly how message lengths are computed. (Sections 3.6, 4.4, 7.2.2, 13.5.2, 14.13, and 14.16)

A content-coding of "identity" was introduced, to solve problems discovered in caching. (Section 3.5)

Quality Values of zero should indicate that "I don't want something" to allow clients to refuse a representation. (Section 3.9)

The use and interpretation of HTTP version numbers has been clarified by RFC 2145. It requires proxies to upgrade requests to highest protocol version they support to deal with problems discovered in HTTP/1.0 implementations. (Section 3.1)

Charset wildcarding is introduced to avoid explosion of character set names in accept headers. (Section 14.2)

A case was missed in the Cache-Control model of HTTP/1.1; s-maxage was introduced to add this missing case. (Sections 13.4, 14.8, 14.9, and 14.9.3)

The Cache-Control: max-age directive was not properly defined for responses. (Section 14.9.3)

There are situations where a server (especially a proxy) does not know the full length of a response but is capable of serving a byte-range request. We therefore need a mechanism to allow byte ranges with a content-range not indicating the full length of the message. (Section 14.16)

Range request responses would become very verbose if all metadata were always returned; by allowing the server to only send needed headers in a 206 response, this problem can be avoided. (Sections 10.2.7, 13.5.3, and 14.27)

Fix problem with unsatisfiable range requests. There are two cases: syntactic problems and range doesn't exist in the document. The 416 status code was needed to resolve this ambiguity needed to indicate an error for a byte-range request that falls outside of the actual contents of a document. (Sections 10.4.17 and 14.16)

Rewrite of message transmission requirements to make it much harder for implementers to get it wrong, as the consequences of errors here can have significant impact on the Internet, and to deal with the following problems:

1. Changing "HTTP/1.1 or later" to "HTTP/1.1," in contexts where this was incorrectly placing a requirement on the behavior of an implementation of a future version of HTTP/1.x.

2. Made it clear that user agents should retry requests, not "clients" in general.

3. Converted requirements for clients to ignore unexpected 100 (Continue) responses, and for proxies to forward 100 responses, into a general requirement for 1xx responses.

4. Modified some TCP-specific language, to make it clearer that non-TCP transports are possible for HTTP.

5. Require that the origin server MUST NOT wait for the request body before it sends a required 100 (Continue) response.

6. Allow, rather than require, a server to omit 100 (Continue) if it has already seen some of the request body.

7. Allow servers to defend against denial of service attacks and broken clients.

This change adds the Expect header and 417 status code. The message transmission requirements fixes are in sections 8.2, 10.4.18, 8.1.2.2, 13.11, and 14.20.

Proxies should be able to add Content-Length when appropriate. (Section 13.5.2)

Clean up confusion between 403 and 404 responses. (Sections 10.4.4, 10.4.5, and 10.4.11)

Warnings could be cached incorrectly, or not updated appropriately. (Sections 13.1.2, 13.2.4, 13.5.2, 13.5.3, 14.9.3, and 14.46). Warning also needed to be a general header, as PUT or other methods may have need for it in requests.

Transfer-coding had significant problems, particularly with interactions with chunked encoding. The solution is that transfer-codings become as full fledged as content-codings. This involves adding an IANA registry for transfer-codings (separate from content-codings), a new header field (TE) and enabling trailer headers in the future. Transfer encoding is a major performance benefit, so it was worth fixing [39]. TE also solves another, obscure, downward interoperability problem that could have occurred due to interactions between authentication trailers, chunked encoding, and HTTP/1.0 clients. (Sections 3.6, 3.6.1, and 14.39)

The PATCH, LINK, and UNLINK methods were defined but not commonly implemented in previous versions of this specification. See RFC 2068 [33].

The Alternates, Content-Version, Derived-From, Link, URI, Public, and Content-Base header fields were defined in previous versions of this specification, but not commonly implemented. See RFC 2068 [33].

20 Index

Please see the PostScript version of this RFC for the INDEX.

21 Full Copyright Statement

Acknowledgment

Funding for the RFC Editor function is currently provided by the Internet Society.

Index

Safari®
BOOKS ONLINE
ENABLED

THIS BOOK IS SAFARI ENABLED

INCLUDES FREE 45-DAY ACCESS TO THE ONLINE EDITION

The Safari® Enabled icon on the cover of your favorite technology book means the book is available through Safari Bookshelf. When you buy this book, you get free access to the online edition for 45 days.

Safari Bookshelf is an electronic reference library that lets you easily search thousands of technical books, find code samples, download chapters, and access technical information whenever and wherever you need it.

TO GAIN 45-DAY SAFARI ENABLED ACCESS TO THIS BOOK:

- Go to **http://www.prenhallprofessional.com/safarienabled**
- Complete the brief registration form
- Enter the coupon code found in the front of this book on the "Copyright" page

If you have difficulty registering on Safari Bookshelf or accessing the online edition, please e-mail customer-service@safaribooksonline.com.

PRENTICE
HALL

Teachers open the door,
But you must enter by yourself